America's Best Day Hiking Series

Hiking ILLINOIS

SUSAN L. POST

Illinois Department of Natural Resources
Illinois Natural History Survey

Human Kinetics

Library of Congress Cataloging-in-Publication Data

Post, Susan L.
   Hiking Illinois / Susan L. Post.
      p. cm. -- (America's best day hiking series)
   ISBN 0-88011-568-8
   1. Hiking--Illinois--Guidebooks. 2. Trails--Illinois--Guidebooks.
3. Parks--Illinois--Guidebooks. 4. Natural history--Illinois-
-Guidebooks. 5. Illinois--Guidebooks. I. Title. II. Series.
  GV199.42.I3P67   1997
  796.51 09773--dc21   96-37721
                                            CIP

ISBN: 0-88011-568-8

Acquisitions Editor: Pat Sammann; **Developmental Editor:** Kristine Enderle; **Assistant Editor:** Coree Schutter; **Copyeditor:** Anne M. Heiles; **Graphic Designer:** Robert Reuther; **Graphic Artist:** Denise Lowry; **Cover Designer:** Jack Davis; **Photographer (cover):** Susan Post; **Illustrator:** Rob Csiki; **Printer:** Versa Press

The maps on the following pages were adapted from Illinois Department of Natural Resources maps: 34, 38, 48, 60, 64, 68, 72, 76, 82, 90, 94, 106, 110, 122, 126, 130, 138, 148, 172, 178, 182, 186, 194, and 198.

Human Kinetics books are available at special discounts for bulk purchase. Special editions or book excerpts can also be created to specification. For details, contact the Special Sales Manager at Human Kinetics.

Printed in the United States of America   10   9   8   7   6   5   4   3   2   1

Human Kinetics
Web site: http://www.humankinetics.com/

United States: Human Kinetics, P.O. Box 5076, Champaign, IL 61825-5076
1-800-747-4457
e-mail: humank@hkusa.com

Canada: Human Kinetics, Box 24040, Windsor, ON N8Y 4Y9
1-800-465-7301 (in Canada only)
e-mail: humank@hkcanada.com

Europe: Human Kinetics, P.O. Box IW14, Leeds LS16 6TR, United Kingdom
(44) 1132 781708
e-mail: humank@hkeurope.com

Australia: Human Kinetics, 57A Price Avenue, Lower Mitcham, South Australia 5062
(08) 277 1555
e-mail: humank@hkaustralia.com

New Zealand: Human Kinetics, P.O. Box 105-231, Auckland 1
(09) 523 3462
e-mail: humank@hknewz.com

To Michael,
Who is not only a great hiking partner
and editor, but also my best friend.
Together, even the flash floods, mud slides,
and bewilderment of being lost could not dampen
each unique experience we shared.

Acknowledgments

As I hiked and wrote, many people made the job easier. My thanks go first to all the staff members and volunteers at nature centers, state parks, and forest preserves for answering innumerable questions and providing maps.

Don and Eileen Dickerson cared for Mr. Pix during my absences, always seemed to have a much-needed reference or map, and provided many words of encouragement. Wayne Frankie gave me expert geological advice, and Cathy Eastman provided me with overall support and Mr. Pix with care. Erin Knight suggested hikes, provided maps, and field-tested several trail write-ups. Joyce Hofmann provided a much-needed second vehicle and was a partner for linear hikes; she field-tested several hikes and provided maps. Thanks to Scott Simon and Bill Handel for their ideas on hiking in northern Illinois. James Seets provided invaluable assistance with maps and advice on hiking in southern Illinois. Jean and Gene Gray provided welcome northern Illinois hospitality. Finally, my appreciation goes to the 1996 purple loosestrife team (especially Rob Wiedenmann and Charlie Helm) for picking up the slack during my sojourns afield.

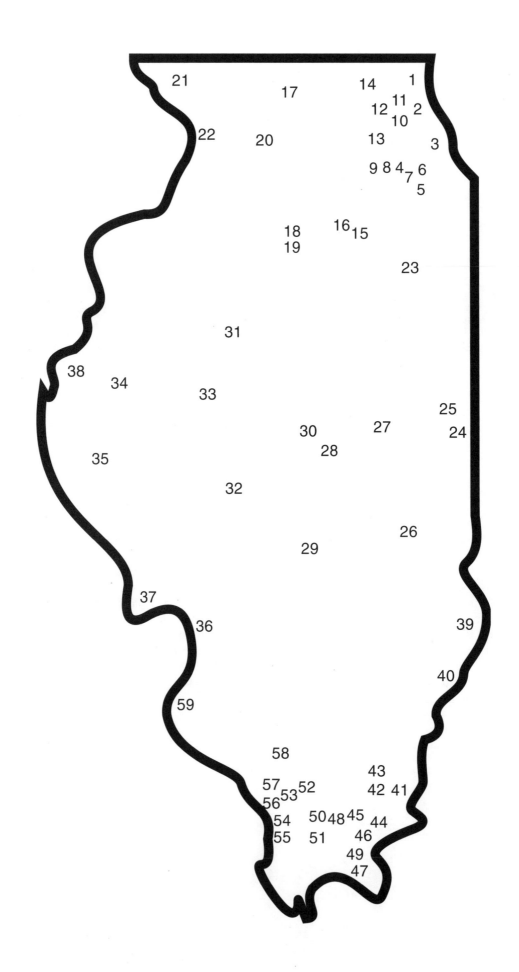

Contents

How to Use This Book

Hiking is an antidote to modern life. It gives the body some much-needed (and enjoyable) exercise, and it gives the mind both rest and stimulation. It even lifts the spirit to connect again with this earth that we're a part of but seldom have time to think about. With the America's Best Day Hiking Series, we hope to provide you with an incentive to start or continue hiking, for the pleasure and the challenge of it.

Each book in the series offers information on 100 or more of the most interesting and scenic trails in a particular state, as well as notes about recreational, historical, and sightseeing destinations located near the trails. The assortment of trails ranges from short, easy hikes for occasional hikers and families with young children to longer, more rugged ones for the experienced trailblazer. None of the trails takes more than a day to hike, although some trails may be linked together to create a hike of several days.

The trails are divided into three main areas—North, Central, and South. Within each area, trails are listed from east to west. Divider pages signal the beginning of each new area, and those pages include information on the local topography, major rivers and lakes, flora and fauna, weather, and best features of the area.

The innovative format is designed to make exploring new parks and trails easy. Information on each park or other nature area always appears on a right-hand page. It begins with the park's name and a small state map that shows the park's general location. Bulleted highlights then point out the trails' most interesting features. A description of the park's history and terrain comes next, with practical information on how to get to the park and the park's hours, available facilities, permits and rules, and the address and phone number of a contact who can give you more information. The section entitled "Other Areas of Interest" briefly mentions nearby parks and recreational opportunities, with phone numbers to call for more information.

After the general information follows a selected list of trails in the park. The length and difficulty of hiking each is given, along with a brief description of its terrain. The difficulty rating, shown by boot icons, ranges from one (the easiest) to five (most difficult).

On the other side of the page is a full-sized map of the park. Our book's larger format allows us to provide clear, readable maps that are easy to follow.

The next right- and left-hand pages are usually

easiest [boot 1] [boot 2] [boot 3] [boot 4] [boot 5] most difficult

descriptions of the two best hikes in that park, along with a trail map at the bottom of each page (a few parks have only one hike, with just one map that primarily shows the trail). Each hike begins with information on the length and difficulty of the trail and the estimated time to walk it, plus cautions to help you avoid possible annoyances or problems. The description of the trail provides more than directions; it's a guided tour of what you will see as you hike along. The scenery, wildlife, and history of the trail are all brought to life. Points of interest along the trail are numbered in brackets within the text, and those numbers are shown on the trail map to guide you. The approximate distance from the trailhead to each point of interest is given.

The park descriptions, maps, and trails are all kept as a unit within an even number of pages. Parks for which only one trail is highlighted take up only two pages; those with the regular two trails cover four pages; and extended trails might take six or eight. We've perforated the book's pages so you can remove them if you like, or you can copy them for your personal use. If you carry the pages with you as you hike, you might want to use a plastic sleeve to protect them from the elements. You also can make notes on these pages to remind you of your favorite parts of the park or trail.

If you want to quickly find a park or trail to explore, use the trailfinder that appears on the next pages. It gives essential information about each highlighted trail in the book, including the trail's length, difficulty, special features, and park facilities.

We hope the books in the America's Best Day Hiking Series inspire you to get out and enjoy a wide range of outdoor experiences. We've tried to find interesting trails from all parts of each state. Some are unexpected treasures—places you'd never dream exist in the state. Some may be favorites that you've already hiked and recommended to friends. But whether you live in a city or in the country, are away vacationing or are at home, some of these trails will be near you. Find one you like, lace up your hiking boots, and go!

Trail Finder

Terrain/Landscape

#	Trail Sites and Trails	Park Facilities	Miles	Trail Difficulty Rating	Hills	Prairie/Grassland	Forest	Lake	Wetlands	Overlook	River/Streams	Page #
1	**Illinois Beach State Park**	RV camping, boating, tent camping, picnicking, fishing, swimming, biking										
	Dead River		2.65	●●		✓	✓	✓	✓	✓	✓	5
	North Unit		2.25	●		✓	✓	✓	✓			6
2	**Chicago Botanic Garden**	picnicking, biking										
	Inside Garden		2.5	●				✓		✓		9
	Outside Garden		2.5	●		✓	✓		✓	✓		10
3	**City of Chicago**	biking										
	Chicago Wilds		9.0	●			✓					13
4	**Wolf Road Prairie**											
	Wolf Road Prairie		2.0	●		✓	✓		✓			16
5	**Edward L. Ryerson Conservation Area**											
	River Woods		3.05	●			✓		✓	✓		18
6	**Palos and Sag Valley Forest Preserve**	fishing, tent camping, picnicking, biking										
	Black Oak		2.0	●●		✓	✓	✓	✓			20
7	**Waterfall Glen Forest Preserve**	biking										
	Waterfall Glen		9.65	●●●		✓	✓	✓	✓		✓	22
8	**Morton Arboretum**	picnicking										
	Prairie		1.8	●		✓						25
	Trail of Trees		3.15	●●			✓	✓	✓			26
9	**The Regional Trail**	RV camping, tent camping, picnicking, fishing, boating, biking										
	Blackwell Forest Preserve		6.75	●●		✓	✓	✓	✓		✓	29
	Herrick Lake Forest Preserve		4.25	●●		✓	✓	✓	✓			30

Continued ☞

#	Trail Sites and Trails	Park Facilities	Miles	Trail Difficulty Rating	Hills	Prairie/Grassland	Forest	Lake	Wetlands	Overlook	River/Streams	Page #
21	**Apple River Canyon State Park**											
	Primrose and Sunset		1.5	3 boots	✓		✓			✓	✓	73
	Pine Ridge–River Route Nature		1.6	5 boots	✓		✓			✓	✓	74
22	**Mississippi Palisades State Park**											
	Sentinel		1.3	6 boots	✓		✓			✓	✓	77
	High Point		5	4 boots	✓		✓			✓	✓	78
23	**Kankakee River State Park**											
	Rock Creek		4.0	3 boots		✓	✓			✓	✓	83
	Area A		3.0	3 boots		✓	✓					84
24	**Forest Glen Preserve**											
	Willow Creek–Deer Meadow–Old Barn		4.0	3 boots	✓	✓	✓	✓	✓	✓	✓	87
	Big Woods		2.5	5 boots	✓		✓			✓	✓	88
25	**Kickapoo State Park**											
	Out-and-Back		7.6	4 boots	✓	✓	✓			✓	✓	91
	Riverview		2.25	3 boots	✓		✓	✓	✓	✓	✓	92
26	**Fox Ridge State Park**											
	River View and No Name		2.15	3 boots	✓		✓		✓		✓	95
	Acorn Avenue–Trail of Trees		3.35	4 boots	✓		✓			✓	✓	96
27	**Champaign-Urbana**											
	In Search of the Big Grove		7.75	1 boot			✓	✓				99
28	**Robert Allerton Park**											
	North River		5.75	2 boots	✓		✓			✓	✓	103
	Buck Schroth Nature		2.4	2 boots		✓	✓				✓	104
29	**Hidden Springs State Forest**											
	Rocky Spring Nature		3.0	2 boots		✓	✓			✓	✓	107
	Big Tree		1.2	2 boots			✓				✓	108
30	**Weldon Springs State Park**											
	Beaver Dam		2.0	2 boots	✓	✓	✓				✓	111
	Lakeside Self-Guiding Nature		2.0	2 boots	✓		✓	✓	✓	✓		112

Terrain/Landscape

Continued ☞

Terrain/Landscape

#	Trail Sites and Trails	Park Facilities	Miles	Trail Difficulty Rating	Hills	Prairie/Grassland	Forest	Lake	Wetlands	Overlook	River/Streams	Page #
31	**Forest Park Nature Preserve**	(camp, picnic)										
	Inside		1.75	4 boots	✓		✓			✓		115
	Outside		2.75	4 boots	✓	✓	✓			✓		116
32	**Where Lincoln Walked**	(RV, camp, picnic)										
	New Salem		5.25	3 boots	✓		✓				✓	119
	Springfield		6.5	2 boots								120
33	**Sand Ridge State Forest**	(RV, camp, picnic)										
	North Section		5.6	4 boots	✓	✓	✓			✓		123
	Henry Allen Gleason Nature Preserve		1.15	2 boots	✓	✓				✓		124
34	**Argyle Lake State Park**	(RV, boat, camp, picnic, fish)										
	Trail of Many Names		5.75	4 boots	✓	✓	✓	✓	✓	✓		127
35	**Siloam Springs State Park**	(RV, camp, picnic, boat)										
	Red Oak Backpack		4.0	4 boots	✓	✓	✓			✓	✓	131
	Hoot Owl		1.5	4 boots	✓		✓			✓		132
36	**American Bottoms**	(RV, camp, picnic, fish, boat)										
	Cahokia Mounds		5.0	3 boots	✓	✓		✓	✓			135
	Horseshoe Lake		4.0	1 boot		✓	✓	✓	✓			136
37	**Pere Marquette State Park**	(RV, camp, picnic, fish, boat, bike)										
	Dogwood–Oak		2.25	4 boots	✓	✓	✓		✓	✓	✓	139
	Fern Hollow		3.0	4 boots	✓		✓					140
38	**Nauvoo**											
	Historic Nauvoo		4.0	1 boot		✓			✓		✓	142
39	**Robeson Hills Nature Preserve**	(camp, picnic)										
	Beech-Maple		1.0	3 boots	✓		✓					146
40	**Beall Woods**	(camp, picnic, fish)										
	Sweet Gum and Schneck		3.0	3 boots			✓				✓	149
	White Oak		1.75	3 boots	✓		✓			✓	✓	150
41	**Rim Rock/Pounds Hollow Recreation Complex**	(RV, camp, picnic, fish, swim, boat)										
	Rim Rock National		2.0	4 boots	✓		✓			✓	✓	153
	Beaver		4.0	4 boots	✓		✓	✓	✓		✓	154

#	Trail Sites and Trails	Park Facilities	Miles	Trail Difficulty Rating	Hills	Prairie/Grassland	Forest	Lake	Wetlands	Overlook	River/Streams	Page #
42	**Garden of the Gods Recreation Area**	(camping/RV/picnic icons)										
	Observation		0.50	🥾🥾						✓		157
	Wilderness		3.5	🥾🥾🥾🥾	✓		✓			✓	✓	158
43	**Northern Shawnee Hills**											
	Gibbons Creek Barrens		2.25	🥾🥾🥾🥾🥾	✓		✓			✓		161
	Stone Face		1.75	🥾🥾🥾🥾	✓		✓			✓		162
44	**Lusk Creek and Hayes Creek Canyons**											
	Lusk Creek Canyon		3.5	🥾🥾🥾	✓		✓			✓	✓	165
	Hayes Creek Canyon		2.0	🥾🥾🥾	✓		✓			✓	✓	166
45	**Bell Smith Springs Recreation Area**	(camping/RV/picnic/fishing icons)										
	Mill Branch		2.0	🥾🥾	✓		✓			✓	✓	169
	Sentry Bluff		3.5	🥾🥾🥾	✓		✓			✓	✓	170
46	**Dixon Springs State Park**	(camping/RV/picnic/swimming icons)										
	Pine–Oak–Bluff		1.7	🥾🥾			✓				✓	172
47	**Fort Massac State Park**	(camping/RV/picnic/boat icons)										
	Hickory Nut Ridge		2.5	🥾🥾			✓		✓		✓	174
48	**Jackson Hollow**											
	Jackson Hollow		3.0	🥾🥾🥾🥾🥾			✓			✓	✓	176
49	**Mermet Lake Conservation Area**	(picnic/boat/fishing/bike icons)										
	Mermet Flatwoods		1.3	🥾			✓		✓			179
	Mermet Lake		4.8	🥾				✓	✓			180
50	**Ferne Clyffe State Park**	(camping/RV/picnic/fishing icons)										
	Hawks' Cave–Blackjack Oak–Waterfall		3.0	🥾🥾🥾🥾	✓		✓			✓	✓	183
	Round Bluff Nature Preserve		1.0	🥾🥾🥾	✓		✓					184
51	**Cache River State Natural Area**	(canoe icon)										
	Heron Pond (Todd Fink)		1.9	🥾			✓		✓		✓	187
	Tupelo		2.5	🥾🥾			✓		✓			188

Continued ☞

xii

North

The northern part of Illinois is defined as the area south of the Wisconsin border and north of an imaginary line from Indiana to the Mississippi River that follows the east-west portion of the Illinois River Valley.

Topography

A drive across northern Illinois from east to west demonstrates a wide range of topography. As recently as six to ten thousand years ago the northeastern region was covered by glaciers, whereas the rugged, western corner of the state was untouched by even the bottom of a glacier. In northeastern Illinois (the most recently glaciated area), glacial landforms are common, and moraines (long ridges of glacial debris) and kames (conical mounds of glacial debris) make for a rolling, hilly terrain. Kettle holes and other depressions scooped out by the glaciers create a montage of complex wetlands. Near Lake Michigan, the lake-bed deposits of the old, glacial Lake Chicago (much bigger than the current Lake Michigan) and old shoreline ridges contribute to a unique landscape of sandy beaches, low dunes, and moist swales.

The Rock River dominates the north-central portion of Illinois. Gravel hill prairies once extended along the eroded bluffs, outcrops of St. Peter sandstone are common in the lower reaches of the valley, and the overall topography is rolling. At one time the Rock River Valley between Beloit and Dixon was nicknamed the "Hudson of the West" because of its many limestone bluffs and rugged, sandstone outcrops.

Extreme northwestern Illinois escaped the effects of glaciation, and consequently the region is called the Driftless Area (drift is glacial debris). The Driftless Area has one of the most maturely developed land surfaces in the state. It is characterized by rugged terrain, including loess-capped bluffs (loess is wind-blown sediment) and high, rocky palisades. The highest point in the state, Charles Mound, occurs here.

Major Rivers and Lakes

Lake Michigan borders the state on the northeast and the Mississippi River forms the entire western boundary of Illinois. The northeast area is home to numerous glacial lakes. These formed when chunks of ice broke off from the glaciers, became buried, and eventually melted or when a depression was created between two moraines. The upper reaches of the Des Plaines River, which lies west of Lake Michigan, provided early French explorers the beginning stretch of an easy and continuous canoe route from the Great Lakes to the Mississippi, at least during periods of high water. Today, most of the Des Plaines watershed is in the greater Chicago metropolitan region.

The Illinois River extends diagonally across the state and drains 45 percent of the state. Other major rivers found here are the Fox, the third-largest tributary of the Illinois; the Rock, which drains part of southern Wisconsin and most of northwestern Illinois; and the Apple, whose two forks unite at Apple River Canyon State Park, forming high cliffs with a unique flora.

Common Plant Life

Three broad types of forests occur in the north: upland, which earlier writers referred to as oak openings, with bur and white oak; mesic upland, dominated by sugar maple and basswood; and floodplain, found along major watercourses and containing silver maple, green ash, and cottonwood. The more unusual tree species found in northern Illinois are the tamaracks (growing in bogs), native white pines, and white birch (native to the Driftless Area).

Common wildflowers to look for in these northern forests include expanses of white trillium, trout lily, Jack-in-the-pulpit, wild geranium, false Solomon's seal, and many other favorite spring ephemerals. The Driftless Area has plants that found a refuge from the glaciers: jeweled shooting star, bird's-eye primrose, and Canada violet.

Fabulous prairies grow here and include wet-to-mesic (moist) tallgrass prairies; dry, gravel hill prairies; and sand prairies. Common wet or mesic prairie plants include little bluestem, compass plant, prairie dock, shooting star, blazing star, and the rare prairie white-fringed orchid. One-third of the country's population of this plant grows here. Dry, gravel hill prairies contain plants more common to the northwest—pasque flower, prairie smoke, bird's-foot violet, and expanses of purple coneflower. Sand prairie species include coreopsis, puccoon, and gentians (both fringed and bottle).

Wetlands make up another significant portion of the landforms in the northeast. Besides the familiar cattail marsh, you will encounter bogs, forested and grassy fens, and seeps. Look for pitcher plants, sundew, grass pink and rose pogonia orchids, white lady's slippers, leatherleaf, marsh marigold, and skunk cabbage.

Common Birds and Mammals

In wetland habitats seek out red-winged blackbirds, great blue herons, great white egrets, little green herons, Canada geese, wood ducks, kingfishers, common yellowthroats, yellow warblers, and swallows. A few of the rarer species that call this area home are yellow-headed blackbirds, black-crowned night herons, sandhill cranes, and black terns. Open grasslands provide habitat for bobolinks, American goldfinches, and various hawks. The Driftless Area provides excellent habitat for wild turkeys. At least one sighting, and usually many more, are guaranteed on any dawn or dusk country drive.

Mammals found throughout the north include white-tailed deer, cottontails, chipmunks, gray squirrels, woodchucks, and muskrat. Red-eared slider, snapping, and softshell turtles may be seen basking on logs in most wetlands. In addition, frogs are universal inhabitants of these wet places.

Climate

As you might expect, this area of Illinois is the last to warm up each spring. The mean average temperature is 23 °F in January and 74 °F in July. Cooler temperatures are found along Lake Michigan in the summer and warmer temperatures occur during winter. Rainfall averages 33.5 inches annually. The mean average snowfall is 27 to 33 inches, and on 20 to 35 days a year this area has 3 or more inches of snow on the ground. As a final statistical note, the Driftless Area has the coldest and driest climate in the state.

Best Natural Features

- Sandy habitats along Lake Michigan
- The only open water bog in Illinois
- Extensive wetlands
- Outcrops of St. Peter sandstone
- Canyons and dells
- Glacial features—kames, moraines, kettle holes, and glacial boulders
- Palisades along the Mississippi River
- Expanses of wildflowers, both rare and common
- Jewels of original prairie landscape

© Michael Jeffords

1. Illinois Beach State Park

- Build a sand castle and kick off your hiking boots as you walk along the lakeshore, dipping your toes in the cold waters of Lake Michigan.
- Study dunesland succession as you go from the sandy beach to a black oak savanna.
- Bring your binoculars to look for birds in the park's 16 different plant communities and to observe avian activity along Lake Michigan.

Area Information

Dubbed the dunesland, Illinois Beach State Park is a remnant of the sand and beach terrain that once lined the state's Lake Michigan shore. The dunesland is home to nearly 700 species of plants that grow on the park's beaches and in its sand dunes, marshes, chalky swales (low area between two dunes), sand prairies, and oak savannas (widely spaced oaks with prairie vegetation underneath).

Here the southwestern prickly-pear cactus mingles with the bearberry and tough, creeping juniper of the far north; southeastern blazing stars coexist with northern fringed gentians. You can see northern orchids, wood lilies, Indian paintbrushes, lupines, and the occasional insectivorous sundew. Because of this area's unique plant diversity, in 1964 it became the state's first nature preserve.

A walk from Lake Michigan back to the parking lot will chronicle how plants have colonized the dunes. Begin by noting the sand-binding grasses along the beach edge and progress to the dune-binding shrubs, such as the creeping and upright junipers. Once these plants have stabilized the dunes (a process over several hundred years) and contributed humus to the sand, other species appear and continue to enrich the coarse sand. The final stage is an oak savanna, a unique and beautiful landscape.

Directions: The south unit of the Illinois Beach State Park is located on the shore of Lake Michigan just south of the Illinois-Wisconsin border. From Zion, take Sheridan Road south about 1 mile to Wadsworth Road; go east to the park. From the south unit turn right (north) on Sheridan Road, follow it to Seventeenth Street, and turn right into the main entrance for the north unit.

Hours Open: The site is open daily from sunrise to 8 P.M.

Facilities: A nature center, located in the nature preserve (south unit), is usually open during weekends. A campground has 40 sites available by reservation. Showers, camp store, boating, jet skiing, fishing, swimming, beach combing, picnic areas with shelters, and playgrounds are some of the amenities.

Permits and Rules: No pets are allowed on the beach; pets must be leashed in all other areas of the park. No skiing or bicycling is allowed on the trails going through the nature preserve.

Further Information: Site Superintendent, Illinois Beach State Park, Zion, IL 60099; 847-662-4811.

Other Areas of Interest

Located in northwestern Lake County near Wadsworth, **Van Patten Woods Forest Preserve** offers fishing and boating on Sterling Lake, picnicking in shelters among the oak forests, youth-group camping, and a rental store for boating, bicycling, and fishing equipment. The preserve offers several trails. For more information call 847-367-6640.

Des Plaines River Trail-Northern Section is a gravel, multiuse trail that parallels the Des Plaines River through Lake County. It can be accessed by Russell Road, east of Route 41, and by each of the forest preserves it traverses. At present, the northern section goes through Van Patten Woods, Wadsworth Savanna Forest Preserves, and the Wetlands Demonstration Project.

Park Trails

Oak Ridge Trail 👢👢—.6 miles—This half-circle trail (south unit) connects with the Loop Trail and the Dead River Trail as it follows a ridge through the oak forest.

Bicycle Trail 👢—10 miles—This asphalt trail (south unit) connects various amenities in the park and provides a nice overview of the area.

Power Line Trail 👢—3.3 miles—Developed from the trailhead near Sand Pond in the north unit, this trail (most of it is on an old asphalt road) uncovers savannas and beach ridges.

Marsh Trail 👢—6.7 miles— This north-unit trail is a continuation of the Power Line Trail. On it, you will skirt the day-use portion of the park and discover a marsh.

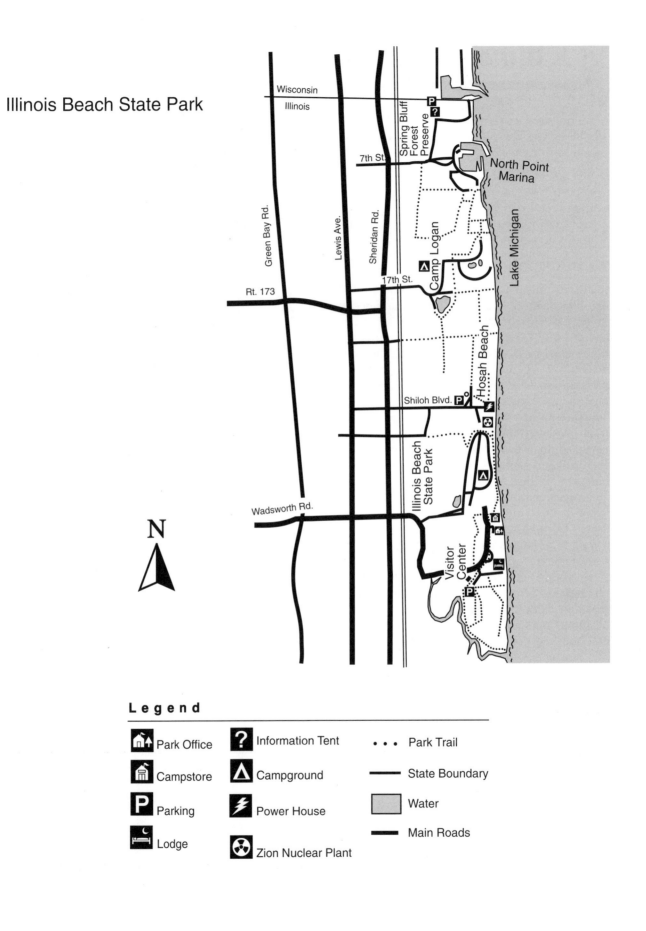

Illinois Beach State Park

Wisconsin

Illinois

Spring Bluff Forest Preserve

7th St.

North Point Marina

Green Bay Rd.

Lewis Ave.

Sheridan Rd.

Camp Logan

Lake Michigan

Rt. 173

17th St.

Hosah Beach

Shiloh Blvd.

Illinois Beach State Park

Wadsworth Rd.

Visitor Center

N

Legend

Park Office	Information Tent	· · · Park Trail
Campstore	Campground	State Boundary
P Parking	Power House	Water
Lodge	Zion Nuclear Plant	Main Roads

Dead River Trail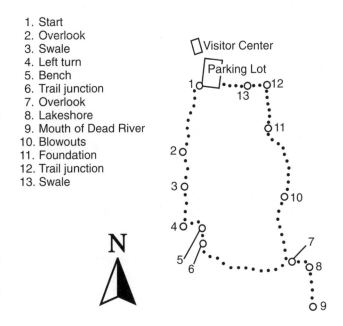

Distance Round-Trip: 2.65 miles

Estimated Hiking Time: 1.75 hours

No matter what the season, the Dead River Trail is alive with color. In the spring, orange and yellow Indian paintbrush mix with red-violet phlox. Summer brings orange wood lilies and the upside-down blooms of hot-pink orchids. In the fall, amid the yellows of goldenrod and red-browns of dying leaves, the area sparkles with the deep blue of gentians.

Caution: Do not try to cross the mouth of the Dead River, which has a dangerous undertow. Poison ivy grows along both sides of the trail so stay on the marked path. After a smelt kill, the beach will smell like an abandoned fish market. Mosquitoes can also be more than a nuisance.

Trail Directions: Begin at a trail-map sign on the southwest corner of the parking area for the nature preserve [1]. The trail is pure sand and all around are low dunes dominated by black oaks. At .25 mile take advantage of the overlook of the Dead River [2].

As you walk along this section, listen for the squeaks of chipmunks and notice the different wildflowers. On your left, low to the ground, note the wild lily of the valley. At .7 mi. the trail crosses a bridge over a swale [3].

Stay on the main trail, even though you will see plenty of unofficial side spurs. Go left at .85 mi. [4], leaving the river and the mosquitoes; within a few steps go right. You are now following the Dune Trail. As you head to the lakeshore, you are walking through an early successional black oak savanna. A bench is provided at 1.0 mi. [5].

The trail intersects another at 1.1 mi. [6]: Continue straight to the lookout tower and the beach. At the overlook (1.15 mi.) climb the steps and observe all the stages of beach and dune succession [7].

Down past the overlook go right. At the lake (1.25 mi.) go right to discover whether the mouth of the Dead River is open or closed [8]. The Dead River seems a short river when its mouth is open to Lake Michigan but a long pond when its mouth is closed by a ridge of sand (deposited by a north-to-south lake current). At 1.4 mi. you will reach the mouth of the Dead River [9]. Turn around and retrace your steps to the observation deck .

Notice how the grasses make perfect arcs in the sand. These grasses are the first stage in dune stabilization; they are resistant to water loss, and their roots hold firm against the wind. At 1.7 mi. you are at [7] again; turn right and continue to follow the Dune Trail. While walking along these stabilized dunes, look for ground cherry, prickly-pear cactus, and small, pale-yellow clumps of an odd-looking Indian paintbrush. The plant, commonly called downy yellow painted cup, is an endangered species in Illinois; this is the eastern limit of its range.

The large indentions in the sand at 1.9 mi. are called blowouts formed by wind erosion in areas where the vegetation has been destroyed [10]. With nothing to hold the sand in place, the wind carries it from the exposed area, forming a hole. A bench on the left marks the 2-mi. point.

At 2.25 mi. [11] you will pass a cement foundation, one of the few remnants of the old town of Beach. On your right will be a sand pond ringed with equisetum (horsetails or scouring rush). Look for mallards along the edge, so still that you'll swear they are decoys.

The trail now curves left, away from the lakeshore, and heads back through a savanna. Another bench is set on the right; stay on the main gravel path. At 2.45 mi. come to a trail junction [12]; go left, coming upon a bridge over a large pond.

The final bridge crossing at 2.55 mi. is over a wet swale [13]. From the bridge, follow the wood-chip path back to the parking area.

1. Start
2. Overlook
3. Swale
4. Left turn
5. Bench
6. Trail junction
7. Overlook
8. Lakeshore
9. Mouth of Dead River
10. Blowouts
11. Foundation
12. Trail junction
13. Swale

North Unit Trail 👢

Distance Round-Trip: 2.25 miles

Estimated Hiking Time: 1.25 hours

Hiking through the fog and mist transports me back 6,000 years. The landscape looks as it did not long after the glaciers disappeared. Sand-prairie species grow next to northern bog species. If not for the old roadbed and nearby subdivision , I wouldn't know what epoch I was in.

Caution: During wet periods, sections of the trail may have standing water. Just take off your shoes—it's worth the wade.

Trail Directions: From the south unit, turn right (north) on Sheridan Road, follow it to Seventeenth Street and turn right into the main entrance of the north unit. Begin the trail at the south parking area [**1**]. The trail starts as a crushed-limestone, multipurpose path. On your left will be Sand Pond and on your right, cottonwoods and oaks. As you hike through a small cottonwood grove, check the shape of the leaves. They are triangular and when crushed, they give off a sweet fragrance. The cottonwood will be the dominant tree on this hike.

Once through the grove go right at a large cottonwood, leaving the crushed-rock path behind [**2**] (.1 mi.). A marsh is on your right, and through the willow on your left is a wet sand prairie restoration with lots of equisetum, or horsetails. An enclosed cattail marsh will soon come into view on the right. At .4 mi. go left at the trail intersection [**3**] and hike along the road to an abandoned housing development. You skirt a preserve on the left; on the right, groves of quaking aspen alternate with a marsh.

Ignore the trail to the right at .65 mi. [**4**]. The area here begins to look like the south unit, black oaks mixing with prairie vegetation—a savanna. Already you can feel the effects of the nearby lake, and fog is a common occurrence. Hiking in the fog gives the feel of the ancient North Woods. You are totally alone, and, given a little imagination, at any moment a Mastodon may materialize from the fog.

At .75 mi. note a trail to the left, but continue straight to the beach [**5**]. On your left is a swale, composed of mucky, sandy soils dominated by rushes and sedges. The soil is alkaline, so its plants are much like those in a bog or marsh. The trail dead-ends at Lake Michigan, which marks .85 mi. [**6**]. Walk along the beach looking for that perfect rock, observing the gulls and an occasional cormorant, and trying to find signs of beach succession. Retrace your steps from the lake, back to point [**5**].

This time at [**5**] go right (.95 mi.). On the right you will have an excellent view of the old beach ridges. When the glacial ice was melting 8,000 to 12,000 years ago, Lake Michigan was part of a much larger Lake Chicago. As the glacier receded farther and farther north, the water level in the lake fell in stages. Each level lasted for several hundred years and formed characteristic beach ridges—the ridges observed in both units of the park.

On the left are evenly spaced trees and a lush, green understory (plants growing under the canopy), dotted with multihued wildflowers. A well-planned and maintained park comes to mind, instead of the natural area that was narrowly saved from being cut up as housing lots. During the late spring look for shooting stars, puccoons, and cedar waxwings in the savanna on your left. At 1.25 mi. you will come to an intersection, but continue on the main trail.

The path comes to a T at 1.5 mi. [**7**]. Go left, skirting an FAA air-traffic-control facility. After this modern-day interruption, look to your left at the swales. Compare the restored area on the left with that on the right, which is in need of help. At 1.75 mi. go left [**8**], and Sand Pond will come into view on the right. The crushed-rock path is soon underfoot again. Look in the willows ringing Sand Pond for yellow warblers. The gravel leads back to where you began the loop (at 2.15 mi.) [**2**] and soon you are back at the parking area.

1. Start
2. Right turn
3. Left turn
4. Side trail (don't follow)
5. Lakeshore
6. Lake
7. Left turn
8. Left turn

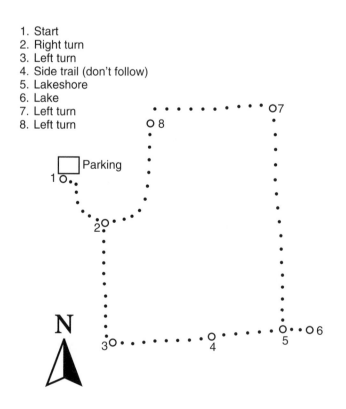

2. Chicago Botanic Garden

- Visit demonstration gardens showcasing the best plants for the Midwest, research gardens holding species being tested for performance in the Chicago environment, and conservation gardens featuring the state's native flora.
- See eye-to-eye with a youthful Linnaeus kneeling to collect a rose.
- Use your binoculars to view some of the 241 bird species found here—from the resident geese that share the trails and garden paths to the migratory spring warblers.
- Contemplate the world as you might imagine it from the quiet of Sansho-En, a Japanese garden.

Area Information

A visit here will fulfill all your garden fantasies. The keys to obtaining that coveted green thumb can be found at this garden, and in epic proportions!

The area, once a large watering trough for herds of cattle, often flooded and was mosquito-ridden. In 1965 the land was drained, and construction of the garden began. The layout of the Chicago Botanic Garden is the work of a landscape architect who envisioned hillocks and waterways reminiscent of the Garden of Perfect Brightness, built in 1709 near Beijing, China. The Chicago Botanic Garden's 300 acres have been reclaimed as a garden showplace. Elevated landforms offer protection from the harsh winds and water, offering a measure of peacefulness as well as tempering the damaging effects of unpredictable frosts. Rolling prairies, woodlands, lagoons, and 20 gardens provide not only beauty but also a friendly habitat for birds, waterfowl, and wildlife.

Directions: The Chicago Botanic Garden is located in Glencoe, about 25 miles north of downtown Chicago. Follow the Edens Expressway (I-94) north onto U.S. Route 41, exit Lake-Cook Road, and travel .5 mile east to the garden's entrance.

Hours Open: The garden is open year-round except on Christmas, from 8 A.M. until sunset. Admission is free, but parking is $4 per car.

Facilities: The Botanic Garden offers an orientation center, food service (open for breakfast and lunch), picnic area, tram tours, plant information services, horticultural library, garden gift shop, greenhouse, and an educational center.

Permits and Rules: The speed limit is 20 mph throughout the garden. No pets are allowed except guide and hearing dogs. Bicycles are permitted on designated bike routes only. No active sports or games (e.g., in-line skating, Frisbee throwing, skiing, swimming, fishing) are permitted. Do not collect plants, flowers, labels, fruits, or vegetables; climb on the trees or shrubs; or stand or walk in the garden beds.

Further Information: The Chicago Botanic Garden, 1000 Lake-Cook Road, P.O. Box 400, Glencoe, IL 60022-0400; 847-835-5440.

Other Areas of Interest

The Chicago Botanic Garden is the northern trailhead for the **North Branch Bicycle Trail** (17.3 miles), a linear hiking-biking trail that follows the north branch of the Chicago River. The bike trail, surfaced mostly in asphalt, wanders through the Skokie Lagoons and several Cook County forest preserves before ending at the intersection of Devon and Caldwell Avenues in Chicago. For more information on this trail contact the Forest Preserve District of Cook County, 536 N. Harlem Ave., River Forest, IL 60305; 708-366-9420.

Early travelers used an old Indian trail to go from Fort Dearborn in Chicago to Fort Howard in Green Bay. The trip took one month on foot. The **Green Bay Trail** is a linear 18-mile, multiuse trail made of crushed gravel and asphalt and leading from Shorewood Park in Wilmette to Lake Bluff. The trail is built on the right-of-way of the old Chicago-North Shore-Milwaukee Railway. For more information call 312-261-8400.

Park Trail

Turnbull Woods Nature Trail 👢—.5 mile—This is a loop trail through a woodland. Spring wildflowers on this former grazing ground include clumps of bloodroot and white trout lily, and carpets of white trillium. Another part of the woods is a true prairie savanna (where trees, such as native oaks, are spaced sufficiently far apart to allow sunlight through to support many prairie wildflowers and grasses).

Chicago
Botanic
Garden

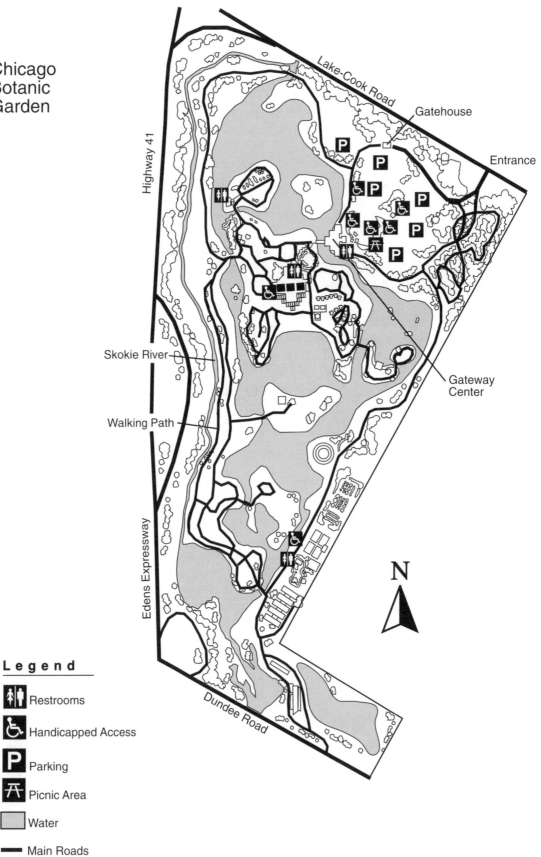

Skokie River

Walking Path

Gatehouse

Entrance

Gateway
Center

Lake-Cook Road

Highway 41

Edens Expressway

Dundee Road

N

L e g e n d

Restrooms

Handicapped Access

P Parking

Picnic Area

Water

Main Roads

Inside Garden Trail 👢

Distance Round-Trip: 2.5 miles

Estimated Hiking Time: 1+ hours

Like Alice in Wonderland, wander through these gardens, gleaning ideas as you go. Instead of a Cheshire cat, meet up with a larger-than-life Linnaeus. Cookies for the tea party are available at the garden's restaurant!

Trail Directions: Begin the trail at the rear door of the Gateway Center and cross the bridge [**1**]. Straight ahead is Flying Geese, the sculpture by the father-and-son team of William and David Turner. Walk straight past the sculpture (.2 mi.), pausing at the Naturalistic Garden on the right [**2**].

The Naturalistic Garden features three types of native Illinois plant communities (oak-hickory forest, prairie, and a combination of the two) that can be duplicated in your own yard. Past the Naturalistic Garden at .3 mi. is a walkway leading to the Fruit and Vegetable Garden [**3**]. Go right, crossing the bridge, and take two additional rights through a hedge with a stone bird on either side of the opening. Explore the best of the old and new fruit, vegetable, nut, and wild food varieties. Use the path on the outside that follows the lake, eventually passing through an arched arbor; turn right and recross the bridge.

After the bridge go right; within a few steps you will be in the Bulb Garden [**4**]. While you're in the Bulb Garden, don't forget to explore the Aquatic Garden; look not only at the plants, but also seek out the dragonflies, fish, and frogs.

Exit the Bulb Garden, stopping to admire the terra-cotta sculpture on the right, which represents the metamorphosis of a bulb. Go straight across (.65 mi.) to the Landscape Garden [**5**], which displays perennial ideas for the home garden and is full of sculptural surprises. When you exit the garden, a fountain is on your right. Within a few steps you should see a directional sign for the Educational Center and the Sensory Garden. Turn right.

Soon you will walk by the entrance to the Educational Center and pass through the parking lot to a path that immediately comes to a T; go right again and at 1.1 mi. enter the Sensory Garden [**6**]. You can pick up an audio wand at the Educational Center, which enables you to listen to how people who have lost one of their senses experience plants. Take the farthest right of the four paths and wind through several woodland environments. Turn right once again, go down the steps, skirt the water, and ascend near the greenhouses.

At this intersection, go right; the greenhouses will be on your left. A large kiosk with crystals marks the entrance to the English Walled Garden (1.35 mi.); go right [**7**], bypassing the Walled Garden, and instead walk by the lake. At 1.6 mi. you will come to an arched bridge—a Japanese symbol for the link between this world and paradise. Cross the bridge (1.6 mi.), turn right, and tour the Japanese Garden—Santo-En, "The Garden of Three Islands" [**8**]. Only two of the islands have paths; the third island, inaccessible to park visitors, symbolizes perfect, everlasting happiness—believed to be unobtainable. By crossing a zigzag bridge to enter the second island, any evil spirits that were following you should have fallen into the water (evil spirits travel in straight lines).

After completing the loop of the garden, recross the arched bridge and go right. Skirt the outside of the Waterfall Garden [**9**] and turn left (2.15 mi.) where the trail forks through an allée of trees, heading to the Educational Center. The trail then comes to a T (2.25 mi.); go right [**10**]. Continue straight through the Heritage Garden, designed after Europe's first botanical garden in Padua, Italy. Here you will come face-to-face with a youthful Linnaeus kneeling to collect a rose—symbolizing the continual search for knowledge.

You have completed a loop walk of the garden and are back at the goose sculpture; go right, back to the Gateway Center.

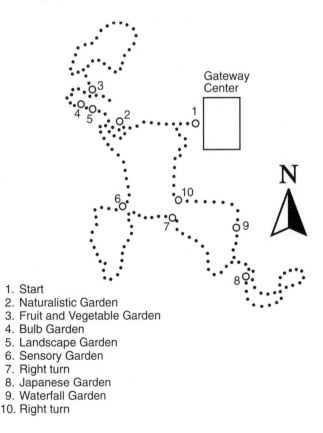

1. Start
2. Naturalistic Garden
3. Fruit and Vegetable Garden
4. Bulb Garden
5. Landscape Garden
6. Sensory Garden
7. Right turn
8. Japanese Garden
9. Waterfall Garden
10. Right turn

Outside Garden Trail 🥾

Distance Round-Trip: 2.5 miles

Estimated Hiking Time: 1 hour

Use the Outside Garden Trail for an overall view and a chance to meet the garden's geese close-up.

Caution: The tram also uses this trail.

Trail Directions: Begin the trail at the Gateway Center (you may pick up maps here). From the Center go right [**1**]. The entire hike will be on an asphalt road with the exception of the trail through the prairie. When you reach the stop sign (.15 mi.), go right and through the gate [**2**].

On the left is the entrance to Turnbill Woods. To the right are the islands of the Japanese Gardens, designed to give the appearance of floating worlds. The large fieldstones that dot the islands are symbols of the earth's bones or skeleton underneath. The body of water that surrounds the garden complex is human-made, although it was originally part of the Skokie Lagoons. As you walk along the path, you'll find plenty of benches provided for quiet contemplation.

At .7 mi. you will reach the Herbaceous Trial Gardens, surrounded by a tall fence to keep out the deer [**3**]. Not even botanical gardens are immune to the browsing of white-tailed deer. Within the next .1 mi. you will come to the Children's Garden [**4**] and the Learning Garden for the Disabled on the left, which demonstrates gardening as therapy for people with emotional and physical disabilities.

Go right at 1 mi., crossing the bridge [**5**] and taking an immediate left on a narrow path through the prairie. During the summer and fall, the tall prairie grasses hide most of the city, giving the sense of wide-open, green spaces. Markers identify many of the plants, so take time to feel their leaves and learn their names. Marvel at the coarseness of the leaves of compass plant and prairie dock. This path parallels

the main trail and is one of several to explore the prairie's many interesting plants. While hiking through the prairie, note the mounds on the left—a reconstruction of a gravel hill prairie.

Exit the prairie (1.35 mi.), staying on the trail (that parallels the larger one) as it takes you through small groves of trees [**6**]. The geese seem to be more abundant in this stretch of the garden and make a good show as they take off from the lake or go about their daily business. The walking path ends at 1.75 mi.; rejoin the larger trail [**7**].

After a few steps you will come to a yellow yield sign. Here the trail comes to a T; go left, parallel to the Skokie River. Look for song sparrows in the grasses along the river and red-breasted nuthatches and dark-eyed juncos in the pines. The 2-mi. point is marked by a river birch on the left just before you round the curve [**8**]. Cross the bridge and leave the Skokie River behind. Go through the traffic gate at 2.35 mi. and turn right, heading through the parking area and back to the Gateway Center.

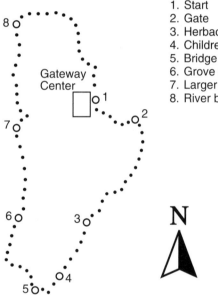

1. Start
2. Gate
3. Herbaceous Trial Garden
4. Children's Garden
5. Bridge
6. Grove of trees
7. Larger trail
8. River birch

3. City of Chicago

- Discover owls, bison, lions, flowers, and birds, all made from stone and incorporated into building facades.
- Admire the many skyscrapers in a city that was the birthplace of this architectural design.
- Have fun riding Navy Pier's 15-story, old-fashioned Ferris wheel and get a great view of the city's skyline.
- Delve into endless museum exhibits.
- Shop and eat to your heart's content.

Area Information

In 1833, the year Chicago was incorporated as a village, a young merchant from New Hampshire named Colbee Benton traveled West to satisfy his curiosity. He wrote in his journal, "I find Chicago a very pleasant place, as I before thought. It is situated on the southwestern shore of Lake Michigan at the mouth of the Chicago River, and already it has the appearance of considerable business."

Location helped this new village grow into one of the largest cities in the world. Chicago lay at the intersection of an inland waterway connecting the east with the west—a city soon to become the nation's middleman. Beginning as a transportation hub, the town quickly developed into a major industrial and manufacturing center. When the Great Fire of 1871 destroyed four square miles of the downtown, the city's infrastructure was spared, and within two years the downtown was rebuilt. The fire spurred a renais-

sance in building and architecture, and by 1885 the first skyscraper in the world was erected—the Home Insurance Building. The recovery of the city was so complete that in 1893 Chicago hosted the Colombian Exposition.

Benton wrote of Chicago, "And finally I have seen a good deal to surprise, interest, and amuse me for the few days that I have remained here." He could have been a modern-day, if somewhat understated, spokesman for Chicago.

Directions: The Field Museum, where the hike begins, is located downtown on Lake Shore Drive (Route 41).

Hours Open: Though the city is open 24 hours daily, year-round, hiking is safest during daylight hours. Sunday morning, when the streets and sidewalks are deserted and quiet, is an excellent time to hike.

Facilities: The museum has a parking lot around it. Restroom facilities, food, and water are available at various sites along the hike.

Permits and Rules: Do not jaywalk.

Further Information: Chicago Tourism Office, 312-744-2400.

Other Areas of Interest

Your imagination and pocketbook are the only limiting factors in a city that offers everything you could imagine or possibly need.

Area Trail

Chicago Park District Bikeway 👢—18.5 miles— This is a linear, multiuse path that provides pan- oramic views of the Chicago skyline and Lake Michigan. The trail includes five parks and 31 beaches as it parallels Lake Shore Drive.

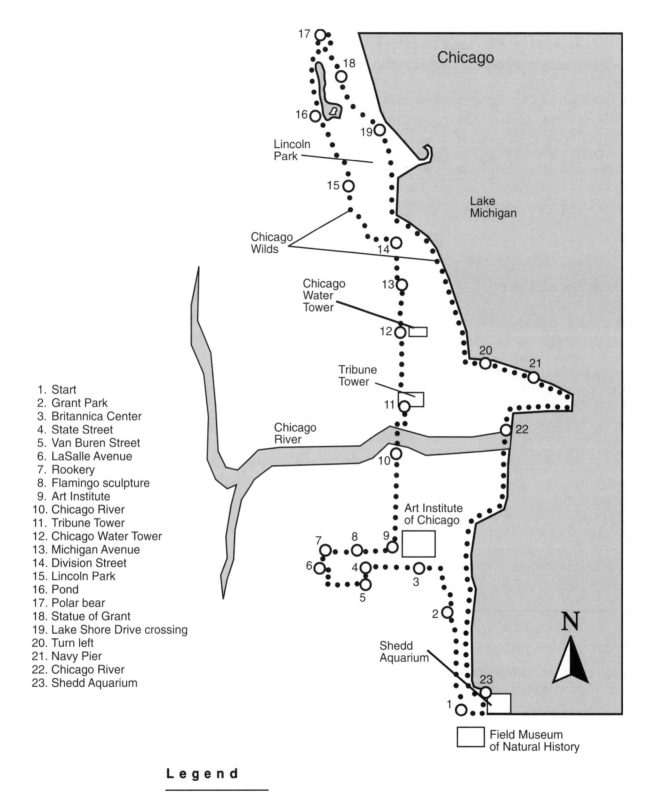

1. Start
2. Grant Park
3. Britannica Center
4. State Street
5. Van Buren Street
6. LaSalle Avenue
7. Rookery
8. Flamingo sculpture
9. Art Institute
10. Chicago River
11. Tribune Tower
12. Chicago Water Tower
13. Michigan Avenue
14. Division Street
15. Lincoln Park
16. Pond
17. Polar bear
18. Statue of Grant
19. Lake Shore Drive crossing
20. Turn left
21. Navy Pier
22. Chicago River
23. Shedd Aquarium

Legend

• • •   Area Trails

   Water

Chicago Wilds—Lions, Bison, and Polar Bears, Oh My! 🥾

Distance Round-Trip: 9 miles

Estimated Hiking Time: 6 hours

A walk in Chicago isn't so different from a hike with Mother Nature. Instead of gazing at tall trees, I admire tall buildings with unique architecture. Adorned with sculpture, these "tall trees" hold not only owls, squirrels, and leaves, but bison and lions as well!

Caution: Except on Sunday mornings, beware of crowds of people on the sidewalks and nonstop noise and traffic.

Trail Directions: Begin the hike at the Field Museum of Natural History parking lot [**1**]. Use the crosswalk west of the museum to cross Lake Shore Drive; go right along Lake Shore Drive and on the east side of Grant Park. This will give you a nice, unobstructed view of the skyline and enable you to admire the park, patterned somewhat after Versailles. After crossing Balboa Drive (.5 mi.), angle left to walk through Grant Park [**2**]. Pause at the Charles Buckingham Fountain, said to be the largest in the world.

Continue through the park, turning left (west) at Jackson Drive. After crossing Columbus Drive, look to your left to see the statue of a seated Lincoln. As you continue west on Jackson (.75 mi.), pause on the overpass over the railroad and look up at the building directly ahead—the Britannica Center [**3**]. At its top is a glass beehive that was the symbol of a banking firm, the original owners of the building. The hive is surrounded by the heads of four bison, representing thrift, industry, strength, and city. The overpass where you are now standing was the eastern edge of the city before the Great Fire.

Continue west on Jackson, crossing Michigan Avenue. As you walk by the Britannica Center (310 S. Michigan), note the flowers, vines, and griffins. At State Street (1 mi.) go left [**4**]. While walking south, look up at the brick-colored building on the right—the Harold Washington Library Center. Crowning the library are huge, blue-green, metal owls of wisdom. Continue south on State to Van Buren Street (1.1 mi.) where you turn right (west) [**5**]. At the corner of Van Buren and Dearborn note the Fisher Building (343 S.

Dearborn) with its aquatic menagerie—fishes, snakes, shells, and crabs—on the facade (cross the street for the best view).

Look for lion heads, corn, vines, grapes, and wheat on the facades of the many buildings around you. Continue straight (west) on Van Buren, and at LaSalle turn right (north). At Jackson Boulevard, LaSalle takes a jog, so go left and then, within a half block, go right (1.4 mi.). You should be back on LaSalle [6]. At the corner of LaSalle and Adams is the Rookery (209 S. LaSalle) [7]. The building, whose name comes from the former city hall located here from 1872 to 1884, was the favorite gathering place for the city's pigeons. Now the only pigeons present are large, silent, and made of stone. Admire the lions' heads that surround the top of the building across the street. Look left from this location for a great view of the Sears Tower.

Go right (east) on Adams and within two blocks come to the bright, orange-red Flamingo sculpture by Alexander Calder [8]. Continuing east on Adams, pass State and Wabash streets to Michigan Avenue. In front of you is the Art Institute (1.75 mi.), flanked by two large bronze lions [9]. The only building allowed in Grant Park, it was constructed for the World's Colombian Exposition as a place for conferences.

Turn left and proceed north up Michigan Avenue. As you pass the Chicago Athletic Association Building, note the owl in the doorway. At the Chicago Cultural Center look up to see the flower facades underneath the overhang and on the undersides of the windows. Cross Wacker Drive (2.2 mi.) and the Chicago River [10]. Note the Fort Dearborn Monument on both sides of the bridge. After the bridge, cross the street to the east side of Michigan Avenue.

At the corner of Illinois and Michigan avenues (2.3 mi.) is the Tribune Tower [11]. It's worth taking time to examine the souvenir bits and pieces from historical ruins and monuments embedded in tower's exterior wall. Look up and find the animal-like gargoyles on the windows. How many different birds, animals, and plants are represented in the archway that surrounds the front entrance? Can you find dogwood, an owl, and a fox, stork, porcupine, parrot, and howling dog?

Continue walking on Michigan Avenue, nick-named the Magnificent Mile at this stretch. After seven blocks (2.75 mi.) approach the Chicago Water Tower and Pumping Station [12], located on Chicago Avenue and flanking both sides of Michigan Avenue. The building resembles a fish-tank castle and was one of the few downtown structures to survive the Great Chicago Fire.

Continuing on Michigan Avenue, cross at Oak Street (2.85 mi.) to the west side of the street [13]. Go left at Division Street (3 mi.) [14], cross Stone Street, and go right at Astor Street. Up and down Astor are brownstone apartments; look at the windows and doorways for interesting stonework. Known as the Astor Street District, this area was constructed over a period of 80 years. Astor Street dead-ends into North Boulevard.

Cross North Boulevard at 3.4 mi. You are now at the south end of Lincoln Park; go right to a path that winds through Lincoln Park; head north [15]. LaSalle Drive will be on your right; take a right and go under LaSalle Drive, using the tunnel. Upon exiting the tunnel, veer left toward the statue of Benjamin Franklin (LaSalle Drive will now be on your left) and then head north. Go left (3.75 mi.) at the pond, home to mallards and geese [16]. After skirting the Farm in the Zoo (but before the bridge), go left and explore Lincoln Park Zoo.

As you wander through the zoo, notice the interesting stone facades on the buildings and the Winken, Blinken, and Nod statue adjacent to the Primate House. Don't neglect to visit the koalas, located north of the Primate House. The northernmost point of the hike is populated by an inhabitant of the far North—the polar bear [17]. It's time to head back, so wind your way south through the east side of the park (5.25 mi.).

Leave Lincoln Park at the imposing statue of Grant [18]. Did you notice that Grant Park had a statue of Lincoln, and Lincoln Park has a statue of Grant? Off to the left and in the distance is a bridge—not over water but over a steady stream of cars. Head toward the bridge, cross it (5.4 mi.), and turn right on the pedestrian lane along the lake shore [19]. You are on the Chicago Park District Bikeway. Explore Lake Michigan and its sandy shore, using the benches to rest or people-watch.

At 7.1 mi. go left toward Navy Pier [20]. Follow the signs for the Lake Front Path. Take a side spur at 7.25 mi. to Navy Pier [21] and ride the Ferris wheel for great views of Lake Michigan and the city's skyline. Returning to the Lake Front Path, go up the stairs and to your left, using the bridge (7.4 mi.) to cross the Chicago River [22]. Continue walking along the lakeshore.

All too soon, the call of seagulls and the lapping of waves are left behind as you leave Lake Shore Path and head up the steps (8.8 mi.) near the Shedd Aquarium [23]. Go right and use the pedestrian underpass to return to the Field Museum. As the final gesture of a devoted naturalist, end your hike at the Beaver Totem.

4. Wolf Road Prairie

- Delight in this hike if you're an engineer—this is a prairie on a grid.
- Bring your prairie plant field guide to help identify the 250 species that grow here.
- Enjoy relief from city noises, drowned out here by katydids, crickets, and cicadas.
- Emerge from the woods to experience the illusion of discovering the prairie for the first time, much as the early settlers did—only from a sidewalk.

Area Information

Like most of the area surrounding Chicago, the early landscape of Wolf Road consisted of savannas and wet or dry prairies. Due to its wet nature, the area was never plowed or grazed. In the 1920s, Wolf Road was slated to become a housing development and sidewalks were constructed. But the Great Depression intervened, the owner was forced to abandon the project, and the prairie was spared—one of the few good things to have come from the depression.

By the 1970s local conservationists discovered Wolf Road. This led them to form the Save the Prairie Society, which has had an active role in the management, restoration, and preservation of the area.

Directions: Wolf Road Prairie is a small oasis in a sea of development. Take the U.S. 34 (Ogden Avenue) exit off I-294 (Tri-State Tollway); go .75 mile on Ogden Avenue to Wolf Road. Take Wolf Road north 1 mile to 31st Street in Westchester. The preserve is north of 31st Street and west of Wolf Road.

Hours Open: The site is open year-round.

Facilities: Parking and a trail and information board are available.

Permits and Rules: Stay on the sidewalks and paths. No pets or vehicles are allowed in the preserve. Do not pick or disturb anything.

Further Information: Save the Prairie Society, 10327 Elizabeth Road, Westchester, IL 60154; 708-865-8736.

Other Areas of Interest

Located in Brookfield, the world-renowned **Brookfield Zoo** features more than 2,300 animals, representing 425 species. Naturalistic exhibits show representatives from rain forests, an African savanna, and the Pacific Northwest. The area has plenty of concessions, restrooms, and paths. For more information call 708-485-0263.

Bemis Woods Forest Preserve is located north of Western Springs and south of Wolf Road. It is the western trailhead for the Salt Creek Bicycle Trail, a 6.6-mile trail that runs from the woods to Brookfield Zoo. Along the way you pass hills, prairies, and sinkholes. For more information call 708-366-9420.

© Michael Jeffords

Wolf Road Prairie Trail 🥾

Distance Round-Trip: 2 miles

Estimated Hiking Time: 1.25 hours

". . . after passing the oak openings & thick forest the first view of an Illinois Prairie is sublime, I must say awfully Grand. . . ."
— *Morris Sleight, 1834, describing the area around Naperville*

Caution: Parts of the sidewalk and trail are very uneven.

Trail Directions: Park at the second parking area by the information board and begin the hike to the right of the board [**1**]. The trail will generally follow old sidewalks, and you will hike this prairie on a grid. Walk through a small grove of bur oak (a savanna), which is carpeted in the spring with wild geranium.

By .15 mi. you will have come to the end of the sidewalk and should go left [**2**]; a large cottonwood will be on your right. Cross the narrow grass path, and you are again on a sidewalk. At .2 mi. turn right [**3**]. Watch your step: This section of the prairie can be quite wet. Look down on your left for glacial boulders. From the wet area you will pass through a problem area. Here brambles and dogwood are trying to take over. At .35 mi. go right [**4**], and within a few feet go right again, in front of the large cottonwood.

At .5 mi. you will turn left, and then left again at .55 mile [**5**]. Touch the grass along the side of the path, but be careful not to cut yourself. This is prairie cordgrass, a native of wet prairies. At .6 mi. enter one of the better areas of the prairie [**6**]. In spring look for shooting star, phlox, and spiderwort; by summer the yellows of the prairie dock, compass plant, and coneflowers will be in their full glory, along with rattlesnake master and blazing star. September brings the final flowering of many plants and flights of butterflies—especially monarchs and tiger swallowtails.

At .65 mi. go right [**7**], and within a few feet, go right again. Continue to walk through one of the better prairie areas. Notice the grass on the right. Even without the wind blowing it gives the illusion of movement, especially in the spring and early summer when it is still short. At .8 mi. go left [**8**] and look to the right to see how many different species of plants you can find. Go left again at .85 mi., not forgetting to look up. The prairie is patrolled by nighthawks and red-tailed hawks.

At 1 mi. turn right; within a few feet, go right again [**9**]. At 1.15 mi. continue straight [**10**] and look around for the grass, little bluestem and, in the fall, the cerulean blooms of prairie gentian. You will now reenter the grove of bur oaks; look to your left in the spring season for large patches of wild hyacinth. You are back at the highway at 1.3 mi.; go right [**11**], past the Nature Preserve sign, and back in through the savanna.

Emerging from the savanna you will enter high-quality prairie on both sides. At 1.45 mi. go left [**12**]; at the crossroads go straight and then left. After viewing prairie you will again enter the savanna (1.65 mi.) and come to the parking area [**13**], but let's discover one more grid before finishing. Turn right, back into the savanna. At 1.8 mi. go left on the grass path [**14**]. Within a few feet go left again and skirt a tree growing in the middle of the sidewalk. Reenter the savanna, and you are back on the road (1.95 mi.); go left [**15**]. Soon you are back where you began.

Wolf Road Prairie

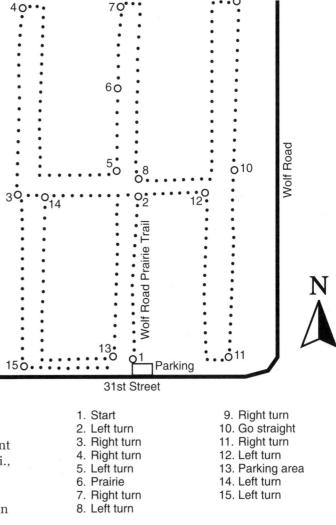

1. Start
2. Left turn
3. Right turn
4. Right turn
5. Left turn
6. Prairie
7. Right turn
8. Left turn
9. Right turn
10. Go straight
11. Right turn
12. Left turn
13. Parking area
14. Left turn
15. Left turn

5. Edward L. Ryerson Conservation Area

- Discover one of the best examples of an old-growth, sugar maple forest in northeastern Illinois.
- Enjoy masses of spring wildflowers.
- Bring your binoculars and scan the canopies of large trees.
- Savor some of the best fall colors in Illinois.
- Hike through a picturesque farmstead.

Area Information

Edward L. Ryerson Conservation Area is a large tract of mature, bottomland forest bordering the Des Plaines River. Two major Indian trails once intersected nearby, and Lake County's first resident, Daniel Wright, built a cabin here. During the 1920s the land was acquired, the intention being to let it sit a while to appreciate and then to sell it for subdivisions. The first parcels that sold, however, went to people who wanted to build weekend cabins, and each of them kept large tracts for their own weekend use.

Edward L. Ryerson acquired land and built a small cabin on the banks of the Des Plaines. In the late 1930s he next purchased a large tract from the descendent of the first settler and built the farm you see today. The Visitor's Center was the Ryerson home during the 1950s and 1960s. Because all the land-owners had grown to love the area, they wished to see it preserved. Beginning with Ryerson, who helped form the Lake County Forest Preserve District, each owner began selling or giving away the land to the Forest Preserve District. Thanks to the former owners' foresight and appreciation of this land, you can enjoy one of the finest deciduous bottomland forests in Illinois.

Directions: Edward L. Ryerson Conservation Area is located west of Deerfield on Riverwoods Road. The entrance is 1.8 miles south of Route 22 and 1.3 miles north of Deerfield Road.

Hours Open: The site is open daily from 6:30 A.M. to 5:00 P.M.

Facilities: Ryerson Visitor's Center has a library, lecture and meeting rooms, water, and restrooms. The Exhibit Cabin contains natural history exhibits, and the site has a working farm.

Permits and Rules: Pets, picnicking, and off-road bicycling are not allowed. Do not collect natural objects. Stay on the trails and do not take shortcuts. For your own safety, view the river only from its banks.

Further Information: Ryerson Conservation Area, 21950 N. Riverwoods Road, Deerfield, IL 60015; 847-948-7750.

Other Areas of Interest

The southern section of the **Des Plaines River Trail** winds through four adjoining forest preserves for a total of 8.75 miles (one-way). Old School Forest Preserve provides fishing, sledding in winter, and an additional 3.5 miles of trails. MacArthur Woods Forest Preserve is a large, undeveloped tract of forest. This is how the eastern edge of the Des Plaines River Valley looked long ago. The trail here has many curves to preserve the large trees. Wright Woods Forest Preserve offers fishing, a playground, and an additional 4.5 miles of trails. At Half Day Preserve, the trail winds through prairie, woods, and wetlands. With the exception of MacArthur Woods, which has no facilities, the other preserves have picnicking, restrooms, phones, and water. For more information call the Lake County Forest Preserve District at 847-367-6640.

Park Trail

North Trail and South Trail Tree Tour 👢—each is < 1 mile—Guidebooks are available for both these trails. The North Trail's describes the changes that have occurred on the land and the South Trail's identifies 15 species of trees encountered on the trail. The tree guide is a handy reference for other areas as well.

River Woods Trail 🥾

Distance Round-Trip: 3.05 miles

Estimated Hiking Time: 1.4 hours

This trail is appropriately named: Especially after a heavy downpour the rivers become torrents, and the trails become rivers. The Des Plaines is up and fast-flowing, and by trail's end my shoes make their own noise—squish, squish, squish.

Caution: The trail can be very muddy after a heavy rain.

Trail Directions: Begin the trail south of the parking area [1]. This access trail intersects with the main trail at .05 mi.; go right and begin hiking through a maple woods. The trail forms a Y at .1 mi.; go left there [2]. At .25 mi. the trail comes to the Des Plaines River [3] and forms a T; go left.

You will encounter the Smith cabin on your left at .4 mi. and also signage about flooding. From the cabin continue on the trail and cross the first of several bridges. At .6 mi. a trail comes in from the left; ignore it and continue straight noting the large willow on the right [4]. At .65 mi. you will come to a pair of bridge crossings; go left after the second one.

At .95 mi. admire the large cottonwood on the right as you cross yet another bridge [5]. After the bridge you will be hiking in a small grove of white oaks. Look on the ground for early meadow rue and great white trillium (the site is famous for it!).

At 1.55 mi. you will cross another bridge and boardwalk; look on both sides for large clumps of marsh marigold [6]. At 1.75 mi. you can expect a five-trail intersection [7]. Just before this intersection, look for shooting star on the right under an oak tree. At the intersection go right, through an oak woods. The trail skirts the boundary of the property (2.1 mi.) and is close to the highway [8]. At the trail intersection (2.25 mi.), go left [9], through a tree-lined allée.

At 2.5 mi. you are back at [7]; take the trail immediately on your right [10]. You will cross two bridges and boardwalks at 2.6 mi., and a spruce grove will be on your left. The trail comes to a grassy open area at 2.75 mi.; go left [11]. The path now skirts the woods, soon entering the forest, and comes to a T at 2.8 mi.; go right [12]. Continue straight through the maple woods at 2.9 mi. On the right is a grassy area partially blocked by a large row of trees. At 3 mi. go right at the large double oak [13]. Within a few yards you will be back at the parking area.

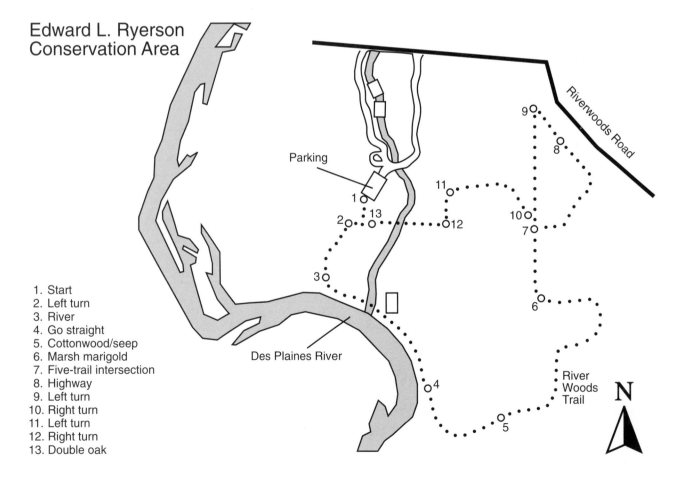

Edward L. Ryerson Conservation Area

Parking

Des Plaines River

Riverwoods Road

River Woods Trail

N

1. Start
2. Left turn
3. River
4. Go straight
5. Cottonwood/seep
6. Marsh marigold
7. Five-trail intersection
8. Highway
9. Left turn
10. Right turn
11. Left turn
12. Right turn
13. Double oak

6. Palos and Sag Valley Forest Preserve

- Discover the largest and most diverse holding in the Chicago Forest Preserve System, containing everything from nature preserves to a nuclear Stonehenge.

- Bring a bird identification guide to help identify the many waterfowl and shorebirds that congregate on and around the sloughs during spring and fall.

- Enjoy the many wildflowers, from the early-blooming skunk cabbage found in Black Partridge Woods to the final goldenrods in the prairie restoration at Little Red Schoolhouse.

- Don't forget your compass! The preserve has many trails, both official and unofficial, and it is easy to become confused or lost.

Area Information

The Palos and Sag Valley Forest Preserve is the largest and most diverse area in any North American urban setting. Here you can find woods, thickets, meadows, sloughs, marshes, and small, twisting streams. The Palos Hills are moraines, an accumulation of earth and stones carried and deposited by the last glacier. The many sloughs found here are also a result of the last glacier. When it receded it left behind large chunks of ice, and as the water melted, it found its way into depressions in the land.

Four of the state's oldest nature preserves are located here. Black Partridge Woods is an area of river bluffs, ravines, and spring-fed streams and is the first place in the Chicago region where wildflowers bloom each spring. Cap Sauers Holdings, the best-defined glacial ridge (*esker*) in the state, is the most undeveloped tract of native landscape in Cook County. A climb to the top of the esker yields a spectacular overlook of the preserve. Cranberry Slough supports a population of cranberries and is the only quaking bog in Cook County. The final preserve in the area is Paw Paw Woods, a bluff and floodplain forest that is the northernmost limit for pawpaws in Illinois.

Despite the peaceful nature of the preserves, a not-so-peaceful enterprise was at one time located here, namely, the original Argonne Lab where the first atomic bomb was developed. Deep in the woods one may stumble on a radioactive burial site. It is marked by six corner markers and a large granite stone—a Stonehenge of the atomic age.

Directions: The Little Red Schoolhouse (where the hike begins) is north of the Cal-Sag channel in Willow Springs. From the Willow Springs Road intersection with Archer Avenue, take Willow Springs south of 95th Street. Here Willow Springs Road becomes 104th Avenue; proceed south and the entrance to Little Red Schoolhouse is on the west side.

Hours Open: The site is open year-round except on Christmas, New Year's Day, and Thanksgiving. The Little Red Schoolhouse is open from 9 A.M. to 4 P.M. Monday through Thursday and from 9 A.M. to 5 P.M. on weekends. It is closed on Fridays.

Facilities: Little Red Schoolhouse has a variety of live mammals, reptiles, and amphibians that are native to the area. Picnickers will find tables, water, reservable shelters, and open places to play. Fishing is allowed on many of the lakes and sloughs. Swallow Cliff has a winter sports center that supports six toboggan slides (including the longest and highest in the Chicago region) and horseback riding is also available.

Permits and Rules: All pets must be leashed. Ground fires are not permitted. Do not pick the flowers.

Further Information: Cook County Forest Preserve Headquarters, 536 North Harlem Avenue, River Forest, IL 60305; 708-366-9420 or 800-870-3666.

Other Areas of Interest

Contact the Cook County Forest Preserve Headquarters for a map of the **Palos and Sag Valley Divisions**. There are many woods, sloughs, and meadows to explore on miles of trails. Just be sure you have a reliable compass before you set out exploring. The trails are not marked well, and unauthorized bicycle trails create a confusing maze.

Park Trails

Swallow Cliff Woods 👢👢👢—7 miles—This is a gravel, multipurpose trail where you will climb small hills, cross streams, and discover large sycamores and ironwood trees.

Maple Lake Trail 👢👢—12 miles—Discover some of the preserve's many sloughs and resident waterfowl as you hike through woods and meadows on this multipurpose path. This trail leads to the Little Red Schoolhouse, as well as to the old site of Argonne Laboratory.

Black Oak Trail 👢👢

Distance Round-Trip: 2 miles

Estimated Hiking Time: 1 hour

What an excellent trail to introduce young children to hiking and nature! While I hiked, proud Canada geese parents introduced their goslings to me—coming in for a closer look, hissing off into the woods, only to return again—keeping the fuzzy yellow goslings always under a watchful eye.

Caution: The trail can be very muddy. The gate to the trail is only open until 5 P.M. Monday through Thursday, and until 5:30 P.M. on the weekends. If you are still on the trail after closing time you may get locked in the preserve. The trail is closed on Fridays.

Trail Directions: Begin the trail behind the Little Red School House Nature Center [1]. The trail is a wide path, and it has plenty of informational signage throughout. At .05 mi. you reach Long John Slough.

At .25 mi. the trail forks; go right and through a gate [2] at .3 mi. that is locked each night. From here you will have open woods on the left and the slough on the right. The trail forks again at .35 mi.; again, go right [3]. By .5 mi. the slough is fairly close to the trail.

At .7 mi. the trail curves to the left and heads up, leaving the water behind [4]. At .9 mi.—and across from station #14—is an American elm, a tree that is fairly rare in Illinois. Note its classical vase shape. A fungus carried by the elm bark beetle has led to the worldwide demise of this species. At the 1-mi. mark, note a black oak and white oak that share part of the same trunk. Look to your right at 1.1 mi. for a very small ravine—the result of rainwater carving into the rock [5].

Pause at the pond on your left and look for aquatic insects—dragonflies, water striders, and damselflies. You will cross a bridge and then pass another pond, this time on the right. Ignore the trails coming in from the right and stay on the wide path. At 1.7 mi. you are back to point [3]; go right and head out the gate. Soon you are back at [2]; go right and follow the sign to the farm pond. On the right you'll find a prairie restoration, so walk slowly by to see how many different insects you can observe. Illinois has an estimated 17,000 species of insects!

At 1.9 mi. the farm pond comes into view [6]. This pond, created in 1921 and then enlarged by the Forest Preserve, sports many different insects. On the left are bee hives. At 1.95 mi. the trail comes to a T; on the left is a garden to explore and old farm equipment. To the right is the parking area and the front of Little Red Schoolhouse.

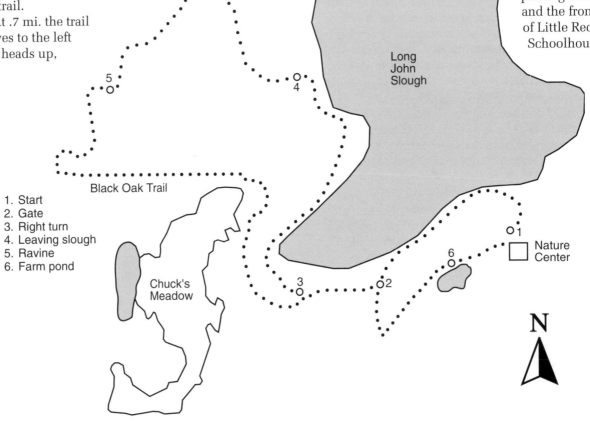

Palos and Sag Valley Forest Preserve

Long John Slough

Black Oak Trail

1. Start
2. Gate
3. Right turn
4. Leaving slough
5. Ravine
6. Farm pond

Chuck's Meadow

Nature Center

N

7. Waterfall Glen Forest Preserve

- Visit a man-made waterfall from the hands of the Civilian Conservation Corps.

- Hike where every big tree is a "wolf" tree.

- Pause at the ponds and look for herons, egrets, turtles, waterfowl, and other water-loving creatures.

- Bring your plant field guide—75 percent of DuPage County's plant species are found here.

Area Information

In 1834, when Harriet Martineau traveled in this area on her way from Chicago to Joliet, what impressed her most were the groupings of trees: "The grass was wilder, the occasional footpath not so trim, and the single trees less majestic; but no park ever displayed anything equal to the grouping of the trees within the windings of the blue, brimming River Aux Plaines [Des Plaines]." As you hike, look for the groupings that Harriet sighted, unusually large oaks with outspread branches.

The forest preserve is part of a 20-mile-long valley enclosed by dolomite bluffs. As glacial Lake Chicago drained through the area, it eroded through the glacial deposits to bedrock and carved bluffs 50 feet in height, deposited low gravel ridges, and left an extremely shallow soil, containing elements from the dolomite bedrock. At one time three quarries were actively mined in the area, taking advantage of the Lemont limestone. The Chicago Water Tower is constructed from limestone from one of these quarries.

In addition, a small area of the park was once used as a nursery by Lincoln Park, a lot of its

topsoil going to create Lincoln Park along the Chicago lakeshore. The pine plantations were planted as a buffer by Argonne Lab. "Waterfall" in the name of the area is not in honor of the CCC-constructed waterfall, but to honor Seymour "Bud" Waterfall, an early president of the District's Board of Commissioners.

Directions: Head toward Darien on I-55. Take the Argonne National Laboratory/Cass Avenue exit (#273A) and head south on Cass. Follow the signs to Waterfall Glen Trailhead parking area.

Hours Open: The site is open year-round from one hour after sunrise to one hour after sunset.

Facilities: At the trailhead you will find horse-trailer parking, water, and toilets, but no picnic tables.

Permits and Rules: Alcohol, collecting, and hunting are prohibited. Pets are welcome; however, they must be on a leash. Please use the trash receptacles.

For further information contact: Forest Preserve District of DuPage County, P.O. Box 2339, Glen Ellyn, IL 60138; 630-790-4900.

Waterfall Glen Forest Preserve

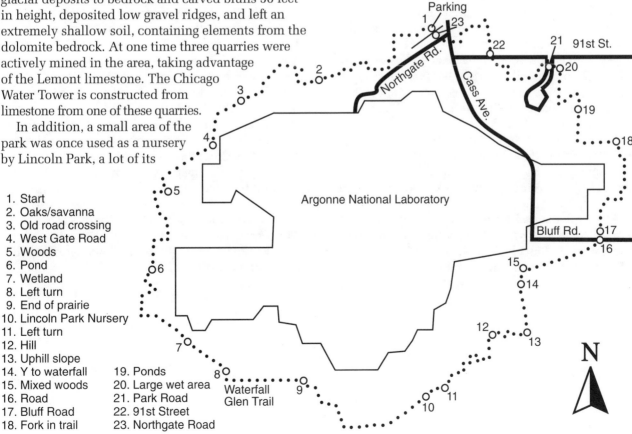

1. Start
2. Oaks/savanna
3. Old road crossing
4. West Gate Road
5. Woods
6. Pond
7. Wetland
8. Left turn
9. End of prairie
10. Lincoln Park Nursery
11. Left turn
12. Hill
13. Uphill slope
14. Y to waterfall
15. Mixed woods
16. Road
17. Bluff Road
18. Fork in trail
19. Ponds
20. Large wet area
21. Park Road
22. 91st Street
23. Northgate Road

Waterfall Glen Trail 👢👢👢

Distance Round-Trip: 9.65 miles

Estimated Hiking Time: 3.75 hours

Hike through history—the ancient oaks, pines planted by the Argonne Lab when it first opened, remnants of an old nursery from the 1920s, a Civilian Conservation Corps waterfall, and pieces of prairie.

Caution: This is a multiuse trail; be alert for bicyclists. There are several road crossings and the trail can be very muddy or flooded. Parts of the trail that aren't crushed rock may be very uneven due to ruts from bicyclists.

Trail Directions: Begin at the information board and head west into the woods [**1**]. A trail immediately comes in from the left; ignore this. Stay on the easy-to-follow main path. The first of several pine plantations occurs at .45 mi. At 1.1 mi., as you head up a small incline, look into the woods [**2**]. On your right are large, evenly spaced oaks with out-spread canopies. This was a savanna, but without fire the understory has grown up.

At 1.4 mi. cross an old road and head into a spruce and pine mixed woods [**3**]. Cross West Gate Road [**4**], at 1.85 mi., noting a fenced area and checkpoint on your left. Angle right and parallel the road. By 2.25 mi. you will leave the road and go left into the woods [**5**]. At 2.65 mi. come to a pond on your left [**6**], ringed with cottonwoods, and inhabited by mallards. Within .2 mi. you will pass another pond, less idyllic than the previous example. After curving left at 3.3 mi., the trail goes through a wetland and is sometimes flooded [**7**].

The trail next enters an open, grassy area. At 3.8 mi. turn left and cross the road [**8**]. Here is the 80-acre, short-grass Poverty Prairie with poverty oat grass, pussytoes, and whorled milkweed. Beyond the prairie in the distance is Poverty Savanna.

At 4.3 mi. the prairie gives way to a pine plantation [**9**]. Soon after, at 4.55 mi., notice the old cement foundations of Lincoln Park Nursery (LPN) on your left [**10**]. Past these, the trail comes to a T; go left. On your right you should see a trail board. Five miles is marked by a huge bur oak on your right. Look on your left at 5.2 mi. for another remnant of the LPN. At 5.25 mi. the trail comes to another T [**11**]; cross the railroad tracks and go left, walking along the road. To the right is a large power station. You will soon come to two trails on your right; ignore the first one and take the second.

At 5.75 mi. you will go up a small hill [**12**] and through a grassy area. The trail promptly comes back down, so be sure to heed the cautionary sign about a steep hill. From here you will cross picturesque Sawmill Creek by an iron bridge. Continue straight, ignoring the trails off to the right and left. At 5.9 mi. the trail forks and heads uphill [**13**]. Take either fork, but the left one has steps that make the climb easier. Once you've reached the top, go left through a woods with large oaks that soon gives way to a pine plantation. A trail spur off to the left at 6.25 mi. offers a nice view of the creek.

The trail forms a Y at 6.3 mi. and the information board [**14**]; go left and then angle farther left, going down stone steps to a man-made waterfall. Look around, explore, and find names written in the cement by the waterfall's creators. Retrace your steps; soon you are back on the gravel path heading northeast. At the crossroads at 6.6 mi. go straight (through the pines). They soon grade into a mixed woods [**15**]. You will come to a parking area and restrooms at 6.8 mi.; go left, with the trail now on the road [**16**]. Turn right and return to the woods just before a house on the right and a major road.

Cross Bluff Road at 7.10 mi. [**17**]. For the next half mile you will hike on a narrow, rutted dirt trail. At 7.7 mi. the trail forks [**18**]; go left, ignoring the prior trail on the right. A water tower will come into view at 7.9 mi., and you will begin to pass a series of ponds at 8.15 mi. [**19**]. At 8.45 mi. you will come to a large wet area [**20**]. Cross the road at 8.5 mi. [**21**].

The last mile of the hike is through a mixed, oak woods. At 9 mi. you will come to the first of three road crossings [**22**]. Cross 91st Street; it is an extremely busy road so use caution (9.4 mi.). Then at 9.55 mi. cross Northgate Road [**23**], head into the woods where the trail will form a T; go right, and you are back at the trailhead.

8. Morton Arboretum

- Bring your tree, vine, and shrub identification guides to help separate the forest into the trees and other things.
- Learn about woody plants from other regions by walking the Geographic Trail.
- Enjoy spectacular spring wildflowers in May and equally notable fall foliage in October.

Area Information

Morton Arboretum was built on the estate of Joy Morton, founder of the Morton Salt Company. In addition to the home, the family grounds had consisted of land used for agricultural crops and grazing plus some undisturbed woodland. The transformation of the estate began in December, 1922. That Joy developed the Arboretum on the Morton grounds seems appropriate: His father was the originator of Arbor Day, and the family's motto was "Plant Trees."

Joy referred to the Arboretum as a ginkgo, meaning it was one of a kind and unrelated to any other institution, just as a ginkgo tree is unique and unrelated to any other plant. In this 1,700-acre, living, outdoor museum, you can see more than 3,000 kinds of trees, shrubs, and vines. Not only is it a museum but also a trial garden for woody plants that can survive the ever-changing continental climate of the Midwest. The plants in the collection—grouped by botanical characteristics, landscape use, or geographic origin—may be seen either by car along 12 miles of one-way roads or by various walking and hiking trails.

Directions: The Arboretum is located just north of Lisle at the intersection of Illinois Route 53 and Illinois Route 88 (the East-West Tollway). Enter it via Route 53.

Hours Open: The grounds are open year-round; inquire at the Visitor's Center for building hours.

Facilities: The Visitor's Center contains an information building, restrooms, theater, restaurant, coffee shop, and a small picnic area. A fee is charged for parking.

Permits and Rules: Park only in designated areas. The speed limit on one-way roads is 20 mph. No bicycles, snowmobiles, or horses are allowed. No pets are allowed, *not even in cars.* No sports, games, fishing, or swimming are allowed; no jogging, except on the roads. Most important, *no collecting* of specimens.

Further Information: The Morton Arboretum, Route 53, Lisle, IL 60532-1293; 630-719-2400.

Other Areas of Interest

Located on the east side of Highland Avenue at 33rd Street in Downers Grove, the **Lyman Woods Natural Area** offers short hiking trails through prairie, oak forest, meadow, and marsh. Spring wildflowers are plentiful and a trail guide will help you with their identification. There are no facilities here. For more information call 630-790-4900.

Located between the communities of Hinsdale and Oak Brook, **Fullersburg Woods Forest Preserve** offers hiking, biking, an environmental education center, and the state's only operating waterwheel–grist mill. A 2.5-mile multiuse trail traverses Salt Creek and the mill and climbs a bluff overlooking the creek. There is also a .3-mile Wildflower Trail, a .8-mile trail through Paul Butler Nature Area, and a 1.3-mile Interpretive Trail running along Salt Creek and its environs. For more information call 630-790-4900.

Park Trails

Geographic Trail —.9 mile—Park in lot 16 to tour the tree collections that are among the oldest in the Arboretum. Most of the plantings were laid out in the early 1920s. Discover the woody plants of the Appalachians, Balkans, Central and Western Asia, China, Japan, and the eastern U.S. wetlands.

Big Rock Trail —.9 mile—Park in lot 14 and then wander through an oak woods to a glacial erratic (a granite rock left at the site by the last glacier).

Forest Trail —.7 mile—Park in lot 14 and take the wood-chip trail through the woods to enjoy spring and summer wildflowers.

East/Maple Woods Trails —1.1 miles—Park in lot 13 and discover a sugar maple woods that has spectacular fall colors. All three trails—Big Rock, Forest, and East—are connected by side trails.

Evergreen Trail —.9 miles—Park in lot 24 and enjoy a fragrant hike through pine, spruce, and other conifers. The trail skirts Lake Marmo and passes a small waterfall. In the winter this trail is popular with birders who scan the evergreens for the northern saw-whet owl.

Morton Arboretum

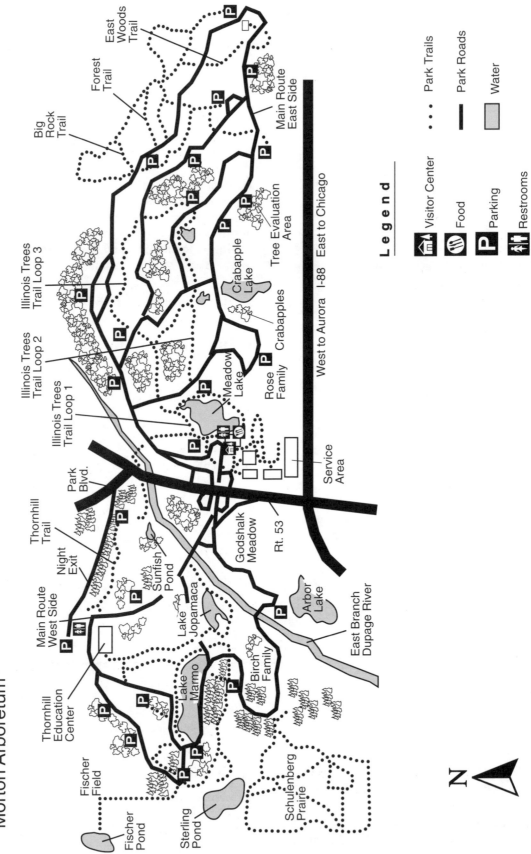

East Woods Trail

Forest Trail

Big Rock Trail

Main Route East Side

Illinois Trees Trail Loop 3

Illinois Trees Trail Loop 2

Illinois Trees Trail Loop 1

Tree Evaluation Area

Crabapple Lake

Rose Family Crabapples

Meadow Lake

West to Aurora   I-88   East to Chicago

Service Area

Rt. 53

Godshalk Meadow

Park Blvd.

Thornhill Trail

Night Exit

Sunfish Pond

Main Route West Side

Thornhill Education Center

Fischer Field

Fischer Pond

Sterling Pond

Lake Jopamaca

Lake Marmo

Birch Family

Arbor Lake

East Branch Dupage River

Schulenberg Prairie

N

Legend

Visitor Center

Food

Parking

Restrooms

Park Trails

Park Roads

Water

Prairie Trail 🥾

Distance Round-Trip: 1.8 miles

Estimated Hiking Time: 1 hour

From the savanna I emerged onto the prairie as the words of Ellen Bigelow, an early settler of Illinois, came to mind. "Nothing can equal the surpassing beauty of the rounded swells and the sunny hollows. The brilliant green of grass, the numberless varieties and splendid hues of multitudes of flowers, I gazed in admiration too strong for words."

Caution: Be sure to stay on the path, walk single file, and proceed clockwise; do not damage or pick plants; do not smoke. The peripheral trail might not have been mowed, so wearing long pants would be a good idea.

Trail Directions: To reach the prairie reconstruction go to the west side of the Arboretum; you can drive or walk to parking lot 25. Begin at the brown sign indicating Schulenberg Prairie and prairie trail [1]. Within a few feet you will come to a paved service road; go left. At .1mi. cross the road; a private park entrance is on the right [2]. A narrow, gravel path appears on the left at .2 mi.; go left where you will encounter posts #1 and #2 from the Arboretum's guide (the guide can be purchased at the Visitor's Center for a nominal fee).

Prior to the prairie entrance a secondary trail goes off to the left; ignore it now. At .3 mi. the path forms a Y; go left on a narrow, concrete-block path and begin your tour [3]. Explore the different textures of the large leaves of prairie dock and compass plant. Feel their coarseness. At post #3 look for clumps of plants with yucca-like leaves; this is rattlesnake master. To the right of the post is wild indigo, a legume. At post #4 the large plant to the right of the sign is compass plant. Its leaves align themselves along a north-south axis so that their huge, flat surfaces

can rotate to follow the rays of the rising and setting sun.

At post #6 you can experience cordgrass: Its edges are extremely sharp, leading to the common name of ripgut. At .5 mi. you will encounter a lone tree in the prairie, a bur oak [4]. From post # 8 the prairie is a thicket of rattlesnake master and prairie phlox. To the left of post #10 in midspring is a large clump of shooting star, called prairie pointers by the early pioneers. After post #10 the path comes to a T; go left [5]. You will soon come to a crossroads; cross it and then cross a cement bridge. This section of prairie is still being reconstructed, as most of the grasses are not native and multiflora rose is everywhere.

At .85 mi. the grassy path comes to a T; go right and skirt the prairie [6]. Within .05 mi. turn left and down a narrow, dirt path. The trail comes to another T at 1 mi.; go left and cross a wooden bridge [7]. As you come off the bridge, look for big bluestem or turkey foot. You reach the end of the property at 1.2 mi.; go left, skirting the hedgerow and the prairie, and follow a mowed (I hope) path [8].

Although the prairie grows quite tall by late summer, each plant's root system is even larger, extending 6 to 7 feet underground—and in the case of compass plants, as much as 14 feet! It is this underground root system that enables prairie plants to withstand fire. At 1.4 mi. you will see houses on the right. Early settlers feared living on the prairie: Because no trees grew on it, they thought the soil must be poor. At 1.5 mi. note a very faint trail to the left; follow it [9] and return near point [3]. Go right on the gravel path, past posts #1 and #2, and then go right again to the road. At 1.75 mi. you leave the pavement, head through the oaks, and retrace your steps to the parking area.

Along the prairie trail you encountered not only many plants but also a myriad of insects. In fact, as you walked you likely stepped on the most numerous and important herbivore (plant eater) on the prairie—no, not the bison, but the lowly grasshopper!

1. Start
2. Private entrance
3. Left turn
4. Bur oak
5. Left turn
6. Right turn
7. Bridge
8. Mowed path
9. Faint trail

Parking

N

Trail of Trees 👢👢

Distance Round-Trip: 3.15 miles

Estimated Hiking Time: 1.5 hours

Who needs a tree identification guide? Most of these large (and small) guys were already identified for me at the Morton Arboretum!

Caution: Beware of neck strain as you look up to see some of the large trees. The path will cross the park road, which can be busy.

Trail Directions: Head down the steps east of the Visitor's Center; the trail begins as an asphalt path with Meadow Lake on your left [**1**]. Within a few steps you will encounter your first tree—a tulip tree on the right (with an informative plaque). The trail forks at .15 mi.; go left, following the symbol for the hike, an oak leaf and acorn embedded in a concrete post and colored to correspond to different sections of the trail. At .2 mi. the trail forms a Y; go right and cross the road [**2**]. On the left is a dolomite prairie restoration site, complete with signage and protected by a chain-link fence.

You soon encounter (on the left side) the Arboretum's largest specimen of a black cherry. Next pass the legume family on the right and the honeysuckle on the left, and head through a grove of pines. Note the large examples of white oak on the left and bur oak on the right at .6 mi. [**3**]. At .7 mi. the trail comes to a T with a trail board on your left; go right [**4**].

Note the grove of oaks on the right (.8 mi.), just before crossing the road [**5**]. Hike under the limb of a bur oak as the trail goes to the right, and then under the limb of a white oak; note its scaly bark. At 1.05 mi. you will encounter Bur Reed Marsh on the right [**6**]. A trail board will be on your left, along with an offshoot trail that should be ignored. The trail now heads back into a woods covered in the spring with trout lily, prairie trillium, and anemone.

At 1.3 mi. the trail crosses the park road [**7**]. On the right is a large, open area with oaks, similar in structure to a savanna; on the left is a dense woods. Look for shooting star under the oaks in the spring. Soon you are walking through open oaks on both sides. The lush spring flora give way to ox-eye daisy and goat's beard (introduced weeds) in early summer. The trail crosses the park road at 1.5 mi. [**8**]. Did you notice the large clump of bloodroot under the oak tree before the crossing?

You will next enter a woods dominated by maples with an open understory (widely spaced shrubs and plants). At 1.65 mi. ignore two offshoot trails. Then cross a bridge at 2.05 mi. [**9**] and look for large Jack-in-the-pulpits growing near the water and mayapples running up the hillside. Off the bridge and to the right is the Arboretum's largest sugar maple. The trail heads uphill past an open area on the right at 2.2 mi. Look for columbine on the rock outcrop here in late spring.

You will cross the road again at 2.25 mi. [**10**]. Down this road on your right is the Appalachian collection. The trail comes to a T at 2.35 mi.; go right [**11**] and to a small area lined with wild hyacinth in late April and early May. At 2.6 mi. watch out for the poison sumac on the left. Look at it but don't touch—you can get a rash from it similar to that from poison ivy. Cross the park road at 2.65 mi. [**12**] and go through a grove of small cork trees. From there you will pass under the branches of a sweet buckeye.

At 2.75 mi. come to a trail board; go right [**13**], where you will be on an asphalt path through red pine. The path winds around Meadow Lake, which has benches and informative plaques by the trees. Go through a picnic area and at the intersection at 3.1 mi., turn left through another picnic area, returning to the Visitor's Center.

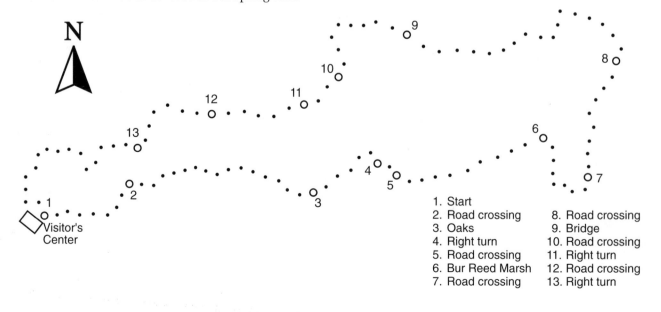

N

1. Start
2. Road crossing
3. Oaks
4. Right turn
5. Road crossing
6. Bur Reed Marsh
7. Road crossing
8. Road crossing
9. Bridge
10. Road crossing
11. Right turn
12. Road crossing
13. Right turn

Visitor's Center

9. The Regional Trail

- Watch bobolinks, one of the state's declining songbird species, as they court mates and defend their territories.
- Catch a glimpse of the past as you hike past large, open-grown oaks concealed in thickets of vegetation.
- Discover the spittlebug.

Area Information

DuPage was the second county in the state to establish an open space district, creating the DuPage County Forest Preserve District in 1915 with the goal of preserving continuous bands of open lands along major waterways.

The Regional Trail is a 7.5-mile, multiuse, linear, limestone path that connects three of the county's 57 preserves—Blackwell, Herrick Lake, and Danada. **Blackwell Preserve** used to be the site of a gravel quarry. Mt. Hoy (Blackwell), created as a winter-sports hill, is also a prime area for hawk sightings.

Herrick Lake was one of the early parcels purchased by the district. Actually a natural pond, Herrick Lake has had little disturbance and is home to 19 mammal and 108 bird species, including Illinois's endangered black-crowned night heron. **Danada Preserve** was once a private estate whose owners' main interest was thoroughbred racehorses. This preserve houses the Danada Equestrian Center.

Directions: To reach **Blackwell Preserve** from Interstate 88 (southwest of Wheaton), go north on Illinois 59 for 1.2 miles to Butterfield Road (Illinois 56). Turn right (east), and in 1.5 miles the entrance for the preserve will be on the left. The parking area and trail information is off to the right. To reach **Herrick Lake** take Butterfield Road and turn south onto Herrick Road. The south picnic and parking area is the second left turn off Herrick Road. To reach **Danada** from Butterfield Road, exit south onto Naperville Road and continue for .6 mile to the entrance.

Hours Open: The sites are open year-round from one hour after sunrise to one hour after sunset.

Facilities: Blackwell has facilities for boat rentals and boating, camping, a dog-training field, fishing, horseback riding, an orienteering course, picnicking, and snow tubing during the winter. At **Herrick Lake** you will find boat rentals, fishing, horseback riding, picnicking, and concessions. At **Danada** an Equestrian Center provides educational and recreational equestrian experiences, hay rides, and sleigh rides; the preserve also has fishing and makes available the Danada House for functions.

Permits and Rules: Alcohol, collecting, and hunting are prohibited in the forest preserves. Pets are welcome, but they must be leashed at all times. Dispose of litter properly. Trail etiquette includes staying in single file on busy days, slower traffic staying on the right, and care in approaching horses. Foot paths or single tracks are off-limits to bicycles.

Further Information: Forest Preserve District of DuPage County, P.O. Box 2339, Glen Ellyn, IL 60138; 630-790-4900.

Other Areas of Interest

Although the **Fermi National Accelerator Laboratory** is a workplace for hundreds of physicists, the grounds are home to a 975-acre tallgrass prairie restoration, 250 species of birds, and the Chicago area's only herd of bison. Fermi also has a 3.6-mile bike path and two prairie trails—.5-mile and 1.2-miles long. For more information call 630-840-3351.

Park Trails

Mt. Hoy (Blackwell) 👢👢👢—.3 mile—This asphalt trail provides access to the top of Mt. Hoy, the highest spot in DuPage County, and is an excellent area to view hawk migration during September and October.

Egret Trail (Blackwell) 👢—1 mile—North of Silver Lake, this trail offers the chance to see waterfowl and an occasional muskrat. It is located near the family camping area.

Lake Trail (Herrick) 👢—1 mile—Encircle Herrick Lake along its shore for some pleasant views of the lake, geese with their goslings, and some large oak trees.

Regional Trail (Danada) 👢—2 miles—This linear path goes through the preserve, passing grasslands, restored woodlands, and the equestrian center.

Parson's Grove Nature Trail (Danada) 👢—1 mile—This double-loop trail winds through an open savanna. Enjoy the large bur oaks and the spring wildflowers.

The Regional Trail

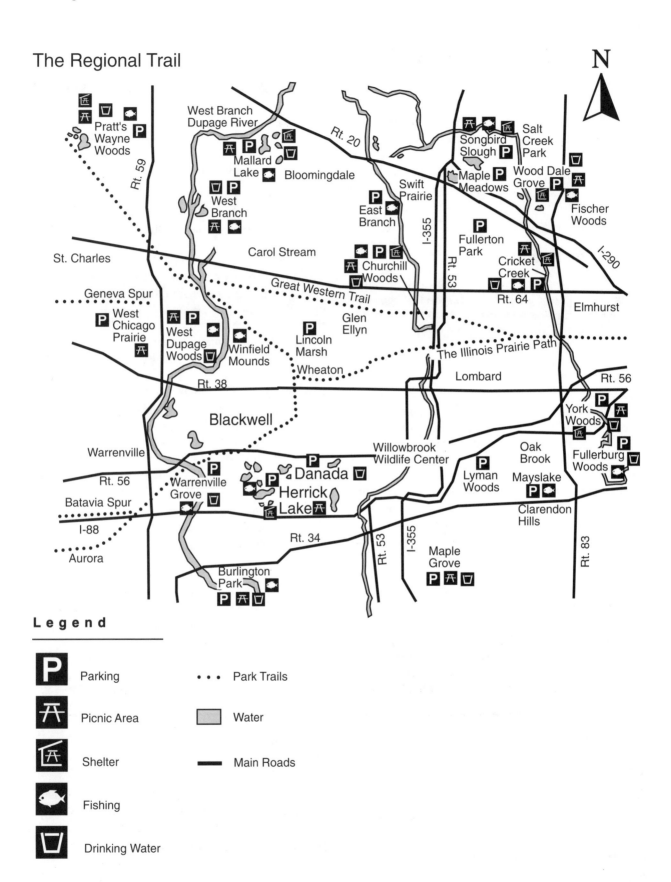

N

Legend

P	Parking
🎋	Picnic Area
🏠	Shelter
🐟	Fishing
🥤	Drinking Water

• • •	Park Trails
�	Water
——	Main Roads

Blackwell Forest Preserve 🥾🥾

Distance Round-Trip: 6.75 miles

Estimated Hiking Time: 2.5 hours

A pair of mallards escorted me for a tenth of a mile down Catbird Trail. While I could outwalk them, I couldn't match their flying prowess.

Caution: This is a multiuse trail shared by hikers, cyclists, horses, and dog walkers—keep alert and watch where you step. You will cross the road twice; remember to look both ways!

Trail Directions: Park by the information board near the Forest Preserve entrance. The trail begins across the road at the McKee Marsh sign and proceeds down on a crushed-rock path [**1**]. Mount Hoy and a pond appear on the right. Ignore the path that comes in from the left; it leads to the highway. You will be walking through an open, grassy area with scattered trees and shrubs. A few large cottonwoods appear here and there, and you will soon pass through a grove of white pines (planted). At .6 mi. the trail goes through a wooded area [**2**]; a small ravine is off to your left, and the trail soon curves left.

Springbrook Creek is on the left at .75 mi., with several spurs providing a closer look [**3**]. Oaks dominate the trail at .8 mi.[**4**], forming a stately avenue. Beginning at 1 mi. and for the next mile, four dirt paths cross the trail [**5**]. Ignore these paths.

You will cross an iron span bridge at 1.1 mi. [**6**], just after the oaks have given way to cottonwoods. From the bridge you hike through a grassy, open area, where every available small tree is occupied by a male red-winged blackbird. Watch barn swallows swoop for insects and listen for the call of the mead-owlark and pheasant. The grass gives way to a black-locust thicket at 1.6 mi. [**7**].

At 1.7 mi. the trail crosses Mack Road [**8**]. On the far side cattails appear immediately on the left, soon lining the trail. Ignore the two trails on the right at 2 mi. [**9**]. A large granite boulder appears off to the right at 2.1 mi. [**10**] with a plaque indicating that this is the Robert and Ada McKee Wildlife Marsh (Robert McKee was the first superintendent of DuPage County).

As you walk along this section of the trail (2.15 mi.) [**11**] in the spring or early summer, you might think you are following a lot of expectorat-ing hikers. Not so, as these masses of "spit" are really caused by spittlebug nymphs excreting liquid waste.

Another trail enters from the left at 2.25 mi.; stay on the main path. At 2.4 mi. the trail enters an old savanna [**12**]. Note how widely

spaced the trees are and how open their crowns. A savanna is usually dominated by oaks, and the understory vegetation is a blend of prairie and forest species.

Take time to marvel at these giant oaks with their outreaching limbs. Immediately after you exit the savanna (2.7 mi.), go left on a wide, mown, grassy path [**13**]. The trail is only subtly visible. You are now on the Catbird Trail and walking through a messy woods with a few large oaks. At 2.9 mi. [**14**] note a double-trunk shagbark hickory on the left as you near the West Branch of the DuPage River. Two large bur oaks can be found on the right at 3.2 mi. [**15**]. The path heads through cottonwood and willows and a grassy area. Once again oak trees line it, and the understory has been overrun by garlic mustard.

At 3.5 mi. you will cross the main trail and join the Bob-o-link trail [**16**]. Although unmarked, the path is mown and fairly easy to follow. The trail forms a Y at 3.65 mi. [**17**]; go right and continue to wander through the grassland. Look for bobolinks. Smaller than red-winged blackbirds, the bobolink male is black with a yellow nape and white on the rump and shoulders.

At 3.85 mi. you will enter a wooded area [**18**], climb a short hill, and enter the grassland. From here you should have a distant view of the marsh and see great blue herons and great white egrets flying in and out of the marsh. The trail curves to the right at 4.1 mi.; at the subdivision (4.3 mi.) it winds right and over a small rise [**19**]. You'll come to a Y at 4.85 mi.; go left and after a few steps you are back on the trail; go left again [**20**].

Retrace your steps: Recross Mack Road [**8**] at 5.15 mi. and the iron bridge [**6**] at 5.75 mi.

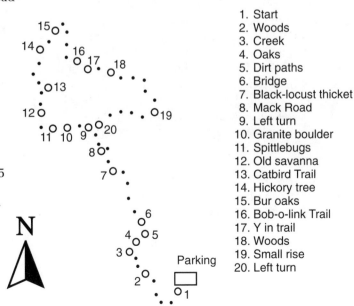

1. Start
2. Woods
3. Creek
4. Oaks
5. Dirt paths
6. Bridge
7. Black-locust thicket
8. Mack Road
9. Left turn
10. Granite boulder
11. Spittlebugs
12. Old savanna
13. Catbird Trail
14. Hickory tree
15. Bur oaks
16. Bob-o-link Trail
17. Y in trail
18. Woods
19. Small rise
20. Left turn

Herrick Lake Forest Preserve

Distance Round-Trip: 4.25 miles

Estimated Hiking Time: 1.75 hours

Although the trail is labeled "green heron," you probably won't find any, maybe because it goes through a grassland! Still, this grassland is alive with the call of meadowlarks from small shrubs, a flash of orange and the song of a Baltimore oriole, gold finches racing across the trail, and the black and white wings of myriads of bobolinks.

Caution: This is a multiuse trail shared by hikers, cyclists, horses, and dog walkers. Keep alert and watch where you step.

Trail Directions: Enter the preserve off Herrick Road and park at the south picnic area. Begin the trail at the information board and go right [**1**]. Within a few steps another trail intersects; continue on the wide path. At .1 mi. go right [**2**]. Although the trail is lined with small oak and hickory trees, look beyond these for larger examples. You'll soon leave the oaks behind and instead find cottonwoods, maples, and elms.

The .5-mi. mark finds you in an open woods with tall oaks and maples [**3**]. The understory is Virginia creeper and false Solomon's seal. At .6 mi. the trail comes onto an open, grassy area. Ignore the dirt trails off to both sides and proceed to a trail intersection at .65 mi. [**4**]. Go right here and enter the Green Heron Trail. Look on either side during late spring and early summer for spittlebugs. That white, spit-like froth the spittlebug nymphs deposit on the plant stems helps maintain high humidity around the soft-bodied nymphs and deters predators. Would you believe spittlebug nymphs have no enemies?

In this grassy area, with the trail stretching out before you, the plant diversity is low but the bird diversity isn't! Listen for distinctive calls and spot the flash of wings, locate them with binoculars, identify them with your field guide, and add them to your life bird list. Seek out meadowlarks, bobolinks, gold-finches, savanna sparrows, and the common yel-lowthroat. As you near more trees, you may spot deer. At the 1.65-mi. trail intersection go left [**5**] and head through the woods. Look for cottonwoods, basswood, and large oaks with outreaching limbs.

A marsh pond area appears on the left at 1.9 mi. [**6**]. You can use the bench there to rest and scan the pond for great blue herons camouflaged against the

dead trees in the pond. Continue on the trail as it wanders through a grove of walnuts and then a mixed woods. At 2.5 mi. come to a trail crossroads; go left and you are back on the regional trail [**7**]. You will pass the Hesterman Drain Project on the left, go through a grassy area, and reenter the woods.

An indigo bunting announced my presence as I entered the mixed woods where large oaks rear from a thicket of honeysuckle and chipmunks scurry across the path. From the woods emerges another grassland. Look for sensitive fern on your left. At the trail crossroads (3.15 mi.) [**8**] go to the right to hike on Meadowlark Trail. Entering the woods again, you can marvel at the tall, straight oak trees, which grade into a disturbed area of young trees and saplings.

At 3.5 mi., barely visible through the vegetation on the right, is a golf course and a reforestation area. A small creek appears on the left at 3.9 mi. [**9**], lined with cottonwoods. Within a few yards is a dirt path on the right, which you should ignore. At 4.1 mi. [**10**] the trail forms a Y; go left—the lake will be on your right. In the late spring, scan this area for geese and their goslings. Within several yards the trail makes another Y; go right and ignore the dirt path leading to the shelter by the lake. When you reach the final trail crossroads at 4.2 mi. [**11**], go straight to the south picnic parking area where the trail ends.

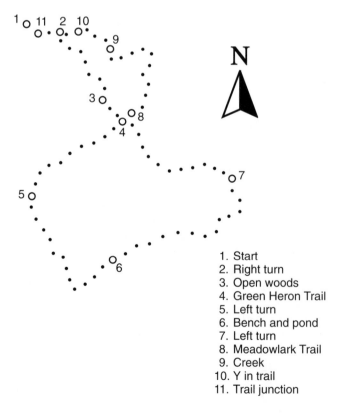

1. Start
2. Right turn
3. Open woods
4. Green Heron Trail
5. Left turn
6. Bench and pond
7. Left turn
8. Meadowlark Trail
9. Creek
10. Y in trail
11. Trail junction

10. Cuba Marsh Forest Preserve

- Sight a black-crowned night-heron or a yellow-headed blackbird, both endangered species in Illinois.
- Watch for the aerial version of a dog fight—a small blackbird warding off a crow.
- Look for showy but nonnative wildflowers, such as hawkweed and dame's rocket.
- Work on your birdcalls as you hike through a variety of habitats.

Area Information

From the name, you might associate Cuba Marsh only with things wet, yet the site presents a mosaic of habitats—lake, marsh, savanna, and prairie. Even a dry, hill prairie is found on its southeast side (accessible only during guided programs), the only such habitat in Lake County. Unlike the rest of the area, which has known much disturbance, the hill prairie has never seen a plow.

When the settlers came here they plowed, logged, and drained the land as best they could. By the 1950s and 1960s, though, descendants of most of these farmers had sold their land to developers. Local residents, however, wanted Cuba Marsh preserved as open space and helped the Lake County Forest Preserve District obtain it. These same local residents, called the Citizens for Conservation, have helped also with tree planting and general care of the land.

The drainage tiles are gone, thousands of trees have been planted, and the regenerative powers of the conservationists' controlled fires have been returned. This is a preserve in the making, so visit it often to see changes as the trees grow, the prairie returns, and the once lush wetland habitat is restored. More and more wildlife—and humans—will likely find this an oasis in years to come.

Directions: Cuba Marsh Forest Preserve is in southwestern Lake County between Barrington and Lake Zurich, west of Route 12. The entrance is on the south side of Cuba Road, just west of Ela Road.

Hours Open: The site is open daily from 7 A.M. to sunset.

Facilities: Restrooms and drinking water are available.

Permits and Rules: Leash and pick up after all pets. Park only in designated areas. Hunting, collecting, firearms, and off-road vehicles are prohibited. Snowmobiles, horses, man-made fires, and camping are not allowed.

Further Information: Lake County Forest Preserves, 2000 North Milwaukee Avenue, Libertyville, IL 60048; 847-367-6640.

Other Areas of Interest

Located near Wauconda, **Lakewood** is the county's largest forest preserve. Here you can find picnic shelters, fishing, playing fields, and winter sports fun. The preserve also has the **Lake County Museum** that traces the county's history and includes a locally discovered mastodon bone. The area has 8.75 miles of hiking trails, including a 6.5-mile horse and hiking trail, a .75-mile fitness trail, and a 1.5-mile cross-country ski trail. For more information call 847-367-6640.

Located east of Ela Road between Barrington and Palatine in Cook County, **Deer Grove Preserve** offers 12.2 miles of hiking trails. At the preserve you will find restrooms, water, picnic tables, and shelters. The 3.9-mile bicycle and hiking trail will help you discover hills, deep ravines, woodlands, and a connection to the Palatine Trail. The 8.3 miles of multiuse trails take you through woods, lakes, and marshes. For more information call 847-366-9420.

For a sneak preview of what Cuba Marsh will be like, visit **Crabtree Nature Center**, located south of Barrington in Cook County. Not so long ago this preserve, like Cuba Marsh, was farmland. Today it is regenerated forests, marshes, lakes, and prairie. More than 260 species of birds have been sighted here. Two trails allow for viewing, a 1.3-mile Bur Edge Nature Trail and a 1.7-mile path through Phantom Prairie. For more information call 847-366-9420.

Cuba Marsh Trail 👢👢

Distance Round-Trip: 3.25 miles

Estimated Hiking Time: 1.3 hours

Before I even set foot on the trail, a red-winged blackbird greeted me from the trail board, a pair of mallards had taken over a large puddle by the parking area, and a kestrel hovered over its kill. With this at the trail's entrance, who knew what surprises lay ahead?

Caution: This is a multiuse trail, so keep alert for bicyclists.

Trail Directions: Begin your hike at the trail board [1]. This hike promises wetlands and, if you are patient and lucky, perhaps even a few uncommon inhabitants. The area surrounding the lake and marsh are open spaces with small oaks. The marsh will come into view at .1 mi., where a bench is provided for your enjoyment [2]. At .2 mi. the trail forks; go right [3] and soon you are skirting a bur oak savanna on the right.

The trail bears right at .4 mi. [4]. In this area look for the bluebird boxes: Not only bluebirds but also tree swallows find these boxes a convenient nest site. At .55 mi. the trail forms a Y in front of a row of white pines; go right [5], through the grove of oaks. In the spring you can find trout lily and waterleaf under the oaks, but be sure to also look up and admire the crowns of these wide-spreading trees.

Soon you reach newly planted trees and, for the next .1 mi., two marshes on the right. Look for the familiar red-winged blackbirds defending their territories from atop a convenient cattail. At 1 mi. a bench overlooks the lake on top of a short incline [6]. Take a few minutes for a short spur to investigate the lake edge from closer range: Look for herons, egrets, ducks, swallows, and even hummingbirds going about their daily routines.

The trail will pass through a wetland corridor not far from the bench. Keep your binoculars ready for a glimpse of a black-crowned night-heron. At 1.45 mi. you'll go through a grove of larger trees—maple and coffee-tree. Here you may spot pockets of dame's rockets in the late spring. The trail comes out at Ela Grove at 1.7 mi. [7].

It's time to retrace your steps and complete several of the loops. Along the way look for any wildlife you might have missed, especially woodchucks along the grassy openings between trees. If you look up, you may discover herons and egrets silently flying overhead, or you may witness a noisy, aerial dogfight between a smaller red-winged blackbird and a larger crow. The blackbird usually comes out victorious. Notice also the native prairie plants attempting to reclaim the old fields.

At 2.35 mi. you are back at the lake and the bench [6]. Turn right at 2.5 [8], soon coming to a shrubby area that goldfinches appear to favor. At 2.7 mi. the trail comes to a Y; go right [9]. In June look for the hawkweed lining the trail. The trail comes to another Y at 2.85 mi.; go right again [10], checking the marshy area for blue-winged teal and yellow warblers. You come to the last Y at 3.05 mi.; once again, go right [11], where you will soon encounter the old bench [2]. Again scan the marshy lake with your binoculars one last time before heading back to the parking area.

Cuba Marsh Forest Preserve

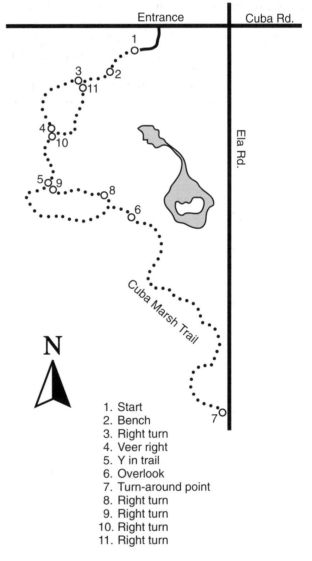

N

1. Start
2. Bench
3. Right turn
4. Veer right
5. Y in trail
6. Overlook
7. Turn-around point
8. Right turn
9. Right turn
10. Right turn
11. Right turn

11. Volo Bog State Natural Area

- Venture forth in an area where heavy bodies are likely to sink!
- Visit a habitat more commonly associated with the northeastern states and Canada.
- Look for orchids, ferns, tamaracks, sphagnum moss, and carnivorous plants along the trails.
- Explore a cattail-filled moat and encounter not alligators but dragonflies, frogs, and muskrats.
- Traverse a bog from the edge to eye.

Area Information

Volo Bog was formed during the Wisconsinan glaciation, about 15,000 years ago. Large blocks of ice broke away from the main mass of the glacier and were pushed into the ground with great force. As the ice melted, it left depressions called *kettle holes*. Volo Bog comprises two kettle holes left after the glacier receded. The kettle holes slowly filled in with partially decomposed plant material called peat. All that remains of the kettle hole is the open water area of the bog, called the *eye*. Volo Bog is the only bog in the state with such an eye.

With all the water around, it's hard to believe that plants experience the bog as a dry habitat, but most have trouble getting water and essential nutrients into their roots because of the water's high acidity level. Yet Volo Bog is lush with ferns, orchids, winterberry holly, tamaracks, and poison sumac. All these plants have developed unique ways of getting nutrients from the bog: Some are able to tolerate the acid waters, some have developed leathery leaves that slow water loss and are not shed each winter, and a few have specialized soil fungi that help them absorb nutrients.

At one time the eye of Volo Bog was 50 feet deep; today it contains only 10 feet of water and 40 feet of muck, marl, and peat. Although the eye is slowly disappearing, it is alive with activity. Kingfishers survey the edges, pollywogs appear to pave the peaty bottom, dragonflies canvas the open water for mates and food, and frogs (camouflaged from the kingfishers) enjoy the sunshine. An eight-year-old being coaxed to leave the boardwalk perhaps summed up Volo Bog the best: "Dad, there's no better place than this!"

Directions: Volo Bog is located 4 miles east of McHenry. From the intersection of U.S. 12/Illinois 59 and Illinois 120 in the town of Volo, go north on U.S. 12/Illinois 59 to Sullivan Lake Road. Turn left and go west 1.4 miles to Brandenburg Road; turn and go north and east .3 mile to the entrance.

Hours Open: The site is open 8 A.M. to 4 P.M. daily, September through May, and 8 A.M. to 8 P.M., June through August. It is closed on Christmas and New Year's Day. The Visitor's Center is open from 9 A.M. to 3 P.M., Thursday through Sunday and on all state holidays except Christmas and New Year's Day.

Facilities: A Visitor's Center houses exhibits, a classroom, natural-history reference library, restrooms, and a book and gift shop. Picnic facilities and a bird-watcher's blind are included on the site.

Permits and Rules: Pay attention to all park signage; it is for your protection. Do not pick or collect any natural object. No pets are allowed anywhere except on a leash in the picnic area. Hunting, camping, and fishing are not permitted. Please stay on the trails.

Further Information: Site Superintendent, Volo Bog State Natural Area, 28478 W. Brandenburg Road, Ingleside, IL 60041; 815-344-1294.

Other Areas of Interest

Less than two hours west of Chicago, **Chain O' Lakes State Park** offers boating, horseback riding, hunting, picnicking, camping, and hiking. A series of natural glacial lakes, Chain O' Lakes State Park offers the largest boat-launch area in any of the state parks. The park has 16 miles of hiking trails and 5 miles of biking trails. For more information call Chain O' Lakes State Park at 708-587-5512.

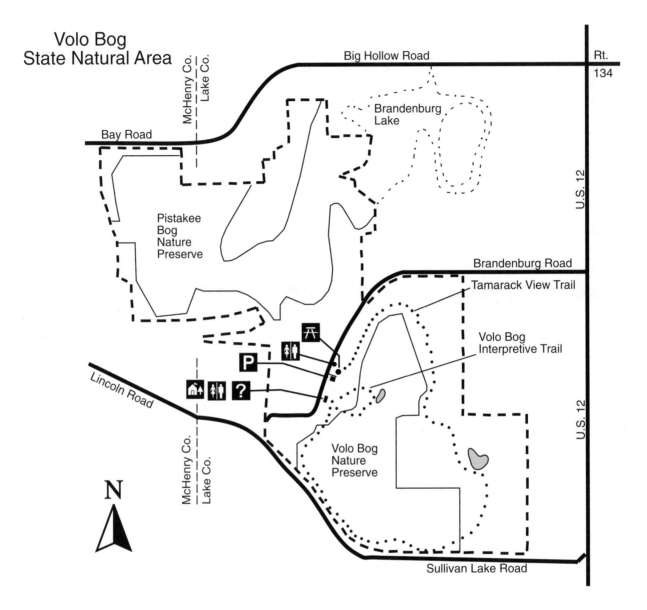

Volo Bog
State Natural Area

Big Hollow Road

Rt. 134

McHenry Co.
Lake Co.

Bay Road

Brandenburg Lake

U.S. 12

Pistakee
Bog
Nature
Preserve

Brandenburg Road

Tamarack View Trail

Volo Bog
Interpretive Trail

Lincoln Road

McHenry Co.
Lake Co.

Volo Bog
Nature
Preserve

U.S. 12

N

Sullivan Lake Road

Legend

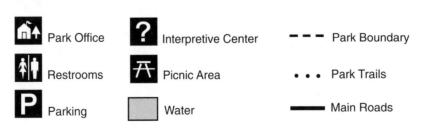

🏠 Park Office	❓ Interpretive Center	– – – Park Boundary
🚻 Restrooms	⛰ Picnic Area	• • • Park Trails
P Parking	▨ Water	━━ Main Roads

Tamarack View Trail 👢👢👢

Distance Round-Trip: 2.75 miles

Estimated Hiking Time: 1.5 hours

This trail introduces you to how the bog was formed, especially if you hike it on an extremely cold day. You feel as if you are part of the Ice Age, waiting for the glaciers to recede.

Caution: Stay on the trail, especially the boardwalks, as some areas can be extremely wet and muddy with unstable soil. Poison sumac may overlap the trail. Learn what it looks like and avoid it.

Trail Directions: Begin the trail at the Visitor's Center. At the bottom of the hill look for a sign for Tamarack View Trail; go right to begin hiking the hummocks (small hills) [1]. The trail distance will be marked every .25 mi. A kettle hole is on your left and an upland, oak-hickory forest on your right. At .25 mi. follow an arrow that points left [2]. On your left is a marsh.

You will cross a bridge and ramp at .3 mi. [3]. In the distance view the hummocky topography associated with glacial terrain. When you think of bogs, oak trees usually don't come to mind, but along this outer trail you'll see many splendid examples of oak (mostly of bur oaks). During the winter and early spring, while the trees are leafless, they look like a gnarled root system turned upside down.

At the intersection a few steps from the .5 mi. marker, go left [4] and leave the adjacent park road behind. You are now hiking around the old margin of the original lake that became Volo Bog. Soon (.9 mi.) you will come to a plastic boardwalk that crosses a marsh [5] lined on both sides by cattails. A "false bottom" often develops around the base of the cattails—silt floating on the water with buoyant plant fragments gives the area a solid appearance. Stay on the boardwalk: Even though the marsh may look solid, it isn't, and wet, muddy feet can result from meandering.

Just past the 1-mi. marker and before the trail curves left, note the large hummock on the right formed by the melting glacier. The flat area to your left is an old lake bed. At 1.4 mi. [6] a hummock on the left obscures all vestiges of civilization for a few minutes. To your right are glacial potholes—shallow depressions gouged by the glaciers and soon filled with water.

At the 1.5-mi. marker [7] go through the small grove dominated by bur oaks. Take time to look on

the ground for their leaves. Bur oaks have the largest leaves of any of the oak trees—6- to12-in. long and 3- to 6-in. wide. The trail then curves to the left, with hummocks and open areas again on either side. As you come off the curve, look straight ahead to see tamaracks, one of the few evergreen trees to lose its leaves in winter.

At 1.75 mi. [8] a bench provides a place to contemplate and look over the bog. Before the 2-mi. marker [9] the trail goes past a grove of quaking aspen, a tree species typical of northern climes. Observe that the moat of the bog (on your left) goes all the way around it, though it isn't always full of water. Soon you approach a bird-blind for observing the many species that surround you and a bench. Pause to look for waterfowl or perhaps a pair of swans struggling to keep other birds away from their nests.

At 2.25 mi. [10] a small trail on the right intersects the path. Stay on the main trail, going to the left, curving around the marsh moat, and heading back into the woods. From here the trail soon comes to a picnic area, and suddenly you are back at the Visitor's Center, ready to explore the mysterious interior of Volo Bog.

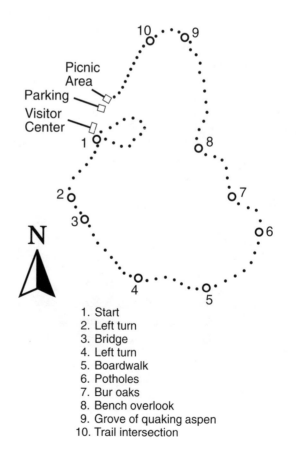

1. Start
2. Left turn
3. Bridge
4. Left turn
5. Boardwalk
6. Potholes
7. Bur oaks
8. Bench overlook
9. Grove of quaking aspen
10. Trail intersection

Volo Bog Interpretive Trail 🥾

Distance Round-Trip: .5 mile

Estimated Hiking Time: .5 hour

A visit to Volo Bog used to require tall boots and a good bit of courage. All you need today to explore the mysterious interior of a bog is a trail map and balance enough to negotiate a floating, wooden boardwalk.

Caution: Stay on the boardwalk! The ground, although it may look solid, is not, and you could find yourself encased in layers of mud, muck, and marl. Learn what poison sumac looks like and do not touch it.

Trail Directions: Due to the trail's short length, mileage distances will not be given.

Begin the hike at the Visitor's Center [**1**]. The barn you have just left is the original barn of the George Sayer farm. Volo Bog, or Sayer Bog as it was originally called because it adjoined the Sayer farm, was the first piece of property acquired by the newly formed Illinois Nature Conservancy in 1958. Downhill from the center is the entrance to the boardwalk [**2**], your path for the hike. Be thankful that a boardwalk exists, for in earlier times visitors jumped from hummock to hummock, causing the trees growing on the floating mat of vegetation to swing like pendulums. You are hiking on the fourth layer of boardwalk, the rest having sunk into the bog!

The first area you encounter is the cattail marsh moat that surrounds the bog [**3**]. The cattail was a veritable supermarket for Native Americans. Every part was edible or useful in some other way.

You soon enter the shrub zone, marked by winterberry holly [**4**]. In late summer this area is spectacular, the bright red berries of holly intermingling with the final yellow-orange flowers of tickseed sunflower. Here you will also encounter four species of ferns: cinnamon, wood fern, royal fern, and sensitive fern. The latter name comes from its being sensitive to cold, and it always succumbs to the first frost.

As you walk through the shrub zone, look on your left for tamaracks: They grow on spongy hummocks, are usually short and scrubby, and have roots that grow sideways instead of straight down. When rainfall is plentiful, tamaracks have little problem. But when the water level is down, their roots, unfortunately, aren't. The result of dry years is the dead trees that you may see off to the left [**5**].

From here to the eye of the bog look for some of the more colorful and unusual bog plants [**6**]. During June the maroon blossoms of marsh cinquefoil and the light pink of the rose pogonia orchid bloom. In July look for the bright pink, upside-down flower of the grass pink orchid.

You will soon reach the eye of the bog [**7**]. Volo Bog is the only bog in Illinois that has an area of open water—the eye. This small, circular expanse is all that is left of the original 50-acre lake. The lake has slowly filled in with peat, and within a century or two the eye will eventually fill in and disappear, a natural process in the life of a bog. From the platform look for pollywogs, kingfishers, dragonflies, large frogs, and water lilies. The eye is ringed with sphagnum moss, and the plants you observe are all growing on a floating mat of sphagnum.

As you come off the platform look to your right [**8**] for a small clump of pitcher plants. Please enjoy them from afar. At one time they were much more numerous, but illegal collecting has taken a toll on the pitcher-plant population. You might also spot leatherleaf in this area, a plant that never loses its leaves. Although they turn brown during the winter, once spring arrives, the leaves turn green again.

From here [**9**] continue on the boardwalk, looking for ferns, bright-orange mushrooms, and, if you are quiet, maybe a glimpse of the bog's resident animals—muskrat, mink, or a turtle. You now cross the marsh moat and the boardwalk ends [**10**]. The trail heads uphill and to the left. A right turn will take you to a picnic area. On the way back to the Visitor's Center you will pass a small pond on the right and go through a prairie restoration area.

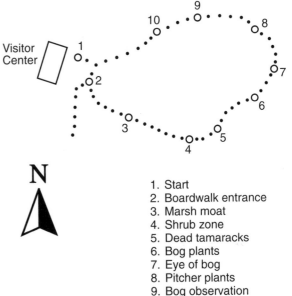

1. Start
2. Boardwalk entrance
3. Marsh moat
4. Shrub zone
5. Dead tamaracks
6. Bog plants
7. Eye of bog
8. Pitcher plants
9. Bog observation
10. Boardwalk ends

12. Moraine Hills State Park

- Listen for the rattle of sandhill cranes and watch them strut like giant chickens in the tall reeds.
- On a sunny day look for hundreds of basking turtles.
- Discover glacial artifacts—marshes, a bog, a fen, a glacial lake, kames, and moraines.

Area Information

The legacy of the Pleistocene glaciers left northeastern Illinois with a mosaic of many different wetland habitats—bogs, fens, marshes, and glacial lakes. Moraine Hills State Park is an excellent place to view many of these, as half the park's acreage is composed of wetlands and lakes.

Lake Defiance, near the center of the park, was formed when a large piece of ice broke away from a glacier and was pushed into the ground with great force. As the ice melted, it left a depression, called a *kettle hole*. The hole filled with water, as it was below the water table. The shore of Lake Defiance is unstable due to an accumulation of peat, and the lake itself is fed by the park's wetlands. Leatherleaf Bog was also formed from a kettle hole, but unlike Lake Defiance, the bog is poorly drained and has no inlet or outlet. The hole gradually filled with ever-thickening layers of peat to form the unstable mat that you see today.

Another area formed from a shallow kettle hole is Pike Marsh, but unlike the Leatherleaf Bog formation, it receives groundwater. The bedrock of gravel near Pike Marsh is high in minerals. Thus, surrounding the marsh is a *fen*, a wetland community that resembles a bog but whose water is alkaline (instead of acidic) from a high mineral content. Its peat is formed from decaying grasses and sedges, not sphagnum moss.

In addition to watery glacial evidence, there are the occasional boulders, kames, and moraines. A *kame* is a circular mound of gravel and sand deposited when holes in the glacier became filled with

debris. *Moraines* formed when the glaciers retreated and left mounds of stones, boulders, and other debris. These appear as the slight ridges and hills in the park. With a variety of plant communities and interesting glacial terrain, Moraine Hills State Park is a great site for a leisurely hike and provides one the opportunity for excellent wildlife viewing.

Directions: Moraine Hills State Park is located in the northeast corner of Illinois and is 3 miles south of McHenry. The park entrance is off River Road.

Hours Open: The site is open year-round from 6 A.M. to 9 P.M., except on Christmas and New Year's Day.

Facilities: Fishing is allowed at both Lake Defiance and the Fox River, and you can rent a boat (see the concession area). Picnicking is a favorite pastime, and some of the day-use areas have playground equipment. Other features include concessions and an interpretive center.

Permits and Rules: Boat trailers are not allowed in the park. Private watercraft are not allowed on Lake Defiance. At Lake Defiance you may fish only from one of the lake's three piers. Pets must be on a leash.

Further Information: Site Superintendent, Moraine Hills State Park, 914 S. River Road, McHenry, IL 60050; 815-385-1624.

Other Areas of Interest

From Algonquin, at the junction of Route 31 and Route 62 (Huntley-Algonquin Road), go west on Route 62 for 1 mile to Pyott Road. Turn north on Pyott for 1.5 miles to the entrance of Barbara Key Park. A trailhead in the park provides access to **Lake-in-the-Hills Fen Nature Preserve**. Here you can continue your discovery of wetland communities and find a calcareous floating mat, graminoid (grassy) fen, low-shrub fen, calcareous seep, and several prairies. For more information call the McHenry County Conservation District at 815-678-4431.

Park Trails

Lake Defiance 👢👢—3.7 miles—On a circuit of Lake Defiance you will encounter several marshes, wooded moraines, and the park's day-use areas.

Lake Defiance Interpretive Trail 👢—.5 mile—Use the guide available from the park office to aid you in the

discovery of plant succession, plant communities, and wetlands. The trail also has an observational blind.

Pike Marsh Interpretive Trail 👢👢—.6 mile—A boardwalk allows you to discover a marsh, fen, and upland forest communities. Look for marsh marigold in the spring and an abundance of cattails during all seasons.

Moraine Hills State Park

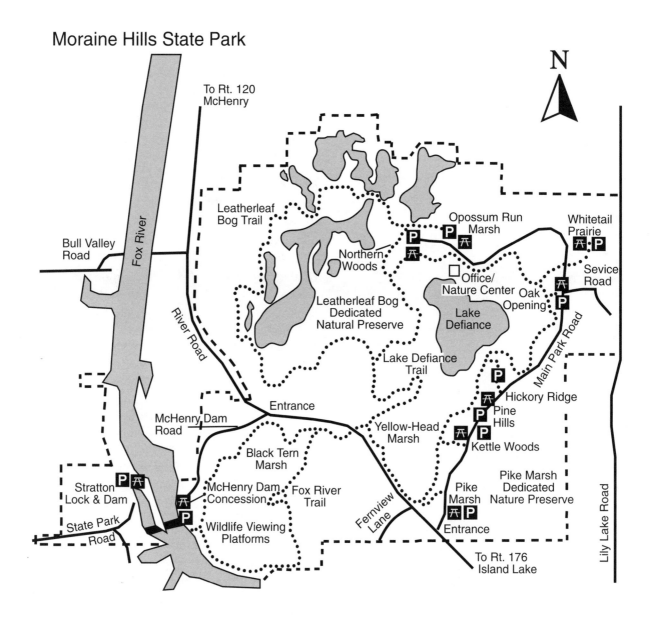

N

To Rt. 120
McHenry

Fox River

Bull Valley
Road

River Road

Leatherleaf
Bog Trail

Northern
Woods

Leatherleaf Bog
Dedicated
Natural Preserve

Opossum Run
Marsh

Office/
Nature Center

Lake
Defiance

Oak
Opening

Whitetail
Prairie

Sevice
Road

Main Park Road

Lake Defiance
Trail

McHenry Dam
Road

Entrance

Black Tern
Marsh

McHenry Dam
Concession

Fox River
Trail

Yellow-Head
Marsh

Hickory Ridge
Pine
Hills

Kettle Woods

Stratton
Lock & Dam

State Park
Road

Wildlife Viewing
Platforms

Fernview
Lane

Pike
Marsh

Entrance

Pike Marsh
Dedicated
Nature Preserve

Lily Lake Road

To Rt. 176
Island Lake

Legend

- • • • Park Trails
- - - - Park Boundary
-         Water
- ▬▬ Main Roads

⛬ Picnic Area

🅿 Parking

Leatherleaf Bog 👢👢

Distance Round-Trip: 3.2 miles

Estimated Hiking Time: 1.5 hours

The trail is a symphony of sound—the cricketing of frogs, honks of geese, the skree of red-winged blackbirds, chattering and chiding of chipmunks, and the off-key rattle of sandhill cranes.

Caution: This is a multiuse trail so the path will be shared by bicyclists and dog walkers.

Trail Directions: Park at the Northern Woods picnic area, where a short access path will take you to the beginning of the trail and mile markers [1]. The trail, which is marked every .25 mi. with blue squares, immediately passes through an oak-hickory woods. By .2 mi. [2] you come down a hill to a cattail marsh on the left and open water on the right. Look for turtles basking in the sun. Not only are they increasing their body temperature, but also exposing their shells to air to reduce algal growth.

The trail soon curves away from the water, and the large oaks disappear to be replaced by a shrubby, old field. At .55 mi. open-water and cattail marshes appear on both sides [3].

From the marsh you will enter an oak savanna restoration. Don't be alarmed if you see evidence of brush cutting or burning in this section. The understory of savannas is burned quite frequently, getting rid of fire-intolerant species and allowing the oaks to grow unimpeded. From the savanna you will hike through a shrubby woods on your left and an old field with lots of bluebird houses. Bluebirds are making a comeback, thanks in part to the widespread use of these houses. Bluebirds are cavity nesters, building their nests near open fields in rotted trees or fence posts. When the farms' fencerows began disappearing, so did the bluebirds.

At 1 mi. [4] note an open water marsh on your left. Scan the area for turtles (both snapping and red-eared sliders) and herons (great blue and little green) as they fish. The trail soon curves to the right. Take advantage of the side spurs that lead down to a closer look of the marsh. At 1.55 observe a glacial boulder on the left and a grove of good-sized white oaks. As the trail heads upward you will come to a narrow spur off to the left [5], affording the opportunity to explore the margin of Leatherleaf Bog.

Wander as far as you like on a linear spur between open water and a leatherleaf bog surrounded by a marsh. Watch the geese come in for a landing with the grace and precision of a 747, and try to identify any warblers flitting around the edge. The plant in

the middle of the bog is leatherleaf—an evergreen shrub. During the spring the plant produces white flowers that dangle from the branches like little bells. Once you have finished your discovery, retrace your steps to the main trail. Now you can see the bog, surrounded by a marsh, on your left. At 1.95 mi. you'll see another spur on the left. At 2 mi.[6] look for two large oak trees on your right—one is a bur and the other a white. Also on the right is a vast grassy area.

At 2.15 mi. look at the woods on the left for large, open-grown oaks and explore the pond on the right for large, fat tadpoles [7]. Another spur trail leads through the woodlands. A drainage channel appears on the left at 2.35 mi. and also a trail junction [8]. The blue and red trails intersect at this point; go left, still following the blue. The trail soon heads over moraines—small hills on both the right and the left (2.6 mi.) [9]. On the moraines you will find an oak-hickory woods, carpeted in the spring with mayapple and toothwort.

At 2.75 mi. the trail skirts the edge of the ill-defined Lake Defiance [10]. Unlike man-made lakes, glacial lakes have no edges. Another trail junction appears at 2.9 mi. [11]; go left and skirt the North Woods picnic area. Soon you will return to where you started and your vehicle.

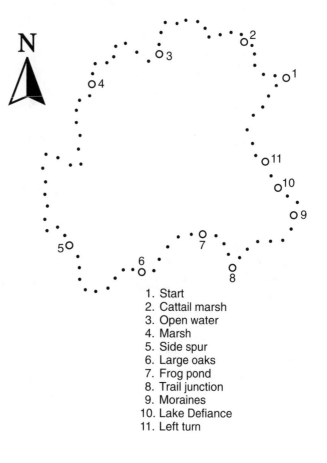

1. Start
2. Cattail marsh
3. Open water
4. Marsh
5. Side spur
6. Large oaks
7. Frog pond
8. Trail junction
9. Moraines
10. Lake Defiance
11. Left turn

Pike Marsh–Fox River Trail

👢👢

Distance Round-Trip: 3.75 miles

Estimated Hiking Time: 2 hours

This trail brings you close-up and personal with large, fat bullfrogs camouflaged by green pond scum; proud geese with new goslings; chipmunks scurrying across the trail; and tall, gangly sandhill cranes.

Caution: This is a multiuse trail; the path will be shared with bicyclists and dog walkers.

Trail Directions: Park at the Pike Marsh parking area and cross the road. Begin the trail at the gate [**1**]. As you begin to hike notice the line of large bur oaks on the right. The trail comes to a T at .15 mi.; go left [**2**]. A marsh will be on your right and the highway on your left. Look for green herons at the edge of the marsh. Open water appears at .3 mi. [**3**]. Scan the pond scum for large bullfrogs trying to hide from herons.

The trail now heads up and away from open water. At .5 mi. you'll come to a trail junction; go left [**4**]. The trail goes through an underpass and comes out on a grassy area. Another trail junction appears at .75 mi. [**5**]. Go right here onto the Fox River Trail. This segment of the trail is marked with yellow squares giving the distances. The trail continues through rolling grasslands, and at .85 mi. you pass a grove of oak trees on a kame to the right [**6**].

On your left notice a small wetland with a creek through it and a line of floodplain trees in the distance. At 1.05 mi., the site of a drainage canal [**7**], you will come upon a very tall plant: This is cow parsnip, a member of the parsley family. The plant may be anywhere from four- to nine-feet tall and have very large leaves with a cluster of white flowers on the top. An open-water marsh comes into view at 1.4 mi. [**8**], part of the Moraine Hills Enhancement Project for the

perpetuation of North American waterfowl. From the trail you can see lots of turtles basking, geese, and perhaps even a mute swan.

At 1.5 mi. take advantage of the observation platform on your left [**9**] to look for muskrats, wood ducks, coots, yellow-headed blackbirds, and black terns. Rejoin the trail, from which the Fox River is now visible at 1.6 mi. [**10**]; it skirts the river for some time. Gone is the quiet, peaceful hike around the marsh, replaced by radios on boats as they zip up and down the river. At 1.8 mi. locate another open-water marsh on the left [**11**]. Look for gatherings of turtles and yellow warblers. At 2 miles the trail curves left, leaving the Fox River behind but not the small marshes.

A levee appears on the left at 2.1 mi. [**12**]; please obey the Do Not Walk On–sign there. By 2.35 mi. the view of open water is gone [**13**]. Instead, you can spot bur oaks on a moraine. At 2.5 mi. you reach a trail intersection; go left to a viewing platform and a wildlife area [**14**]. (The viewing platform is on the left down a few steps.) From this vantage point look to your right to locate any sandhill cranes. They are tall, gray birds with a patch of red on the crown. Then go back up the steps and to the left. At 2.75 mi. you will come to another trail intersection; again go left and come down off a moraine into a willow flat [**15**].

Three miles brings you back to [**5**]; go right and begin to retrace your steps. At 3.25 mi. you are at [**4**]. Go right again, ignoring the wrong-way signs (intended for bicyclists and cross-country skiers). As you pass the open water, don't forget to look for any new activity. At 3.6 mi. you will return to the Pike Marsh junction [**2**]; go right, and soon you are back to the trailhead, hopefully with some new bird sightings to add to your Illinois life list.

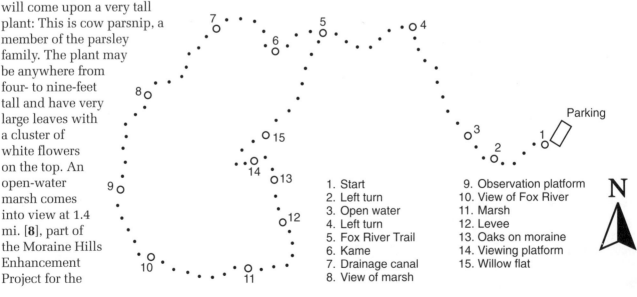

1. Start
2. Left turn
3. Open water
4. Left turn
5. Fox River Trail
6. Kame
7. Drainage canal
8. View of marsh
9. Observation platform
10. View of Fox River
11. Marsh
12. Levee
13. Oaks on moraine
14. Viewing platform
15. Willow flat

13. Trout Park Nature Preserve

- Discover a unique wetland community—a forested fen.
- Bring along your plant field guide to help you identify the unusual species found here.
- Come out of winter hibernation to celebrate the early-blooming skunk cabbage, the state's first flower of spring.
- See watercress—not on bread, but in a brook.

Area Information

Trout Park's name dates from the mid-1800s, when a former owner stocked the streams with trout. In the early 1900s the park was part of a popular amusement park. A roller coaster was located on the shore of the Fox River, and a concession stand sold bottles of spring water from the park. By the 1920s the city finally realized the unique botanical characteristics of the area and took steps to preserve it.

The park contains a forested fen, one of only two in the state. The water that comes from the porous hillsides in a relatively constant supply flows through limestone before it emerges, thus making it chemically alkaline. The park's location, along the northeast side of the Fox River and nestled deep within the enveloping ravines, protected it from the prairie fires that swept the area before settlement. Over time a fen (an alkaline wetland) developed, with a climax forest of white cedar, a tree species normally found farther to the north. A climax community is the final stage in ecological succession that results in a stable community, achieved over time through adjustment to a particular environment.

Yet as the ranks of humanity swelled, the park shrank: Tollway construction in the area destroyed the richest ravine and seep-spring community. Today, the area is an Illinois Nature Preserve, and although that offers it political protection, erosion from unofficial trails and runoff water remain problems. As you hike the short trail, admire the unique plant communities but tread lightly, for this is a piece of our natural heritage just as important as Lincoln's Home or the Field Museum—a piece of botanical history.

Directions: From Elgin at the junction of I-90 (Northwest Tollway) and Highway 25 (Dundee Avenue), take Dundee Avenue south one block to Trout Park Boulevard, then west one block to Trout Park. The nature preserve is on the north side of the park.

Hours Open: The site is open year-round, but closes daily at 10 P.M.

Facilities: There are no facilities within the nature preserve. The adjacent city park has restrooms, water, and a picnic area.

Permits and Rules: The trails are located in a dedicated Illinois Nature Preserve. No pets are allowed on the trails. Do not pick the flowers. No bicycles are allowed on the trail. Do not hike off the trail as this causes erosion and could lead to the park's being closed for hiking.

Further Information: Elgin Area Convention and Visitors Bureau, 77 Riverside Drive, Elgin, IL 60120; 800-217-5362 or 847-695-7540.

Other Areas of Interest

Fox River Bicycle Trail is a 36-mile multipurpose trail that runs from Crystal Lake in the north past Aurora in the south, traveling the banks of the scenic Fox River. The trail passes Trout Park Preserve and also connects with the Illinois Prairie Path, the River Bend Trail, and the Great Western Trail. Restrooms, water, and food are available along the path. For more information call 800-217-5362.

Located in the northwest corner of DuPage County, **Pratt's Wayne Woods Forest Preserve** contains marshes, meadows, savannas, and prairie. Restrooms and water are available. Popular activities include picnicking, horseback riding, fishing, and model-airplane flying. Two hiking trails are located here, in addition to the northern arm of the Illinois Prairie Path that bisects the preserve. The West Loop Trail is 4.6 miles long and travels through the youth campground area and equestrian jumping area. The East Loop Trail is 4.5 miles long and leads through meadows and prairie. For more information call 630-790-4900.

Trout Park Trail 🥾🥾🥾

Distance Round-Trip: .75 mile

Estimated Hiking Time: .75 hour

The amusement park's roller coaster may be gone, but taking its place is nature's roller coaster for feet and legs. You provide the power.

Caution: The trail can be very muddy. Tree branches sometimes block the trail, and roots protrude from the ground.

Trail Directions: Begin at the wooden, arched entrance, reminiscent of an Adirondack Camp [1]. Immediately after your entry, look to the left for a clump of twinleaf, a fairly rare occurrence in Illinois. You next encounter steps leading down; once off the steps, you are in a fen/seep (.05 mi.).

Look on your left for large expanses of the two major plants on the hike— skunk cabbage and marsh marigold.

Within a few steps you are above the wet area and have a better view of its vegetation. At .1 mi. come to an intersection; go left and down steps [2]. The trail to the right is closed due to erosion. You will now cross a bridge over a spring run. The trail then comes to a T; go right and circle the skunk cabbage (.15 mi.)

[3]. At .2 mi. the trail forms another T; go right [4] and cross a railroad-tie bridge. The trail comes to yet another T; go left. From here you will encounter a bridge: Angle right, cross another bridge, and head upward (.25 mi.) [5]. At .35 mi. the trail forks; go right [6]. Note the large patches of bloodroot as you pass by.

Within a few steps you should encounter a small grove of white cedar just before another bridge crossing. These trees are extremely old, although they don't look it. They grow about one inch every 10 to 20 years. As you cross the bridge, look for watercress, an exotic, mat-forming plant that clogs the streams and reduces oxygen in the water. Off the bridge, go right and up another plank bridge. At .4 mi. head up some steps and then go right, continuing to circle the fen [7], which is on your right (on your left is the forest—look for spring wildflowers here). Before the trail heads up, you will walk through a small thicket of witch hazel.

At .5 mi. the trail comes to another T; go left and up a small hill where four trails come together; take the one farthest right [8]. The fen will still be on your right. Note how the large oak has become part of the trail. All too soon you are back where you first encountered the fen. Retrace your steps to the parking area.

Trout Park Nature Preserve

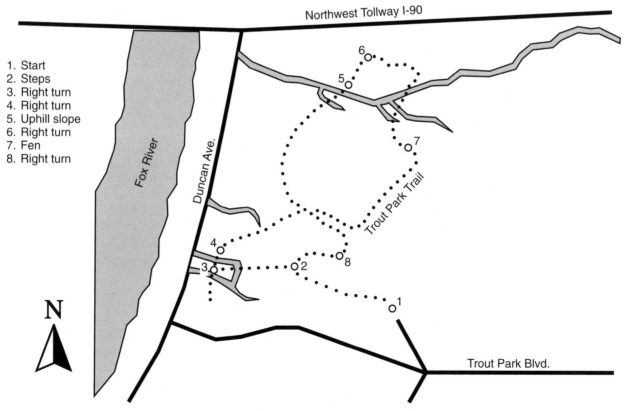

1. Start
2. Steps
3. Right turn
4. Right turn
5. Uphill slope
6. Right turn
7. Fen
8. Right turn

14. Glacial Park

- Discover kames, kettle holes, and erratics in a park where glacial history comes alive.
- Climb a 100-foot camelback kame to enjoy a bird's-eye view.
- Walk in the ancient bed of glacial Wonder Lake.
- Bring your binoculars to watch the aerial acrobatics of swallows, the day-to-day drama in the lives of red-winged blackbirds, and the creek-patrolling behavior of kingfishers.

Area Information

The Pleistocene glaciers and their meltwaters forever changed the Illinois landscape. Nearly 90 percent of the state was once covered by one or more sheets of glacial ice. When the last of the glaciers began to melt from Illinois about 14,000 years ago, the country that emerged looked far different from preglacial lands. The glaciers had scraped and smeared the landforms they overrode (much the same way a person kneads dough). The moving ice carried colossal amounts of rock and earth, and when the ice melted, it dumped whatever it was carrying in place. Here at Glacial Park, remnants of the last glacier—the Wisconsinan—are everywhere in evidence.

Outwash deposits (a mixture of sand, stone, and gravel) of the glacier created distinctive landforms called *kames*. Kames are circular mounds of outwash that resulted when holes in the glacial ice were filled with debris from the streams that flowed along the surface of the glacier. Today, kames have great value and a new name—sand-and-gravel pits.

Kettle holes were formed when large pieces of ice became detached from the glacier and were buried by outwash. When the blocks of ice melted, the outwash fell downward, creating craters, and pockmarks. Leatherleaf Bog and Kettle Hole Marsh are both examples of kettle holes. The reminders of this great ice form an ancient and interesting part of Illinois history.

Directions: Glacial Park is located in northeastern Illinois, in McHenry County. From the town of Richmond, go south on Route 31 until you reach Harts Road and a sign for the park. Follow Harts Road to the Wiedrich Barn Education Center.

Hours Open: The site is open year-round from 8 A.M. until sunset.

Facilities: Wiedrich Barn Education Center has an environmental educator, seasonal displays, and interpreters who conduct walks through the area. Restrooms are also located here. Picnic facilities with fire grates are located at the visitor parking lot. Canoeing, as well as bank fishing, is allowed on Nippersink Creek.

Permits and Rules: Part of the trail at Glacial Park is in a dedicated Illinois Nature Preserve. Due to this status, no pets are allowed on the trail.

Further Information: McHenry County Conservation District, 6512 Harts Road, Ringwood, IL 60072; 815-338-1405 or 815-678-4431.

Other Areas of Interest

Located north of Marengo on Route 23, **Marengo Ridge** is situated on a glacial-end moraine. The south end of Kunde Woods, located in the area, provides an excellent vantage point for studying the geological history of McHenry County. The area offers camping, picnicking, and cross-country skiing. A nature trail to the eastern edge of the woods will take you to one of the highest points in McHenry County. For more information contact the McHenry County Conservation District.

Located south of the town of McHenry, the **Fox River Conservation Area** contains a number of sites, two of the more popular being the Hollows and Hickory Grove. The Hollows, formerly a sand-gravel mine (an old kame), now has fishing and picnicking. Three miles of hiking trails provide a close-up look at the county's gravel-mining industry and the healing powers of nature. Hickory Grove includes not only diverse natural areas but also Fox River frontage and a state nature preserve. While there is no public access to the nature preserve, the conservation area offers picnicking, fishing on the river front, and a 1.5-mile nature trail. For more information contact the McHenry County Conservation District.

Park Trail

McHenry County Prairie Trail 👢—7 miles—This linear trail is open to hikers and equestrians in the spring and summer and to snowmobilers in winter. The trail, on an old railroad bed, has patches of prairie along its length and offers nice views of Nippersink Valley. The path begins north of Ringwood and ends at the Illinois-Wisconsin border.

Glacial Park

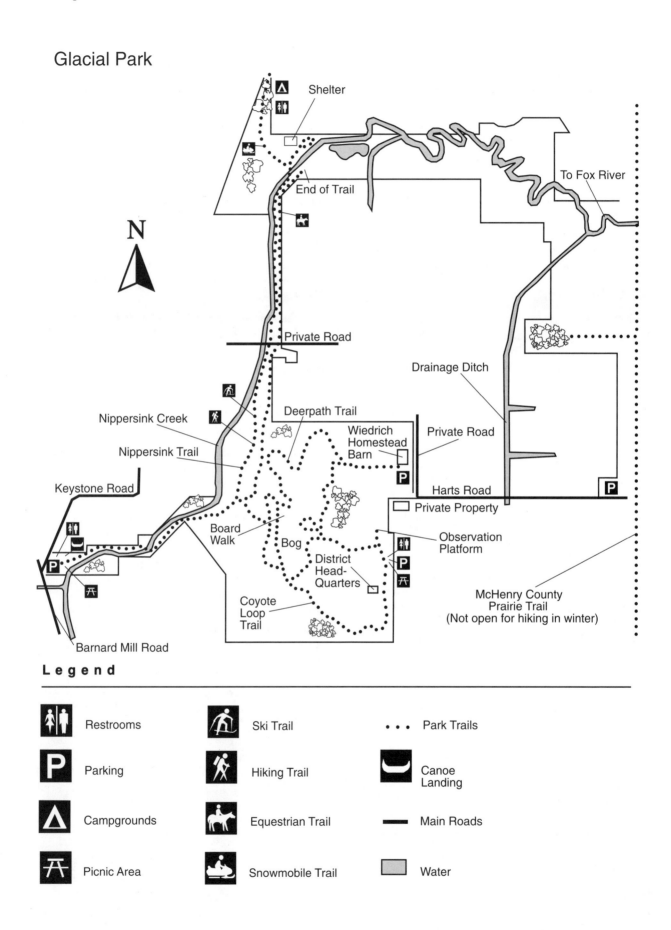

Shelter

End of Trail

To Fox River

N

Private Road

Drainage Ditch

Nippersink Creek

Deerpath Trail

Private Road

Wiedrich
Homestead
Barn

Nippersink Trail

Keystone Road

Harts Road

Private Property

Board
Walk

Observation
Platform

Bog

District
Head-
Quarters

Coyote
Loop
Trail

McHenry County
Prairie Trail
(Not open for hiking in winter)

Barnard Mill Road

Legend

Restrooms	Ski Trail	• • •	Park Trails
Parking	Hiking Trail		Canoe Landing
Campgrounds	Equestrian Trail	—	Main Roads
Picnic Area	Snowmobile Trail		Water

Deerpath Trail 👢👢👢👢

Distance Round-Trip: 2 miles

Estimated Hiking Time: 1 hour

While the kame looms in the distance, the hike is a "one-booter" When I hiked over it , however, it quickly acquired three more boots. Kames are far easier to admire than to climb.

Caution: Stay on the boardwalk at the bog: The ground is very unstable and a heavy body is likely to sink!

Trail Directions: Park at Wiedrich Barn and begin at the trail board [**1**] on a mown path. Go left from the trail board and hike up the small kame. At .1 mi. the trail forms a Y; go left along a park road. Kettle Hole Marsh is on your right [**2**]. If your visit coincides with a spring-burn year, the new growth of grass clothes the glacial features in a cloak of bright green. Take advantage of the Marsh Observation Deck on the right at .3 mi. [**3**].

This marsh was formed by the slow fill-in of an old kettle hole. From the observation deck come to a crossroads and go right, skirting the edge of the marsh.

As you hike look to your left for a series of kames topped with bur oaks. Your opportunity to climb a kame will soon come. At .55 mi. note another trail intersection [**4**]; go straight across to discover a bog. Use the boardwalk to look for sphagnum moss and the dominant plant of this bog, leatherleaf, a plant that keeps its leaves year-round.

The boardwalk ends at .65 mi. [**5**]; go right and walk through a savanna, a plant community charac-terized by large, open-grown oaks with an understory of woodland and prairie plants. A few yards bring you back to [**4**], go left this time. At .75 mi. is another intersection, go right on Coyote Loop Trail [**6**]. You are hiking through a bur oak savanna. Look on the ground on either side to note the glacial debris (rocks and gravel). These rocks were hauled in—not by trucks but by glaciers!

The trail curves to the right around the bog and at .9 mi. comes to a T [**7**]. Go right at a bench and a large bur oak. The trail will take you by another savanna. While you will see several examples of this commu-nity here, it is a very rare plant community within the whole state. Savannas, with their park-like settings, were a favorite area for pioneers to settle. Without fire to maintain them, woody plants, such as sugar maple and buckthorn, soon grew up and turned the area into a closed forest.

At the southwest corner of the savanna are three trails; take the center one and begin the trek up the kame (1.05 mi.) [**8**]. Local people call these 100-foot kames you are climbing *camelback kames*. More than 10,000 years ago the edge of the glacier rested here. During the summers, meltwaters carried sand and gravel over the edge, resulting in these unique landforms. Think of the cold, glacial ice while climbing. It may help you cool off. At the top enjoy a vulture's-eye view of the surrounding savanna and valley of Nippersink Creek.

Down from the kame at 1.3 mi. [**9**], the trail first goes right and then left. As you hike along this stretch, look for kames on both sides and stop to admire the huge bur oak on the left at 1.4 mi. [**10**]. From the bur oak you begin to hike through an oak-hickory savanna. In the spring the ground is covered with mayapple. Note that only the plants with a pair of leaves bear a flower. The trail goes upward to an overlook and a bench (1.65 mi.) [**11**].

From here you can see the broad valley shaped by the ancient Fox River. The savanna is left behind and at 1.9 mi. the trail comes to a T; go left [**12**] and soon you will be back on the flat ground of the parking area.

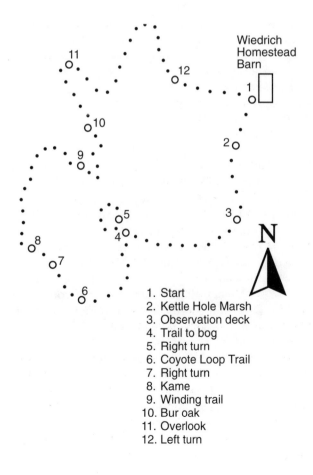

Wiedrich Homestead Barn

1. Start
2. Kettle Hole Marsh
3. Observation deck
4. Trail to bog
5. Right turn
6. Coyote Loop Trail
7. Right turn
8. Kame
9. Winding trail
10. Bur oak
11. Overlook
12. Left turn

Nippersink Trail 🥾

Distance Round-Trip: 4.2 miles

Estimated Hiking Time: 1.75 hours

Enjoy a pleasant hike along a stream where you can watch swallows, herons, and warblers while looking for muskrat and beaver. Along the way discover kames and an ancient river valley.

Caution: This linear trail can be very muddy and wet due to low spots. Watch for traffic at the rural road crossing.

Trail Directions: From the intersection of highways 12 and 31, go west on Tryon Grove Road. Follow this until it intersects with Keystone Road. Go south on Keystone to the trailhead at the intersection of Keystone and Barnard Mill Road. Begin at the trail board, hike toward the creek [1], and go left. While passing through a willow thicket, check the goldenrod for galls. These are swellings on the plants' stems. Galls are caused by a fly that lays its eggs here in the summer.

At .2 mi. the trail has partially eroded [2]; go left through a thicket of box elder. Cross the bridge over the creek [3] and then go left (.35 mi.). Nippersink Creek is now on your left and will be until you reach the turnaround point. To your right are distant kames and, closer to the trail, a marsh. While walking along the creek and marsh, observe the red-winged blackbirds. Watch belted kingfishers as they patrol up and down the creek. A kingfisher will dig a tunnel into the creek bank with its bill and place its nesting chamber at the end.

At .7 mi. come to signage about the camelback kames and an intersection [4]; go left and continue to follow the creek. The broad valley you are hiking in, dotted with kames on the right, was shaped by the ancient Fox River that flowed in the opposite direction of Nippersink Creek. A shallow lake, known as Wonder Lake, occupied this region after the kames were deposited. As it drained, it left the flat land between these kames.

Note the large, solitary cottonwoods on your right. At .95 mi. the trail curves right, away from the creek. On the left is an aspen grove [5], and within a few yards you will come to a trail crossroads; go left on a gravel path (1 mi.) [6]. Ahead of you are two kames, one an almost-perfect cone. At 1.35 mi. come to the first kame on your right. It has water and a bench [7]. After a cool drink, go through a fence and cross a private road to rejoin the hiking trail on the opposite side, the one closer to the creek (the other is a snowmobile and equestrian trail).

Observe how straight the creek now is. It has been made into a straight channel (channelized) in an attempt to move water quickly. Note also along this section that the activity near the water has slowed—there are few birds. On your right is an isolated kame, a textbook example of this glacial landform. At 1.5 mi. [8] and beyond the kame, look to the right at what remains of the old creek bed (especially visible during wet periods). Two miles bring you across an old iron bridge [9]. To the right is a shelter, picnic table, restroom, and water, all set in a grove of bur oaks. As this is a linear trail, it's soon time to retrace your steps and look for anything you might have missed.

On the way back, again watch the red-winged blackbirds. Watch the aerial acrobatics of the swallows—tree, barn, and rough-winged. These creatures of the air feast on insects captured while on the wing. If you follow one of them long enough with your binoculars, you can observe that they have short, wide bills that open and close with precision. Their long, narrow, pointed wings, and notched or deeply forked tails facilitate fast turns in pursuit of prey.

At 2.9 mi. recross the road [6] and you will have a great view of the camelback kames. Wild turkey like this section of the trail, so keep your eyes open and don't be surprised if one flies or runs across the trail. Look on the right near the water for beaver (a house and lots of stumps indicate their presence). That bright flash of yellow near the water is a yellow warbler. As you near the large cottonwoods (at 3.45 mi.) note the lightning strike on the trunk of one. At 3.8 you will recross the bridge [3], and the trail soon leads back to the parking area.

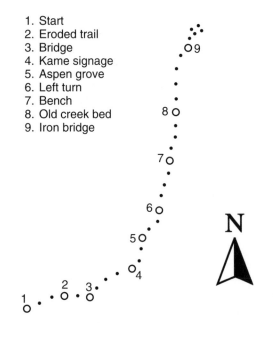

1. Start
2. Eroded trail
3. Bridge
4. Kame signage
5. Aspen grove
6. Left turn
7. Bench
8. Old creek bed
9. Iron bridge

15. Goose Lake Prairie

- Visit the largest prairie remnant in the state of Illinois—a place of grasses, wildflowers, and ceaseless prairie winds.

- Walk the trails in late summer to experience grasses taller than a person on horseback.

- Bring forb and grass guides to help identify more than 200 species found growing here.

- Discover how the prairie changes through the seasons, from the diminutive prairie violet on a gentle spring day to the reddish brown of big bluestem, harsh against the snow during an early February cold snap.

- Catch sight of deer, fox, grassland birds, and hawks.

Area Information

Goose Lake Prairie is indeed a habitat of wildflowers, tall grasses, and relentless prairie winds—once home to the buffalo, wolf, prairie chicken, and otter. Today, abundant numbers of rabbits, muskrats, deer, and small rodents substitute for the fauna of old. Huge boulders scattered in the area are evidence of the geologic history. These boulders were not formed in Illinois but were brought more than ten thousand years ago by glaciers down from the north.

Goose Lake itself no longer exists; it was drained before the turn of the century for farming and to mine the underlying clay. In its day, the lake that extended some one thousand acres often was covered so thickly with geese and ducks that the water was not visible. Today what remains is a series of ponds and marshes, outstanding examples of a once-common habitat—the prairie pothole. In 1840 Eliza Steele exclaimed, "I was in the midst of a prairie! A world of grass and flowers stretched around me, rising and falling in gentle undulations, as if an enchanter had struck the ocean swell, and it was at rest forever." This is Goose Lake.

Directions: From Morris, take Highway 47 south across the Illinois River (.7 mile) to the blacktop road known as Pine Bluff-Lorenzo Road; turn left (east) and travel 6 miles to Jugtown Road; turn north to the park entrance.

Hours Open: The site is open year-round except on Christmas and New Year's Day. During the winter (December - February) the Visitor Center is closed during the weekends, but the park is open.

Facilities: Visitor Center with exhibits, picnic area, cross-country ski trails, and restrooms.

Permits and Rules: Pets should be confined on a leash and are not allowed in the nature-preserve part of the park.

Further Information: Site Superintendent, Goose Lake Prairie State Natural Area, 5010 N. Jugtown Road, Morris, IL 60450; 815-942-2899.

Other Areas of Interest

Heidecke State Fish and Wildlife Area features Heidecke Lake (formerly called Collins Lake), which serves as a cooling lake for Commonwealth Edison. Only boats used for fishing and hunting are allowed on the lake. The fishing season opens April 1 and closes the second Sunday in October; deer hunting and waterfowl hunting are allowed during season. For more information call 815-942-6352.

Ten miles south of Joliet, the Des Plaines River joins the Kankakee River to form the Illinois River at the **Des Plaines Fish and Wildlife Area**. This area offers picnicking, fishing, boating, camping, and hunting. The largest pheasant-hunting site in the state is located here. Eighty acres of the area make up a dedicated nature preserve. For more information call 815-423-5326.

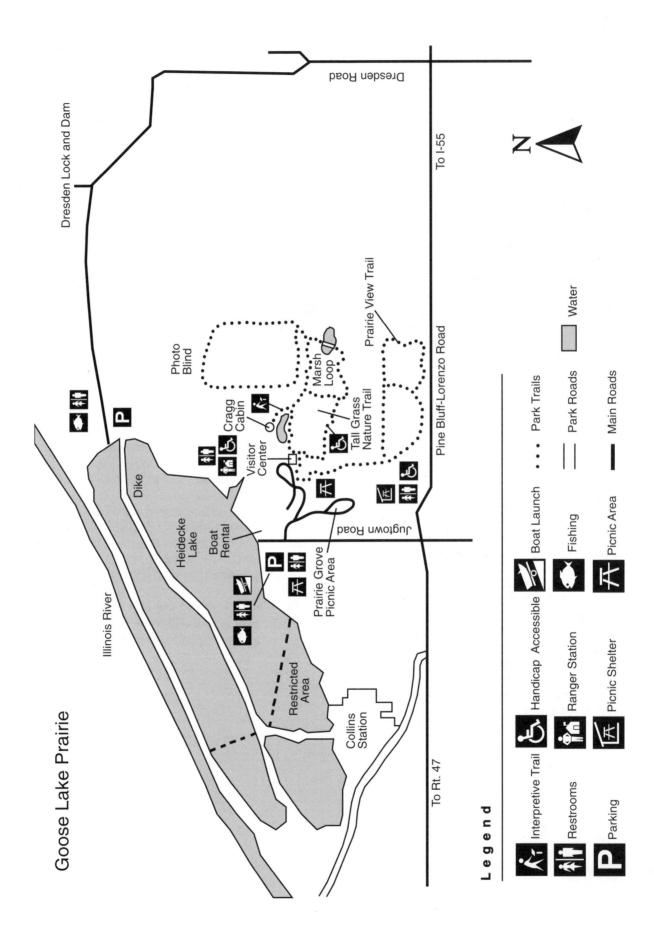

Goose Lake Prairie

Dresden Road

Dresden Lock and Dam

To I-55

Illinois River

Dike

Heidecke Lake

Boat Rental

Restricted Area

Collins Station

Photo Blind

Marsh Loop

Cragg Cabin

Visitor Center

Tall Grass Nature Trail

Prairie View Trail

Pine Bluff-Lorenzo Road

Jugtown Road

Prairie Grove Picnic Area

To Rt. 47

Legend

Interpretive Trail	Handicap Accessible	Boat Launch · · · · Park Trails
Restrooms	Ranger Station	Fishing — Park Roads
Parking	Picnic Shelter	Picnic Area — Main Roads
		Water

Tall Grass Nature Trail 🥾

Distance Round-Trip: 3.5 miles

Estimated Hiking Time: 1.75 hours

Hiking this trail in late summer with prairie grasses and forbs towering overhead gives one the feeling of "being lost in a sea of grass," a phenomenon undoubtedly like that experienced by early pioneers.

Caution: The bridge over Goose Lake sometimes is in disrepair due to muskrat damage. The trail is a fairly level, mowed path with occasional slabs of bedrock embedded in it. Many mammals other than humans use the area's trails—watch for their scat.

Trail Directions: Pick up a trail guide at the Visitor Center—it provides useful tidbits about the prairie landscape. Begin the trail at the sign board directly behind the Visitor Center [**1**]. Take the trail to the left. The numbers on the trail-guide map do not correspond to those found in this book.

A pond carved out by the Wisconsinan Glacier is on your left. At .25 mi. [**2**] the trail forks. Go left for a short side spur to a replica of one of the first cabins in Grundy County. Retrace your steps to the main trail.

On the left note the small grove of hawthorn trees (.5 mi.) [**3**]; although they are native to the prairie, without seasonal prairie fires they would take over and choke out the prairie vegetation. At .7 mi. the trail forks [**4**] at a metal sign with the #8 on it; go right. Within a short distance the trail will fork again; go to your left [**5**] and enter the marsh loop of the trail. Straight ahead is a prairie pothole—a shallow depression made by the glaciers that quickly filled with water. Along this section of the trail notice the large granite boulders embedded in the ground. Called glacial erratics, they are not from Illinois but were brought in from the north by the Wisconsinan Glacier.

This is a wetter part of the preserve, and the composition of the prairie has changed. Plants that need more moisture now dominate the landscape—cordgrass, swamp milkweed, and blue vervain. At 1 mi.[**6**] you will cross a bridge over all that remains of Goose Lake. Surrounding the water is bur reed and saw grass. During summer look for the small white flowers of arrowleaf emerging from the quiet water.

After crossing the bridge, go up a short incline. The trail forks at 1.1 mi.; go right [**7**].

Within .1 mi. the trail forks again; go right again and begin the Sagashka Trail loop [**8**]. The path looming ahead is arrow-straight and very quiet. Only whistling winds and rustling grasses can be heard. On the horizon are the towers of the Dresden Nuclear Power Plant and the General Electric Midwest Fuel

Recovery Plant—sites early settlers would not have seen. This part of the trail is excellent for viewing deer in a prairie. Other wildlife, although abundant here, are usually in evidence only by their tracks, scats, or an occasional feather.

The path curves to the left at 1.6 mi. On your right is a large pothole [**9**]. Note the restoration work underway in this area. The large cottonwood trees have been felled in an effort to encourage prairie vegetation. At 1.9 mi. the trail intersects a service road; go left [**10**]. To the right are impressive expanses of native prairie grasses—Indian grass and big bluestem. To the left is a weedy field dominated by foxtail.

At 2.5 mi. you return to [**8**]; go right and retrace your steps to [**7**]. Go right at [**7**], skirting the edge of the pothole. Soon (at 2.9 mi.) you will come back to [**4**]; go left to [**5**], where you will go to the right and enter the final leg of the trail. You'll sight excellent stands of big bluestem, switch grass, Indian grass, and little bluestem. In the summer this area should be a riot of colorful forbs, such as sunflowers, rattlesnake master, and thistles.

On your left note the windmill and the large glacial boulder (3.2 mi.) [**11**]. The area around the windmill is somewhat wet, as evidenced by stands of prairie cordgrass and bluejoint grass. Soon you will return to the trail board [**1**], leaving the tall grasses and incessant winds behind.

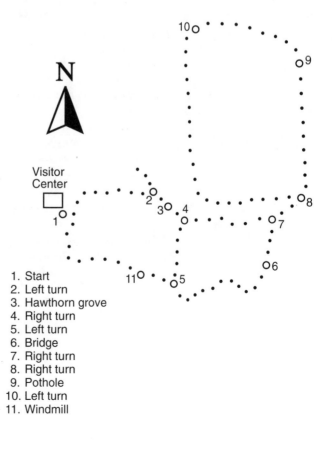

1. Start
2. Left turn
3. Hawthorn grove
4. Right turn
5. Left turn
6. Bridge
7. Right turn
8. Right turn
9. Pothole
10. Left turn
11. Windmill

Prairie View Trail 👢👢

Distance Round-Trip: 3.5 miles

Estimated Hiking Time: 1.75 hours

Hiked in the winter, the low sun gives the ubiquitous grasses a golden glow. The ice on the ponds is a bright, cold blue. Animal tracks are permanently embossed in the mud, at least until the next thaw.

Caution: Watch your step at the beginning of this trail: Culverts are embedded in the path and part of the trail may be very wet during any season.

Trail Directions: The trail begins at the south side of the parking lot, to the left of the pay phone. Cross a wooden footpath bridge and begin your hike [1]. The trail is a mowed swath through prairie grasses—Indian, big bluestem, and switch. During late summer the path is lined with gold—the blooms of goldenrod and sunflowers.

At .1 mi. [2] a small grove of trees on the left, hawthorn and chokecherry, is being removed. Prairies are sustained by fire; with the suppression of fire trees and shrubs begin to colonize, choking out the prairie vegetation. Removing trees and shrubs and beginning a fire regime allows the prairie to come back.

At about .4 mi. [3] look on the left for the remnants of a stone fence, made from the many glacial boulders as the land was cleared. Keep alert for hawks in this wide expanse of grassland; the occasional tree provides a perch from which they search for their next meal. Where the trail forks at .8 mi.[4], go left, following an old fencerow. The vegetation on either side is old field. Straight ahead and to the right are the old spoil heaps of a strip mine.

A marsh with a pond appears on your left at 1 mi. [5]. Large expanses of common reed (*Phragmites*) interspersed with cattails are the dominant plants. In less than .1 mi. the trail forks where a sign explains strip mines and the reclamation of the land [6]. Go to the right and pass small ponds on both sides. Begin a gradual uphill ascent.

To your left a short observation spur, uphill at 1.3 mi. [7], leads to a great panorama of the spoil ponds and the prairie beyond. Continue on the trail and walk by a series of spoil ponds. Contrast these ponds with the potholes on the prairies. The spoil ponds are lined with cattails and European weeds, whereas prairie potholes are lined with native reeds and grasses.

The trail forks at 1.45 mi. [8]. Go left. During this part of the trail you are walking on top of spoil heaps. This part of the trail can be muddy, so check the ground for animal tracks, scat, or feathers from a predator's recent meal. Once off the spoil heaps, the trail enters a mud flat (1.9 mi.) [9]. A wooden boardwalk traverses the wettest area.

Soon you return to [6]; take a left, retrace your steps to [8], and go right. The trail parallels the road and will take you past the remnants of an old grove: Look for weathered stumps and piles of wood chips on the right. At 2.75 mi. you have completed the loop and are back at [4]. Continue straight back to the Visitor Center and the parking lot.

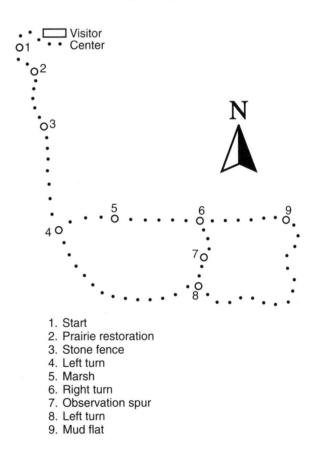

1. Start
2. Prairie restoration
3. Stone fence
4. Left turn
5. Marsh
6. Right turn
7. Observation spur
8. Left turn
9. Mud flat

16. Illinois and Michigan Canal

- Hike at about the same speed and on the same path as the mules and horses that towed the canal boats.
- Although the "King" is dead (the largest cotton-wood in the state), find its many heirs apparent along this trail.
- Bring your binoculars. Who knows what mysteries you might see?
- Play an ongoing game of tag with a green heron as it flies along the canal—stopping just long enough for you to focus your binoculars before it flies on, just out of your range.
- Walk on giant, geometric depictions of Illinois Valley aquatic animals. Would you believe an 1,800-foot-long by 26-foot-high water strider?
- See an aqueduct for a canal over a stream!

Area Information

The National Heritage Corridor of the Illinois and Michigan Canal (I & M) extends more than 100 miles, from Chicago to LaSalle/Peru, and encompasses some 450 square miles of industrial heartland and prime Illinois farmland. Quarries, cornfields, and refineries rest on the dolomite and St. Peter sandstone of the Des Plaines and Illinois River valleys. Here, the northern forests ended and the prairie began in the days when early settlements along the canal were mere pinpoints dotting the prairie, forests, and wetlands.

Today the situation is reversed, and remnants of wilderness are pinpoints among the urban and agricultural sprawl. Within the National Heritage Corridor lie 8 state parks or recreation areas and at least 39 significant natural areas. Even after extensive development, this area retains one of the richest concentrations of natural areas and open lands in the entire state, providing clues to what once was here. Threads of wilderness exist like capillaries along the vein of development that is the I & M Canal.

Directions: For Aux Sable access at Morris, take Cemetery Road east to Tabler Road. Go north on Tabler to the parking area. For the Gebhard Woods access, exit I-80 south on Route 47. Turn right (west) onto Bedford Road (Route 6), go to Union Street, turn left (south) and follow the signs. For Ottawa access take Route 6 (west) through Ottawa and go south onto Boyce Memorial Road. The access entrance is before the railroad. Buffalo Rock State Park is located on Dee Bennett Road, west of Ottawa.

Hours Open: The I & M Canal is open year-round. Buffalo Rock State Park opens at 8 A.M. and closes at sunset.

Facilities: The Gebhard Woods Information Center is well-stocked with information about the trail and other sites around the area. It is staffed by friendly volunteers who are able to give trail conditions. Gebhard Woods has toilets, picnic shelters, and horseshoe pits. Buffalo Rock State Park has three primitive campsites, two baseball diamonds, and picnicking with shelters. Fishing is allowed along the canal. Canoe access is available from Channahon State Park, Gebhard Woods, Utica, and LaSalle.

Permits and Rules: Pets must be leashed at all times. No horses are allowed on the trail.

Further Information: Illinois and Michigan Canal State Trail, P.O. Box 272, Morris, IL 60450; 815-942-0796.

Other Areas of Interest

Within the corridor's 100 miles are many attractions. A sampling includes Isle a la Cache Museum, Illinois State Museum-Lockport Gallery, Messenger Woods, Pilcher Park, McKinley Woods, W.G. Stratton State Park, Goose Lake Prairie State Natural Area (see park #15), Seneca's Old Grain Elevator, Illini State Park, Starved Rock State Park (see park #18), Matthiessen State Park (see park #19), and the Illinois Waterway Visitor Center.

Park Trail

Illinois and Michigan Canal State Trail 👢—61 miles—This long multiuse, linear trail begins in Channahon and ends in LaSalle, but it can be accessed from many points.

Illinois and Michigan Canal

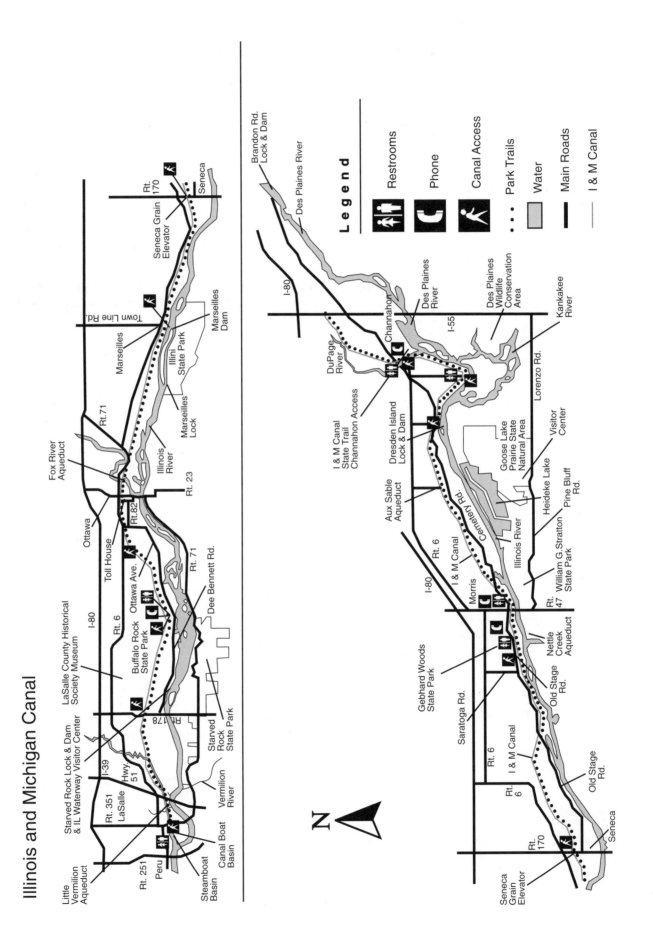

Legend

Restrooms

Phone

Canal Access

Park Trails

Water

Main Roads

I & M Canal

N

Aux Sable to Gebhard Woods

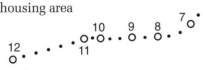

Distance Round-Trip: 7 miles (one way)

Estimated Hiking Time: 2.75 hours

Unlike a passenger on the old canal, I was inspired not by reaching my destination but by watching a mother catbird defend her nest against a fox snake tangled in a shrub along the shore. First pretending to be injured, and then pecking the snake until it slithered off, the catbird won! The nest was safe.

Caution: You will cross the highway or city streets three times; remember to look both ways. This is a multiuse trail so keep alert for bicyclists. This is also a linear trail, so you might want to hike it with friends and have a vehicle at both ends.

Trail Directions: Park at the brown sign for the Aux Sable Access. Cross the bridge over the flume (inclined channel), go left, and begin the trail at the information sign at the head of Lock #8 [**1**]. All that remains of the small village of Aux Sable is the lock tender's house. Head west from Aux Sable (left if facing the canal). Throughout the hike the canal will be on your right. At .2 mi. you will cross a bridge and skirt a marsh on the left.

Notice at .3 mi. how the canal has broken out of its walls [**2**]. One mile is marked by a bench on the left and a trash receptacle [**3**], coming just after some glacial boulders on the right. Your hiking speed is likely to be just a little slower than the speed of the canal packets (boats) of the 19th century. They traveled about 5 mph; any faster a pace caused waves that undermined the banks.

Next the trail skirts a marsh on the left. Look at the edge for tall meadow rue, spiderwort, and Canada anemone. Further on, Angelica can be found. This tall plant with maroon stems is very aromatic, and its oils have been used in cordials and medicines. Keep alert, for along the trail great spangled fritillaries (butterflies) seek nectar, small rabbits hop in front of you, squirrels argue with each other, and chipmunks continually chatter. In the canal, fish jump, red-eared sliders and softshell turtles sun on logs, and damselflies skirt the edges. Be sure to keep an eye out for impressive examples of mulberry and cottonwood trees.

At 2 mi. you hike through a small housing area

on the left [**4**]. Look for kingfishers patrolling the canal. These birds require a fairly clean stream, as they need to spot their prey within two feet of the water's surface. At 3.15 mi. you'll find another bench on the left [**5**], and at 3.6 mi., a campsite on the left.

By 4.5 mi. you become aware of Morris. Arthur Cunynghame, a traveler on the canal in 1850 wrote:

> At about nine A.M., we reached the small town to which I had previously alluded, called Morris, as being a particularly good spot for "hunting prairie chickens"; and from the general appearance of this settlement, I can readily believe that it abounded in game. Morris is surrounded by fine prairies, with quite enough grain to feed the game.

At 4.75 mi. the trail crosses a road [**6**] and is lined with small houses. You will cross a bridge at 5.15 mi., and by 5.4 mi. the floodplain of the Illinois River comes into view. Then at 5.55 mi. the Illinois River can be seen on the left [**7**]. The trail skirts William Stratton State Park (5.75 mi.) [**8**], which provides public access to the Illinois River for boats, fishing, and picnicking. You cross another street and then walk under the bridge over Route 47 (6.1 mi.) [**9**].

Glance left at the Illinois River and its barges—they obviously wouldn't fit in the canal. Cross another street at 6.4 mi. [**10**]. Then check out the Nettle Creek aqueduct at 6.65 mi. [**11**]. From the aqueduct, Gebhard Woods will soon come into view. The largest tree in Illinois, an eastern cottonwood, used to reside here. Although the tree met its demise during a bad wind and lightning storm, you may have noticed many cottonwoods along this segment of the canal that are heirs apparent! At 7 mi. cross the bridge on the right over the canal and enter Gebhard Woods, visit the I & M Canal Visitor Center [**12**], and, hopefully, find a friend's waiting vehicle.

Aux Sable Aqueduct

1. Start
2. Broken dike
3. Bench
4. Houses
5. Bench
6. Road crossing
7. Illinois River
8. William Stratton State Park
9. Bridge
10. Road crossing
11. Aqueduct
12. Visitor Center

N

Ottawa to Buffalo Rock State Park 🥾🥾

Distance Round-Trip: 4.65 miles

Estimated Hiking Time: 2 hours

This is a two-part hike. The first focuses on a functional, man-made structure. The second portion features artistic, bulldozer-made sculptures!

Caution: This is a multipurpose and linear trail; be alert for bicyclists. You may want to hike this with a friend and have a vehicle at each end. At Buffalo Rock State Park stay on the trail; do not attempt to climb the sculptures.

Trail Directions: To reach the Ottawa Access trailhead, go right on Route 6 and turn left onto Boyce Memorial Road. The entrance to the Ottawa access is before the railroad. Begin the trail here and head west [1]. The canal here is just a wet spot and is hidden by black locust trees.

After you cross the railroad tracks at .45 mi., Lock #11 will be on your right [2]. At .7 mi. admire the giant mounds of pure silica sand (from St. Peter sandstone) of the Ottawa Silica Company on your left. The canal on the right is only a verdant depression. At 1.1 mi. a large lake is on the left [3]. At 1.25 mi. two early modes of transportation have converged—the railroad and the canal [4]. Look to your right at the exposed sandstone bluff that was cut through for the railroad.

Continue to occasionally look on the right where the bluffs increase in height. A spoil heap makes up part of the bluff, so it isn't all natural. You'll have abundant opportunities for viewing wildlife. Check any portion of the canal that still holds water: Why is that water smartweed moving against the current? Because it's being carried along by a muskrat! Turtles usually are basking on logs and black-winged damselflies are catching those pesky mosquitoes.

Lock #12 is on the right at 2.05 mi. [5], with a bridge passing over the lock (look in both directions as you stand on the bridge). At 2.25 mi. you will walk under an overpass and enter a corridor of floodplain woods before crossing a bridge at 2.45 mi. [6]. Before Lock #12 a stream incorporated the canal into its bed. Where the stream meanders off to the left at the bridge crossing, the canal becomes nothing more than a moist depression again. On the left and right you will also pass the Illinois version of Mayan ruins—old overpass arches!

The trail now parallels the road on the left. The canal, to the right of the dirt wall, is just a wet

spot. The access parking area to Buffalo Rock State Park is at 3.15 mi. [7]. Get in the car that you ought to have parked here and drive to the park entrance (on the right, heading east on the main highway). The park road has no shoulder and is too narrow for safe hiking. As you drive, look on the right at the fern-lined sandstone cliffs. Park on the far right of the parking area.

Continue your hike at the observation deck [8], first reading about the sculptures you are about to see. Along the mile-and-a-half bluff are five sculptures depicting animal life of the Illinois River. These are some of the largest earthen sculptures ever built—and the largest built since Mt. Rushmore. Go right, off the deck, and follow a gravel footpath. At the trail intersection go right and follow the Effigy Trail. At 3.3 mi. (this only includes hiking mileage), the first sculpture will be in front of you—a water strider [9]. Stay on the main gravel path as it curves left; part of the frog is now visible. At 3.8 mi. you will pass the tail of the catfish on the right [10].

At the intersection at 3.9 mi. [11] go left and follow River Bluff Trail. (If you want to "see" the rest of the sculptures, continue to the right. The trail will dead-end at the snake.) Observe the Illinois River on your left and the islands covered with *Phragmites*. Soon you will come face-to-face with a 140-foot-long frog at 4.1 mi. [12]. At the intersection at 4.4 mi. continue straight [13] and skirt the water strider on your left. You will have completed the loop at 4.65 mi. Before heading back to the parking area, visit the two bison in the pen on your right. These are not effigies but the real thing!

1. Start
2. Old lock
3. Lake
4. Railroad
5. Old lock
6. Bridge
7. Buffalo Rock access
8. Observation deck
9. Water strider
10. Tail of catfish
11. Left turn
12. Frog
13. Water strider on left

17. Rockford Area

- Within the second largest city in the state, experience the illusion of nothing but hill after hill, each covered with prairie grasses and forbs.
- Hike through a kaleidoscope of spring warblers.
- Explore a gravel terrace prairie and discover pasque flower, prairie smoke, and purple coneflowers.
- Bring your field guides for the prairie plants and grassland birds at Harlem Hills and the woodland plants and spring warblers at Rock Cut.

Area Information

The city of Rockford is located in a region of rolling topography drained by the Rock River. If you were to look at the soil of the area, you would find not the deep, fine particle soils of areas to the east and south but glacial *till* and *outwash*—a mixture of sand, gravel, and dolomite with only a thin layer of soil on top. On a topographical map the city looks as if it resides on a lion's paw. These knuckles were originally gravel terrace prairies, and all but one of them—**Harlem Hills**—have succumbed to the ever-growing city.

Rocks, whether the tiny particles that make up the gravel terrace prairies or larger examples found along the Rock River, played a significant part in the development of the area. Rockford is where wagons once forded the Rock River—hence, its name. **Rock Cut State Park** is the site of the old Rockford-Kenosha Rail Line. Most of the railroad bed is now covered by the waters of Pierce Lake. To provide a suitable roadbed, railroad crews conducted vigorous blasting in the area. Thus, the park's name came to be Rock Cut.

Directions: To reach **Harlem Hills** drive from the intersection of Highway 251 and Windsor Road on the north side of Loves Park, turn east onto Windsor Road and go 1.3 miles to a T that Windsor Road forms at Forest Hills Road. Turn north on Forest Hills Road and go .1 mile to Flora Drive. Turn east on Flora Drive and go another .1 mile; the preserve is on the south side of the road. **Rock Cut State Park** is located 7 miles northeast of Rockford, and the park is accessible from Illinois Route 173.

Hours Open: The sites are open year-round, except on Christmas and New Year's Day.

Facilities: There are no facilities at **Harlem Hills**. **Rock Cut State Park** offers campgrounds with electricity and showers, fishing, boating, swimming, picnicking, a concession stand, and two fishing piers accessible to the disabled.

Permits and Rules: The trail at **Harlem Hills** is located in a dedicated Illinois Nature Preserve: No pets are allowed on the trail. All plants, animals, and natural features are protected. No camping, firearms, vehicles, or horses are allowed. **Rock Cut State Park** does not allow alcoholic beverages in the park from March 1 through May 31. Do not pick any of the flowers, and keep your pet leashed at all times.

Further Information: (for both sites) Site Superintendent, Rock Cut State Park, 7318 Harlem Road, Loves Park, IL 61111; 815-885-3311.

Other Areas of Interest

Winnebago County has 31 **forest preserves** that offer day-use areas, ball fields, and hiking trails. For more information call 815-877-6100.

Located only 30 minutes from Rockford, **Long Prairie Trail** begins north of Illinois Route 173. The 9.5-mile linear asphalt trail, marked every half mile, highlights natural-history features and points where interesting human events occurred. For a trail map and more information call 815-547-7935.

Park Trails

Pierce Lake Trail (Rock Cut Trail) 🥾—4.25 miles—Circumnavigate the shoreline of Pierce Lake at Rock Cut State Park on this loop trail. You will hike not only by the water's edge but through wooded areas as well.

Cross-Country Ski, Bike, and Hiking Trail 🥾🥾🥾—6 miles—This trail connects with the Pierce Lake Trail, but it also takes a loop into a restored prairie, along small streams, and through woods with large oaks. Use caution as there are many unmarked side spurs created by off-trail bicyclists.

Rock River Recreation Path 🥾—3.3 miles—This recreation corridor in downtown Rockford includes four parks, a rose garden, sculptures, a trolley, and museums. The trail has markers every half mile. Call 815-987-8694 for a map.

Rockford Area

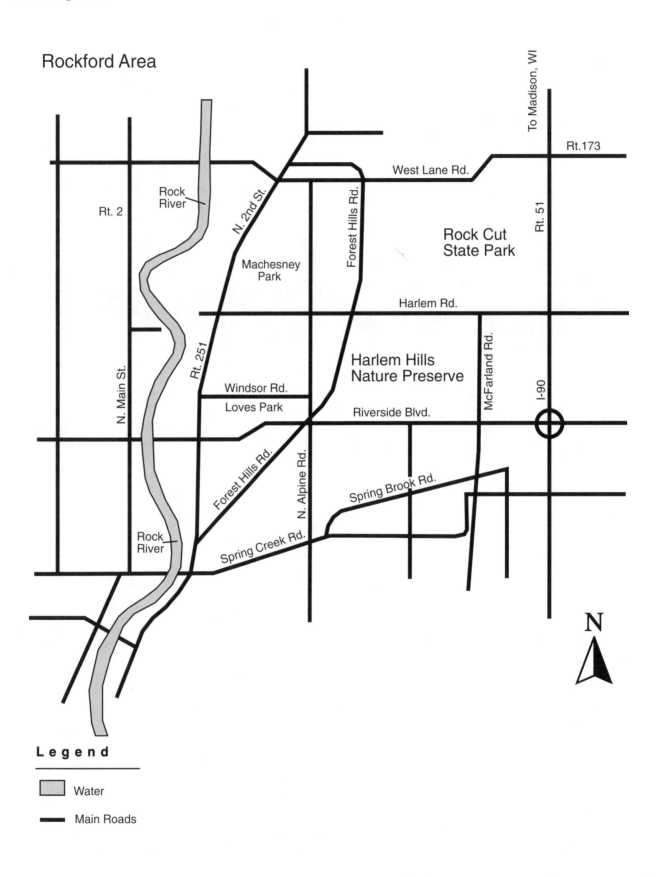

Harlem Hills Nature Preserve

Distance Round-Trip: 1.4 miles

Estimated Hiking Time: 1 hour

Periodically, the grass-covered gravel terraces are invaded by pink- and purple-clothed armies. Early spring brings the fuzzy lavender of pasque flowers, low to the ground and protected from the cold. By early summer hundreds of purple coneflowers erupt and flow down the terraces like pinkish-purple lava. Summer's end is signaled by the bright pink of Liatris, each concealing brilliant yellow spiders in their tall, pink spikes.

Caution: The path is periodically mowed, and cut stems of brush protrude from it. Beware of groundhog holes concealed by the grass.

Trail Directions: Begin the trail at the gate in front of the Nature Preserve sign [1]. Although there is no official trail, there is a well-worn path that is easy to follow. In the early spring you will encounter pasque flowers within a few steps: Come back in May and all that is left are their silky plumes.

Go up a small hill; the trail soon curves to the right. At .15 mi. the path comes to a T; go left, or east [2]. Experience the prairie. Look at its rolling, gravel hills; walk through the pervasive grasses; discover bird's-foot violets, the prairie buttercup, and prairie smoke; and watch the antics of American gold-finches. Walk as far as the two dead willows on the right (.25 mi.) [3]. As you face west on the walk back, the landscape appears to be nothing more than a series of hills—a vast, dry prairie. During late June at this spot hundreds of purple coneflowers explode into bloom.

At .35 mi. note a low thicket [4]. Here the path is easily lost, but within a few steps you come over a gravel hill and can once again see the city. By .4 mi. you are back at the intersection [2]; continue straight. During July this is a thicket of purple coneflowers, but by fall all that remain are the dead seed heads, waving like gearshift knobs above the ever-growing grasses. Soon you will encounter a fire lane; cross it and continue straight, following the narrow path that heads uphill and to the left.

The path comes out at a housing development on a wide path; go right (.55 mi.) [5]. On your left is a work in progress (prairie restoration); on the right is what that parcel should eventually look like. With the absence of natural fires, some fire-intolerant species, such as sumac and other small shrubs, were able to gain a foothold. It will take many hours of sweat to cut and remove all traces of these invaders. By

midsummer, when blazing stars (*Liatris*) and flowering spurge are in bloom, this section of the prairie is a riot of pinks and white. The trail curves right, following the prairie contours. You may think you are merely on a gravel road, when you are actually walking on glacially deposited gravel, the main component on which this gravel terrace prairie grows.

The path ends at the fence (.85 mi.) [6]. Go right and follow the fencerow, prairie on the right and housing on the left. At the electric line go left, still skirting the fence. At .95 mi. [7], another power pole, go left. This is a great corner for pasque flowers in the spring and coneflowers in the summer. Within a few yards turn left and continue following the fence. Look for shooting star in this corner.

At 1 mi. you are back at the parking area [1], but continue to follow the fence on your left. Look on your right for the legume, cream wild indigo, that blooms in late spring. At the corner of Thompson and Nimitz roads go right (1.15 mi.) [8]. Within a few yards you will go right again, always following the fence.

By 1.25 mi. the fence has disappeared [9]; continue to circle the prairie on the mowed path and head southeast and uphill toward the fence. This part of the prairie was once a horse pasture. In spring, patches of pasque flower decorated it like crocuses and dodged the horses' hooves. Now it provides a buffer for the prairie. You reach the corner of the old pasture at 1.3 mi. [10]; turn right and go through a large patch of shooting star that bloom in spring. Head back to the gate and parking area. Your discovery and exploration of a gravel prairie are over.

1. Start
2. Left turn
3. Dead willows
4. Low thicket
5. Right turn
6. Fence
7. Left turn
8. Right turn
9. Circle prairie
10. Right turn

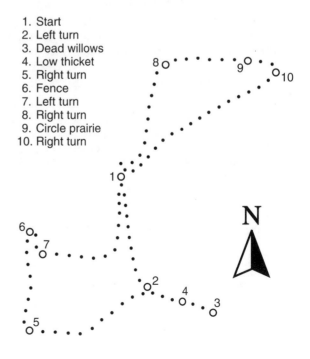

Rock Cut State Park

Distance Round-Trip: 3.75 miles

Estimated Hiking Time: 2 hours

By trail's end I had witnessed two male turkeys displaying for a coy female, observed countless colorful spring warblers flit and rest by the flowing streams, and watched a muskrat emerge from the water onto the trail before me.

Caution: At several points the trail comes very close to the edge of a bluff. Roots and rocks have eroded from the trail. Remember that some parts of the trail are shared with bicyclists; be careful.

Trail Directions: Park at the Lakeview Picnic Area and begin the trail by heading toward the spillway [**1**]. Go right (before the spillway) and across an old, paved parking area that soon becomes a gravel, multiuse (hiking and biking) trail. At .1 mi. [**2**] go left on a grassy path that will lead you down the spillway's watercourse; at the water go right.

At the intersection at .3 mi. go right, soon walking parallel to the stream [**3**]. Within .1 mi. climb a small hill and go left to merge with a wide path [**4**]. At .75 mi. the trail comes to a Y; go left [**5**].

Soon you are hiking on a ridge overlooking the water and passing an old foundation on the right. Within a few steps two trails will cross; go left and downhill (.85 mi.) [**6**]. At 1.1 mi. come to an intersection; you'll see a clump of silver poplar trees on your right just before you should go left across a bridge [**7**]. From the bridge you will enter a paved parking area. From here go left and walk on an old park road.

At 1.3 mi. go left and leave the old road before it curves [**8**]. You are now walking through a narrow allée of elm trees. Leave the allée at 1.45 mi.; go left and you are soon skirting the same creek, only on the opposite side [**9**]. The path comes to a T at 1.65 mi.; go left and uphill [**10**]. On your left is the edge of the bluff. Use caution as the trail is close to the edge, and many roots are exposed.

The trail forks at 1.75 mi.; go left [**11**]. You soon come down out of the woods and skirt the creek. First you skirt the bluff, but soon the trail heads up and provides a closer view (1.85 mi.) [**12**]. Within a few yards come to a trail intersection. Go straight across and use the stairs to head up into the woods [**13**]. You are now hiking through a white oak forest. The trail comes to a Y at 2 mi.; go right. On your left is Lone Rock, a solitary rock outcrop [**14**].

The trail is now marked with blue and passes through an oak woods with nice spring wildflowers. Although this part of the trail has many narrow side trails, stay on the main, wide, well-trod path. The trail comes to a T at 2.25 mi; go left [**15**]. Soon the trail heads upward.

At 2.4 mi. the trail enters a grove of white pines and a picnic area [**16**]. Go right as the trail skirts West Lake Picnic Area. Within a few yards the trail heads back into the woods, again with several offshoot trails; stay on the main marked path. A bike path joins the trail at 2.7 mi. [**17**] near a large oak. You are now hiking through an oak forest on a wide trail. The oaks give way to pines, and at 3 mi. you can see a concession area on the left, through the trees [**18**].

Go left, leaving the pines, crossing the road, and following the sidewalk along the lakeshore. Once the sidewalk ends, continue to skirt the lake. At 3.25 mi. cross a bridge [**19**] and go right and around the lake. Soon the trail heads into the woods, where, in the spring, it is lined with buttercup. You emerge in an oak grove picnic area near the lake (3.40 mi.) [**20**]. Past the picnic area the trail is a path alongside the park road that crosses a bridge over the spillway (3.65 mi.) [**21**]. The Lakeview Picnic Area will soon come into view; cross the road and return to your vehicle.

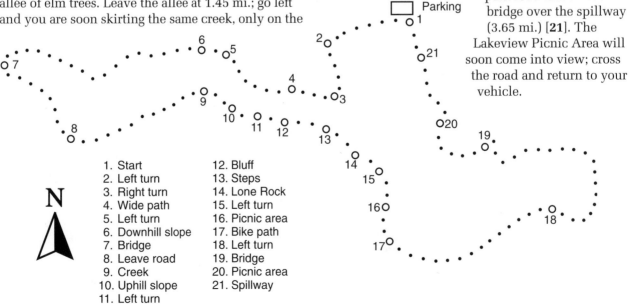

N

1. Start
2. Left turn
3. Right turn
4. Wide path
5. Left turn
6. Downhill slope
7. Bridge
8. Leave road
9. Creek
10. Uphill slope
11. Left turn
12. Bluff
13. Steps
14. Lone Rock
15. Left turn
16. Picnic area
17. Bike path
18. Left turn
19. Bridge
20. Picnic area
21. Spillway

18. Starved Rock State Park

- For a challenge—in and out of canyons, up and down steps, and along ridge tops suitable for a mountain goat—the trails of Starved Rock State Park will test any hiker's nimbleness.

- During the winter, canyon trails lead to canyon waterfalls that have become icefalls—statuesque, sculpted towers of ice.

- If you're satiated with the wide vistas of the Illinois landscape, the canyons and imposing walls of Starved Rock State Park will afford welcome relief.

- You can find harebell, reindeer lichen, yew, and mountain holly on the cool, craggy surfaces of the canyons. Called *survivor species*, these plants were left behind when the last glaciers receded.

Area Information

Starved Rock and the adjacent canyons are eroded from porous St. Peter sandstone, laid down millions of years ago by a shallow, inland sea. The sandstone was brought to the surface as a result of a huge upfold, known as the LaSalle Anticline. Streams have cut across the anticline and sunk their channels to considerable depth, giving rise to narrow, blind canyons and cliffs surrounded by a closed, canopy forest.

Waterfalls are found at the canyon heads. By summer these falls have slowed to a mere trickle or completely dried up. The waterfall at St. Louis Canyon is the exception. Fed by springs, this canyon stream never dries up, and in winter its fall is transformed into a column of ice, enhanced and constantly changed by the water's continuously trickling down the column and freezing.

Water falling on the porous sandstone rock quickly soaks in; thus, the sandy surface remains essentially dry. The plant communities found in the canyons are restricted to those species able to gain a foothold on the steep rock walls—usually lower forms of plant life—such as liverworts grasping the canyon walls like moist fingers. At least one third of all Illinois fern species are part of the flora of Starved Rock.

Whether you want to hike the many trails, observe the waterfalls and unique flora, or simply enjoy the entertainment of chipmunks cavorting among the crevices and along the trails, Starved Rock State Park offers a unique area of Illinois.

Directions: The park is located on the south bank of the Illinois River. From I-80 take Route 178 south to the entrance. From I-39 follow State Route 71 through Oglesby to the park entrance.

Hours Open: The site is open year-round except on Christmas and New Year's Day.

Facilities: A campground, lodge, and conference center are available, as well as picnicking, boating, and fishing activities.

Permits and Rules: Climbing, rappelling, or scrambling on the rocks is prohibited. Pets must be kept on a leash at all times. Hikers must be off the trails by dark.

Further Information: Site Superintendent, Starved Rock State Park, Box 116, Utica, IL 61373; 815-667-4726.

Trail Information: Here are some tips to help you interpret the trail signs. Metal trail maps are located at all trail access points, intersections, and points of interest to help keep you on track. Colored dots and posts along the trails correspond to the colors found on the metal maps (brown dots or posts indicate bluff trails; red dots or posts indicate river trails, and green dots or posts indicate interior canyons or connecting trails.) The yellow dots on trees or posts show that you are moving *away* from the lodge; white dots mean you are returning *to* the lodge.

Other Areas of Interest

Starved Rock State Park is located adjacent to **Matthiessen State Park** (see park #19) and along the historic **Illinois and Michigan Canal** corridor (see park #16).

Park Trail

Illinois, Kaskaskia, and Ottawa Canyons

—3.5 miles—This lightly used trail is away from the more heavily used portions of the park. The bluffs here are unlike those in southern Illinois in that no big chunks have broken off. Illinois and Kaskaskia are multilevel canyons. On the way from Illinois Canyon to Kaskaskia Canyon you will hike through Council Overhang, a shelter cave that resembles the Hollywood Bowl. Check with the park staff on the condition of these trails. Only the trail leading to Illinois Canyon was open in 1996 due to the storm damage of 1995; by spring, 1997, all these trails should reopen.

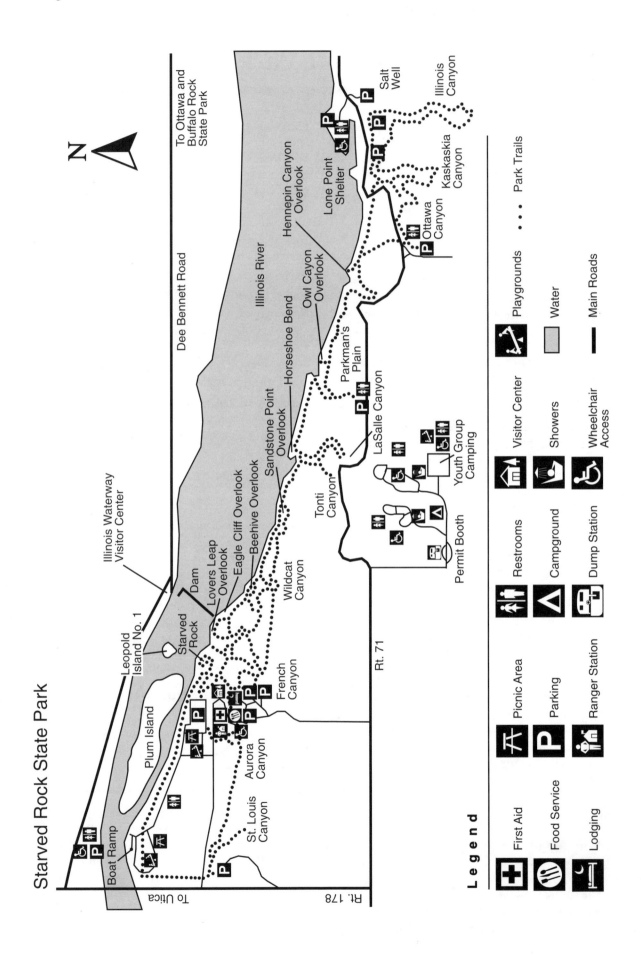

Starved Rock State Park

N

To Ottawa and Buffalo Rock State Park

Salt Well

Illinois Canyon

Kaskaskia Canyon

Hennepin Canyon Overlook

Lone Point Shelter

Illinois River

Dee Bennett Road

Ottawa Canyon

Owl Cayon Overlook

Horseshoe Bend

Parkman's Plain

LaSalle Canyon

Sandstone Point Overlook

Illinois Waterway Visitor Center

Tonti Canyon

Beehive Overlook

Eagle Cliff Overlook

Lovers Leap Overlook

Youth Group Camping

Dam

Leopold Island No. 1

Starved Rock

Permit Booth

Wildcat Canyon

French Canyon

Plum Island

Rt. 71

Aurora Canyon

St. Louis Canyon

Boat Ramp

To Utica

Rt. 178

Legend

First Aid

Food Service

Lodging

Picnic Area

Parking

Ranger Station

Restrooms

Campground

Dump Station

Visitor Center

Showers

Wheelchair Access

Playgrounds

Water

Main Roads

Park Trails

Starved Rock–Sandstone Point–LaSalle Canyon

Distance Round-Trip: 6 miles

Estimated Hiking Time: 3.5 hours

During a January thaw the air smells of spring, the bluffs are white, orange, and gray-green, accentuated against a too-blue sky. A blanket of newly fallen snow covers the canyon floors, erasing any trace of previous visitors.

Caution: Use extreme caution on the steps during the winter: They are very icy. During summer, moss growing on them can also cause slick conditions. Hike only where there are trails! Off-trail hiking destroys the vegetation, causes erosion, and is very dangerous for the hiker.

Trail Directions: Begin at the eastern edge of the lower parking lot [**1**]. This lot can be reached by going north on Route 178 to the entrance of the park. The lot is the final one past the playground areas. After a few steps find a trail board (map). Take a right, walking through the concession area and proceeding around the base of a small hill. The trails are well marked; area maps appear at many intersections. At .2 mi., when you come to a sign listing the various canyons or the Lodge, go to the left and up a hill [**2**].

The upward climb has taken you to Starved Rock (.4 mi.) [**3**]. After a series of wooden steps, go right and follow the wooden boardwalk around and upward. Upon completing the circle, retrace your steps back to [**2**] and go to your left toward the canyons. The trail is wide and flat, and Starved Rock is on the left. At the trail map at .75 mi. [**4**] go to the right for a side trip to French's Canyon. This part of the hike will be marked with green poles. Proceed to the end of the canyon, but

ignore the steps to your right, which go to the lodge. Enter the canyon using the steps carved into the sandstone. The trail is a narrow path that dead-ends at a waterfall (or icefall). At the canyon's end (1 mi.) [**5**] retrace your steps back to the main trail.

At 1.1 mi. [**6**] go to the right and follow red trail markers. A trail map appears at 1.3 mi. [**7**]. Go left toward Lover's Leap and Eagle Cliff (the trail markers will still be red.). After .1 mi. a trail appears off to the right, but continue straight ahead to the top of a bluff. You will have reached the river (1.5 mi.) [**8**] and the first of several overlooks. This one is called Lover's Leap.

Continue along the bluffs to Eagle Cliff. At 1.85 mi. the river (red) and a connecting trail (green) intersect [**9**]; go left, downhill, toward the river and hike along the river bank. Cross a wooden bridge, come to a trail split, and go left up the steps to Beehive Overlook (2 mi.) [**10**]. Admire the view, descend a series of steps, and go left. Soon you will cross a bridge over a canyon, with another trail map at 2.15 mi. [**11**]. Go right on a narrow path with steps leading downward into Wildcat Canyon.

Retrace your steps out of the canyon and return to [**11**]. Continue along the river; the bluffs are getting closer to the trail. Sandstone Point, where the river meets the bluff, is at 2.8 mi. [**12**]. A few steps past Sandstone Point cross a bridge and scramble up steps carved from sandstone.

At 3.2 mi. find a trail junction with a map [**13**].Take the right fork and do not cross the arched bridge in front of you. At 3.35 mi. [**14**], cross the bridge and go right, using a series of steps and bridges. The trail dead-ends at Tonti Canyon [**15**], the deepest canyon of the park. Retrace your steps to [**14**].

Returning from Tonti Canyon, go right, off the steps to a trail that leads to LaSalle Canyon. The trail winds around a bluff and comes perilously close to the edge. At 4.1 mi. [**16**] you will come upon LaSalle Canyon and its falls. The trail skirts the overhang, and you can walk behind the falls. Continue onward using a series of steps and bridges. Soon the trail leads to the arched bridge that will be on your left at 4.35 mi. [**17**]. Cross the bridge and continue walking straight on the trail back to Sandstone Point [**12**].

At Beehive Junction [**18**] go left, hiking around the hill. At 5.3 mi. [**9**] go to the left—following a green marker—and proceed uphill away from the river between the bluffs. After .1 mi. climb a series of steps and go to your left [**19**]. You have returned to [**7**]; go right, then left over the bridge. Soon you will return to [**2**], having explored some of the notable features of the park, and then to the parking area.

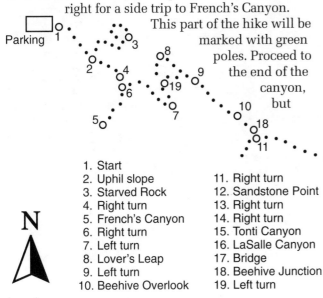

1. Start
2. Uphil slope
3. Starved Rock
4. Right turn
5. French's Canyon
6. Right turn
7. Left turn
8. Lover's Leap
9. Left turn
10. Beehive Overlook
11. Right turn
12. Sandstone Point
13. Right turn
14. Right turn
15. Tonti Canyon
16. LaSalle Canyon
17. Bridge
18. Beehive Junction
19. Left turn

St. Louis Canyon 👢👢👢👢

Distance Round-Trip: 3.1 miles

Estimated Hiking Time: 2 hours

During the hot summer, the coolness of the canyons beckons, especially St. Louis Canyon, with its ever-flowing waterfall. Chipmunks scamper and cavort among the canyon crevasses. In the dry streambed adjacent to the trail, a groundhog gathers leaves, preparing for colder days ahead.

Caution: The trail will cross a park entrance road, so watch for cars. The rocks near St. Louis Canyon are slippery when wet; watch your step.

Trail Directions: Begin at the large trail map near the eastern edge of the lower parking lot [**1**]. Hike north toward the river and turn left (west) at the riverbank (.2 mi.) [**2**]. This first segment of the trail skirts the river and is very flat. Across the river, what appears to be the opposite shore is actually Plum Island. The main channel is on the far side.

At the tip of Plum Island the trail bears left (.7 mi.) [**3**], and soon you are hiking amidst a loop road. At 1 mi. go right across a small wooden bridge [**4**] and immediately turn left. The path is asphalt with a floodplain forest to your left.

Climb a vertical staircase leading to a main park road (1.3 mi.) [**5**]. At the top of the stairs cross the park road and proceed down the other side on another staircase. At the bottom the path winds around a bluff. A parking area will be visible on the right. Continue straight ahead on the trail marked with a brown hiker silhouette.

A trail map appears at 1.4 mi. [**6**]. Take a right and go downhill into St. Louis Canyon. The well-traveled trail will be a series of ups and downs as it winds its way to the canyon. The trail is marked with a green post and a yellow dot. If it is spring, look along the trail for mayapple, Solomon's seal, wild geranium, Jack-in-the-pulpit, and the park's many fern species.

St. Louis Canyon and its waterfall come into view at 1.7 mi. [**7**]. Take time to explore the falls and the canyon walls. In winter the frozen falls are spectacular—they are off-limits to ice climbers, so the beauty is unspoiled. Retrace your steps back to [**6**]. At the trail map, go right and up a series of winding steps.

At the top, go to the right (2.1 mi.) [**8**] and hike on top of a bluff that overlooks the park road. The trail is fairly narrow and winds up and down, but mostly up. Within a short distance you will encounter more steps up that skirt a sandstone bluff. The wooden steps soon become sandstone steps, and the view also changes. The trail, marked with brown and white circles on trees, now follows a bluff overlooking the wide Illinois River Valley.

At 2.5 mi. look toward your left at a canyon that suddenly appears below. After 2.7 mi. a series of steps leads down to a bridge across Sac Canyon [**9**]. Once across the bridge, take a short detour to an overlook into the canyon. Continue to a series of steps and bridges overlooking Aurora Canyon, whose twists, turns, and curves mimic the trail.

The trail comes out behind the lodge (where refreshments are available). Next go left and continue the hike (2.85 mi.) [**10**], the trail now marked with a green pole. With a series of steps and bridges the trail winds downward. A junction appears at 3 mi. with a trail map. Go left for a short side spur into Aurora Canyon [**11**]: The trail makes a large S-curve to the canyon. Retrace your steps back to [**11**]. Go north (left), and the trail will soon cross the park road and return to the parking lot.

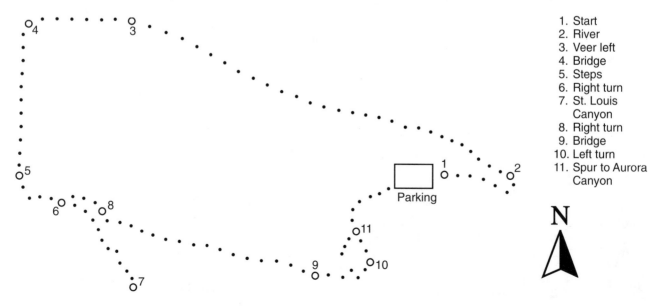

1. Start
2. River
3. Veer left
4. Bridge
5. Steps
6. Right turn
7. St. Louis Canyon
8. Right turn
9. Bridge
10. Left turn
11. Spur to Aurora Canyon

Parking

N

19. Matthiessen State Park

- Revel in a geological paradise of sandstone canyons gracefully carved by flowing water.
- Discover Devil's Paint Box, Giant's Bath Tub, and Cascade Falls.
- Enjoy the cool, moist canyons where mosses, ferns, and liverworts cover the walls, and where frogs, toads, and salamanders find refuge on the canyon floors.
- Relax in the park's serene beauty and solitude.
- Explore waterfalls that turn into icefalls each winter.

Area Information

Formed by water erosion, the canyons of Matthiessen State Park (cut from St. Peter sandstone) consist of two levels, the Upper and Lower Dells. Water-based activity is constant in the canyon; as groundwater seeps from the canyon walls, it evaporates and deposits the minerals it carried to add color to the canyon walls.

Huge deer populations enjoyed these mineral deposits, called *licks*, and led to the park's first name—Deer Park. The original owner of the park was Frederick Matthiessen. With a large work crew, he oversaw the construction of the park's first bridges, trails, and stairways; some of these are still in use today.

Matthiessen State Park is just as spectacular as its sister park, Starved Rock, but less crowded. Here you can relax and enjoy the spring and summer wildflowers along the trails. During twilight hours, be on the lookout for flying squirrels.

Directions: Matthiessen State Park, located in central LaSalle County on Route 178, can be easily reached from either I-39 or I-80.

Hours Open: The site is open year-round except on Christmas and New Year's Day.

Facilities: A concession stand, picnic shelter, picnic area, field archery range, toilets, and a radio-controlled model-airplane field are available. During winter weekends, cross-country skis may be rented.

Permits and Rules: No camping, rappelling, or rock or ice climbing are allowed. Do not remove any archeological material of Native American origin. All pets must be on a leash.

Further Information: Site Superintendent, Matthiessen State Park, Box 381, Utica, IL 61373; 815-667-4868.

Trail Information: Bluff trails are marked with a brown post, river trails with a red post, and connecting or interior canyon trails with a green post. These posts also carry a colored dot: White indicates travel toward the parking area and yellow designates travel away from the parking area.

Other Areas of Interest

Matthiessen State Park is located adjacent to **Starved Rock State Park** (see park #18) and along the historic **Illinois and Michigan Canal** corridor (see park #16).

© Michael Jeffords

Matthiessen State Park

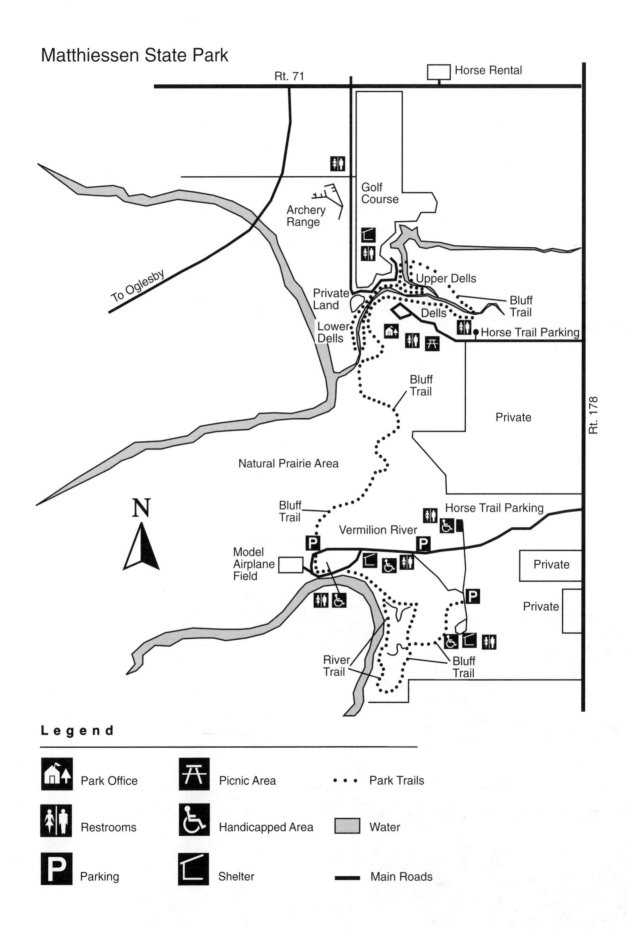

Rt. 71

Horse Rental

To Oglesby

Golf Course

Archery Range

Private Land

Lower Dells

Upper Dells

Dells

Bluff Trail

Horse Trail Parking

Bluff Trail

Private

Rt. 178

Natural Prairie Area

Bluff Trail

Vermilion River

Horse Trail Parking

Model Airplane Field

P

P

P

Private

Private

River Trail

Bluff Trail

N

Legend

Park Office	Picnic Area	• • • Park Trails		
Restrooms	Handicapped Area	Water		
Parking	Shelter	Main Roads		

Dells Trail 👢👢👢👢

Distance Round-Trip: 3 miles

Estimated Hiking Time: 2 hours

Even though the Dells Trail of Matthiessen State Park has icefalls in the winter, the water does not give up easily and continues to flow, eroding the ice. As a result, huge chunks of ice crack off and tumble into the canyon, leading the imagination to places far away where pieces of glaciers break off and tumble into the sea.

Caution: The trails crisscross slippery streambeds, expect to get your feet wet.

Trail Directions: Begin the trail at the reconstructed fort, northwest of the parking area. Descend a long wooden staircase to a bridge; a trail-map board is to your right [**1**]. Cross the bridge and proceed to the right. The trail gradually ascends and is marked with a yellow dot on a brown pole.

At .3 mi. come to a trail junction [**2**]; go to your right. The forest, which had been dominated by oaks, now is a mixed woods with pines. The trail follows a ridge between two deep canyons. At .5 mi. a series of steps lead down. At the bottom a sign points right to Cedar Point; go left [**3**], and soon find yourself hiking through a narrow canyon, looking upward at the sandstone bluffs.

The trail leads through a boulder-strewn streambed to a waterfall. Climb a set of steps to the left and walk into the streambed (.65 mi.) [**4**]. You are now atop Giant's Bathtub. Your feet are likely to get wet as you cross the streambed (despite the concrete stepping stones); skirt it on the right. While you're in the canyon, take a side trip to Lake Falls; in winter marvel at the spectacular icefall. On your return from the falls (.7 mi.) cross the stepping stones [**5**] and go up the staircase to your right. At the top of the steps is a trail board. Continue straight and climb another set of steps.

At the next landing go right and cross a large stone bridge over Lake Falls (.85 mi.) [**6**]. To the left is Lake Matthiessen. After crossing the bridge continue straight. The trail marker is brown, and the trail passes through an oak-dominated, mixed woods. In spring check the woods for wildflowers— hepatica and spring beauty.

At 1.15 mi. [**7**] round a point and go to the right; a ski trail goes off to your left. You are hiking on a bluff top overlooking the canyon. By 1.55 mi. you have completed the first half of your hike and are back at the original bridge [**1**]. Go down the steps and recross the bridge, going left after the crossing [**8**].

At 1.85 mi. [**9**] take a long series of steps to the left. Cross a cement bridge and go to the left down more steps at 2 mi. [**10**]. The bridge and steps are part of the original trails that Matthiessen constructed, and the steps lead to a side spur where you can explore the interior of the canyon.

Go right (straight) off the steps. The trail skirts the bluff and enters a stream; cross over it, using the stones. Continue walking to the end of the canyon, where the trail dead-ends in a huge bowl with another waterfall (2.15 mi.) [**11**]. Past water activity has carved out shelter and erosion caves, like catacombs, in the canyon walls.

Retrace your steps to the cement staircase and ascend. You are now back at the bridge and steps [**10**]. Go straight and climb a set of wooden stairs; at the top go left (the trail to the right continues and eventually becomes a horse trail). You will pass Strawberry Rock and a state nature preserve. At 2.7 mi. [**12**] go to your right as the trail straight ahead will lead back to the bridge where you started the hike. Soon you will come to more steps; go right and start the long climb back to the fort.

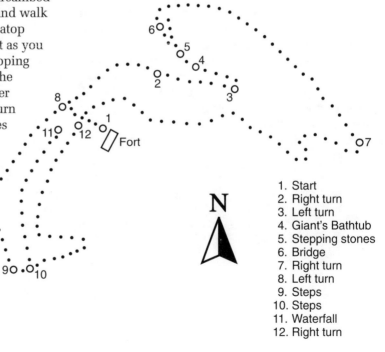

1. Start
2. Right turn
3. Left turn
4. Giant's Bathtub
5. Stepping stones
6. Bridge
7. Right turn
8. Left turn
9. Steps
10. Steps
11. Waterfall
12. Right turn

Vermilion River Trail 👢👢👢

Distance Round-Trip: 1.75 miles

Estimated Hiking Time: 1 hour

Discover the river terraces of Illinois's other Vermilion River. In summer the cool, rock-bottomed stream may soothe tired feet. In winter, partially frozen and with snow-covered boulders strewn along the edge, this stretch of river landscape is stark and beautiful.

Caution: The steps leading downward can be slippery when wet, even in the summer when they are coated with fine green moss.

Trail Directions: The entrance road for this trail is south of the Dell's Area. It is lined with little bluestem that turns a rust color each fall. Park in the far loop and begin at the trail board located on the west side of the parking area [1]. Initially, the trail marker will be green. After a few steps the trail forks; go left (the trail marker is now brown with a yellow dot). The trail begins a gradual uphill climb.

While passing through the mixed woods, watch out for (and avoid!) the large vines of poison ivy climbing the trees. At .2 mi. the trail forks; go left [2] and follow the brown marker with the yellow dot. The trail follows a ridge. On your right you will see a series of river terraces. The steps that soon appear lead down over these terraces. At .4 mi. [3] another set of steps leads downward. At the bottom, the trail marker has changed color and is now red. To your left is a nice view of the Vermilion River.

The quality of the woods improves as you head downward. The trail intersects with a connecting trail (marked in green) at .7 mi. [4]. Continue straight ahead on the river trail (marked in red). Finally, you cross the last terrace and are near the river. The only obstacle between you and the water is the river's

narrow floodplain. At .9 mi. [5] cross a wooden bridge; immediately afterward the trail forks. Take the left fork and follow the river—the trail marker is red. At 1 mi. the trail begins to head back [6]. Note the large, rock outcrop high on the bluff directly ahead.

The red- and green-marker trails have now joined. Go left, up the incline, and climb the river terraces again (1.2 mi.) [7]. After a steep, uphill climb, a picnic area will be on your left. Within a few steps you will cross a bridge, the trail appearing immediately on your right (1.35 mi.) [8]. Follow the trail with brown markers.

Once again you are walking on top of the ridge, with nice views of the valley below. At 1.5 mi. go to the left [9]; this will lead you back to [2], the beginning trail sign, and the parking lot.

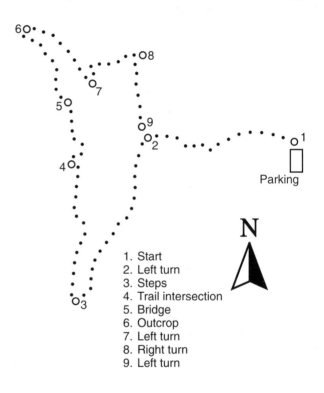

Parking

1. Start
2. Left turn
3. Steps
4. Trail intersection
5. Bridge
6. Outcrop
7. Left turn
8. Right turn
9. Left turn

20. Rock River Valley

- Look closely at limestone (dolomite) outcrops for the mysteries each conceals.
- Hike along trails that support the southernmost natural population of white pines in the United States—not the uniform plantations found in much of Illinois but massive, natural examples.
- Discover firsthand what happens to St. Peter when he ages.

Area Information

White Pines Forest State Park is known as the southern boundary of the old Chicago-Iowa Trail. Nowhere else in Illinois can one experience such a mixed hardwood-conifer forest. None of these trees grew in the open, for each white oak and white pine is straight and tall, specimens that obviously grew amid other trees. When European settlers first encountered this park, it extended more than 700 acres along Pine Creek; today it supports nearly 400 acres of trees and open lands.

As early as 1903 Ogle County residents were petitioning their politicians to save this southernmost and last Illinois remnant of white pines. Although they failed initially, in 1927 Congress finally appropriated funds to purchase and preserve the area. Any season is a good time to visit the pines, but spring and winter are particularly beautiful—spring for its displays of wildflowers, winter for the soft, silky blanket of snow that creates a stark contrast with the dark green needles of the pines.

Although **Castle Rock State Park** was named for a large butte of St. Peter sandstone located along the Rock River, the main reason for its becoming a park was to preserve remnant habitats of biological importance. In this 710-acre nature preserve, many plant associations of more northern climates exist in deep ravines. One ravine, in fact, supports 27 species of ferns! Another unique feature of the area is the rock itself. The St. Peter sandstone, which underlies much of the state, comes to the surface in only a few places. While you follow the trails, notice when they abruptly change from packed earth to fine, white sand. This sand, the result of erosion of the St. Peter sandstone, would be welcome on any Florida beach. Bring along a hand lens and look closely at any rocky outcrop; a microscopic inspection reveals perfectly round grains of sand cemented together into a soft, easily eroded rock. With its unique rock formations, deep ravines, and river overlooks, it's no mystery why Native Americans called the river that traverses the park "Sinissippi" or rocky waters. Today, we simply call it the Rock, one of the most scenic rivers and river valleys in Illinois.

Directions: White Pines Forest State Park is located east of Polo and 8 miles west of Oregon on Pines Road. The featured trailhead is off the parking area near the park headquarters.

Castle Rock State Park is 3 miles south of Oregon on Route 2. Its featured trailhead is off the Valley View picnic area.

Hours Open: Both sites are open year-round.

Facilities: White Pines Forest State Park offers picnic areas, camping, cross-country skiing, and restrooms. Its 1930s, CCC-constructed lodge (with cabins), the White Pines Inn, houses a gift shop and restaurant. For lodge reservation call 815-946-3817. **Castle Rock State Park** offers picnic areas, restrooms, fishing along the Rock River, and limited hunting.

Permits and Rules: No pets are allowed in the nature preserves. In other areas of the parks, pets must be kept on a leash at all times.

Further Information: White Pines Forest State Park, Park Office, 6712 West Pines Road, Mt. Morris, IL 61504; 815-946-3717. **Castle Rock State Park**, 1365 W. Castle Rock Road, Oregon, IL 61061; 815-732-7329.

Other Areas of Interest

Nachusa Grassland, a Nature Conservancy preserve south of Oregon on the east side of the Rock River (along Lowden Road), is a 1,200-acre, natural area that features a mosaic of forest and prairie. Listed as a major work in progress, the site is undergoing extensive restoration activities.

Park Trails

White Pines Forest State Park has seven developed trails, six of them less than a mile long. All provide excellent viewing of the tall pines. **Castle Rock State Park** has 6 miles of marked hiking trails divided into northern and southern groups.

Rock River Valley

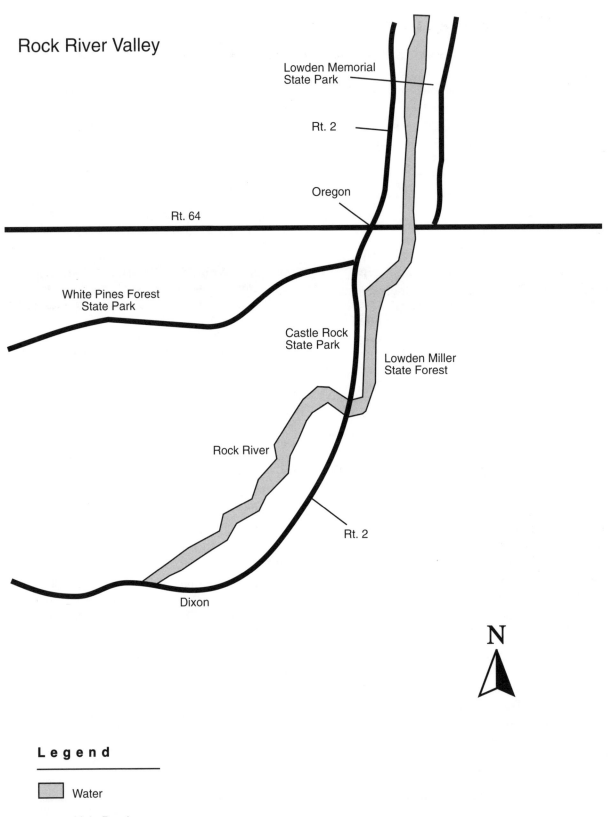

Lowden Memorial
State Park

Rt. 2

Oregon

Rt. 64

White Pines Forest
State Park

Castle Rock
State Park

Lowden Miller
State Forest

Rock River

Rt. 2

Dixon

N

L e g e n d

Water

Main Roads

North Trails of Castle Rock State Park 👢👢👢

Distance Round-Trip: 3.25 miles

Estimated Hiking Time: 2 hours

About midway along the trail a beautiful, pastoral valley manifests itself, complete with meandering stream. For a moment I return to an earlier time. If I were a settler traveling west to find my place in the sun, it just might be here.

Caution: Beware, this is deer-tick country!

Trail Directions: Begin your hike at the Wildlife Viewing Trail board, just northwest of the Valley View Picnic Area parking lot. The trail passes through an old field and soon forks as it enters the woods [1]. Go right (straight) and begin hiking through a grove of big-tooth aspen. Along here the forest is recovering.

At .25 mi. the trail passes through a very young forest and soon enters another aspen grove, this one made up of two species—big-tooth aspen (named for the large teeth along the edge of its leaves) and quaking aspen (tiny teeth along edge). At .3 mi. [2] a large "wolf tree" (a tree that grew apart from other trees) is on the left, an indication that these woods once had a parklike quality (called a savanna). The trail crosses a stream. Near .4 mi. bracken fern appears in the understory and you see an overlook of an open area [3] surrounded by forest. Notice a U-shaped valley in the distance, likely formed by glaciers.

You next head down through another aspen grove and enter a cool valley at .55 mi. Soon you will come to a sign for Nature Trail and Heather Valley Trail [4]. Go right on Heather Valley Trail and take the right fork soon afterward. Notice that you are suddenly hiking on pure, white sand. At .7

mi. climb a ridge and notice that St. Peter is at the surface along the climb. On top [5] a dry, oak forest appears with many oak seedlings in the understory. Around .9 mi. the understory has several different kinds of ferns. The trail soon enters a thick grove of aspen seedlings that are reminiscent of western, mountain habitats [6]. At 1.15 mi. the trail passes an open meadow lined with large aspens. At 1.2 mi. the trail descends into a large, grassy valley and intersects with the Timber Ridge Trail. Go right and stay on Heather Valley Trail; look for deer grazing in this idyllic valley. Soon you will cross a willow-lined stream on a wooden bridge [7]. A slow, uphill climb begins (1.35 mi.). A short downhill respite leads to a sandy stream crossing (more white sand) and then back uphill. At about 1.6 mi. a side trail leads to a scenic overlook of Heather Valley [8]; take it for a breathtaking view of the landscape. Return to the main trail and pass through ferns at 1.9 mi., including maidenhair and the northern interrupted fern. Castle Rock Nature Preserve is now on your right [9].

As you cross the stream by the bridge at 2.1 mi., see if you spot black-winged damselflies along its margins [10]. A large apple tree at 2.2 mi. suggests the former use of this land and that someone found this valley an appealing place to live. The trail bridges another stream at 2.3 mi., presenting a good view of St. Peter sandstone; it soon comes out on the same large meadow and passes the other end of Timber Ridge Trail. Go right, skirting another meadow on the right, and enter yet another aspen grove (2.4 mi.). At 2.5 mi. observe a stand of large aspens on the left that grade uphill into an oak forest. At 2.55 mi. return to a trail junction (near [4]) and retrace your steps to Wildlife Viewing Trail. Go right at 2.8 mi., checking the trail for the fibers from cottonwood trees.

At 2.9 mi. the trail parallels the park road. Go left and pass the sign for Castle Rock Nature Trail [11]. Continue on; as you head uphill, note the signs of a controlled burning to restore an oak opening. At 3.2 mi. [1] go right and retrace your steps to the parking area.

Picnic Areas

N

1. Start
2. Wolf tree
3. Overlook
4. Heather Valley Trail
5. Top of ridge
6. Aspen seedlings
7. Bridge
8. Overlook
9. Nature preserve
10. Stream
11. Sign for nature trail

Red Squirrel and Gray Squirrel Trails of White Pines Forest State Park 👢👢

Distance Round-Trip: 1.1 miles

Estimated Hiking Time: 1 hour

I looked into a cavity in the limestone wall only to meet the eyes of its patrons, a group of startled, naked nestlings. A view into another cavity yielded quite a different sight—an aggregation of leggy crane flies preparing for a peaceful night's sleep.

Caution: Many large trees have been toppled in recent years, and portions of the trail may be littered with their branches. This is deer-tick country, so take precautions (light clothes, socks over pant legs, and tick repellent).

Trail Directions: Park in the lot between the park headquarters and the lodge. The trailhead for Red Squirrel Trail, on the northeast corner, is designated by brown posts with a blue top. Enter the trail and soon turn right. Note a CCC-constructed stone wellhouse on the right [1]. Signs designating a nature preserve will be along the trail on the left. This area appears to be a typical Illinois forest, at least until you look up! The canopy, far overhead, is made up of large oaks and white pines—the latter not planted but native to the site. The forest around you is a curious mixture of several species of hardwoods and large pines. At .13 mi. a trail leads to the right. Ignore it, continue on for a short distance, and take the next trail (brown pole with blue top) to the right [2]. You will soon come to a sunny area with an open canopy. Severe windstorms have topped some of the large trees, creating this opening. Here is also a good place to observe that these trees are "forest-grown." The clues are their long, straight trunks and fan-shaped canopies reaching far overhead.

At .25 mi. the trail forks; go left. At the bottom of a ravine [3] note the limestone rocks in the path: Many have fossils in them, especially spiral gastropods. Continue straight ahead along a creek bed to a small bridge, turn left, and head up a series of stairs. A bench [4] next to a large black oak will appear at the top (.3 mi.). Note the clumps of lady fern along the trail here. Soon after, large expanses of wild ginger line the trail. At .54 mi. you will come to a signboard for Red Squirrel Trail. Go left and follow brown posts, now with green tops. You are on the Gray Squirrel Trail. At .6 mi. note a large open area of pines [5],

many of which have been topped by severe winds. A river overlook (Pine Creek) comes into view at .65 mi. Go right along the bluff overlooking the creek.

At .7 mi. the trail passes through three very large white pines [6] and heads downhill on steps. Both sides are again a carpet of wild ginger. Cross an intermittent stream on a boardwalk at .73 miles and note the huge pines at the top of the stairs. You are now hiking along a very narrow ridge. At .8 mi. a small shelter with a bench is provided. The trail now begins to head down to the creek bed [7]. On quiet mornings look for great blue herons feeding in the shallows. At the bottom of several steps notice a large limestone (dolomite) outcrop [8] with numerous holes, or dissolution cavities (formed by groundwater passing through the rock). Along the base of the outcrop look for karst features (sink holes) and ponder the mystery of where they might lead.

The trail now passes along the creek and at .91 mi. heads up set-in steps. Soon the trail forks; go right and follow the signs. You are now hiking along a ravine. Here the rich understory should provide good spring wildflowers [9]. At 1.05 mi. identify a very large ash on the left. The trail ends at the southwest corner of the parking area.

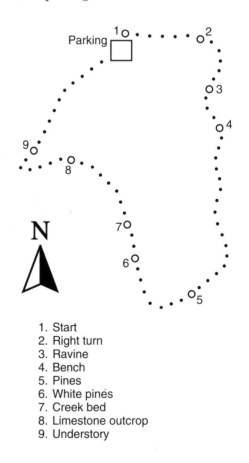

1. Start
2. Right turn
3. Ravine
4. Bench
5. Pines
6. White pines
7. Creek bed
8. Limestone outcrop
9. Understory

21. Apple River Canyon State Park

- Climb dolomite bluffs, carved not by glaciers but by Apple River.
- Bring a plant identification guide to help identify more than 60 species of trees and 600 species of plants found in this small park.
- Discover glacial relicts—plants surviving at the southernmost tip of their geographic range.
- Enjoy the picturesque Apple River and its surrounding canyon.
- Find Pepoon's primrose cliffs.

Area Information

In 1823 a geologist from Pennsylvania, W. H. Keating, traveled through this area and observed that the huge granite boulders characteristic of much of the glaciated Midwest were missing. He found ravines and valleys crisscrossing the land in every direction and slopes that dominated the landscape. Few lakes and ponds were present. From this evidence he deduced that Jo Daviess County and part of Carroll County escaped the glaciers of the Pleistocene. The area must have been an island in a sea of ice; it became known as the "Driftless Area" (drift is glacial debris).

Although the glaciers missed this area, their meltwaters blocked the southeast outlet of Apple River, causing it to cut a new channel. As the river cut through the masses of limestone, dolomite, and shale to form its new channel, it also formed the rugged and picturesque canyon. This iceless region provided a haven that allowed certain plants and animals to survive the glacial periods. Dozens of species managed to survive the Pleistocene in the Driftless Area while their neighbors were being driven to extinction. Both paper birch and bird's-eye primrose are examples of these relicts.

The river changes course at about the center of the park. The small town of Millville, so-named because it contained two sawmills, took advantage of the river's power here. By 1838 Millville had a population of 330 and a post office, and the stagecoach went through the town. The town had begun to rival Chicago, which only had a population of 550. Unfortunately, the railroad later bypassed the town, and in 1892 a flood drove the people away, forever.

Directions: Apple River Canyon State Park is only 3 miles from the Wisconsin border. From Route 78 take East Canyon Road west into the park.

Hours Open: The site is open year-round except on Christmas.

Facilities: The park has camping (no electrical hookups), fishing, a concession stand, and picnic facilities.

Permits and Rules: Pets must be kept on leashes at all times. Do not pick or remove any wildflowers.

Further Information: Site Superintendent, Apple River Canyon State Park, 8763 E. Canyon Road, Apple River, IL 61001; 815-745-3302.

Other Areas of Interest

Eighty-five percent of **Galena** is a National Register Historic District, encompassing Main Street and adjacent residential streets. Here you will find numerous examples of 19th-century architecture. Galena was home to Ulysses S. Grant, and his home is a state historic site open for tours. For more information call 800-747-9377.

Located near the town of Lena in Stephenson County, **Le-Aqua-Na State Park** offers modern campsites, boating, fishing, swimming, and a small restaurant. Le-Aqua-Na has 7 miles of hiking trails; the 13-mile Stephenson–Black Hawk Trail passes through the park. In spring, the park's marsh area hosts nesting geese and a large expanse of marsh marigold. For information about the park call 815-369-4282; for information about the trail call 800-369-2955.

Park Trail

Tower Rock River Trail 👢👢👢—1 mile—This linear trail, through primarily oak woods, offers a panoramic view of the park. It shares a trailhead with River View Trail.

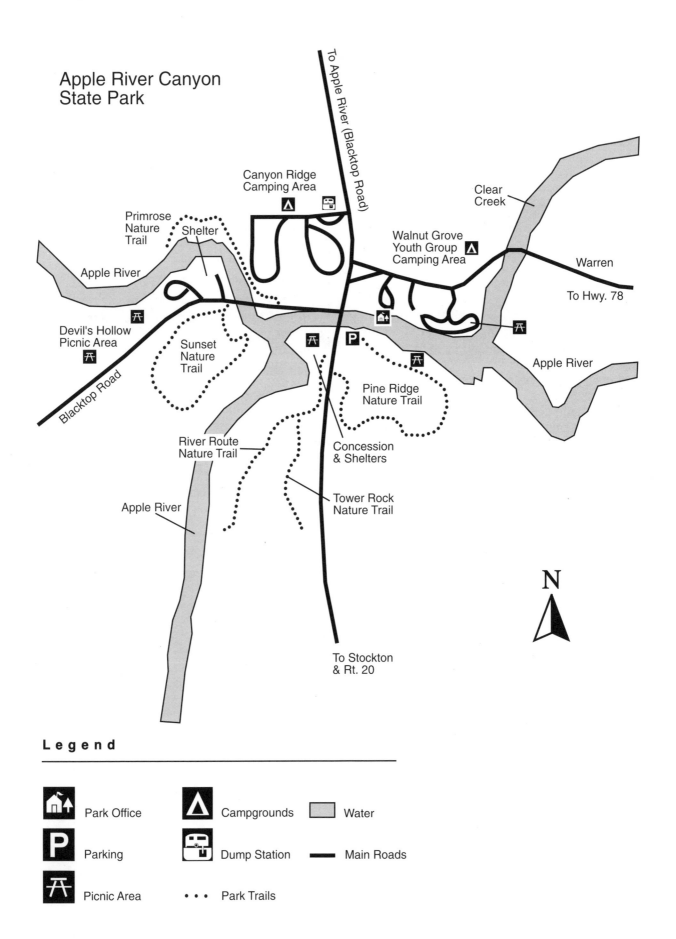

Apple River Canyon State Park

Canyon Ridge
Camping Area

Clear
Creek

Primrose
Nature
Trail

Shelter

Walnut Grove
Youth Group
Camping Area

Warren

To Hwy. 78

Apple River

Devil's Hollow
Picnic Area

Sunset
Nature
Trail

Apple River

River Route
Nature Trail

Pine Ridge
Nature Trail

Blacktop Road

Concession
& Shelters

Apple River

Tower Rock
Nature Trail

To Stockton
& Rt. 20

To Apple River (Blacktop Road)

N

Legend

Park Office

Campgrounds

Water

Parking

Dump Station

Main Roads

Picnic Area

• • •   Park Trails

Primrose and Sunset Trails

🥾🥾🥾

Distance Round-Trip: 1.5 miles

Estimated Hiking Time: 1 hour

While heading down to see the primrose cliffs, I was scared out of my wits by a wild turkey exploding into the air in front of me on the trail. I don't know who was more frightened, but we quickly headed in opposite directions!

Caution: The trail can be very muddy. Logs and roots pose tripping hazards, and a stream crossing has no bridge.

Trail Directions: Begin at the Primrose trail board and immediately climb steps [**1**]. During the upward trek check out the spring wildflowers on the bluff. At the top go left and pass a grove of pines and the campground on your right. Lots of shooting star occur along this trail through the pines. The campground is out of sight at .2 mi., and the trail passes an overlook of Apple River on your left [**2**]. Almost the entire river basin lies in the driftless (unglaciated) area, but the river cut a new channel and created the canyon when glacial meltwaters blocked its outlet.

At the overlook watch swallows swooping for insects; they are very helpful in keeping mosquitoes and biting flies at bay. From the overlook the trail curves right, going through a grove of big-tooth aspen. A bench is provided just before you head downhill. The trail crosses a bridge at .3 mi. [**3**] and then heads back uphill. You hike through an oak woods with lots of aspen. In spring look for hepatica, wild geranium, and wild ginger in this area. Within a few yards you reach another bridge crossing. When the formal trail ends at .4 mi., you enter a picnic area [**4**]. Go left, meeting with a springtime profusion of wildflowers. Cross a small creek, and skirt the bluff on the far side.

These bluffs are unglaciated dolomite, and where pockets of soil form, plants have been able to gain a foothold. Look for columbine, ferns, and bird's-eye primrose in the crevices. In 1909 Herman Pepoon, a botanist, described bird's-eye primrose as "tinting the bare rock a lavender purple with the multitudes of its blossoms." Bird's-eye primrose, a northern relic of cooler times, blooms in early May. Walk along these bluffs to discover these unique plants [**5**], but be careful not to fall in the river.

Then retrace your steps across the creek back to where the formal trail ended [**4**]. (At times you may be able to cross Apple River at a ford to access Sunset Trail.). Before heading up, look for chipmunks with full cheeks scurrying under large, moss-covered boulders. On the bluff look for Solomon's seal, Jack-in-the-pulpit, and prairie trillium. Retrace your steps back to the trail board (1 mi.) [**1**]. From here go right, walking along the edge of the park road. Cross the bridge, taking time to enjoy the canyon from this other angle; on your left is the trail board for Sunset Trail (1.1 mi.) [**6**].

Climb upward; after a few steps the trail goes left and up again. In the spring it is lined with wild ginger and multitudes of anemones. The latter are called wind flowers because their slender stalks always blow in the wind. The trail follows a narrow ridge that overlooks the river and the park. At 1.2 mi. [**7**] the low, sprawling evergreen on either side is Canada yew, a plant that occurs only in North America. On the left is a short spur to an overlook; after viewing, go right and continue upward. You will encounter a pair of benches on the left near 1.25 mi.

You have been hiking among mixed hardwoods and big-tooth aspen. At 1.35 mi. come to another bench where the trail heads downward [**8**]. You have completed the loop, and the path soon ends at the trail board (1.5 mi.) [**6**]. Recross the road and retrace your steps to the parking area.

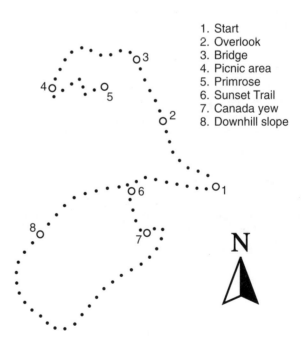

1. Start
2. Overlook
3. Bridge
4. Picnic area
5. Primrose
6. Sunset Trail
7. Canada yew
8. Downhill slope

Pine Ridge–River Route Nature Trails 👢👢👢👢👢

Distance Round-Trip: 1.6 miles

Estimated Hiking Time: 1 hour

Although the trail may be rated difficult, the climb up the dolomite bluff has plenty of benches for resting, carpets of native pine needles, nice views, and a scenic walk along the Apple River.

Caution: The trail can be very muddy and the rocks very slippery.

Trail Directions: Begin at the Pine Ridge trail board and head upward [**1**]. In spring, note a thick stand of white trout lilies on both sides of the trail. Appreciate each flower, for it requires a long period of growth before the plant blooms—as long as seven years from seed to blossom. For five years the plant sends up a single leaf, the sixth year finds two leaves, and in its seventh year, the plant finally blooms. Try to spot the plants that will bloom next year, but don't pick any flowers, destroying seven years of botanical labor!

Once you reach the top, find a bench. The trail soon comes to a T; go right, through an aspen grove. At .1 mi. observe a stand of native white pine on the right [**2**] and the trail leading through an aspen and pine forest. Another bench is set nearby on the right with a nice view of Apple River and the park. At a large cedar on your left you'll hike upward again.

The trail emerges on an open area with sumac, where the wind whistles through the pines (.3 mi.) [**3**]. When you see the trail fork; go left. As you hike, note the pine plantation on your left (the trees, planted in rows, are of uniform age). On your right is a grove of native pines mixed with aspen. These trees are mixed in age and randomly scattered. Head upward and to the left through lofty pines. You will soon exit the pines, pass through an open field, and hike through another pine plantation.

At .6 mi. [**4**] you'll find a bench on the right by a large, native white pine. Head downward, cross a bridge and the park road, and pick up the River Route Nature Trail on the opposite side (it has a trail board). During spring the moss-covered rocks by the trail's entrance are covered with Dutchman's-breeches. Head upward through an oak woods (with an occasional white pine). You will come to a T at .8 mi. [**5**]; go right onto the River Rock Trail. At the next intersection, near a wooden observation deck, go left to a narrow trail that might be more appropriate for a mountain goat.

As you descend, Apple River will be on the right at the 1-mi. point [**6**]. Just before you reach the river, look on either side of the trail for equisetum, commonly known as horsetails. They are also called scouring rushes (because their stems contain abrasive silica) or puzzle plants (as they can be pulled apart and reassembled at their gray bands). Once the river has been reached, a faint trail skirts the water. Look for large clumps of Jacob's ladder along here, across from beautiful bluffs on the other side.

Trail and river come together at 1.2 mi. and, unfortunately, the river wins and the trail disappears [**7**]. Retrace your steps back to [**6**] and head up the narrow goat path you just descended. At 1.5 mi. you are likely winded and back at the observation deck [**8**]; linger, looking at the river below. Go left off the deck and hike downhill. Be cautious, as this is a very steep, downhill grade. The trail ends at the trail board, just across the road from the parking area.

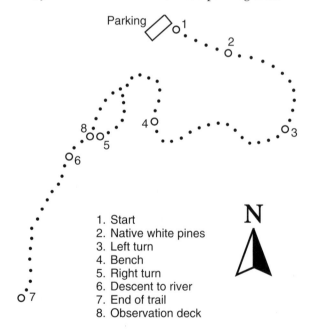

1. Start
2. Native white pines
3. Left turn
4. Bench
5. Right turn
6. Descent to river
7. End of trail
8. Observation deck

22. Mississippi Palisades State Park

- View unique rock features eroded from the dolomite, with names like Indian Head, the Sentinel, and Twin Sisters.
- Climb the bluffs to enjoy a great view of the Upper Mississippi River valley and its floodplain.
- Get caught in a river of bluebells flowing down the steep valley, capped with great white trilliums.
- Bring your binoculars and field guide to observe and identify some of the park's 150 bird species.

Area Information

Mississippi Palisades State Park, near Savanna, is in the southern part of the geologic region known as the "Driftless Area," a section untouched by glaciers during all the Ice Ages. With bitterly cold winters, the park also is slow to warm in the spring, allowing for late viewing of spring wildflower assemblages.

The unglaciated topography of the park contains steep, limestone bluffs and rock palisades that overlook the Mississippi River. The bluffs are cut by wooded ravines. The name *palisades* was given to the steep bluffs because of their resemblance to similar geological formations along the Hudson River.

Contained within the park is Sentinel Nature Preserve, dedicated as the 200th preserve in the state. This preserve is named for a geologic feature called the Sentinel, a freestanding dolomite column rising nearly 200 feet above the talus (rock) slopes. In addition to its geologic features, the preserve also contains expanses of wildflowers. Extensive stands of Virginia bluebell, great white trillium, and bellwort grow on the north-facing slopes and in ravines. Large concentrations of jeweled shooting star line the bluff tops and southern exposures. They clothe the rocky slopes in a blanket of pink visible from the highway below.

Whether a hillside of amethyst-colored shooting stars, expanses of trillium in deep and lush valleys, wild turkeys at dusk, or 400-million-year-old rock palisades, a unique mix of wonders awaits the visitor to Mississippi Palisades State Park.

Directions: Mississippi Palisades State Park is located north of Savanna on Illinois Route 84.

Hours Open: The site is open year-round except on Christmas and New Year's Day.

Facilities: A modern campground with showers operates from May through October. Boating, fishing, an auto tour, a campground store, picnicking, and rock climbing are also featured.

Permits and Rules: The Sentinel Trail lies within a dedicated Illinois Nature Preserve: No pets are allowed on the trail. On all other trails pets must be leashed. Rock climbers should check in with the site superintendent.

Further Information: Site Superintendent, Mississippi Palisades State Park 16327A, Route 84, Savanna, IL 61074; 815-273-2731.

Other Areas of Interest

The Upper Mississippi River National Wildlife and Fish Refuge extends more than 260 miles from Wabasha, Minnesota, to Rock Island, Illinois. Its many ramps offer boating and canoeing opportunities, and the hunting of ducks and geese is allowed during season. It is a great area for watching wildlife, boasting 292 species of bird and 57 species of mammals. For more information call 815-273-2732.

A large sign in the shape of Illinois, made from angle iron, greets visitors at the entrance to **Morrison-Rockwood State Park.** Located north of Morrison, the park offers recreational opportunities from camping, picnicking, fishing, and boating to a remote-control airstrip. A 3.5-mile hiking trail winds through the park, affording views of the lake, an old quarry, and spring wildflowers. For more information call 815-772-4708.

Park Trails

North Trail System 👢👢👢—5.9 miles—The system includes these trails: Rocktop, Goldenrod, Aspen, Bittersweet, and Deer. The trails' accesses are near the campground. Goldenrod offers pieces of prairie; the other trails are mainly forested.

South Trail System 👢👢👢👢—3.3 miles— The south trails include Sunset, Uptons, Indian Head, Heron, and Pine. Several of these trails traverse the bluff edges; use extreme caution. Sunset offers grand vistas, Pine should be hiked in the spring to enjoy the diverse wildflowers, Uptons leads you to a cave, and Indian Head features a view of an eroded bluff in the shape of its namesake.

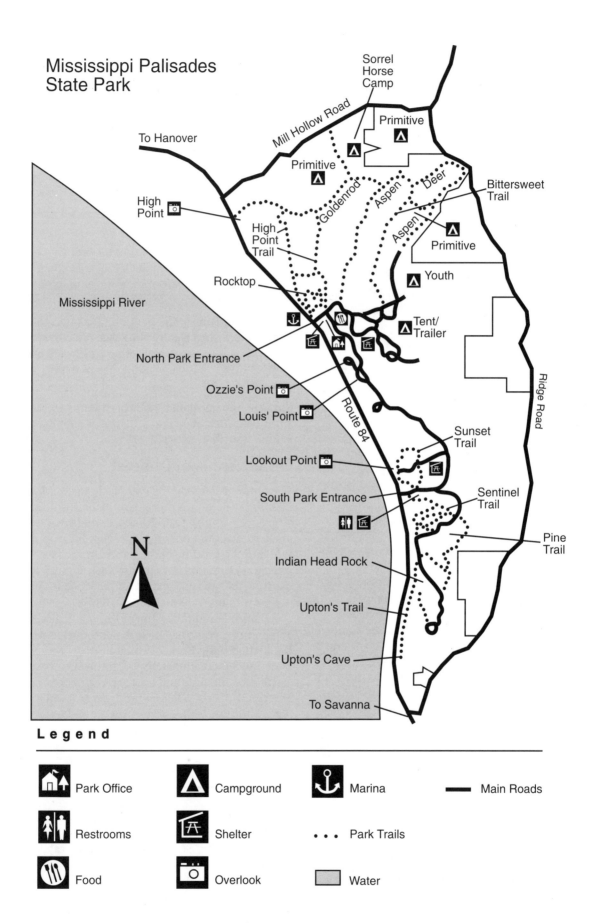

Mississippi Palisades State Park

To Hanover

Sorrel Horse Camp

Mill Hollow Road

Primitive

Primitive

High Point

Goldenrod

Aspen

Deer

Bittersweet Trail

High Point Trail

Aspen

Primitive

Rocktop

Youth

Mississippi River

Tent/ Trailer

North Park Entrance

Ozzie's Point

Louis' Point

Route 84

Sunset Trail

Lookout Point

Sentinel Trail

South Park Entrance

Pine Trail

N

Indian Head Rock

Upton's Trail

Ridge Road

Upton's Cave

To Savanna

Legend

🏠 Park Office

⛺ Campground

⚓ Marina

— Main Roads

🚻 Restrooms

⛺ Shelter

••• Park Trails

🍴 Food

📷 Overlook

Water

Sentinel Trail 👢👢👢👢👢

Distance Round-Trip: 1.3 miles

Estimated Hiking Time: 1 hour (a lifetime, if you like flowers!)

Instead of giving your mother flowers for Mother's Day, take her to see the colorful explosion of wildflowers on the Sentinel Trail. Peak bloom is usually on Mother's Day.

Caution: The trail climbs over rocks that can be very slippery with moss and mud. The bridge entering the trail is also very slick when wet. Tree roots are prominent in the trail, especially near bluff edges. Portions of the trail are also very steep.

Trail Directions: Begin at the Sentinel trail board and immediately cross the arched stone bridge [1]. Go left off the bridge and enter an Illinois Nature Preserve—one of the state's finest. Although not marked, the trail is a narrow, well-trod path. If you are hiking in late April or May, by .1 mi. you should have encountered a fantastic array of wildflowers [2], at least 10 to 15 species blooming simultaneously.

Identifying and enjoying the wildflowers should keep you occupied as you gradually climb. At .15 mi. stone steps lead upward, and the trail forks; go right [3]. On your right will be two large, moss-covered chunks of sandstone. Continue to climb along a narrow ledge. Look on your left for a bluff, covered with wildflowers in spring and draped with ferns by summer. On the right will be an overview of the carpet of wildflowers you just walked through.

At .25 mi. [4] go up stone steps and note the cave-like structure on your left. Skirt a huge boulder, and climb more steps. If you visit in mid-May, look to the left where jeweled shooting stars usually carpet the hillside a bright pink. At one time it was classified as a threatened and endangered (T & E) species in Illinois. The state's botanist used binoculars to search likely habitats from roads and was able to locate several new populations of this plant, which turns inaccessible hillsides pink each spring. His search led to removing the jeweled shooting star from the state's T & E list.

Before the overlook of the Mississippi River, you will encounter several human-made spur trails on both the left and right. Please stay on the main path! Pause at the overlook (.3 mi.) [5]. You should see a trail intersection; go straight and take advantage of spectacular views of the Mississippi River. At .4 mi. the trail forks; go left [6]. You have been hiking on a ridge, and the trail now leads down through a ravine

forest. In spring, this area is a river of Virginia bluebells cascading down the slopes. Innumerable great white trillium break up the blanket of pale blue.

The .5-mi. point brings you to another intersection; go left [7] and head upward (very steep) to a hillside covered in May with jeweled shooting star. On your way up look to the left for white birch—a native tree in this area. At the hilltop, on the left you'll see a hill prairie and on the right, a grand view of the Mississippi. At .6 mi. three trails converge at the overlook [8]. Enjoy the view, then face all three trails and take the center one that leads up through the hill prairie and through the woods. Look again for white birch.

At the trail intersection at .7 mi., go right [9]. Another intersection will appear at .85 mi.; go left [10] (straight takes you to the park road and Pine Hill Trail.). You are hiking once again on a narrow ridge with a bluff on your left and a ravine on your right. The 1-mi. point resembles the old-growth forests of the Pacific Northwest [11]. The hillside is clothed with ferns, and the fallen logs are covered with thick, green moss. While passing the rock outcrops, look for doll's eye (very colorful berries in the fall) and wild columbine.

You'll encounter a series of slick rock steps leading down at 1.1 mi. [12] until finally you are back at the first intersection [3]. You have completed the loop, so continue downward, retracing your steps through the wildflower-strewn valley, over the bridge, and back to the trail board.

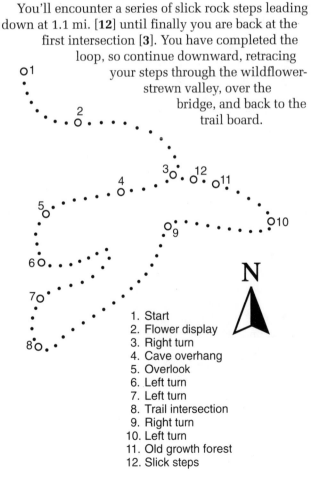

1. Start
2. Flower display
3. Right turn
4. Cave overhang
5. Overlook
6. Left turn
7. Left turn
8. Trail intersection
9. Right turn
10. Left turn
11. Old growth forest
12. Slick steps

High Point Trail 👢👢👢👢

Distance Round-Trip: 5 miles

Estimated Hiking Time: 2 hours

This trail is for the birds—from the bird's-eye view of the Upper Mississippi River National Wildlife Refuge to the hermit thrushes darting back and forth and from side to side along the trail. During my hike I also encountered a turkey vulture that took off, spooked from the hollows, to begin its daily ride on the thermals, plus a pair of fuzzy, but naive, great horned owlets.

Caution: The trail is very steep and slick, especially after a heavy rain.

Trail Directions: Begin at the trail board, hiking on a one-lane gravel road [**1**]. You will soon go through a gate; the trail on the left leads to Rocky Point, but continue on your original path. Note the white birch and "wolf" tree (a large oak with outspread branches) on the left. The trail begins to head upward at .2 mi. [**2**]. Look for loess (wind-blown silt) and notice its uniform texture and how it is free from rocks. If you touch it, you will find that while it holds together, it is also crumbly and good for digging and nest-building—just ask the local swallows.

A bench is on your left at .4 mi. [**3**]; the gravel and asphalt trail has become a level, grassy path. Within a few yards you will encounter Rocktop Trail on your left; continue to the right, noting the shrubby vegetation on either side of the trail. During spring, for the next .25 mi., you will encounter large clumps of bellwort, likely one of the best stands in the state. The yellow-petaled flowers that hang down reminded early naturalists of a bell; wort means plant. At .85 mi. Goldenrod Trail comes in on the right [**4**]; continue straight on High Point.

At the trail intersection at 1.1 mi. go right [**5**]. As you hike to the overlook, the trail narrows; you'll reach a sheltered overlook at 1.5 mi. [**6**]. Take time to scan the backwaters of the Upper Mississippi River Wildlife Refuge. From the shelter go right; soon you are back on the original trail, retracing your steps. You encounter another trail intersection at 1.9 mi. [**7**]; go right again.

A major intersection appears at 2.1 mi. [**8**]. Go right .25 mi. to the overlook at a dead-end. You will hike on rolling terrain until the trail comes to a wide area with a danger sign—steep cliff ahead (2.3 mi.) [**9**]. Walk on the narrow path, but use caution. In May the slopes are carpeted pink with jeweled shooting stars.

Through the fence of cedars look at the marsh across the way and listen to the geese. This part of the trail is very steep and slick. Just explore a little way and then retrace your steps back out and to the intersection [**8**].

Back at [**8**] (2.65 mi.), take the first right downhill. You will be walking through a valley, dwarfed by the large bluffs on either side. Rock outcrops and more shooting stars appear on the right. The trail forks at 3.1 mi. [**10**]; go left and up. On the left you will see a bluff with cedars and an overlook. On the right is a fence, shed, and the road. You will pass a house at 3.2 mi. [**11**]; go left. By 3.25 mi. you are away from development and hiking through wooded bluffs on either side again.

Look to your right at 3.3 mi. to see a nice valley [**12**]. The bluffs are lush with ferns, and farther down the trail on the left is a sandstone outcrop. At 3.65 mi. the grassy path curves left and goes up [**13**], and in .1 mi. you are once again back at [**8**]. Go right and uphill this time. Mile 3.9 brings you back to [**5**] and the main trail; go right. As you retrace your steps, look for stands of white birch in the forest and amazing expanses of bellwort. At 4.5 mi. you are back to where Rocktop Trail comes in; continue on High Point and back to the trail board.

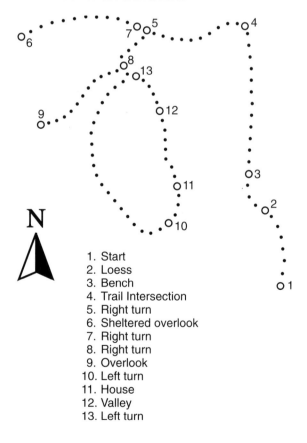

N

1. Start
2. Loess
3. Bench
4. Trail Intersection
5. Right turn
6. Sheltered overlook
7. Right turn
8. Right turn
9. Overlook
10. Left turn
11. House
12. Valley
13. Left turn

Central

The central part of Illinois is defined as the area north of Interstate 70 and south of an imaginary line from Indiana to the Mississippi River that follows the east-west portion of the Illinois River Valley.

Topography

The central portion of the state is dominated by a vast and flat or gently rolling plain—a product of recent glaciers. What was the Grand Prairie now has towns with such characteristic names as Flatville and Broadlands. Towns in this area of Illinois were also named after prairie groves (islands of trees amidst the prairie): Groveland, Table Grove, Forest City, and Middle Grove. Yet the whole area is not flat, as most outsiders believe; west of the Illinois River the terrain is older and more rolling and peppered with ravines.

Illinois' eastern-central border, along the Vermilion River, has a fairly rugged landscape. Its western border, along the Mississippi River, has a narrow, imposing band of river bluffs and limestone cliffs. In Calhoun and parts of Pike and Adams counties, the topography is rugged because (like the Driftless Area in the north) it escaped the crunching, leveling effects of the glaciers.

The soils are a unique feature of central Illinois. Most are comprised of windblown sediment called loess. In some areas near road cuts or where erosion has exposed the loess, you can see and feel this most unique material. Sand deposits along the Kankakee and the Illinois rivers are a result of the meltwaters of the last glacier. The water cascaded down old river channels carrying loads of sand and gravel, and when it reached and passed a narrow spot in the river, the water slowed and dumped its load of sand. Other sandy deposits occur in old glacial lake beds.

Major Rivers and Lakes

The Mississippi River borders the central area of Illinois on the west and the Vermilion and Embarras are among the rivers in the east. The Middle Fork of the Vermilion is the state's only federally designated wild and scenic river.

The major river in the center of the state, however, and the largest tributary of the Mississippi River above the mouth of the Missouri, is the Illinois River. It was the most frequently traveled interior waterway used by early explorers, traders, and settlers. Thomas Jefferson portrayed the Illinois River in 1787 as "a fine river, clear, gentle, and without rapids." Settlements along its banks are among the oldest in the state.

The Kankakee, Mackinaw, Spoon, and Sangamon rivers are all tributaries of the Illinois. Clinton Lake, an impoundment (reservoir), is part of the Sangamon River drainage. The other major river in this area is the Kaskaskia, which flows into the Mississippi. Two of the state's largest impoundments are found in its drainage: Lake Carlyle and Lake Shelbyville.

Common Plant Life

In the early 1800s Henry Blevins described the prairie as "an ocean of flowers of every possible hue, glittering and blazing in the sunlight." Although grasses—including big and little bluestem, Indian grass, and switch grass—form 90 percent of prairie vegetation, it is the wildflowers that provide a welcome relief to the infinite shades of green. More than 200 species of plants can be found on Illinois prairies. A gradual procession of blooms begins in springtime with diminutive violets and blue-eyed grass; the yellows and pinks of late summer and fall come from sunflowers, such as tall prairie dock and compass plant, and from the common blazing stars.

Two unique types of prairies occur here: hill and sand. *Hill prairies* occur on the windswept bluffs above the major rivers and their tributaries. Look for little bluestem, sideoats grama, obedient plant, purple prairie clover, and ladies' tresses (orchids). *Sand prairies*, growing on the sand deposits of the Illinois River, include prickly pear cactus, cleft phlox, puccoons, butterfly weed, and blackjack oaks—which together bind the sand.

Savannas are prairie-forest associations that are not quite woods and not quite prairies, but have the best of both—an understory (plants growing under the tree canopy) of prairie grasses and forbs along with scattered trees, usually oaks. The oaks, which resist fire, are usually huge and have outstretched branches, an indication that they grew with no competition from surrounding trees: Biologists call them "wolf trees." Look for prairie plants such as shooting star, lupine, rattlesnake master, and little bluestem in the understory.

Like islands in an ocean of prairie grasses, *prairie groves* usually occur along water courses, protected from the sweeping prairie fires. These woods are usually oak, hickory, or maple, and in the spring they have a wonderful display of blooming wildflowers: Virginia bluebells, trilliums, trout lilies, spring beauty, phlox, and blue-eyed Mary. By summer the wildflowers have been replaced with stinging nettle. *Floodplain forests* are forests that grow where a river or stream periodically floods. Floodplain forest species include silver maple, cottonwood, and sycamore. Masses of jewelweed, with spring-loaded seeds, bloom in the summer.

Along the Vermilion River are two unique plant communities—beech-maple forests growing in ravines (complete with tulip trees) and seeps. The first is a forest associated with the northeastern United States. *Seep springs*, in turn, are wet areas that support skunk cabbage, marsh marigold, and bog twayblade orchid, plants that here are at the southern limit of their range.

Common Birds and Mammals

Grassland birds to look for in central Illinois include horned lark, dickcissel, meadow lark, pheasant, quail, and American kestrel. Bald eagles roost during the winter along the Mississippi and Illinois rivers. Hummingbirds are abundant in floodplain sites that have jewelweed. In wet areas and along watercourses, great blue herons and wood ducks are common. The area along the Illinois River is also temporary home to thousands of waterfowl during spring and fall migrations. Waterfowl species to sight include canvasbacks, mallards, shovelers, scaup, coots, greenwinged teals, and Canada geese.

Mammals are plentiful, too, including the ever-present white-tailed deer, cottontails, raccoons, gray squirrels, coyotes, beaver, woodchucks, thirteen-lined ground squirrels, and muskrat. Look for a myriad of insects in the prairies and grasslands—monarch butterflies, grasshoppers, katydids, bees, and colorful beetles.

Climate

The mean average temperature in January is 27 °F and in July, 77 °F. Rainfall averages 36 inches annually, with the highest totals occurring in June (4.3 inches). The mean average snowfall is 17 to 25 inches annually; 10 to 15 days a year have 3 or more inches of snow on the ground. This central-Illinois area experiences the highest of the highs and the lowest of the lows in temperatures and is in the middle of the tornado belt.

Best Features

- Prairie pieces
- Spectacular spring wildflowers
- Loess bluffs
- Lincoln memorabilia and historic sites
- Sculptures on the University of Illinois campus and at Allerton Park
- Middle Fork of the Vermilion River
- Illinois' version of deserts

© Michael Jeffords

23. Kankakee River State Park

- Marvel at how large trees can grow on dry sand.
- Revel in the summertime companionship of nymphs and satyrs (butterflies, that is).
- See a waterfall in a square-bottomed canyon.
- Come to enjoy spring wildflowers and fall colors.

Area Information

The Potawatomi called the Kankakee "wonderful land": The river's clear water and surrounding wetlands provided a hunting, trapping, and fishing haven for several Indian nations. By 1770 the Potawatomi, Ottawa, and Chippewa tribes dominated the area and were known as "The Three Fires." One of the most extensive villages was near the mouth of Rock Creek. An unusual feature of the park can be found on the Chief Shawwawnasee Trail—his burial spot. The last of the Potawatomi left the area in 1833 except for the Chief. When he died the following year, he was laid to rest above ground, in a sitting position facing west with a pen of logs surrounding him. Shortly after his family left, his remains were buried. A huge granite boulder now marks the spot.

By the early 1920s the area had become popular for summer cottages, and with the addition of roads on both sides of the river people flocked to the site. Opened in 1948, the state park today envelopes the Kankakee River for 11 miles. People still come to enjoy the many water activities, seek the quiet beauty of Rock Creek and its sculpted, fern-lined shore, or perhaps catch a rare glimpse of the Kankakee mallow, a plant found nowhere else in the world but here.

Directions: The park is located 6 miles northwest of Kankakee along Routes 102 and 113.

Hours Open: The site is open year-round.

Facilities: The park has two campgrounds. Potawatomi has showers, a dump station, and gravel pads. Chippewa has electricity. Boating is allowed in the river from the park's two launching ramps. Canoes may be rented, and you can be bused to the put-in point and picked up when the trip is completed. The Kankakee River is a Class 1 canoeing stream. Fishing is extremely popular here, and hunting is allowed. The park also offers a small nature center, picnic area with grills, concessions, a bike path, and lots of wide-open spaces for playing.

Permits and Rules: Nonhunters are not allowed on the Area A trails from October 1 to November 30. Pets must be kept on leashes at all times.

Further Information: Site Superintendent, Kankakee River State Park, P.O. Box 37, Bourbonnais, IL 60914; 815-933-1383.

Other Areas of Interest

Located in the extreme northeast corner of the adjacent county, **Iroquois County State Wildlife Area** contains an extensive prairie marsh, dry sand ridges, and a large savanna that is a dedicated Illinois Nature Preserve. During migration, the marshes are visited by numerous species of birds, including sandhill cranes. The area offers several picnic areas, drinking water at area headquarters, pit toilets, an archery range, hunting, dog training, a hand-trap shooting range, snowmobiling, and a small concession stand that operates during hunting season. There are also two short hiking trails. For more information call 815-435-2218.

Park Trail

Bicycle Trail 👢—8 miles (one-way)—This is a paved, linear trail that begins at the Davis Creek Area and ends at the Chippewa Campground. The trail skirts the river in several places and crosses a suspension bridge.

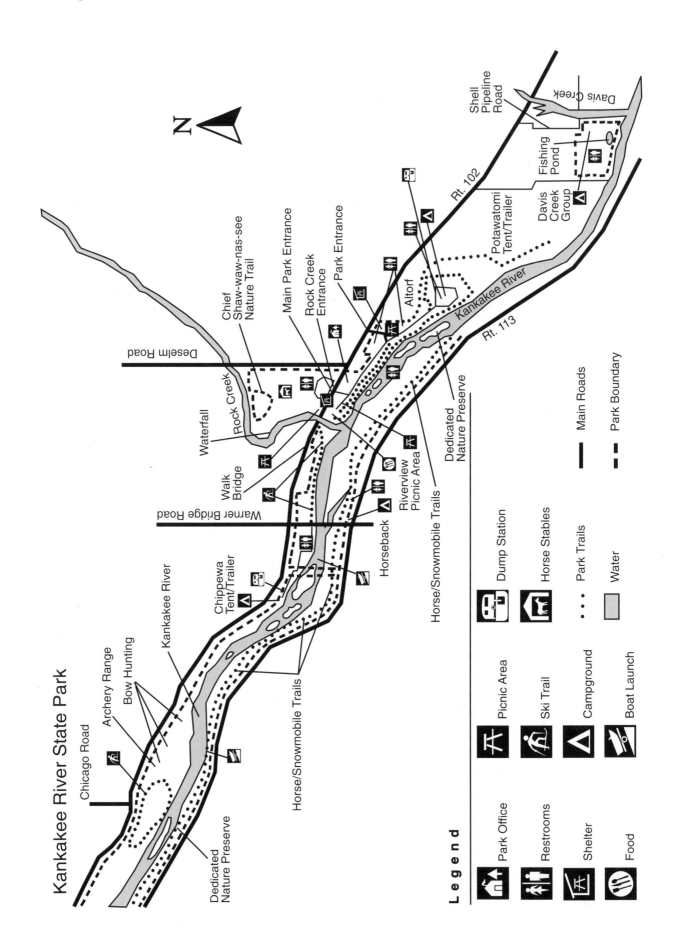

Kankakee River State Park

N

Chicago Road

Archery Range

Bow Hunting

Kankakee River

Dedicated Nature Preserve

Horse/Snowmobile Trails

Chippewa Tent/Trailer

Warner Bridge Road

Horseback

Riverview Picnic Area

Dedicated Nature Preserve

Horse/Snowmobile Trails

Walk Bridge

Waterfall

Rock Creek

Deselm Road

Chief Shaw-waw-nas-see Nature Trail

Main Park Entrance

Rock Creek Entrance

Park Entrance

Altorf

Rt. 102

Kankakee River

Rt. 113

Potawatomi Tent/Trailer

Davis Creek Group

Shell Pipeline Road

Fishing Pond

Davis Creek

Legend

Park Office

Restrooms

Shelter

Food

Picnic Area

Ski Trail

Campground

Boat Launch

Dump Station

Horse Stables

Park Trails

Water

Main Roads

Park Boundary

Rock Creek Trail 👢👢

Distance Round-Trip: 4 miles

Estimated Hiking Time: 2 hours

While hiking, I kept encountering the same family, wandering about in the maze of trails. I found my way out, but I'm not sure about them!

Caution: The trail can be very muddy and rutted, and horses share parts of it. Lots of tree roots lie near the surface. The trail crosses Route 102, which can be very busy. This area is a maze of trails, most of them unofficial.

Trail Directions: Park at the Riverview Picnic Area near the concessions building and begin the trail at the northwest corner of the parking lot near the suspension bridge [1]. This gravel path goes through a grove of oak trees and crosses Route 102 near the service road (the bridge over Route 102 will be on your left when you cross the road.). Walk along Rock Creek on the asphalt service road. Trees along the side obscure your view of this picturesque stream and canyon, unfortunately, but you can take advantage of many spurs to catch glimpses of it. Can you find a rock pillar protruding from the bank at .1 mi.? At .6 mi. you hear the waterfall before it comes into sight [2]. Take a short spur on your left to get a good view of the falls. Note how the streambed is encased in bedrock and squared off.

From the falls the path forks; go right into the woods and away from the creek. You are now on a narrow path through a shrubby, old field. Look for large dragonflies sunning along the path and green tiger beetles ahead of you on the trail. At 1.05 mi. the trail forks; go left [3]. Within a few feet another trail comes in; continue straight. The path forks again at 1.15 mi.; again go left and walk through a silver maple woods [4]. Ignore a path to the left and another to the right. At 1.4 mi. you will encounter an open, horse-camping area on the right [5]. After this camp you will find several unofficial trails leading off the one you are on. Continue to hike straight ahead.

After traversing a large bend in the trail, you will encounter a horse and hiker sign at 1.65 mi. [6]; go right, into the woods. At a post labeled #18 you will be on part of the self-guided Chief Shawwawnasee Trail. Look for large trees and spring wildflowers in this area. At 1.8 mi. the trail forks near an outdoor toilet; go to your left [7]. Within .1 mi. the trail forks again; go left, cross a bridge, and head up. The trail will curve to the right and soon come to a T; go right. At 1.95 mi. the trail dead-ends above Rock Creek, so

go left, skirting the creek on the right [8]. A large, granite boulder appears in the trail at 2.05 mi.—Chief Shawwawnasee's burial site. He was the last Potawatomi chief to remain in this area [9].

The trail forks at 2.2 mi.; go left [10] but don't forget to look down at the crotch of a large tree for Jacob's ladder. Within .05 mi. you will come to an intersection; go left. The path then goes left again and leads across a bridge. At a T, go left. The trail makes another T, so again go left (2.5 mi.) [11]. At yet another T, go left and pass a pine plantation on the right. At 2.65 mi. take a short spur to a nice pond on the left [12]. It is obvious from the tracks indenting the shore that many other creatures have taken this spur! Back from the pond stay on the wide path, ignoring trails coming from both directions.

At 2.95 mi. you will pass [6], where you joined Chief Shawwawnasee Trail; continue straight and begin retracing your steps. At 3.15 mi. the trail forks, and you are back at [5]. Soon you will re-enter the silver maple woods. You'll see several trails, but take the first one on your right, still retracing your steps. At 3.5 mi. the trail forks; go left [13], following a horse trail. A pine plantation will be on your right; continue straight, ignoring the many offshoot trails crossing your path. At 3.75 mi. go right on a wide-mown path [14] and ignore a path on the left. Within a few yards you are back on the asphalt; go left, and soon you recross Route 102. Hopefully, you have safely navigated the maze of trails, but just to be safe, bring along a compass!

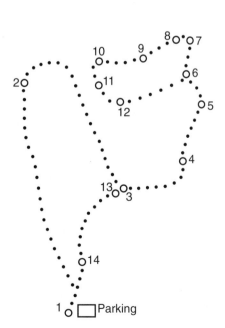

1. Start
2. Waterfall
3. Left turn
4. Silver maple woods
5. Horse camp
6. Right turn
7. Left turn
8. Creek
9. Chief's burial site
10. Left turn
11. Left turn
12. Pond
13. Left turn
14. Right turn

Area A Trail—A Sand Forest

Distance Round-Trip: 3 miles

Estimated Hiking Time: 1.33 hours

Keep your mouth shut while hiking this trail during the summer or you could end up like the lady who swallowed a fly—only you would have swallowed a spider.

Caution: This trail is not always well maintained. I would advise wearing long pants as protection against the grass, which can be quite high. Branches and limbs also lie or droop across the trail. The trail is closed to nonhunters from October 1 to November 30.

Trail Directions: Area A trails are located 5.5 miles west of the Park Office on Route 102. The parking area and trailhead are on the south side of Route 102, near the junction of Chicago Road and Route 102. Begin at the large trail board and head up into the woods [1]. Within a few feet come to a trail intersection; go right on the poorly maintained but well-marked (with a skier) sandy trail through the woods. At .25 mi. go to the right (after admiring the sinuous stand of sassafras in front of you) [2]. Within a few yards, go left (do not follow the skier sign), passing through the sassafras. Open any folded sassafras leaves and look for spicebush butterfly larvae. You'll know them when you see them, as the caterpillar resembles a rough, green snake!

The sassafras leaves lining the trail are like hands in mittens reaching out to touch you. Look in the understory for bracken fern and Virginia creeper. At .55 mi. the trail goes right and then immediately left [3]. Watch for unusual grasshoppers in the sun-dappled understory. You will soon pass an open area full of sumac on the left. Go left at .75 mi. [4], and enter an open, savanna-like area with lots of spiderwort. Once in the woods, be on the lookout for open, grown oaks (wolf trees). You will pass a grove of quaking aspens on the left. You are, and have been, hiking through a dry, oak forest growing on pure sand. Search for puccoon, which bloom in late May. In August this area is ablaze, hopefully not with fire but with the pink blossoms of rough Liatris or blazing star.

At 1.75 mi. [5] you have completed the blue loop; retrace your steps and head right on the orange trail (1.8 mi.) [6]. You will briefly hike through an open area with sumacs on the right and oak trees on the left. The trail goes down into a forest of slender sassafras and big white oaks. The trail makes a T at 1.9 mi. [7]; go right. At 2.1 mi. you will enter a grove of white oaks. Go left at 2.25 mi. [8], from where the trail first traverses an open, sandy area, and then head back into the woods. Continue to follow the path straight ahead, ignoring trails to the right and left.

At 2.4 mi. you will enter an open area, alive with color in August when the Liatris and flowering spurge bloom. The trail soon reenters the oak-sassafras woods. At 2.75 mi. it comes to a T; go right [9] and undulate with it along a ridge. At 2.8 mi. go left at the trail intersection; you are soon back at the large trail board.

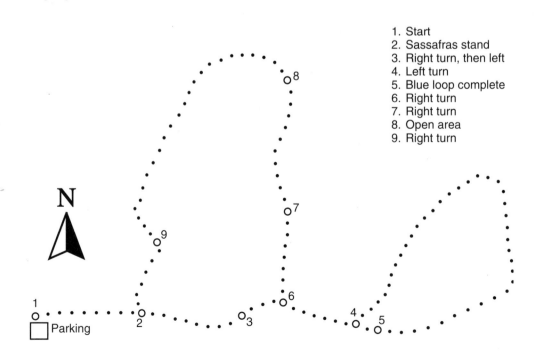

1. Start
2. Sassafras stand
3. Right turn, then left
4. Left turn
5. Blue loop complete
6. Right turn
7. Right turn
8. Open area
9. Right turn

24. Forest Glen Preserve

- Journey to where north meets south and east meets west, at least botanically.
- Climb a 72-foot tower for a panoramic view of the Vermilion River valley.
- Discover seeps—but stay on the trail, lest the water in the supersaturated soil seep into and fill up your shoes.
- Hike along wooded ravines, the Vermilion River, a tallgrass prairie, grassy meadows, and quiet ponds.

Area Information

Forest Glen Preserve, dedicated in 1968, is located in the Vermilion River Basin, with the river forming its eastern boundary. Some of its unusual features are calcareous seep springs with their own unique vegetation; tulip trees growing in the beech-maple forests of the ravines and adjacent uplands; and occasional hill prairies on west-facing bluff tops. These diverse features result from the Vermilion River lying in a tension zone between the beech-maple forests of the east and the prairie peninsula and oak-hickory vegetation to the west.

The area's seeps are a type of wetland (often at the base of a hill) in which groundwater flows down through a porous material until it reaches an impermeable layer, such as clay, that channels it back to the surface. The seeps of Forest Glen support skunk cabbage—the state's earliest flowering plant and one that makes its own heat to protect its precious bud and warm the winter ground around it. Marsh marigold, sweet flag, and bog twayblade orchids are also found here. Two of the seeps at Forest Glen are Illinois Nature Preserves: Forest Glen Seep and Howard's Hollow Seep.

Beech-maple woods are more typical of forests in the eastern United States and reach only a few miles into Illinois. American beech and tulip trees are not found in the central and western parts of Illinois. Take advantage of the Beech Grove and Big Tree Trails and the Russell Duffin Nature Preserve to see these stately giants, especially the beeches with their smooth, gray bark. These two plant communities and many others make Forest Glen a natural jewel to be discovered and rediscovered on a regular basis.

Directions: Forest Glen is located in southern Vermilion County and is 7 miles northeast of Georgetown. From the junction of Highway 1 and blacktop road 1200N in Westville, turn east and follow the blacktop road east and south 5 miles; then turn and go east 1.8 miles to the entrance of the preserve.

Hours Open: The site is open year-round. The observation tower closes at dark.

Facilities: Shelter Houses are available for picnicking, plus each picnic site is furnished with a charcoal grill. Tent, RV, and group camping sites are available, and some of the sites have electricity. There is also a central water supply, restrooms, and a dump station. Fishing in two stocked ponds is allowed. In addition, the park has an arboretum, a tree and shiitake mushroom research area, a pioneer homestead, and an education campus. Below Hawk Hill Trail is an access point for canoeing.

Permits and Rules: No bicycles, horses, snowmobiles, or motorcycles are allowed on the trails. No collecting of plant, animal, or mineral specimens is allowed (although you may collect leaves, nuts, fruits, and mushrooms). All pets must be leashed. Park only in the lots. No swimming is allowed in the park.

Further Information: Forest Glen County Preserve, 20301 E. 900 North Road, Westville, IL 61883; 217-662-2142 or 800-383-4386.

Park Trails

Hawk Hill Trail 👢👢👢—<1 mile—The trail begins at the observation tower and ends at the Vermilion River. It follows a ridge edged by deep ravines on each side and heads down a steep hill to the river valley below.

Hickory Ridge Trail 👢👢—1.5 miles—This trail is only accessible from other trails— Hawk Hill or Tall Tree Trail—and passes through open fields and woods with two stream crossings.

Spring Crest Trail 👢—.33 mile—Exceptional spring wildflowers highlight this trail as you walk through woods and skirt the edge of several ravines.

Crab Tree Trail 👢👢—1.5 miles—The trail passes through open woods, successional fields, beech woods, and deep ravines. During wet weather parts of the trail may require boots. This is an excellent trail for wildlife observation.

River Ridge Backpack Trail 👢👢👢👢—11.5 miles—You must preregister at the park office before hiking. The trail takes in a variety of habitats (including a restored tallgrass prairie, wooded ravines, beech forests, several ponds, and seeps) and terrain (steep climbs and descents and many stream crossings).

Forest Glen Preserve

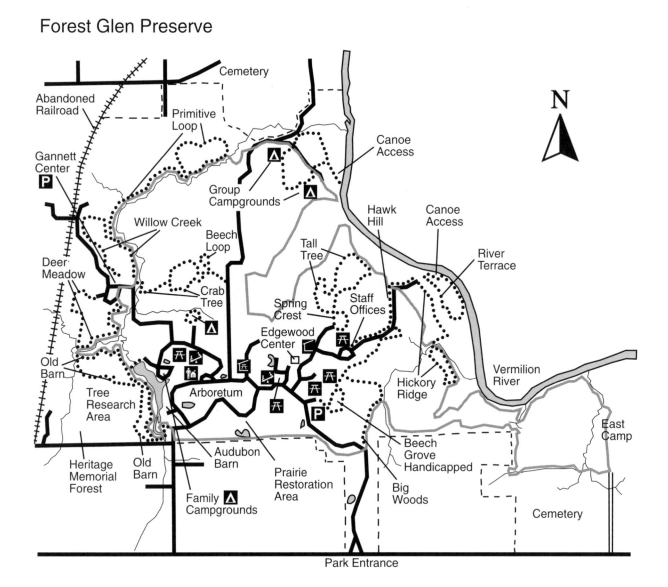

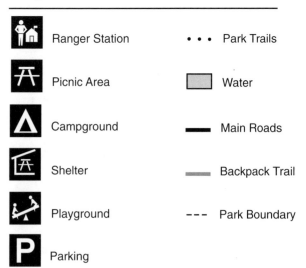

Legend

Ranger Station		• • • Park Trails	
Picnic Area		Water	
Campground		—— Main Roads	
Shelter		—— Backpack Trail	
Playground		- - - Park Boundary	
Parking			

Willow Creek–Deer Meadow–Old Barn Trails 👢👢👢

Distance Round-Trip: 4 miles

Estimated Hiking Time: 2.25 hours

While walking I saw deer, rabbits, fox, squirrels, and chipmunks and I stepped on mole tunnels. But the best by far was seeing the skunks, scurrying toward the stream—skunk cabbages, that is.

Caution: The trail can be very muddy. It is quite narrow in a couple of places, so watch your step.

Trail Directions: Park at Sycamore Hollow Campus at Gannet Center parking area and head east (downhill) on the road. Find a large, open area on your left. Willow Creek Trail starts on the northeast corner [1]. Begin at the trail sign and pick up a trail guide to further enhance your hiking experience. At .1 mi. ignore a trail on the left and hike along a ridge above the stream. Head into a woods filled with large sugar maples. On the left you will begin to see the large, caladium-like leaves of skunk cabbage.

At .25 mi. take a short spur to the right to view a coal deposit and get a close look at Willow Creek [2]. Back on the main trail, look left and you will see the nature preserve's sign for Howard's Hollow Seep, a one-acre wetland within the forested hills. At .35 mi. the trail intersects with the primitive loop [3]. Continue to the left on Willow Creek. At .4 mi. you will see a large white oak on your right; on the left a few steps further on is the opening to old "Dog Mine," a one-person coal mine. At .55 mi. the trail curves left and passes through a grassy area and back through the woods.

At .75 mi. take time to admire a large sugar maple [4]. The trail now heads up and back through the woods. At .85 mi. come to a trail intersection; go left and head toward the campus area [5]. As you round a bend you are struck by a sinuous line of sassafras. The trail comes out behind the Gannet Center [6] at 1 mi. Go right, skirt the woods, cross the park road, and enter Deer Meadow Trail on the right at 1.05 mi. [7].

At 1.25 mi. cross the road [8]; the trail is off to the right. Within a few yards, go left and pass between the house and barn of the original settlers of the area, James and Anna Ogden. From the homestead the trail goes left. The trail forms a Y at 1.6 mi. [9]. Go right, coming on Old Barn Trail (there is a guide for this trail). After walking under the branches of a large oak, you will see a stream on the right lined with scouring rush—nature's pop beads.

At 1.75 mi. you will come to a trail intersection; go right and cross the creek [10]. Black-winged damselflies skirt the edge, and the water is so clear you can see small minnows along the sandy bottom. Once uphill, go right and take the short spur on your right to discover a seep (not a bog, as the sign says), where skunk cabbage literally run down the slope. From the seep continue through oak woods that have many maple seedlings (maple takeover). Since oak woods need fire to help maintain their composition, maples will dominate the oaks if fire is suppressed. The trail comes out into a large, open area at 2.1 mi. [11], the tree research area; go left. The trail curves right at 2.45 mi.

A wetland-pond appears on the right at 2.6 mi. [12]. Sit on the nearby bench to observe any animal interactions. Farther down the trail, catch a glimpse of the dam of an efficient wetland engineer, the beaver. Soon you will cross a bridge. The woods conceals the lake on your right; on your left is an open meadow. At 3 mi. the trail curves away from the lake, and soon a deep ravine appears on the right.

At 3.15 mi. the trail forms a T; go left [13] through a woods littered with maple seedlings. You will soon head down into the ravine (a railing is provided), cross a bridge, and head back up the other side. At 3.4 mi. you will have completed the loop and come back at [10]; go right and recross the plank bridge. After the bridge go right again. The trail comes out at the creek, then heading left on a narrow path that is precariously close to the edge. At 3.7 mi. the trail curves left and heads up and away from the stream [14]. An overlook will appear on the left at 3.9 mi. [15]. Admire the view, then go right and down, but do not cross the creek. The trail now forks, but continue heading up (to the right), following a red arrow. The trail comes out near the bird's-of-prey exhibit at the education center, near where you parked.

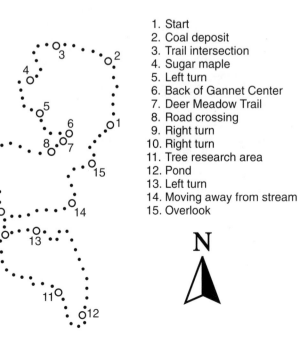

1. Start
2. Coal deposit
3. Trail intersection
4. Sugar maple
5. Left turn
6. Back of Gannet Center
7. Deer Meadow Trail
8. Road crossing
9. Right turn
10. Right turn
11. Tree research area
12. Pond
13. Left turn
14. Moving away from stream
15. Overlook

N

Big Woods Trail

Distance Round-Trip: 2.5 miles

Estimated Hiking Time: 1.33 hours

Instead of a Stairmaster, try this trail that goes up and down the rolling terrain, up the many steps of the observation tower, and then back along the rolling trail. When you hit that final downhill climb, you'll feel the burn!

Caution: Roots are exposed on the trail. Watch your step as you climb the observation tower: Some of the boards are loose.

Trail Directions: Park at the Beech Grove parking area and begin the trail at the board [**1**] on an asphalt path. Use the trail guide to enhance your enjoyment of the hike. At .05 mi. you will begin to see the smooth, gray bark of large beeches and a trail fork; go right [**2**]. Look for tiny green frogs (tree frogs) the size of a nickel on the foliage along here, find daddy longlegs under the leaves, and don't forget to look down at your feet: You just might see a bright brown and yellow millipede saunter by. An overlook for the ravine is set at .1 mi. [**3**]. At .2 mi. you'll find a large tulip tree to admire just before the trail intersection for Big Woods Trail, where you go right [**4**].

On the right is a black oak and a white oak, the two trees literally growing together. Note the different color barks. On your right as you walk on a narrow ridge are ravines cloaked with Christmas fern, maidenhair fern, and wild ginger. At .4 mi. come to another trail intersection [**5**]; go left and up, examining the bluff on your left for hepatica (which blooms in March). By .5 mi. you are in an open woods where most of the trees have double or triple trunks. A pair of benches appears at .6 mi., and if you use them and are quiet, you should be rewarded with a visit from the resident chipmunks. The trail now heads down into the ravine.

From the bridge crossing at .7 mi. the trail undulates [**6**] and is lined with numerous beech trees. At a large black oak the trail goes right and then heads down (.85 mi.) [**7**]. At .95 mi. it emerges in an open area, the observation tower on your right [**8**]. If it is open, climb up, catch your breath, and enjoy the view. If

you're lucky, you may be eye-to-eye with a turkey vulture! Head back down and retrace your steps to [**8**]. Return on the Big Tree Trail and catch up on things you missed the first time. Watch your step along here, at least until you get back your land legs after your trek up the tower.

Retrace your steps to [**5**] (1.7 mi.) and go left. Take time to read the sign about Indian Trails. You will immediately come to a signpost (# 7) that points out the large beech tree on the left, which is at least 100 years old. At 1.75 mi. go down the steps, cross the creek on a log bridge, and head up the steps and to the right [**9**]. As you walk on a narrow ridge between two ravines, look for the long, oval leaves of pawpaw, a shrub in the understory. The trail now heads up more steps. Look at the bluffs on both sides, covered with hepatica and wild ginger.

At the top, you are walking in an open woods with a fairly clean understory. Again note that many of the trees have double trunks. Look for a row of tall, straight tulip trees and take a final glance at the smooth, gray bark of the beech trees. At 2.05 mi. pass the trailhead for Big Tree Trail [**10**] and go right, walking along the road. It has nice, wide shoulders. By 2.35 miles the woods have disappeared and you are walking through an old field with planted trees next to the road. At 2.5 mi. go right and you will be back at the Beech Grove parking area.

1. Start
2. Right turn
3. Overlook
4. Right turn
5. Left turn
6. Beeches
7. Downhill slope
8. Observation tower
9. Creek crossing
10. Road

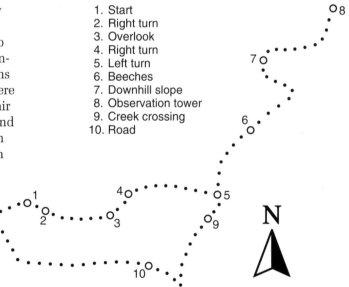

25. Kickapoo State Park

- Visit the first park in the nation to be built on strip-mined land, which now is healing from the damages.

- Pause at the old iron span of the Johnson Hill Bridge, which crosses the Middle Fork of the Vermilion River—the state's only National Wild and Scenic River.

- Wind through the woods, along ridge tops, and through flatlands on trails that will definitely keep the feet busy.

- Brush up on aquatic natural history and look for whirligig beetles, blue-breast darters, kingfishers, and bald cypresses in more than 20 deepwater ponds and along the river.

Area Information

Kickapoo State Park is located at the northeast boundary of a great Illinois coalfield. Between 1850 and 1940 most of the park was strip-mined for coal, leaving a landscape scarred by spoil piles and mine pits. During the past 50 years, however, the landscape has been reclaimed by nature. The strip lands are covered with bottomland forests of sycamore, soft maple, bur oak, and walnut. The understory contains a profusion of spring wildflowers from hepatica to squirrel-corn. During spring migration, the park is excellent for warbler watching.

Kickapoo State Park offers a variety of recreational activities, ranging from the usual fishing, canoeing, and hiking to the more novel, such as scuba diving.

Directions: Kickapoo State Park is 6 miles west of Danville and can be reached via exit 206 or exit 210 off I-74. Follow the brown signs along the road to the park.

Hours Open: The site is open daily from 8 A.M. to 10 P.M.

Facilities: The park offers camping, fishing (including rainbow trout), boating, canoeing, scuba diving, picnicking, hunting, cross-country skiing, sledding, ice skating, and mountain biking. During the summer a concession stand operates on the weekends. Canoes and rowboats may be rented daily except for Wednesdays.

Permits and Rules: Swimming is one of the few water activities not allowed in the park. Pets must be kept on leashes.

Further Information: Site Superintendent, Kickapoo State Park, 10906 Kickapoo Park Road, P. O. Box 374, Oakwood, IL 61858; 217-442-4915.

Other Areas of Interest

Located 6 miles north of the Oakwood exit off I-74, **Middle Fork State Fish and Wildlife Area** offers fishing, hunting, picnicking, canoe access to the Middle Fork River, camping, a trap range, and an archery trail. The area includes 35 miles of equestrian, cross-country skiing, and snowmobiling trails. Among bird watchers this area is known for its hawks, owls (long-eared, short-eared, and northern saw-whet are winter residents), breeding warblers, and sparrows. In the fall witness one of the largest gatherings of ruby-throated hummingbirds in the state. For more information call 217-442-4915.

Located 5 miles north of Penfield in northeast Champaign County, **Middle Fork River Forest Preserve** is a prime nesting spot for migratory waterfowl. The Middle Fork River winds through the area, which also includes 6 miles of hiking trails and a fitness trail. For more information call 217-586-3360.

Park Trails

Mountain Bike Trail 👢👢👢—6.5 miles—For visitors who would rather bike than hike, this trail parallels a portion of the Out and Back Hiking trail. The trail varies from prairie flatlands to winding ridge tops.

Nature Trail 👢—.75 mile—Located near the White Tail Day-Use Area, the trail explores the western arm of High Lake.

High Pond Trail 👢—.75 mile—Located near the High Lake Day-Use Area, this trail explores the southeastern edge of High Lake and the area south of the lake.

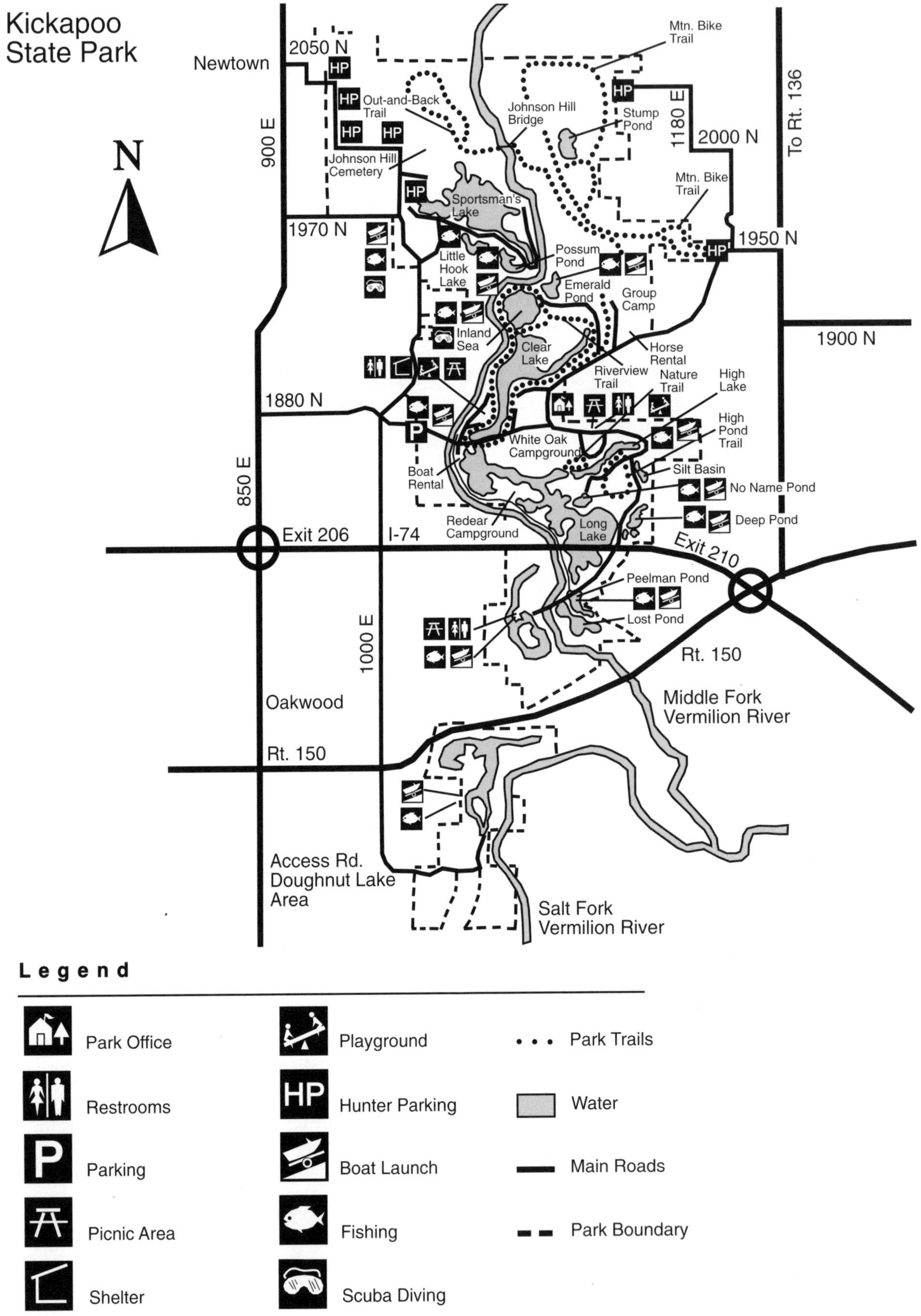
Kickapoo
State Park
N
Newtown
2050 N
HP
Out-and-Back
Trail
Johnson Hill
Cemetery
900 E
Mtn. Bike
Trail
Johnson Hill
Bridge
Stump
Pond
1180 E
2000 N
To Rt. 136
Sportsman's
Lake
Mtn. Bike
Trail
1970 N
1950 N
Little
Hook
Lake
Possum
Pond
Emerald
Pond
Group
Camp
1900 N
Inland
Sea
Clear
Lake
Horse
Rental
Riverview
Trail
Nature
Trail
High
Lake
1880 N
High
Pond
Trail
P
White Oak
Campground
Boat
Rental
Silt Basin
No Name Pond
850 E
Redear
Campground
Long
Lake
Deep Pond
Exit 206
I-74
Exit 210
Peelman Pond
Lost Pond
1000 E
Rt. 150
Middle Fork
Vermilion River
Oakwood
Rt. 150
Access Rd.
Doughnut Lake
Area
Salt Fork
Vermilion River
Legend
Park Office
Restrooms
Parking
Picnic Area
Shelter
Playground
Hunter Parking
Boat Launch
Fishing
Scuba Diving
Park Trails
Water
Main Roads
Park Boundary

Out-and-Back Trail 👢👢👢👢

Distance Round-Trip: 7.6 miles

Estimated Hiking Time: 3.5 hours

For an invigorating, postholiday, pre-Super Bowl workout, try the 7.6-mile Out-and-Back Trail at Kickapoo State Park. It climbs hills, scampers over trees, fords creeks, and is guaranteed to work off those holiday cookies and snacks.

Caution: Downed trees are often found on the trail; be on the lookout for them. Several creeks must be crossed without the aid of a bridge. During and after wet weather, dry feet are a rarity. A very steep—and often slick—hill must be climbed at the midpoint.

Trail Directions: The parking area is near the park office. Across the road is a signboard designating the trail [**1**], which is marked with white hiker silhouettes or orange blazes on trees. This is an official cross-country trail, so you'll also see red mile markers.

The trail starts as a narrow foot path, shared by the Clear Lake Trail. You hike on a ridge overlooking Clear Lake far below. At .25 mi. go right at a T [**2**]. At the end of a small incline a white marker with a black arrow will appear. Go left, crossing the asphalt park road, and head up a small hill. Atop the hill you will come to another T; go left. Here the trail widens and is no longer a narrow path.

The trail forks at .7 mi. [**3**]. Take the path leading straight ahead through an old field of goldenrod and Queen Anne's lace. Within a short distance (.1 mi.) a major intersection of the horse, hiking, and biking trails will appear. It is well marked; continue straight, following the hiker silhouette.

At 1.14 mi. the trail curves to the left and traverses a fencerow with an old strip mine on the right [**4**]. The rounded mounds are the old spoil heaps. Within .2 mi. you will again cross the bike and horse trails, but plenty of signage will help you along the correct path. After this intersection, the trail will again narrow and follow a ridge top, with a steep ravine on the left.

The bike path parallels the hiking trail at 1.5 mi. [**5**]. The trail snakes its way through the woods along a ridge top. At 2.1 mi. [**6**] you will come upon a heavily disturbed area; make an S-curve by entering the valley (this is a steep walk downhill). You'll immediately have another steep climb uphill; at the top note the hiker silhouette so you stay on the trail. Within .1 mi. the trail goes down a steep incline. Here

you have entered a deep valley with high, wooded spoil heaps on either side.

Johnson Hill Bridge appears at 2.43 mi. [**7**]: It is an old, one-car, steel-span bridge over the Middle Fork of the Vermilion River. Watch the river flow underneath and be alert for wildlife. Off the bridge the trail is a wide, long straightaway—a respite before the hill ahead.

At 2.7 mi. [**8**] take a hard right and head uphill. Prepare yourself for the steep, uphill climb. While climbing you'll pass the red 3-mile marker. Descend another steep hill at 3.8 mi. [**9**]; watch your step, as there are few handholds. While descending, note the large patch of Christmas fern to the right. At the bottom you will pass between large, tree-covered spoil heaps and begin to follow a creek.

Several creek crossings begin at the 4-mi. point [**10**]; some have a footbridge, but others must be crossed on rocks. The trail travels up and down as it follows the creek. At 4.85 mi. you have completed the hill loop [**11**]. Now retrace your steps and go left, hiking on the long straightaway to the bridge. You will recross the bridge, climb uphill, encounter the S-curve, and again parallel the bike path. While wandering back, look for wolf trees, which are large oak trees with a wide-spreading canopy.

Use caution while returning from [**2**] where the trail parallels the road. The trail slopes downhill with a steep drop-off and offers a treacherous challenge for tired hiking legs! The trail ends at the signboard near the parking lot.

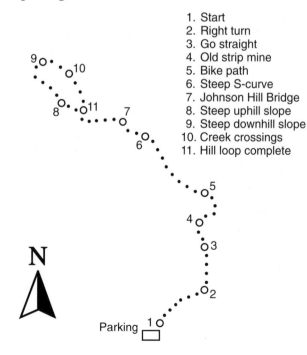

1. Start
2. Right turn
3. Go straight
4. Old strip mine
5. Bike path
6. Steep S-curve
7. Johnson Hill Bridge
8. Steep uphill slope
9. Steep downhill slope
10. Creek crossings
11. Hill loop complete

Riverview Trail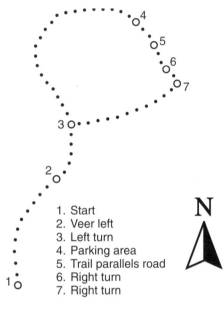

Distance Round-Trip: 2.25 miles

Estimated Hiking Time: 1 hour

After a spectacular view of the Middle Fork of the Vermilion River, the trail winds through a recovering woods—up and down narrow, winding ridges that will keep your feet busy, if not your mind.

Caution: Watch your step as the footing can be tricky in the woods. A wooden fence skirts the trail along the river bluff to keep errant hikers from falling off the edge and tumbling downhill into the river.

Trail Directions: Park at the Clear Lake Day-Use Area and begin the trail at the brown Riverview Trail sign [**1**]. The Middle Fork will be on your left as you hike uphill on a fairly wide trail. If it is late fall or winter, look for bittersweet berries that will provide a bit of color in an otherwise drab landscape. After .1 mi. the trail heads downward and curves to the left [**2**]. The path has narrowed, and Clear Lake is visible on the right.

At .45 mi. the hiker silhouette appears and the trail angles to the left in front of a pine tree [**3**]. Go left and head uphill. At the top is a wooden fence to protect you from falling into the river far below. Take time to appreciate the great view! Inland Sea now appears on your right. Note the cypress trees that have been planted. The trail follows a ridge between the river and Inland Sea for .3 mi. In the spring look for wildflowers—toothwort and hepatica—on the hill across the river. You'll likely need binoculars for this. Observe that the hillside appears to be sliding downhill. This is called slumping.

The ridge-top trail comes out in a parking area (.85 mi.) [**4**]. Cross the parking lot (black arrows lead you). Once on the other side, the trail resumes with a series of steps and becomes very narrow. At the 1-mi. point it comes out at the road, goes immediately back into the woods, and parallels it for a few steps [**5**]. You soon are following a winding trail through a recovering woods that skirts the edge of Inland Sea. The trail is up and down, narrow and winding; it traverses small ridges.

The trail comes to a T and changes into a wide path again at 1.25 mi. [**6**]. Go to your right; on the left is a parking area with an outdoor toilet. The trail here is marked with black arrows on a metal sign. After descending a hill, the trail forks (1.45 mi.) [**7**]. If you continue straight, you will be hiking on the Clear Lake Trail that covers some of the same ground as the Out-and-Back Trail. Go right to continue on the Riverview Trail. Before turning, note the sinuous

forms of the trees on your left, clearly visible in winter.

As you hike along a series of little ponds on both the right and left—remnants of the park's strip-mining past—keep a sharp eye for wading birds, muskrats, and insects in the summer. At 1.85 mi. you have completed the loop around Inland Sea and are back at [**3**]. Go left, retracing your steps to reach the parking area.

1. Start
2. Veer left
3. Left turn
4. Parking area
5. Trail parallels road
6. Right turn
7. Right turn

N

© Michael Jeffords

26. Fox Ridge State Park

- Bring your insect field guide and practice your entomological skills in summer.
- Hike on ridges with clean understories and descend into valleys where you are engulfed by vegetation.
- Develop an appreciation for the diversity of daddy longlegs.
- Enjoy the brilliant fall colors of the park's abundant maples.

Area Information

Nestled along the Embarras River, Fox Ridge State Park belies its prairie heritage. It is a series of ravines along a glacial moraine. Simply translated, this area is very hilly! The Embarras forms the western boundary of the park. In olden days it provided early settlers with food, water, and transportation. Flatboats carried the settlers' goods to the Wabash River and from there to points beyond. This small parcel of land was taken over by the state during the late 1930s.

The park is used not only for recreation but also for research. The Illinois Natural History Survey maintains a laboratory here, with scientists studying the lake, streams, and ponds in order to improve fishing. Ridge Lake was the first lake where scientists were able to control the water level. They have studied the effect that drawdowns have on fish, whether supplemental feeding of the lake's fish is helpful, and what happens with the introduction of predators, such as walleye and muskellunge. These fishery studies have been some of the longest and most continuous in the country.

Civic pride is strong locally. The Fox Ridge Foun-
dation is very active in promoting and improving the park so that visitors will have a good time and return often.

Directions: Fox Ridge State Park is located off Route 130, 8 miles south of Charleston.

Hours Open: The site is open-year round.

Facilities: Recreational offerings include camping (which includes a rent-a-camp) and five reservable picnic shelters. Fishing is allowed from 6 to 10 A.M. and 3 to 8 P.M., Wednesday through Sunday, by reservation only. Fishing and canoeing in the Embarras are open to all.

Permits and Rules: No bicycles are allowed on the trails.

Further Information: Site Superintendent, Fox Ridge State Park, RR 1, Charleston, IL 61920; 217-345-6416.

Other Areas of Interest

Located 20 miles northeast of Charleston, **Walnut Point State Fish and Wildlife Area** offers fishing, camping, hunting, and picnicking. Take advantage of a tree-lined drive to learn your native Illinois trees and to enjoy the spring wildflowers. Two trails total 2.25 miles. For more information call 217-346-3336.

The **Lincoln Log Cabin** historic site features the 1840s farm and home of Thomas and Sarah Lincoln, Abraham Lincoln's parents. From June through August the farm comes to life with crops, livestock, and costumed living-history interpreters. Located south of Charleston, the site is open year-round. For more information call 217-345-6489.

Park Trails

Wilderness and Family Trails 👢👢👢—.25 mile each—Both of these are linear trails through oak,
hickory, and maple woods. Both are lined with mayapples and Jack-in-the-pulpits in the understory, and both provide good views into the ravines.

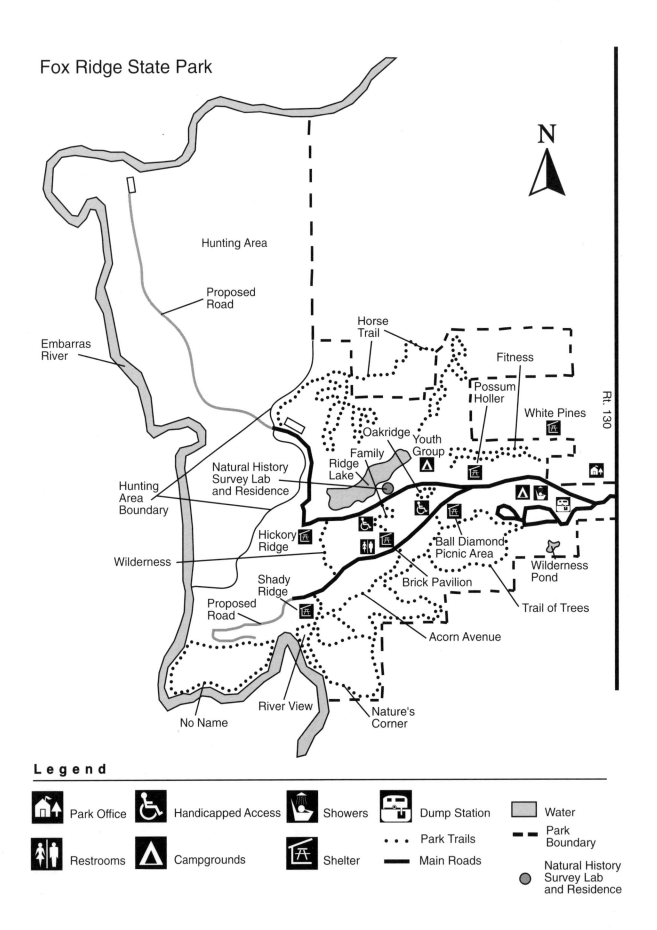

Fox Ridge State Park

N

Hunting Area

Proposed Road

Embarras River

Horse Trail

Fitness

Possum Holler

White Pines

Oakridge

Youth Group

Family Ridge Lake

Natural History Survey Lab and Residence

Hunting Area Boundary

Ball Diamond Picnic Area

Wilderness Pond

Hickory Ridge

Wilderness

Brick Pavilion

Trail of Trees

Shady Ridge

Proposed Road

Acorn Avenue

River View

Nature's Corner

No Name

Rt. 130

Legend

🏠 Park Office   ♿ Handicapped Access   🚿 Showers   🚐 Dump Station   ▢ Water

🚻 Restrooms   ⛺ Campgrounds   ⛩ Shelter   • • • Park Trails   — Main Roads

- - - Park Boundary

● Natural History Survey Lab and Residence

River View and No Name Trails 👢👢👢

Distance Round-Trip: 2.15 miles

Estimated Hiking Time: 1.5 hours

During the summer this is a place to practice your entomological skills. Dragonflies and damselflies flit about on vegetation along the river, crane flies hang motionless on stinging nettle, butterflies form puddle clubs on the trail in front of you, and all are accompanied by the inevitable yet familiar drone of mosquitoes.

Caution: The trail can be very muddy. Logs sometimes block it and roots are everywhere. Some of the wooden steps are beginning to decay, so use caution as you go up and down. Part of the trail is very close to the edge of the river, and the trail footing is quite loose here.

Trail Directions: Park your vehicle at Shady Ridge Shelter and begin the trail on the south side of the loop parking area. At the River View trail board head down a series of steps [1] and look at the vegetation and insects concealed along the stairs. Look for daddy longlegs, hanging crane flies, and green katydids. As you continue down, look for the large, oblong leaves of pawpaw.

Come off the steps and go straight [2]. Within a few yards the trail will go right; follow the arrow for Nature's Corner. By summer, any remnants of the spring wildflowers are gone, and left in their place is stinging nettle. Don't get too close to this plant, for any contact will cause some of its hairs to break off and become embedded in your skin.

At .25 mi. you come to a trail intersection with a map; go right [3] and hike along the Embarras River on a path that eventually disappears into the river (erosion). Where the trail is missing, continue to skirt the river, and soon you will come to another trail; go right. This trail forms a T at .35 mi.; go left on this connector [4]. Within .05 mi. there will be another trail intersection; take the left fork [5]. Keep the river on your left as you follow No Name Trail. The white fuzz that litters the trail during the early summer is seed from the cottonwood tree.

As you hike along the river, look for black-winged damselflies (the males have metallic green bodies) and notice how they hold their wings when at rest. Check the trail for tracks. Although you may not

meet another hiker during the day and you certainly won't see many mammals, this place is a veritable highway of activity in the evenings! Watch where you step also, as the trail is littered with tiny toads about half an inch long and the color of mud.

At .85 mi. the trail goes right, away from the river into a grassy area, and then left, skirting a weedy field [6]. Here you are walking among ambrosia—not the salad, but a severe allergen-causing plant called giant ragweed. The path soon reenters the woods, where you can see big hackberry trees on either side of the trail. It leads through a mixed floodplain forest with lots of small buckeye trees. As the trail curves to the right note the large pappaws on either side.

At 1.2 mi. the trail goes right, away from the river [7], and is very subtle (it almost disappears altogether). Then it emerges from the woods, and a hiker sign directs you to the left. The woods will be on the left and a field on the right. The large, mosquito-like insects in the woods are crane flies. They don't bite; in fact most do not feed at all as adults. The trail crosses a series of low spots and is very faint, so continue to skirt the woods, keeping to the left.

At 1.5 mi. the road to Shady Ridge is on your left; continue straight (right) [8]. While hiking this section look for butterflies—great spangled fritillaries, hackberry, and swallowtails. On the left the forest conceals a ridge; to the right is an open field. You complete the loop at 1.75 mi. and are back at [5]. Go left into the woods.

At 1.8 mi. you return to [4]; go left. Two miles puts you back at the steps [2]. Head up and back to Shady Ridge Picnic Area, looking for any new insects along the way.

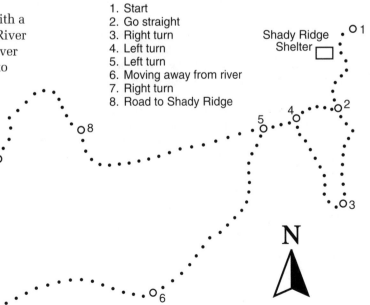

1. Start
2. Go straight
3. Right turn
4. Left turn
5. Left turn
6. Moving away from river
7. Right turn
8. Road to Shady Ridge

Shady Ridge Shelter

N

Acorn Avenue–Trail of Trees

👢👢👢👢

Distance Round-Trip: 3.35 miles

Estimated Hiking Time: 1.75 hours

This hike provides a complete workout—large and small steps, twisting switchbacks (zigzags), and flat stretches. Even your neck gets a workout as you strain to look up at the lofty trees.

Caution: Logs are sometimes blocking the trail and roots protruding from it. Respect all signs telling you to stay off an area due to erosion!

Trail Directions: The Acorn Avenue Trail starts across the road from the Brick Shelter. Begin at the trail board and go right and down the dirt stairs [**1**]. At the bottom, go left and cross a bridge (the first of many crossings). At .15 mi. [**2**] you will come to a trail intersection; go right and cross another bridge. Look for an unusual, multitrunk sycamore on the right, as well as fragile fern and Christmas fern.

At .3 mi. [**3**] note a pair of cottonwoods and a huge, leaning sycamore on your left, and walk under the arch of a bending buckeye. The trail forks at .45 mi. [**4**]; go right, noting the sycamore (also on the right) with large trunks. The species (recognized by its peeling, scaly bark) has the largest single-blade leaf of any North American tree. Sycamore leaves can be up to 10-inches long. The trail forms a T at .55 mi. [**5**]; go left and follow the sign to Eagles Nest. Within a few yards the trail forks; take the left fork that will lead to a stream.

Cross the stream and head up a series of steep steps. At the top on the right is an overlook (built around an oak tree) for Gobbler's Knob. From here, continue uphill along a narrow path on top of a ridge. The trail comes to another T at .85 mi.; go right [**6**]. As you hike along this segment of the trail, take notice of all the maple seedlings and saplings. These woods were once dominated by oaks, evidenced by the large examples that remain. Oak seedlings cannot tolerate shade as well as maple seedlings can, so the once-stately oak forest is being taken over by maples.

The trail forks at .95 mi. [**7**]; go left. Look for brown tiger beetles with white markings that are twice the size of the green ones. The trail begins to head down, and you encounter a switchback, log steps, and a bridge crossing. After the bridge [**8**] at 1.15 mi. look to your right for pappaw trees before heading up the steps. Look on either side of the trail for Christmas ferns and false Solomon's seal. At the top observe the white splotches on the bark of the oaks, caused by a fungus.

The trail now heads down with the help of a switchback at 1.4 mi. [**9**]. Once on level ground note a small patch of ostrich ferns on your left and maidenhair ferns on your right. You will cross four bridges before coming to a trail intersection [**10**] at 1.8 mi. Go right. Within a few feet the trail will fork; go right again. Along this connecting trail note the fern-covered ridges. At 1.9 mi. the trail forks yet again; go right and up the stairs [**11**]. A profusion of hepatica and bloodroot grow along the stairs; both species bloom in very early spring. The wooden steps soon become dirt steps that require a giant's stride to reach them.

At the top is a bench on which to sit to catch your breath and admire the moss carpeting the area. The trail is now on a ridge dominated by oaks and maples. Did you notice the large oak with four trunks? Look and listen for pileated woodpeckers here, and don't neglect the impressive ravine on the right. By 2.35 mi. the solitude of the hike and the open understory of the woods both are gone. The trail is near the campground [**12**] where the woods have been disturbed. The trail forks again at 2.5 mi.; go left and skirt the campground [**13**].

Once you are away from the campground, the openness of the woods returns. You will see a bench before the trail heads down with the help of switchbacks. Look at decaying branches and logs for brightly colored mushrooms. At 3 mi. cross the bridge and go left [**14**]; soon you will cross another bridge, and the trail will fork. You are back at [**11**]; go right, retracing your steps. The trail comes to a T at 3.2 mi.; go right, cross the creek, and head up the numerous steps to your vehicle.

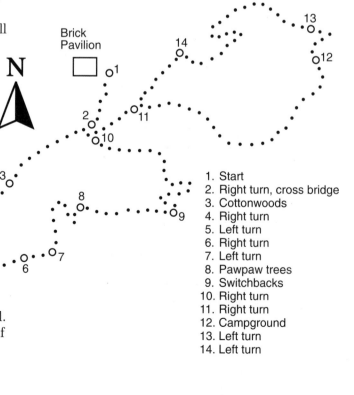

Brick Pavilion

N

1. Start
2. Right turn, cross bridge
3. Cottonwoods
4. Right turn
5. Left turn
6. Right turn
7. Left turn
8. Pawpaw trees
9. Switchbacks
10. Right turn
11. Right turn
12. Campground
13. Left turn
14. Left turn

27. Champaign-Urbana

- Walk along and cross streets with names reminiscent of a Monopoly board. Your goal here, however, isn't to acquire the most money, hotels, or the coveted Boardwalk, but to find the biggest trees.
- See the second-largest English oak in the United States and the largest in Illinois.
- Traverse the gamut from very formal gardens to nature's wildness.

Area Information

When settlers first came to Champaign County, they found huge expanses of prairie with forests growing along rivers and streams. Near what was to become Urbana grew the "Big Grove," an area of timberland along the Salt Fork. To create farmland, settlers preferred clearing trees from the woods over breaking the tough, prairie sod. A cabin was built on the edge of the Big Grove in 1822. Senator John Vance, who represented Vermilion County, named the town that grew up there Urbana, after the name of his boyhood home in Ohio.

The land that became Champaign was low, swampy prairie. Avoided at first, the land was settled in large part because of the railroad and called West Urbana. Like many other small towns of the time, Urbana was passed over by the railroad, which instead located a depot in West Urbana. Railroad administrators wanted to avoid construction of bridges over the Salt Fork and Embarras rivers.

The town took the name Champaign in 1860 so it would no longer be construed as being part of Urbana. Champaign means "level expanse of open country," which accurately described the view from anywhere in town. In 1867, after much politicking and rumors of champagne dinners, the two towns landed what was to become the University of Illinois. From the University's humble beginnings—a single building with a faculty of two, a first class of 50, and a swampy campus where students waded through mud to attend classes—the school and the two communities have blended economically, socially, and culturally as all three have grown.

Directions: Champaign-Urbana is located off I-74. To reach the starting point for the hike, take the Lincoln Avenue exit and go south through Urbana. You will cross major intersections at University, Springfield, and Green streets. Go right at the four-way stop at Lincoln and Pennsylvania avenues. Take another right after several blocks onto Sixth Street. From Sixth Street take the first left (Peabody Drive) and park at the meters in front of the Krannert Art Museum.

Hours Open: The site is open year-round.

Facilities: Restrooms, water, and a small cafe are located inside the Art Museum. During the hike, water and restrooms may be also be found at Crystal Lake Park and the Anita Purves Nature Center. Crystal Lake Park has picnic shelters, fishing, and boating.

Permits and Rules: All dogs must be leashed. As this is an urban hike, you will be hiking past homes, so please respect the owners' privacy.

Further Information: Champaign-Urbana Convention and Visitors Bureau, 40 East University, P.O. Box 1607, Champaign, IL 61824; 800-369-6151.

Other Areas of Interest

Located along the Salt Fork River, east of Urbana and near Homer, **Homer Lake** was created to provide water recreation in a predominately agricultural area. In addition to fishing, boating, and picnicking, several of the small ponds offer the opportunity to watch the age-old ritual of toad courting and mating. Hiking is offered on several short trails. For more information call 217-896-2455.

Located near the Vermilion River, 6 miles northeast of Gifford, **Patton Woods** is a remnant of the once-extensive forest along the Middle Fork of the Vermilion River. Here you can find a showy display of spring wildflowers and migratory birds. The best time to visit is during late April and early May. A quarter-mile trail loops through the woods. For more information, trail guides, and plant and mammal checklists call Parkland College, Natural Science Department, at 217-351-2285.

Area Trail

Champaign Volksmarch 🥾—6.2 miles—The hike starts at the Hometown Pantry at 2402 West Springfield Avenue where you can pick up a trail map and register. The trail goes around Kaufmann Lake and through four urban parks, including Centennial where you can see a petting zoo. For more information call 217-355-1704.

Champaign-Urbana

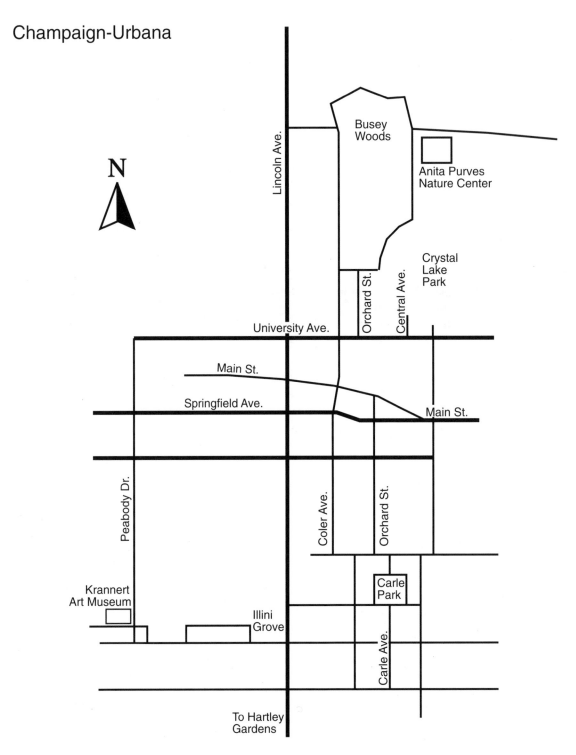

In Search of the Big Grove 👢

Distance Round-Trip: 7.75 miles

Estimated Hiking Time: 3.25 hours

The Big Grove extended from what is now Main Street in Urbana, north to the present town of Leverett, and east as far as Mayview. Looking for remnants of this prairie grove shouldn't be too hard, especially in a town that prides itself on being Tree City, USA.

Caution: There are many street crossings.

Trail Directions: Park in front of the Krannert Art Museum, located at 500 E. Peabody, Champaign. Obtain a permit from the Museum to park extended hours at the meters from 8 A.M. to 5 P.M. Mondays through Fridays; parking is free at other times. Begin the hike in the courtyard by the large, sculpted feet [1] that serve as benches. Go left from here onto Peabody, cross Sixth Street, and continue east. As you walk by the Natural Resources Building observe the frieze work and that each story has a different style of window.

Continue east, passing an open area (Agriculture Quad) and a large orange sculpture on the left (.25 mi.) [2] called *Aurora I* (created by Bruce White). Walk under the Agricultural Engineering walkway, continuing until the sidewalk dead-ends onto Pennsylvania Avenue (.35 mi.) [3]. Go east (left) on Pennsylvania, past the tennis courts, to the Illini Grove (on your left) [4]. Unfortunately, this is not a remnant of the Big Grove. The Illini Grove was planted in 1871 as a demonstration to show farmers the value of tree planting on the prairie; a century ago this was one of the best-known forest plantations in the Midwest. For many years the area extending from Nevada Street to this corner was called The Forestry.

Cross Lincoln Avenue at .6 mi. and take a right, heading south. Once you cross Florida Avenue (.75 mi.) [5], the sidewalk disappears and is replaced by a grassy path. In the distance on the right note the three classic round barns on the hill. At .9 mi. [6] you have come to the Hartley Selection Gardens of the Arboretum. Head east toward the garden and under the trellis on the red and white rock path. Walk along the maze of paths in the garden, studying and comparing plants for use in your home garden. Then retrace your steps back to Lincoln Avenue (1.45 mi.) [5] and turn right (east) on Florida Avenue

As you head east note the mansion on the right, the residence of the president of the University. Cross Orchard Street; at Carle Street, go north or left (1.8 mi.) [7]. Carle Street dead-ends into Carle Park. Cross the street and walk through the park on the wood-chip path (2.05 mi.) [8]. You will encounter large trees here, but this also is *not* part of the Big Grove. The wood-chip path rejoins the sidewalk on the far side of the park (you are still on Carle Street); continue north. Go left on Washington, and after a half-block turn right onto McCullough (2.25 mi.) [9]. Continue north on McCullough.

As you walk through this residential neighborhood, note the original brick-paved streets and the flower-filled yards. At 2.55 mi. [10] cross Green Street and continue north on McCullough. On your left note the large ginkgo tree: The apartment complex was built around it due to community support for the tree! Cross Springfield Avenue and at Main Street go left (2.65 mi.) [11]. As you walk west on Main you will pass several historic houses on the right and left. Go right on Coler and then take another right at University Avenue. Notice the park area to the left— this is Leal Park, and at one time this area was a pioneer cemetery. After the third block, which should be Central Avenue, cross University Avenue (3.05 mi.) [12].

Enter Crystal Lake Park from Central Avenue at 3.2 mi. [13] and go to your right, taking the stairs down to the boathouse. Cross the footbridge and go left on a wide, asphalt path through the park. Note the grove of bur oaks on your left. These, finally, might be remnants of the Big Grove! At 3.35 mi. note a fountain on your left [14]. About 100 feet from the fountain sidestep a gate, cross a park road, and join the footpath that winds north, parallel to the road. On your left you will see the county fairgrounds. The path soon ends so continue north, through the parking lot, to the Anita Purves Nature Center.

Enter the Nature Center at 3.75 mi. and take a break [15]. You will find water, restrooms, interesting exhibits, and a helpful staff. After the center go out the door you came in, turn right, and go downhill. Go left across a suspension bridge into Busey Woods (3.85 mi.) [16]. Take the trail to the right and within 100 feet go right again. You have found the *Big Grove*! Busey Woods is one of the few remaining remnants. The southern half was cleared and used as pasture and a farmstead. With the help of volunteers conducting cleanups, controlled burns, and brush cutting, the land is being reclaimed as woodland. As you walk through the woods, look for carpets of trout lily and other spring flowers in April. Check for owls, evidenced by their pellets and calls—or an actual sighting.

At 4 mi. [17] go left at the sign indicating a short loop. Soon you will come to a small boardwalk on your left (ignore this). Go right and skirt the pond—a remnant of a stream that once flowed through the woods. Within .1 mi. another boardwalk appears on the left (4.15 mi.) [**18**]. Take a few moments to kneel down and look into the water. Look for diving beetles, tadpoles, and fairy shrimp. After the boardwalk the trail comes to a T; go left, up a small incline, and left again. The trail now crosses through a honeysuckle thicket. Proceed left and follow the power line. A trail intersection and a big oak appear at 4.4 mi. [**19**]; continue straight. Soon you are back where you entered the woods. Angle right and recross the suspension bridge.

Retrace your steps back to the fountain in Crystal Lake Park (5 mi.) [**14**]. Continue on the asphalt path, recrossing the concrete footbridge and then walking around the lower level of the boat house. From here you will come to a parking area where you can soon exit the park at Race Street (5.35 mi.) [**20**]. Cross Race Street and continue south, crossing 11 streets before coming to Washington Street, where Race Street jogs to the right (6.25 mi.) [**21**]. In less than a half a block, cross Washington, and continue on Race.

Across from the entrance to Urbana High School turn right, into Carle Park. On your right is a statue of Lincoln by Lorado Taft (6.4 mi.) [**22**]. The statue commemorates Lincoln's many visits to the community while riding the circuit, portraying Lincoln as the young lawyer Urbana had known. Continue straight into the park, going left before the Pavilion (6.55 mi.). Pause here [**23**] in front of the largest English oak in Illinois—and the second-largest in the United States. Continue straight west past the fountain and rejoin the chip path; go left.

Cross the street (Indiana) and go right at 6.65 mi. [**24**]. You will be walking west on Indiana. Cross Orchard Street and go left. At Pennsylvania Avenue go right (6.8 mi.) [**25**]. Before reaching Mt. Hope Cemetery, you will pass the former residence of

Lorado Taft on the left. This is not the house's original location; it was moved here from John Street to make room for the University expansion. If it is near dusk, look in the large trees of Mt. Hope Cemetery for hawks and great horned owls. They hunt here regularly for the abundant ground squirrels. Turn right onto Sixth Street (7.6 mi.) [**26**], cross Peabody, and turn left. You are back at the museum courtyard, so use the big feet to take a load off your own.

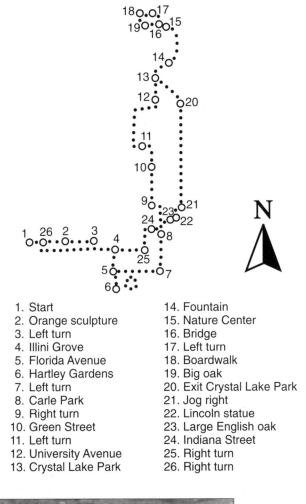

1. Start
2. Orange sculpture
3. Left turn
4. Illini Grove
5. Florida Avenue
6. Hartley Gardens
7. Left turn
8. Carle Park
9. Right turn
10. Green Street
11. Left turn
12. University Avenue
13. Crystal Lake Park
14. Fountain
15. Nature Center
16. Bridge
17. Left turn
18. Boardwalk
19. Big oak
20. Exit Crystal Lake Park
21. Jog right
22. Lincoln statue
23. Large English oak
24. Indiana Street
25. Right turn
26. Right turn

28. Robert Allerton Park

- Discover wonderful sculptures as you walk through the woods and gardens.
- Enjoy not only a profusion of spring wildflowers but also well-manicured gardens.
- Take peaceful, pleasant hikes and encounter birds, butterflies, wildflowers, and wildlife.
- Gaze upward at the 15-foot *Sunsinger* as he embraces the morning sky.
- Walk and learn.

Area Information

Allerton Park, located near Monticello, began as a series of land holdings along the Sangamon River purchased in 1863 by Samuel Allerton. The land, known then as "The Farms," was a model production-stock and crop farm. In 1946 this land was given to the University of Illinois for research and educational purposes. In addition to the farmland, the grounds contained landscaped gardens and more than 100 sculptures.

The Sangamon River divides the park into two sections. The north contains the gardens and sculptures, whereas the south is a relatively undisturbed example of an Illinois stream-valley ecosystem. The southern section supports a 600-acre floodplain that includes a nearly primeval forest and has been declared a National Natural Landmark. River bluffs are dominated by red and bur oak, and some 75 acres of reclaimed prairie (complete with the prairie rattlesnakes) are there for the exploring. The park is a sanctuary for plants and animals: 1,042 species of plants, 60 species of breeding birds, 30 species of animals, and 28 species of reptiles and amphibians.

Directions: Robert Allerton Park is located off I-72 near Monticello. From exit 63, take Market Street to Monticello; turn right on Marion, then left on Allerton Road. From exit 61, take Bridge Street east to Monticello; turn right on Market Street, right on Marion, then left on Allerton Road. Follow the signs into the park.

Hours Open: The site is open year-round from 10 A.M. to sunset (except Christmas and New Year's Day).

Facilities: A visitor center has snacks, restrooms, and information about the park and the Allerton family. Picnicking is permitted, but no special areas are set aside for it. The hiking trails may be used for cross-country skiing during the winter. Allerton House, the family mansion, is used as a conference center and is usually not open to the general public.

Permits and Rules: All pets must be leashed. Motorized vehicles are not allowed on the trails. No alcoholic beverages or firearms are allowed. No fishing or hunting is permitted. Nothing is to be removed from the park. Do not swim or wade in the river or ponds.

Further Information: Robert Allerton Park, RR 2, Box 135, Monticello, IL 61856; 217-762-2721 or 217-244-1035.

Other Areas of Interest

Holiday Showcase is held the weekend before Thanksgiving, and at this time Robert Allerton House is open to the public and lavishly decorated. Explore the many rooms that normally can only be glanced at through curtained windows. For more information call 217-762-7011.

Located near Monticello, **Lodge Park—Piatt County Forest Preserve** offers camping, primitive toilets, fishing, and hiking. In the spring a veritable artist's palette of color awaits you in the form of wildflowers along the banks of the Sangamon. For more information call 800-952-3396.

Park Trails

North-Side Trails 👢👢—total 17.4 miles—Four of the five north-side trails circulate around the landscaped gardens. The park's sculptures can be seen on these trails: Fu Dog Garden Trail, 1.92 mi.; Centaur/Woodland Trail, 3.24 mi.; Short trail by the river, 4.26 mi.; Centaur/Sunsinger Trail, 3.56 mi.; and Bottomland River Trail, 4.4 mi.

South-Side Trails 👢👢—total 12.5 miles—Experience a near primeval, central Illinois forest, a prairie, and profuse wildflowers by taking one of the loop trails—Short Loop, 2.98 mi.; Medium Loop, 4.24 mi.; and Long Loop, 5.28 mi.

Robert Allerton Park

N

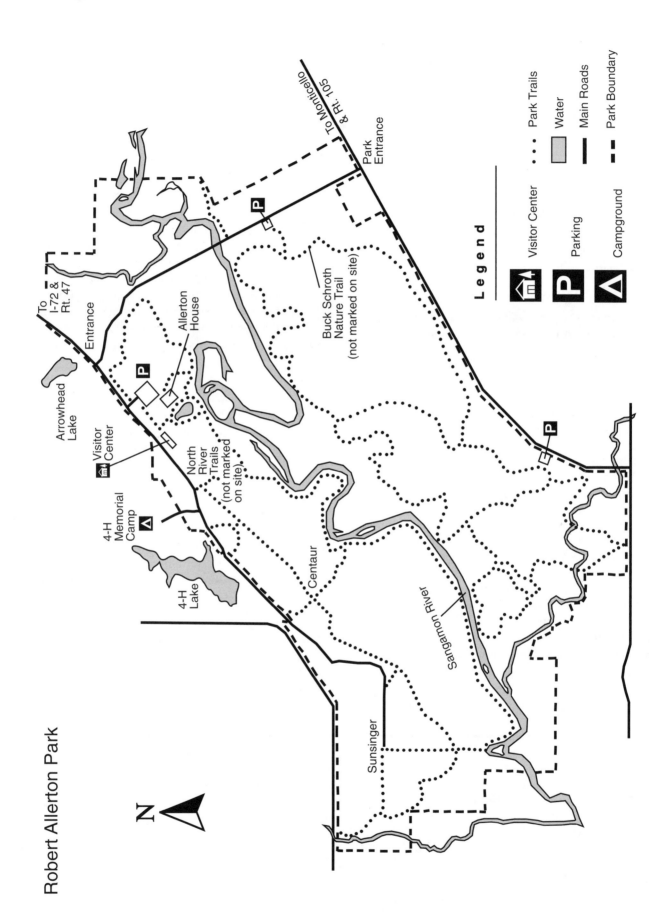

To Monticello
& Rt. 105

Park
Entrance

Buck Schroth
Nature Trail
(not marked on site)

To
I-72 &
Rt. 47

Entrance

Allerton
House

P

Arrowhead
Lake

Visitor
Center

North
River
Trails
(not marked
on site)

4-H
Memorial
Camp

4-H
Lake

Centaur

Sangamon River

Sunsinger

P

Legend

Visitor Center

Parking

Campground

Park Trails

Water

Main Roads

Park Boundary

North River Trails 🥾🥾

Distance Round-Trip: 5.75 miles

Estimated Hiking Time: 3 hours

Hiking these pieces of several trails allows one to discover some of the many treasures of the park—the bottomland forest of the Sangamon, a larger-than-life Apollo, acres of wildflowers, finely manicured gardens, and blue Fu dogs.

Caution: The trail can be very muddy near the river. Poison ivy and stinging nettle are everywhere.

Trail Directions: From the main parking lot near Allerton House, walk back toward the entrance, turning right just before the road and then walking down a vine-lined allée [**1**]. Straight ahead is the *House of the Golden Buddhas.* From here go right and through the Fu Dog Garden (.15 mi.) [**2**]. From the Fu Dog Garden enter the woods and continue on the trail. Pass to the right of a small pond. On your immediate left is a seep.

At .4 mi. the trail turns right and heads toward the river [**3**]. Floodplain forest will be on your left. At the trail intersection at .85 mi. go left again, toward the river [**4**]. (The trail straight ahead will lead back to Allerton House.) At 1 mi. another trail intersection appears; go left and up the wooden steps [**5**]. A dam for a pond will be on your right. Here you will find a bench overlooking the scenic Sangamon as well as another series of steps. Once at the top, follow the trail to the left. The Sangamon River is on the left; to the right is a small patch of woods backed by Allerton's open vista of grass.

Go left at 1.3 mi. and continue to walk along the river [**6**]. At 2 mi., go left and continue to skirt the river [**7**]. You will be hiking through an excellent example of a bottomland forest. At 2.4 mi. you will approach a point of land that juts out into the river [**8**]. Left and across the river is an upland, oak-hickory forest.

At 3.3 mi. observe a large opening with an oak tree; turn right, heading away from the river [**9**]. In the distance straight ahead you may spot the famous *Sunsinger.* You are walking on the remnants of an old road. Another trail intersects your path (3.5 mi.) [**10**], but continue straight and go uphill to the statue. The trail emerges on a road that circles the statue (3.6 mi.) [**11**]. Go right, walking along the wide, grassy shoulder.

The *Sunsinger* is actually Apollo greeting the morning sky with song and extended arms. Continue to walk on the grassy shoulder, away from the *Sunsinger,* and follow the park road. As the wide grassy shoulder begins to narrow, you will come upon a sign. The other side reads Pioneer Cemetery, and just past this sign are concrete pillars; go right, downhill, and into the woods (3.7 mi.) [**12**].

This short trail soon comes to a T; go left and hike between upland forest on the left and floodplain forest on the right (4 mi.) [**13**]. Soon the *Death of the Last Centaur* appears in the distance; head uphill to enjoy this unusual depiction (4.5 mi.) [**14**]. Continue northeast on the rolling trail, which is lined with tall oaks that arch over the path. At 4.7 mi. you will pass a trail to the House in the Woods, but continue straight [**15**] and into an allée of spruce trees. The natural portion of the hike has ended.

At 4.85 mi. you will enter the sunken gardens, marked with fish-topped pillars [**16**]. Cross the garden and go up the steps on the other side along a path lined with statuary of Chinese musicians. You may now navigate the hedge maze and pass through a cedar allée with a statue of *Adam* in the center. At the statue of the *Girl with a Scarf,* take a right (5.15 mi.) [**17**]. You will soon pass through a brick-wall gate topped with baskets of stone fruit and bronze figures of *Sea Maidens.* Continue straight on the path, walking toward Allerton House and the pond on a trail of pea gravel. Walk down the steps and pass between the house and the pond. At the end of the path continue straight, going down a metal, spiral staircase. Ignore the stairs on the right and go down the wooden, terraced steps toward the river. At the trail intersection, go left and uphill (5.45 mi.) [**18**]. You will soon be back at [**5**]; go left and uphill again, returning to the parking area.

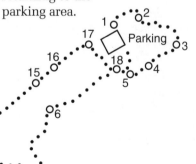

1. Start
2. Fu Dog Garden
3. Right turn
4. Left turn
5. Steps
6. Left turn
7. Left turn
8. Island in river
9. Right turn
10. Trail intersection
11. *Sunsinger*
12. Right turn
13. Left turn
14. *Death of the
    Last Centaur*
15. Spruce trees
16. Sunken gardens
17. Right turn
18. Left turn

Buck Schroth Nature Trail

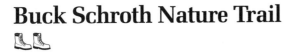

Distance Round-Trip: 2.4 miles

Estimated Hiking Time: 1.15 hours

Although Buck is no longer around to guide you on his popular nature walks through the park, his legacy lives on with interpretive signs and his presence is still felt.

Caution: During late spring and summer the mosquitoes can be very pesky. Don't forget to wear repellent.

Trail Directions: Begin the trail at the parking area just south of the Sangamon River [**1**] and hike through a recovering woods. Cross the bridge and head uphill. Parts of the trail are old asphalt, remnants of a trail laid out by the Allertons. The interpretive trail is an on-going project. The trail comes to a T at .15 mi. [**2**]; go right, and a sign describes Schroth and the purpose of his trail. Eugene "Buck" Schroth, biology teacher, former director of Allerton House, and Allerton volunteer extraordinaire, was attracted by the park's diversity. He spent more than 50 years here, walking, studying, learning, and imparting his knowledge through popular wildflower talks and tours of the nature trails. This trail is a fitting memorial to him.

At .25 mi. you enter the floodplain forest. The first station is at .3 mi. [**3**] and concerns fungi (mushrooms). One of the most popular activities in the park is mushroom hunting, and here you can learn more about morels and some ten thousand other species of fungi that thrive here. The Sangamon River soon comes into view on the right. At .4 mi. you have arrived at the Sangamon River station [**4**]. The Sangamon remains a natural stream: Stop here to learn more about the ecology of the river and its floodplain.

The floodplain forest is soon replaced by more upland species; look for "wolf" trees on the right. (Wolf trees are usually oaks with large outspread branches, indicating they grew in the open.)

You will soon pass a small, temporary pool on the right, but it isn't what it appears. In reality, at least when the Allertons were here, this was a hog wallow (.55 mi.). The wildflower station appears at .7 mi. [**5**]. April through May is a wonderful time to visit the park and walk among the profusion of

spring flowers. Virginia bluebells, blue-eyed Mary, violets, and phlox carpet the park. Here Buck reaches forth from the past and tells you what will be blooming when. At .75 mi. come to a trail intersection [**6**]; go left. Look for deer as you hike this stretch. Exit the woods at .95 mi. to encounter the savanna station [**7**]. Learn more about savannas and the clues used to identify this habitat in the park and elsewhere. Now go left and skirt the prairie (the trail is in development and will eventually form a loop).

As you walk by the prairie, feel the leaves of the compass plant. At one time pioneers used this compass to tell direction; luckily, you have a nice, wide trail. Like the woods-in-progress you have just passed through, this is a prairie-in-progress. Another station at 1.05 mi. [**8**] provides information on a group of beasts you've undoubtedly encountered on the trail—the insects. Come to a trail intersection at 1.2 mi. [**9**] and go right. As you continue to skirt the prairie, note examples of ongoing restoration. The dead "trees" on the left are the remains of invading sumac.

At 1.45 mi. go right and take the short path to discover the prairie—a landscape that once covered 60 percent of the state [**10**]. Return to the trail and continue on, eventually heading into the woods. To discover why Allerton Park may be the ultimate butterfly garden explore butterfly alley (1.60 mi.) [**11**]. One-third of the state's butterfly species can be found in the park. From butterfly alley, retrace your steps (in the future the trail will loop) and look for deer, admire the prairie flowers, watch dragonflies sun themselves, and, if you are really lucky, encounter a prairie rattlesnake. (It belongs here, so admire but leave it strictly alone!)

Back at [**9**] (2 mi.), continue straight and through the woods. At 2.05 mi. you will pass the station on exotic plants [**12**]. Isn't it ironic that in the exotic landscape of Allerton, exotics should be a problem. By 2.25 mi. you are back at [**2**]. In the words of Buck, hopefully you learned not only about the "various and sundry plants, but [also about] trees, birds, and nature." Go right and retrace your steps to the parking area. Whether or not you saw any of the things highlighted by the interpretative signs, you certainly feel like you have. If you come to Allerton Park often enough, though, it is a foregone conclusion that eventually you will see everything that Buck saw.

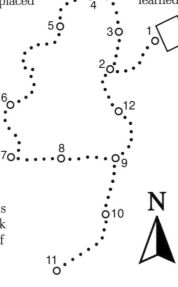

1. Start
2. Right turn
3. Fungi station
4. River station
5. Wildflower station
6. Left turn
7. Savanna station
8. Insect station
9. Right turn
10. Prairie station
11. Butterfly station
12. Exotics station

29. Hidden Springs State Forest

- Hike on a trail where you see the oaks of Illinois, but have the smell of the North Woods.

- Enjoy some of the best fall colors in Illinois.

- Walk on pure sand surrounded by waist-high stinging nettle and discover a floodplain woods.

- Learn to identify the native Illinois trees by picking up a trail guide at Big Tree Trail. Four of the eight species of Illinois oaks are found in this forest.

Area Information

This area was originally known as Shelby State Forest. Planners intended to develop the area as a state lake but changed course because of the construction of Lake Shelbyville. The forest is now called Hidden Springs after the seven springs on the property (which Native Americans and early pioneers used for drinking water). The springs no longer run freely; they now are covered with natural siltation and vegetation and are mostly hidden. Two of them, however, Rocky and Quicksand springs, are visible from the trails.

From the flat, floodplain woods along Richland Creek to the dry, oak-hickory stands on the ridge tops, the forest not only covers varied terrain, but also has varied uses. Tree plantations of both native and introduced species are maintained, and this forest is the seed orchard for both white and scotch pines. Experimental burn plots also are maintained to show the effects of fire on woods. In addition to timber research and management, the area offers a variety of recreational opportunities and meets its goal of sound timber management complemented by recreational activities.

Directions: Hidden Springs is located 10 miles southeast of Shelbyville. Follow Route 16 east from Shelbyville to Route 32; go south on Route 32 to Strasburg, and follow the signs to the forest.

Hours Open: The site is open year-round except on Christmas and New Year's Day. The day-use areas open at 6 A.M. and close at 10 P.M.

Facilities: There are picnic areas (with a shelter, stoves, fire ring, and playground), camping (class C and group), fishing, and hunting, but no modern restrooms.

Permits and Rules: No swimming is permitted in the ponds. No camping, horses, bicycles, or motorcycles are allowed on the trails. Keep vehicles on the gravel roads, pads, or parking areas. No plants, flowers, shrubs, or trees may be damaged or removed.

Further Information: Forest Superintendent, Hidden Springs State Forest, Box 200, RFD 1, Strasburg, IL 62465; 217-644-3091.

Other Areas of Interest

Located on the eastern shore of Lake Shelbyville, **Wolf Creek State Park** specializes in water recreation—fishing, water skiing, pontoon boating, wind surfing, or just plain swimming. The area has both recreational vehicle and tent campgrounds with showers, as well as horse and group camps. Seven hiking trails total 8.75 miles; most are near the lake. For more information call 217-459-2831.

Located on the western shore of Lake Shelbyville, **Eagle Creek State Park** offers the same water recreation as Wolf Creek. Both recreational vehicle and tent camping are offered, but no showers are provided. A full-service resort and golf course are found here. Five hiking trails include the 11-mile Chief Illini Trail along the edge of the lake. For more information call 217-756-8260.

Park Trail

Possum Hollow 👢👢—.75 mile—Be sure to pick up a brochure for this self-guided nature trail that highlights and identifies many of the forest's native trees. In addition, two short side spurs lead to a pond and to the white- and scotch-pine seed orchard.

Hidden Springs State Forest

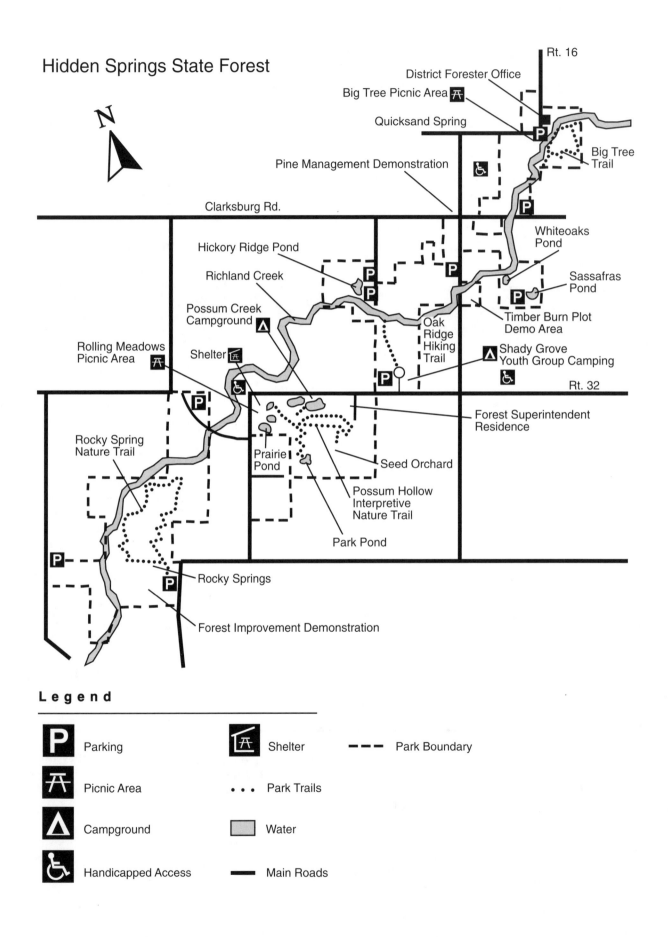

Legend

P Parking		𝐀 Shelter		- - - Park Boundary	
𝐀 Picnic Area		⋯ Park Trails			
△ Campground		▢ Water			
♿ Handicapped Access		— Main Roads			

Rocky Spring Nature Trail

Distance Round-Trip: 3 miles

Estimated Hiking Time: 1.5 hours

Even during a sultry summer day this is a magical place to hike. Cloaked in the sassafras leaves are swallowtail caterpillars that mimic first a bird dropping, later a green snake. Damselflies with slender green bodies flit in front of you while a battle-worn, male luna moth silently waits for evening to resume his never-ending search for a female.

Caution: Logs sometimes block the trail and many roots are exposed. The trail goes through a designated hunting area from August 1 through January 31: Check with the ranger on hiking availability.

Trail Directions: Begin at the trail board and follow a wide, mown path [1]. A pine plantation is on the right and mixed woods on the left. In the summer look for deptford pinks, a European wildflower. At .25 mi. the trail forks; go left [2], crossing a bridge and then curving left. As you head downward, look at the large multibranch white oak on the left. Within a short distance you will see a trail off to the right; ignore it and continue on.

Rocky Spring appears on the right at .35 mi. [3], an area covered with jewelweed, a favorite flower of hummingbirds. Look for both the flower and bird beginning in late July. From the spring the trail heads up, and at .45 mi. [4] a hiker sign appears and a trail goes off to the right. Continue hiking straight. At .55 mi. [5] go right at the sign. Note the large sugar maple on the right and the understory of fragile fern and mayapple.

Richland Creek comes into view by .7 mi. with a bench on your right and a large oak. At .85 mi. [6] you come off a small hill; the large trees on the right are ashes, and one has a split trunk. Within a few steps you will encounter large sugar maples and a very large red oak, which the trail skirts. Periodically, notice how the clean understory and large trees disappear, replaced by lots of shrubby growth and saplings. These areas have been disturbed either by pasturing or old home sites.

At 1.1 mi. skirt Richland Creek on the left [7]; the trail crosses a bridge and

gradually heads upward. At 1.35 mi. you will encounter a series of curves marked by a hiker sign. An overlook with a bench is set at 1.6 mi. [8] with a bird's-eye view of Richland Creek and a farm field. From the overlook the trail curves right. Listen for the squeaks of chipmunks and look for green dragons—rare cousins of Jack-in-the-pulpit that are downright abundant, however, on this trail! The plants have a single, compound leaf with 5 to 10 leaflets arranged in an arch around the top. The leaves begin appearing in early May.

If you are hiking in June, the blade-shaped seeds that litter the path are ash seeds. The trail begins to descend at 1.9 mi. [9], and soon you will cross the first of seven bridges. While you crisscross the creek, take time to look at its bottom. In many places the bed is slabs of bedrock. An area nearby the creek is carpeted with green dragons; look also for a large clump of Jacob's ladder in front of a large oak. The last bridge crossing is at 2 mi. Two steps up and the trail heads higher and away from the stream; the clean woods are gone.

At 2.25 mi. the trail comes into an open area with three paths; take the middle one and continue straight [10]. The open, grassy area is full of sassafras, oak, and hickory seedlings. At 2.35 mi. you will encounter paths to the left and right; ignore both and continue straight into the woods. You will pass a bench on your left and again come out into the open field. If you should happen to venture off the trail, look in the grass for crayfish mounds and frogs. During summer, the two major blooming plants in this area are purple milkweed and beardtongue (penstemon), both favorites of butterflies. Look for great spangled fritillaries and several species of swallowtails as they cluster around these beautiful flowers.

At 2.45 mi. [11] the trail goes back into the woods and through a pine plantation, becoming a cushion of pine needles: The smell is wonderful! Within a few steps the trail goes right, still a carpet of pine needles. The pines eventually disappear and you pass through a mixed, sapling woods. At 2.6 mi. [12] cross a bridge, go up, then down, and left. You have completed the loop. Cross the bridge and go right; within a quarter of a mile you are back at the trail board.

1. Start
2. Left turn
3. Rocky Spring
4. Straight
5. Right turn
6. Large ashes
7. Richland Creek
8. Overlook
9. Downhill slope
10. Go straight
11. Pine plantation
12. Bridge

N

Big Tree Trail 👢👢

Distance Round-Trip: 1.2 miles

Estimated Hiking Time: .75 hour

Pick up a trail guide—more than 25 species of native Illinois trees have been identified here. While you learn about the trees, your feet will be treated to a roller-coaster trail.

Caution: Logs and limbs sometimes block the trail, and roots are exposed. By summer the stinging nettle is waist high, so stay on the trail.

Trail Directions: Begin the hike at the trail board at the end of the parking area [1]. This trail is wheelchair accessible. Pick up a trail guide to add to your enjoyment of the hike (its numbers do not correspond to the bracketed numbers in this guide). You are hiking through a floodplain woods dominated by cottonwoods and silver maples, and you can spot the first of these very large cottonwoods on the right just before you cross the bridge. Cross Richland Creek on the bridge and go right.

At .1 mi. you come to the big sycamore [2] (or what's left of it). Its circumference used to be 19.9 feet and it reached over 116 feet. At present, the largest sycamore in Illinois is found in Logan County and has a circumference of 23 feet and a height of 106 feet. As you walk around the fenced tree, note that it was, and is, hollow. This is a characteristic of sycamores when they reach middle age (200 to 300 years old). Their sapwood no longer is involved with water and mineral transport, but instead gradually fills with metabolic wastes and resins that harden to form the dead central core of the tree, known as heartwood. If the heartwood rots, which frequently happens with sycamores, the tree can still live a long life.

Retrace your steps from the big tree and go right. After crossing a bridge you will go under an arching branch at .2 mi. [3]. Look for emerald-bodied, black-winged damselflies, yellow jewelweed, and hanging crane flies. At this point you are on higher ground, and the trees are no longer floodplain species but oak-hickory. Have you noticed the round holes in the leaves? These are made by native, leaf-cutting bees.

At .45 mi. [4] you will have just come down a hill; go right and cross the bridge. The trail guide calls this area fern valley: The creek banks are lined with Christmas fern. Fragile fern and rattlesnake fern can also be found here, although not as abundantly as Christmas fern. The trail now heads up. As you hike,

look down now and then at the ridged, underground mole trails. Since the soil here contains a lot of sand, it is perfect for moles—soft, moist, friable, and with considerable humus that contains grubs, millipedes, centipedes, and earthworms. As moles tunnel and dig, they aerate and turn over the soil—a valuable service.

At .55 mi. look for a tree with a fence mark in it; take advantage of Richland Creek overlook here [5]. Notice also the exposed tree roots gripping the banks. Soon you will be hiking through a jungle of pawpaw—small trees with very large leaves that are food for zebra swallowtail caterpillars. Look for these boldly patterned butterflies during April and mid-summer. At .65 mi. cross a bridge [6]; the trail curves right. Within .1 mi. you will cross another bridge; this time, the trail curves left. One mile brings you back to the first bridge [1]. Before crossing it, you might take one last, lingering look at the Big Tree (who knows how long it will last?). Go right and cross the bridge. Once back at the trail board go left and uphill to the parking area, though you're not finished with your hike.

Cross the park road (1.05 mi.) [7] and follow the grassy path to discover Quicksand Spring. Within .1 mi. you will come to an observation platform at the spring. Like all the springs here, this one is hidden by cloaking vegetation. Look for iris and sweet flag, whose leaves look like those of the cattail. After examining the spring, retrace your steps, recross the road, and return to the parking area. Now you're finished.

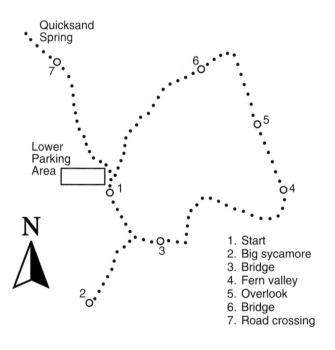

1. Start
2. Big sycamore
3. Bridge
4. Fern valley
5. Overlook
6. Bridge
7. Road crossing

30. Weldon Springs State Park

- Walk the same ground that popular Chautauqua speakers William Jennings Bryan, William Howard Taft, Helen Keller, Eugene Debs, and Carrie Nation did.

- Visit a restored country schoolhouse where the question "Just how sharp are a beaver's teeth?" can be answered. Later as you hike, look for evidence of those sharp teeth in action around the lake.

- Look for hummingbirds feeding at large patches of jewelweed near the marsh's observation deck.

- Enjoy a profusion of spring beauties (flowers, that is) near the old springs for which the park is named.

Area Information

Weldon Springs is named both for the natural springs that seep from numerous spots and feed the human-made lake, and for Judge Weldon, the original owner of this land and a friend of Abraham Lincoln's.

During the early 1900s, Judge Weldon leased his land to a group of Clinton residents for the establishment of a Chautauqua—an outdoor educational assembly that combined lectures and entertainment. During 10 days each summer from 1901 through 1922, hundreds of visitors were enlightened by Chautauqua speeches held on these grounds.

All that remains of this popular event is the lake, the name of a picnic shelter, and old handbills preserved in the Union School, a former country schoolhouse used as an interpretive center. Here modern-day visitors are encouraged to ask questions and touch and feel the exhibits. Outdoor recreational pursuits abound at the park, including tournament-quality horseshoe pits, hiking trails, ice fishing, and an impressive sledding hill.

Directions: Weldon Springs is in DeWitt County, east of Route 51 and 2 miles southeast of Clinton, off Route 10.

Hours Open: The site is open year-round except on Christmas and New Year's Day.

Facilities: Camping (including a well-equipped tent campsite for rent), fishing, boating, concession stand, and an outdoor education center are among the options.

Permits and Rules: Pets must be kept on leashes at all times.

Further Information: Weldon Springs State Recreation Area, RR 2, P.O. Box 87, Clinton, IL 62727; 217-935-2644.

Other Areas of Interest

Clinton Lake State Recreation Area is an impoundment of nearly 5,000 acres that was created as a cooling lake for the Clinton Nuclear Power Plant. The area, located 3 miles east of Clinton, offers camping, boating (including unlimited horsepower recreation boats), fishing, water skiing, and day-use areas with picnic facilities and playgrounds. The 3.5-mile Houseboat Cove trail loops north of the beach and goes through the woods. A 12-mile trail follows the hilly shoreline along the perimeter of Clinton Lake between North Fork Boat Access and North Fork Canoe Access Area. The latter trail is not maintained. For more information call 217-935-8722.

Located on the southern edge of Lincoln in Logan County, **Edward R. Madigan State Park** offers canoeing along Salt Fork Creek, wildlife watching, picnicking, and short trails. For more information call 217-735-2424.

Park Trails

Whitetail Cross-Country Skiing and Hiking Trail 👢👢—3 miles— This trail leads you past second- and third-growth oak-hickory forest and down a hill into a grassland restoration that follows an old fencerow of honey locust and Osage orange. Ulti-mately, the trail leads to Salt Creek and its floodplain woods.

Salt Creek Backpack Trail 👢👢—1 mile—This trail connects with the Whitetail Trail and leads into Salt Creek's floodplain forest, where backpacker camping sites are available.

Weldon Springs State Park

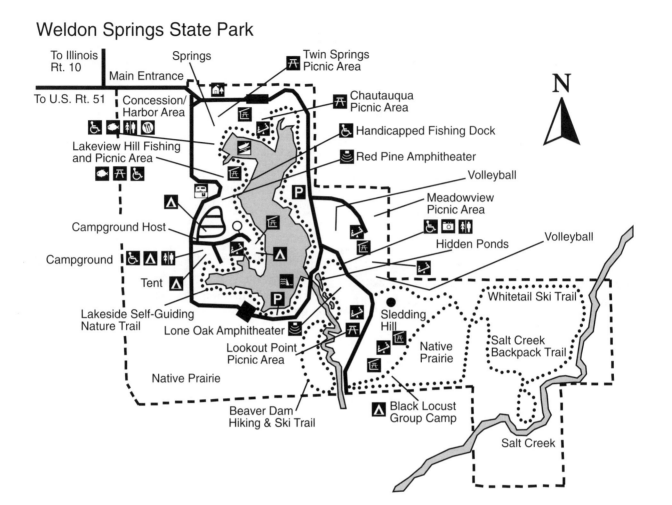

To Illinois Rt. 10

Springs

Twin Springs Picnic Area

Main Entrance

To U.S. Rt. 51

Concession/ Harbor Area

Chautauqua Picnic Area

Handicapped Fishing Dock

Lakeview Hill Fishing and Picnic Area

Red Pine Amphitheater

Volleyball

Meadowview Picnic Area

Campground Host

Volleyball

Campground

Hidden Ponds

Tent

Lakeside Self-Guiding Nature Trail

Whitetail Ski Trail

Lone Oak Amphitheater

Sledding Hill

Native Prairie

Salt Creek Backpack Trail

Lookout Point Picnic Area

Native Prairie

Black Locust Group Camp

Beaver Dam Hiking & Ski Trail

Salt Creek

N

Legend

 Park Office

 Restrooms

P Parking

 Picnic Area

 Shelter

 Dump Station

Campground

Handicapped Access

Playground

Food

Viewing Area

Boat Launch

Fishing

Amphitheater

Dam

• • • Park Trails

Water

Main Roads

▬ ▬ Park Boundary

Beaver Dam Trail 👢👢

Distance Round-Trip: 2 miles

Estimated Hiking Time: 1 hour

While hiking this trail I kept hearing the who-cooks-for-you call of a barred owl. By trail's end the call was louder, without a sighting of the owl as yet. Then a closer inspection with binoculars revealed that one of those dark gray "squirrel nests" in the trees above wasn't a squirrel's nest at all, but rather the largest barred owl I had ever seen!

Caution: Use caution while walking on the narrow ridge top overlooking the hidden ponds. During periods of high water your feet are apt to get a soaking at the creek crossings.

Trail Directions: Begin the trail to the right of the entrance to the Lone Oak Amphitheater near a small parking area. The trail board is framed by large red cedars [1]. Within .1 mi. you can see the amphitheater with the lone white oak butted up against it—thus its name.

Immediately after the amphitheater (.15 mi.) a short side spur will lead to the edge of the hidden ponds [2]. As you walk this spur in spring, look in the water for large, lazy tadpoles and for dragonflies patrolling the water's edge for prey. At .25 mi. the side spur rejoins the original trail (near three cotton-woods); after a few steps cross a creek using its flat rocks [3]. (Some of the rocks are loose so use caution.) The trial now forms a loop—go right.

After you pass a large, rounded hill with oaks arching down its slope, a trail will appear on the right

(.5 mi.). Go right [4], immediately crossing a bridge, and hike through a picnic area. Proceed to the right and follow a fencerow. As you hike, there will be several offshoot trails that lead to the picnic area, but stay near the fencerow.

At .8 mi. walk around a wooden gate [5]. Here the trail skirts a prairie restoration on your left and a floodplain forest on your right. The trail will occasionally be marked with the blue silhouette of a cross-country skier (at least in the winter). The prairie has a nice stand of Indian grass, which turns golden brown in the fall. At 1.05 mi. you will come to the first of two trail intersections [6]. Continue on the trail, going straight ahead. The trail off to the right is the White Tail Ski Trail. In less than .1 mi. the second intersection will appear. Go left at this one, skirting the base of a hill.

Cross the base of this sledding hill (1.2 mi.) [7]. Watch around you in the winter to avoid getting smacked by an out-of-control sledder! Immediately after crossing the sled path, the trail enters an old, gated area. Picnic grounds are on your left and forest is on your right, and the trail here is on an old gravel road lined with honeysuckle. During the winter its bright red berries are enjoyed by numerous cardinals and chickadees.

Cross an open field (mowed area) at 1.5 mi. [8] and leave the gravel path, which continues uphill and to your right. Return instead to the bridge and the remainder of the beaver-dam loop. Cross the bridge and proceed right, with the creek on your right as you hike. At 1.65 mi. you are back at [3]; recross the creek on the stones. Follow the main trail back to the trail entrance, keeping a wary eye out for owls. (Remember that the final .25 mi. is uphill.)

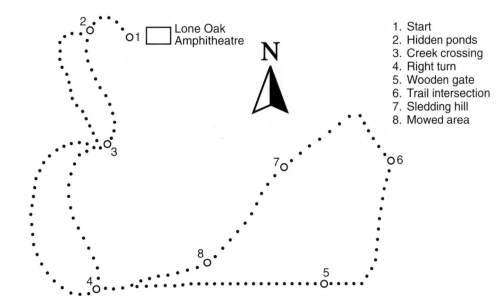

1. Start
2. Hidden ponds
3. Creek crossing
4. Right turn
5. Wooden gate
6. Trail intersection
7. Sledding hill
8. Mowed area

Lakeside Self-Guiding Nature Trail 🥾🥾

Distance Round-Trip: 2 miles

Estimated Hiking Time: 1.25 hours

After petting the large stuffed beaver and feeling its teeth at Union School Interpretive Center, I was ready for a beaver encounter on the trail. The only encounters, though, were numerous views of beaver-created stumps and an occasional trip over a forgotten, beaver-chewed branch across the path.

Caution: The trails can be slippery and have several stairs and relatively steep slopes to navigate.

Trail Directions: Begin the hike near the concession area and large parking lot. First pick up a trail guide at the park office and use it to add to your enjoyment of the hike. The trail starts immediately after you cross the bridge over the spillway (at a signboard outlining the hike) [**1**]. Many of the numbers in the book identify trees along the trail (although the numbers on the trail-guide's map do not correspond to those found in this book).

At .3 mi. [**2**] find a series of wooden steps off to the left. Take these and walk out to the lake's edge, now three times the size of the original one constructed in 1900 by Clinton's Chautauqua entrepreneurs. After admiring the lake, continue on the path. At .6 mi. cross a set of wooden bridges [**3**] and continue onward. The woods around the lake are oak-hickory, and signposts 10 to 12 (.65 mi.) examine some of these trees. A series of steps then climb uphill [**4**].

The earthen dam and spillway are crossed at the 1-mi. point [**5**]. In the winter this area affords a nice view of the resident ducks and geese. During the summer look for barn-, tree-, and rough-winged swallows as they skim the water for a drink while on the wing. After the spillway the trail skirts a picnic area. For the next .5 mi. look for evidence of beavers (gnawed stumps of trees), observe the playful antics of gray squirrels, and listen for the pump-handle squawk of the blue jay.

At 1.5 mi. [**6**] the trail leads away from the lake to a marsh. Within .1 mi. a series of steps will lead downward. As you come off these steps, a large cypress tree is on the left. Cypress trees are more typical of the swampy areas of southern Illinois than of central Illinois, and this one was probably planted here. Although cypresses are related to evergreen pine trees, the conifers lose their needles each fall. Surrounding the tree are knobby structures called *knees*. The height of the knees corresponds to the average high-water level for the area.

After 1.7 mi. [**7**] look for hummingbirds, acrobats of the air that are attracted to the large patches of jewelweed growing in the marsh. An open-area overlook for the marsh provides a ringside seat to watch for muskrats, hummingbirds, and several species of frogs (1.8 mi.) [**8**]. Immediately after the overlook a set of wooden stairs leads down toward the lake. The path now becomes crushed gravel and skirts the lake.

Before you return to the concession area, note an oak grove at 1.9 mi. [**9**]. Within this grove are the springs that gave the park its name! People liked to pitch a tent during the Chautauqua and let the springs keep their food cool. Pink- and white-striped spring beauty carpets this area in early April. To finish the hike, continue through the concession area and back to where your vehicle is parked.

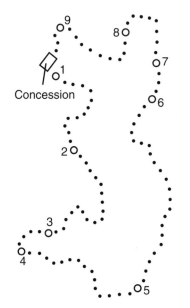

1. Start
2. Steps
3. Wooden bridges
4. Steps
5. Dam
6. Marsh in view
7. Jewelweed
8. Overlook
9. Oak grove

31. Forest Park Nature Preserve

- Enjoy spectacular views of the Illinois River Valley.
- Become a Hundred-Mile Hiker after reaching the century mark on the preserve's trails.
- Visit a woodland oasis located in the third-largest metropolitan area in Illinois.
- See wildflowers decorating the bluffs and ravines each spring and unparalleled color spectacle each fall.

Area Information

In 1839 J. Gould wrote of Peoria, "The bluff comes near to the river, and is covered, as is the narrow strip of bottom land, with a thick growth of timber." In Gould's time, the bluffs overlooking the Illinois River were a mix of oak woodlands and prairie openings that supported a diverse mix of wildlife and plant species. The bluffs at Forest Park Nature Preserve have similar rich woods and prairie openings, providing a window across time to that 1840s landscape.

Forest Park Nature Preserve was dedicated as the 13th nature preserve in Illinois. Although the entire area had been lumbered in the mid-19th century, the forest was allowed to grow back. A few of the old trees are still present in the preserve. Called "wolf trees," these old specimens have the large, outstretched branches indicative of trees that grew in the open. This type of habitat doesn't maintain itself, however, and as you hike you might notice the telltale evidence of fire, used to keep the land open and healthy.

Gould concluded his visit by stating, "On the whole it is the finest site for a town that I ever saw." Forest Park, an oasis of woodland in a busy city and a small remnant of that fine site, today provides a glimpse of what Gould saw and the potential he envisioned.

Directions: From Peoria at the junction of Highways 29 and 150, take Highway 29 north for 3 miles; turn and go west on Gardner Lane .5 mi. to Forest Park Nature Center. The nature preserve is located to the west of the nature center.

Hours Open: The site is open year-round from dawn to dusk. The Nature Center and Nature Store are open Monday through Saturday from 9 A.M. to 5 P.M. and on Sundays from 1 to 5 P.M.

Facilities: The site maintains a Nature Center that houses displays, an area for programs and classes, a well-stocked gift shop, and mileage cards for participants in the hiker club. Water, restrooms, juice and soda machines, and trail maps are also found here. Picnic tables are outside the center.

Permits and Rules: Please leave your pets at home; they are not allowed on the trails or in the area. Dispose of litter properly. Stay on the trails—off-trail hiking only causes erosion and destroys plants. No biking or skiing is allowed.

Further Information: Forest Park Nature Center, 5809 Forest Park Drive, Peoria Heights, IL 61614; 309-686-3360.

Other Areas of Interest

North of I-74 in East Peoria, **Bennett's Terraqueous Gardens** is a small remnant of a seep, complete with spring runs. A boardwalk provides the opportunity for close views of marsh marigold and skunk cabbage. The area is maintained by the Fond du Lac Park District. For more information call 309-699-3923.

Located in northeastern Peoria, **Detweiller Park** contains not only play areas, a golf course, BMX competition area, and an archery range but also a nature preserve. The preserve has lush, spring-blooming wildflowers and two trails, the Ridgetop and Pimiteoui. The area is maintained by the Peoria Park District. For more information call the Forest Park Nature Center.

Wildlife Prairie Park, 10 miles west of Peoria, is home to bison, bobcats, badgers, and 30 other species of mammals that are or were native to Illinois. The grounds are a reclaimed strip mine, its native vegetation once again encouraged. The park includes a visitor center, restaurant, small railroad, and a gift shop. Ten miles of trails visit the animals and tour the park grounds. The longest trail is 4 miles. For more information call Wildlife Prairie Park at 309-676-0998.

Park Trail

Pimiteoui Trail (Forest Park Section) 👢👢👢👢—2.5 miles—A 1.25 mi. linear trail, Pimiteoui begins south of the nature center. The trail hikes along the top of a bluff. Lots of wildflowers may be found here in the spring.

Forest Park
Nature Preserve

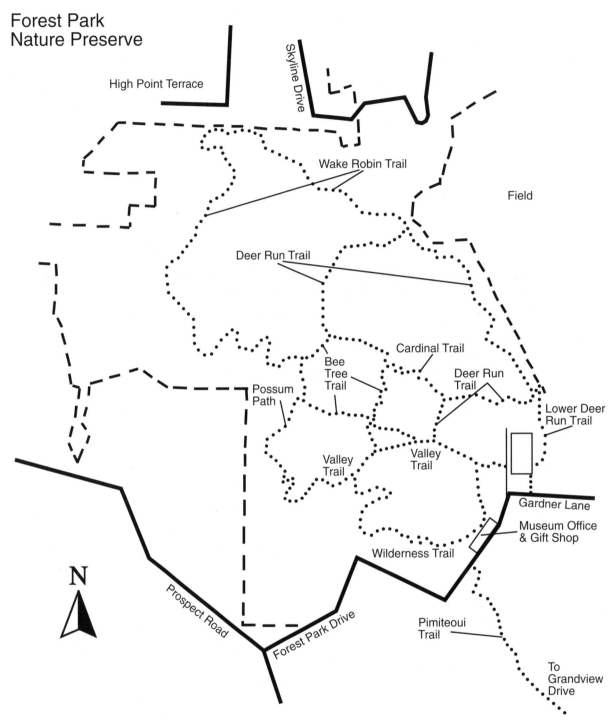

High Point Terrace

Skyline Drive

Wake Robin Trail

Field

Deer Run Trail

Cardinal Trail

Bee
Tree
Trail

Deer Run
Trail

Possum
Path

Lower Deer
Run Trail

Valley
Trail

Valley
Trail

Gardner Lane

Museum Office
& Gift Shop

Wilderness Trail

N

Prospect Road

Forest Park Drive

Pimiteoui
Trail

To
Grandview
Drive

Legend

• • •   Park Trails

━━━   Main Roads

━ ━ ━   Park Boundary

Inside Trail (a Combination)

Distance Round-Trip: 1.75 miles

Estimated Hiking Time: 1 hour

Hiking the trails at Forest Park is like riding a roller coaster—up one ridge, down another, then back up again, and around a switchback. All that's missing is an upside-down, loop-the-loop!

Caution: The trail can be very muddy. Logs sometimes block the way and roots are exposed.

Trail Directions: The trail begins at the southwest corner of the parking lot. The first trail marker is for the Wilderness Trail [1]. Take advantage of several "listening points" along the trail, defined in the trail brochure as "places of quiet where the world can be contemplated with awe." At the start, immediately after crossing a bridge, note a tree with three huge trunks on your right At .15 mi. [2] begin an upward climb on a series of switchbacks (zigzag trails to help the climb). On the climb enjoy the view of the valley below.

The trail emerges on a ridge top, and you soon encounter the first listening point (.3 mi.) [3]. The trail descends, intersecting at .4 mi. [4] with another; go left, winding along a creek on your left. The trail has changed names: It now is called Possum Path (.6 mi.). Along here note the large boulders in the forest understory [5]. Called glacial *erratics*, the boulders lie scattered where the glaciers left them.

At 1 mi. the trail becomes Bee Tree and forks, to the right or straight; proceed straight ahead [6]. As you hike, look for familiar wildflowers but notice the absence of ferns. This is a drier woods, and ferns in the understory have been replaced by woodland grasses and sedges. At 1.2 mi. [7] you will come to two more intersections. Bee Tree Trail intersects with Wake Robin; continue on Bee Tree, going straight. After a few yards, the Bee Tree Trail intersects with Deer Run; go to your right and continue to hike on Bee Tree.

Pause at the River Outlook (1.3 mi.) [8] for a great view of the Illinois River valley. From this vantage point the water is a deep blue and looks like a distant lake. The trail begins a descent and soon intersects with Cardinal Trail. Go straight on the Cardinal Trail and continue to walk downward over a series of switchbacks.

While hiking you'll pass several Restoration Area signs. Although the hike appears to be only through woods, on top of the south-facing ridges there used to be hill prairies. Fires are helping to bring the prairie plants back and restore this habitat. Cardinal Trail soon becomes Deer Run and you have the option of going left or right. Go right (1.5 mi.) [9], and soon you'll enter a prairie restoration on the right.

At 1.6 mi. [10] Deer Run makes a T into Valley Trail; go left on Valley Trail and follow it back to the Nature Center where you can log in your miles as a new member of the Hundred-Mile Hikers.

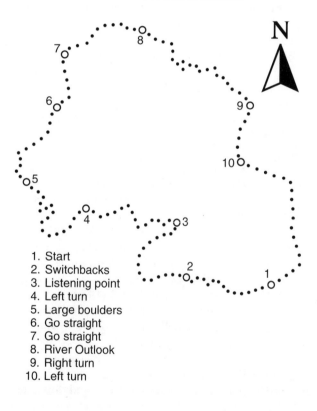

1. Start
2. Switchbacks
3. Listening point
4. Left turn
5. Large boulders
6. Go straight
7. Go straight
8. River Outlook
9. Right turn
10. Left turn

Outside Trail (a Combination)

Distance Round-Trip: 2.75 miles

Estimated Hiking Time: 2 hours

While hiking you could forget the nearby city—except for the noise. This can be remedied if you shuffle your feet through the deep carpet of leaves, although any nearby wildlife will likely scatter.

Caution: The trail can be very muddy. Logs sometimes block the way and tree roots are exposed. Several stream crossings must be navigated on slippery rocks.

Trail Directions: Begin the trail behind the Nature Center [1]. Note the listening points scattered throughout the trail, usually adorned with a bench. The trail, marked with an occasional arrow and the trail's name, begins as a fairly wide path but soon narrows at the base of a bluff.

Before the first listening point the trail intersects with the Valley Trail; take the Valley Trail. At .1 mi. [2] it intersects with Deer Run Trail. Continue straight on Valley Trail. On your right is a prairie restoration. Within .05 mi. Valley Trail and Valley Loop intersect; continue straight and head upward through a rolling, oak-hickory forest.

At .25 mi. [3] cross a bridge and continue straight. You are now on Bee Tree Trail and are continuing the upward trek. Notice the restoration work here—the use of fire and selective plant removal—to bring the area back to original conditions. At the top of the climb (.5 mi.) [4] stay on Bee Tree and go to your right. Within a few steps the trail again intersects another one; this time go left on Wake Robin Trail.

Wildflowers are abundant here in the spring. Dutchman's-breeches are everywhere; mayapple, bloodroot, and prairie trilliums (also called wake robins) are also fairly common.

As you begin the Wake Robin Trail, hike along the edge of a ridge. Note the shaggy bark of the shagbark hickory in this dry forest area. Log steps lead down the ridge, and within .1 mi. you can cross a creek on a makeshift bridge of logs and stones (.75 mi.) [5]. Scramble up the other side and go to the right, heading back uphill. At .9 mi. the trail is again on top of a ridge. Look off into the distance; when there are no leaves on the trees, you can see the Illinois River valley far below [6]. You will also encounter a trail marker near here; go right.

At 1.4 mi. you reach the Wake Robin listening point [7]. On either side is an oak-hickory forest, while straight ahead is a deep, cool ravine with sycamores and a creek. Begin the descent using a handrail and steps, and enter a ravine forest. Gone are the big oaks and in their place are sycamores, cottonwoods, and maples. Look for the yellow blossoms of buttercups here in the spring, and the flowers of blue lobelia in the summer.

Cross the creek the best way you can (no boards or rocks are provided) (1.5 mi.) [8] and scramble up the other side. Note the row of large trees—perhaps part of the original forest. They stand out because the other trees are much smaller. In this section of the trail you can also see the many vines that use the trees for support as they reach for the sun. The vines provide food and cover for animals and enhance the habitat.

Cross another creek (1.65 mi.) [9], this time on stepping stones. Within .1 mi. the trail intersects with Deer Run Trail; continue hiking straight, and you'll reach a farmstead on the left. Remember that the preserve was grazed and is just now recovering. Within a few steps the trail curves to the right. The forest has given way to an old field that has grown up, and you are hiking through maple and elm saplings. Soon the narrow path reenters the bluff forest.

At 2 mi. come upon another listening point [10], and a few yards away note a pair of large, open-grown oaks (wolf trees) on the left. One has a large hole that provides a nesting place for small mammals and a home for a species of mosquito.

Deer Run Trail divides at 2.25 mi. [11]. Take the path to the right and climb uphill. Within .25 mi. you encounter another intersection [12]; proceed to your left, still on Deer Run Trail. At .1 mi. you're back to [2]; go left and retrace your steps back to the Nature Center. Just outside it watch the antics of chipmunks as they steal seed from the numerous bird feeders.

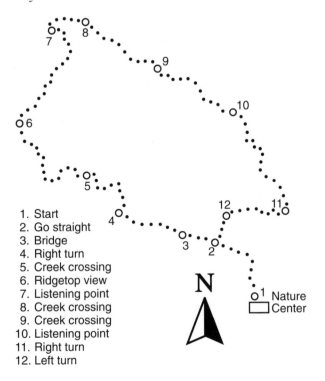

1. Start
2. Go straight
3. Bridge
4. Right turn
5. Creek crossing
6. Ridgetop view
7. Listening point
8. Creek crossing
9. Creek crossing
10. Listening point
11. Right turn
12. Left turn

32. Where Lincoln Walked

- See Lincoln depicted in statuary at various stages in his life.
- Tour the only home Lincoln ever owned and marvel at how Mary Lincoln was able to entertain from the smallest of kitchens.
- Admire the stained glass high up in the state's capitol.
- Even in the city you will find deer, although not necessarily in conventional form.

Area Information

New Salem was founded in 1828 on a ridge above the Sangamon River. Near the many streams in Sangamon County and amid a rich mix of tallgrass prairie and timber, the town's location looked promising, situated as it was on an apparently navigable river and on a road connecting Springfield with Havana. Yet the village never prospered. The needed improvements to make the river navigable never happened. At the village's peak, it had 25 buildings and 100 residents. By 1840, New Salem had ceased to exist.

The village's most famous resident was Abraham Lincoln. Here he studied, worked at several different trades, made his reputation for physical prowess and fairness, and began developing his talent for leadership. After six years in residence, he left the village to begin practicing law in Springfield.

Springfield has been called "the city Lincoln loved." He practiced law here, and he delivered his famous "House Divided" speech in the Old State Capitol. Here he also made key decisions that affected his personal life: He fell in love, married, and bought a home.

Lincoln lived in Springfield for 24 years, and when he left, he said, "To this place, and the kindness of these people, I owe everything." But Springfield is more than Lincoln. Government buildings, museums, statues, and parks wait to be discovered and explored.

Directions: New Salem is 20 miles northwest of Springfield on Route 97. Take Route 125 out of Springfield for 5 miles until it joins Route 97. Turn north on Route 97 and travel north to the park entrance. **Springfield** is located in the center of the state, on I-55 and I-72 .

Hours Open: New Salem is closed on holidays but otherwise is open daily from 9 A.M. to 5 P.M., April to October, and from 8 A.M. to 4 P.M., November to March. Most of the **Springfield** sites are also closed on holidays, but open daily from 9 A.M. to 5 P.M. Check with the city's Visitor Center for individual site hours.

Facilities: New Salem has a Visitor Center, picnic area, restaurant, craft shop, and campground. The city of **Springfield** also has a Visitor Center. A National Park Service Visitor Center is associated with Lincoln's home, and free tickets may be obtained there for the home tour.

Permits and Rules: Put all litter in the nearest available trash container. No flowers, plants, shrubs, or trees may be removed or damaged. Children must be accompanied by adults.

Further Information: Lincoln's New Salem, RR 1, Box 244A, Petersburg, IL 62675; 217-632-4000. Superintendent, Lincoln's Home NHS, 413 S. 8th Street, Springfield, IL 62703; 217-492-4150. Springfield Convention and Visitors Center, 109 North Seventh Street, Springfield, IL 62703; 217-789-2360 or 800-545-7300.

Area Trails

Carpenter Park 👢👢—4.5 miles—Located 3 miles north of Springfield off Business 55, Carpenter Park has 10 interconnecting trails. The 4.5 miles of trails travel through intermittent streams and floodplain forests dominated by large sycamores, silver maples, and box elder trees; by small seeps; and around sandstone and bedrock outcrops. Parts of the park have been dedicated as an Illinois Nature Preserve. For more information contact Springfield Park District, 2500 South 11th Street, P.O. Box 5052, Springfield, IL 62705; 217-554-1751.

Lincoln Memorial Garden 👢—5 miles— The garden is located on the southeast side of Lake Springfield in Springfield. Eighteen interconnecting trails total 5 miles and lead you on a journey through an Illinois landscape similar to what Lincoln experienced. The gardens, designed by the famed landscape architect Jens Jensen, are a living memorial to Abraham Lincoln. For more information contact Lincoln Memorial Garden, 2301 East Lake Drive, Springfield, IL 62707; 217-529-1111.

Springfield

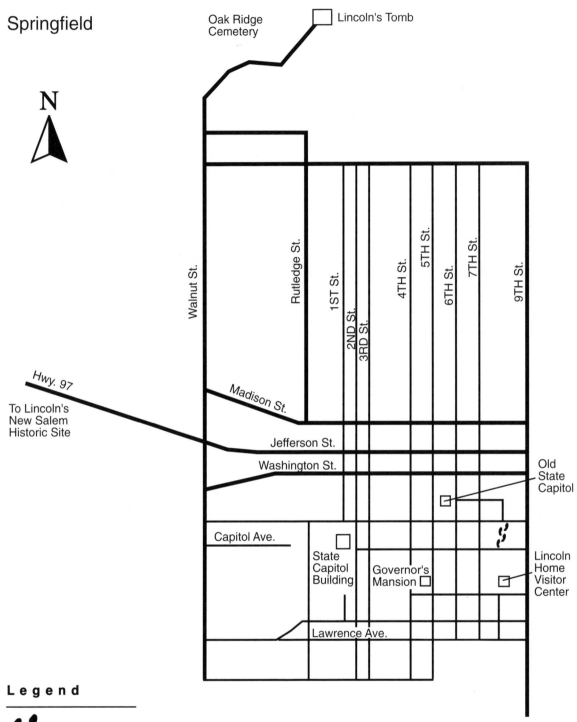

Legend

Foot Path

Main Roads

New Salem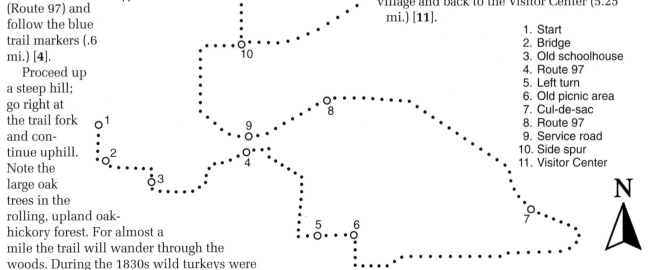

Distance Round-Trip: 5.25 miles

Estimated Hiking Time: 2.5 hours

I wandered in the woods adjacent to the village, walked along the Sangamon River, and strolled the village streets. The thought that came to mind was "from humble beginnings. . . ."

Caution: The trail crosses the highway. During periods of rain, the path will be muddy. Also, beware sticktights, plant seeds that attach to your clothing (especially sweaters) and won't let go.

Trail Directions: After an introduction to the area at the Visitor Center, begin at the south end of the parking lot near a trail board for Mentor Grahams Footsteps [1]. Mentor Graham, a self-educated man, taught school at New Salem for a nickel per pupil per day. He told Lincoln that he "most needed to study grammar." Later, Graham was to comment that Lincoln was the "most studious, diligent, strait forward [sic] young man in the pursuit of knowledge and literature than any [sic] among the five thousand I have taught in schools."

The trail, marked with blue markers with a white hiker silhouette, traverses second- and third-growth oak woods along a meandering stream. At .15 mi. [2] the trail crosses a bridge where the stream's bank is lined with Christmas ferns. Immediately after crossing the bridge, the trail splits; go uphill, following the blue trail marker.

At .30 mi. [3] you'll come upon the remnants of an old schoolhouse; on your left, surrounded by a split-rail fence, is an old cemetery. Cross another bridge and exit the woods near the main park entrance. Turn right, and soon cross the road (Route 97) and follow the blue trail markers (.6 mi.) [4].

Proceed up a steep hill; go right at the trail fork and continue uphill. Note the large oak trees in the rolling, upland oak-hickory forest. For almost a mile the trail will wander through the woods. During the 1830s wild turkeys were plentiful in here, whereas deer were scarce. Today, the opposite is true; the turkeys have vanished, but deer are everywhere.

Exit the woods (1.5 mi.) [5] and turn left, following a park road. After a few steps the trail goes right onto a grassy path through a sumac thicket. You are now hiking through a late successional old field with lots of shrubs. At 2.3 mi. [6] come to a grassy area that once may have been a picnic area. The restrooms on the right are nonfunctional. Continue onward for another .1 mi., where the trail crosses the road. This is not well marked; all that is left of the marker is the pole. Cross over the drainage ditch, cross the road, and hike along it.

The road winds downhill, turns left, and ends in a cul-de-sac; the Sangamon River is on your right. The blue markers are few and far between along this stretch.

At 3 mi. [7] you reach the cul-de-sac. Continue straight ahead, and after a few steps a trail marker will direct you to the right. Here you will join the old Pritchetville road. Turn left onto this old, one-lane asphalt roadbed that winds along the Sangamon. Cross Route 97 again at 3.6 mi. [8], using caution, and pass by a statue of Abraham Lincoln on horseback. A nearby log cabin structure has restrooms.

The trail now runs along the park entrance road, but within .25 mi. turns to your right and onto a service road (3.8 mi.) [9]. Hike up a hill to the village. Turn left and begin to wander through, exploring the buildings and marveling at the large ram. After passing the tavern, the trail marker indicates left; instead, go right for a side spur at 4.2 mi. [10] to the saw and grist mill.

Go to your right, down the steps and across a bridge to the grist mill, and explore the first structure in the village of New Salem. Retrace your steps back to [10] and continue your tour of the village.

Take time to peer into the log houses and read the signage above them as you wander through the village and back to the Visitor Center (5.25 mi.) [11].

1. Start
2. Bridge
3. Old schoolhouse
4. Route 97
5. Left turn
6. Old picnic area
7. Cul-de-sac
8. Route 97
9. Service road
10. Side spur
11. Visitor Center

N

Springfield 👢👢

Distance Round-Trip: 6.5 miles

Estimated Hiking Time: 4 hours

As you hike, try to find the state's symbols—big bluestem, white oak, deer, cardinal, violet, and monarch—all present when Lincoln walked here. While you may find it difficult to spot the last three, depending on the season, you will find huge specimens of white oaks and even an urban deer (the heavy metal kind!).

Caution: The parking lot may be crowded during summer weekends. Some street crossings may be busy.

Trail Directions: Park at Lincoln's Tomb, where there is free parking, restrooms, and water. Begin at the bust of Lincoln in front of his tomb [**1**]. Walk through the tomb and observe the various statues of Lincoln in the alcoves.

Exit the tomb and go left and down an asphalt path. Halfway around, take a staircase to the right for a side spur. Turn left at the bottom of the steps. Within a few feet you will encounter the public receiving vault for Abraham Lincoln. Retrace your steps to the tomb and continue circling it to the right.

Go to your right and through the parking lot (.2 mi.) [**2**]; follow the cemetery road down the hill. Go right and follow the signs leading to the Illinois Vietnam Veterans Memorial. After visiting the Memorial, exit the cemetery from the west gate onto North Walnut Street and go left (.7 mi.) [**3**]. No sidewalk is present, so walk on the grassy border between the cemetery fence and the street. After one block turn left on Yates Street, again using the grassy strip. Follow Yates to Rutledge Street and turn right.

Stay on Rutledge for 1 mi. until it dead-ends into Madison; turn left on Madison (2 mi.) [**4**]. Follow Madison to First Street and take a right. Follow First to Monroe Street. Cross Monroe Street and go right (2.4 mi.) [**5**], following Monroe to College Street. On College, walk past the Illinois Visitor Center and note the huge metal deer made from car bumpers.

Follow College Street to Edwards and turn left. On Edwards you will walk past the Illinois State Museum. Follow Edwards to Second Street and turn left (3 mi.) [**6**]. Inside the State Capitol a block ahead you can obtain a brochure about the statues that line Second Street [**7**].

Follow the granite path into the Capitol. After you have finished exploring, exit the same way you entered and return to Second Street.

Cross the street and follow Capitol Street to Fifth; go right (3.4 mi.) [**8**]. After one block the Governor's Mansion will be on your right. Take Fifth Street to Edwards and turn right. Walking on Edwards you will pass by the Governor's Mansion.

Follow Edwards to Fourth Street and turn left on Fourth. Follow Fourth to Lawrence and take a side spur (right) to the Dana-Thomas house [**9**]. After viewing the house, retrace your steps to Fourth and Lawrence (3.75 mi.) and continue east (straight) on Lawrence.

Follow Lawrence to Seventh Street and turn left. Follow Seventh to the Lincoln's Home Visitor Center (4 mi.) [**10**]. At the Center obtain a free ticket to tour the house.

From Lincoln's Home go left on Eighth Street (the home faces Eighth Street). Cross Capitol Street and walk through a complex of city buildings and a minipark. Turn left on Adams Street (4.6 mi.) [**11**] and follow it to Sixth. Turn right on Sixth—the Old State Capitol is on the left (4.7 mi.) [**12**]. In the rotunda of the Capitol is an original copy of the Gettysburg Address. Across the street at Bank One is the original ledger (on display) of Lincoln's account at Marine Bank.

Follow Sixth Street to Jefferson and turn left. Continue to Second Street and turn right (5.2 mi.) [**13**]. Follow Second for about a mile to North Grand Avenue. Go left on North Grand and follow it to Monument Avenue (less than one block) (6.2 mi.); go right [**14**].

Once you have arrived at the entrance to Oak Ridge Cemetery, continue straight on the cemetery road. You can see the tomb ahead. Before taking the asphalt trail to your right, look at the unique John Tanner monument on your left. An asphalt trail leads to the front of the tomb where you began the hike.

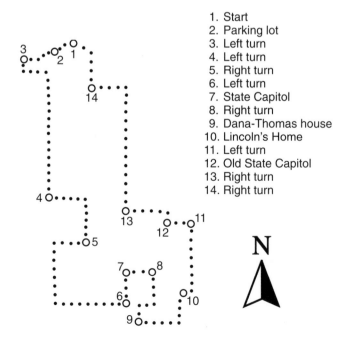

1. Start
2. Parking lot
3. Left turn
4. Left turn
5. Right turn
6. Left turn
7. State Capitol
8. Right turn
9. Dana-Thomas house
10. Lincoln's Home
11. Left turn
12. Old State Capitol
13. Right turn
14. Right turn

33. Sand Ridge State Forest

- Climb a 60-foot-high sand dune in central Illinois.
- Find a prairie in a round bowl (*quiver prairie*).
- Relive a piece of botanical history, walking in the footsteps of the famous botanist Henry A. Gleason.
- Celebrate the beginning of summer with the waxy, yellow blossoms of prickly-pear cactus.
- Enjoy a different group of fall colors—russet prairie grasses, red-brown blackjack oaks, and gray-green prickly pears.

Area Information

The gently rolling sand dunes, expanses of oak-hickory forest, and stretches of sand prairie found at Sand Ridge State Forest contrast sharply with the black-soil landscape of central Illinois. The sand, deposited in the Illinois River valley a few thousand years ago by the meltwaters of the Wisconsinan glacier, creates a special home for a unique collection of plants and animals. The flora here is a combination of plants common to the tall grass prairie of Illinois—little bluestem, butterfly weed, and rough blazing star—and western plants usually associated with drier open habitats—prickly-pear cactus and silvery bladder pod.

The growing conditions here are strikingly different from those found on the black-soil prairies. Although the sandy areas receive the same amounts of heat, light, rainfall, and wind as the rest of the state, they experience larger variations in day-to-night and surface-to-subsoil temperatures. The water-holding capacity of the sandy soil is very low, and in open areas the surface sand is constantly shifting, sometimes forming dunes or blowouts (areas where the sand and vegetation are blown away by the wind). All these contribute to the landscape that Gleason found so fascinating and explored for nearly 60 years.

Directions: Sand Ridge State Forest is located in Mason County, about 25 miles southwest of Peoria. From Manito, go west on 2500 N and follow the directional signs. Once past the road to the Jake Wolf Fish Hatchery, the trailhead for the North Section hike is at .8 mile. The Henry A. Gleason preserve is on the western edge of Sand Ridge State Forest.

Hours Open: The site is open year-round.

Facilities: A picnic area provides grills, water, toilets, and a shelter. Campsites feature water, pit toilets, and a dump station. There is no electricity. Group camping and equestrian camping are also available. A hand-trap shooting range, hunting, horse trails, cross-country ski trails, and snowmobiling are also featured.

Permits and Rules: No horses or pets are allowed in Henry Allen Gleason Nature Preserve. In other areas of the forest, pets must be kept on a leash at all times.

Further Information: Sand Ridge State Forest, P.O. Box 111, Forest City, IL 61532; 309-597-2212.

Other Areas of Interest

Located in Mason County, the **Chautauqua National Wildlife Refuge** each fall and winter offers some of the greatest concentrations of wild ducks and geese to be observed along the Illinois River. In addition to wildlife watching, the refuge provides fishing, mushroom and berry picking, boat access, and hunting. An interpretive hiking trail is located at the site headquarters. For more information call 309-535-2290.

Dickson Mounds Museum, situated between Lewistown and Havana, is a center for the study and interpretation of the prehistory of the Illinois River valley. Here you can explore the world of the Native Americans who lived in the Illinois River valley. For more information call 309-547-3721.

Rock Island Trail State Park is a 26-mile linear, rail-to-trail from Alta, in Peoria County, to Toulon, in Stark County. This trail is a railroad which was converted into a hiking trail after the track was removed. The pathway is well marked with directional signs and mile markers. Along the way you will pass Kickapoo Creek Recreation Area where you can find water and primitive camping, old railroad depots, and vistas of the Spoon River. For more information call 309-695-2228.

Park Trails

Sand Ridge offers 44 miles of marked trails ranging from 1.6 to 17 miles each, and 120 miles of fire lanes affording plenty of hiking opportunities. Most of the trails are on sand and are shared by horses.

Sand Ridge State Forest

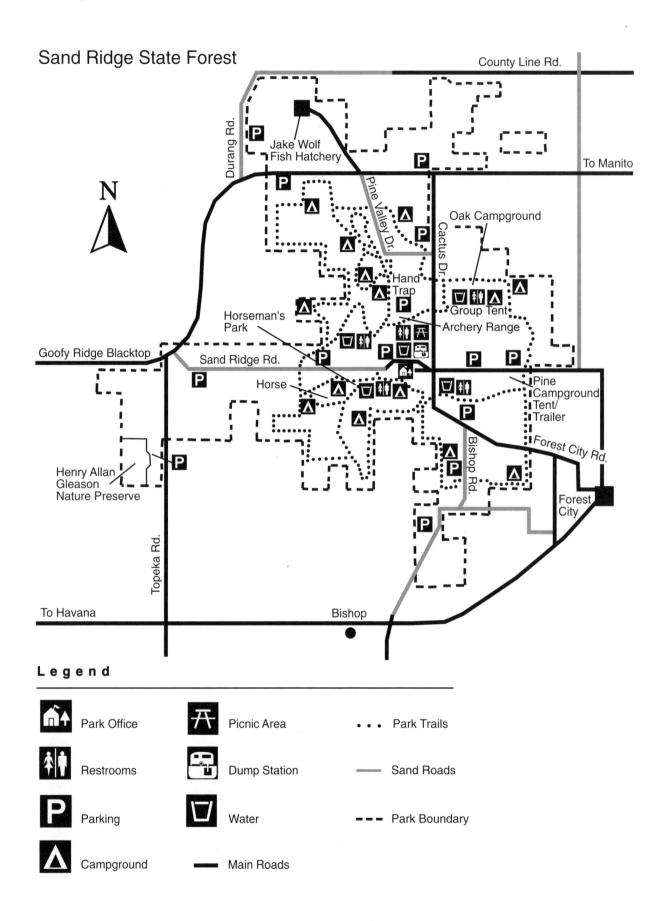

Legend

🏠 Park Office	🔼 Picnic Area	• • • Park Trails
🚻 Restrooms	🚐 Dump Station	── Sand Roads
P Parking	🥤 Water	─ ─ ─ Park Boundary
⛺ Campground	── Main Roads	

North Section 👢👢👢👢

Distance Round-Trip: 5.6 miles

Estimated Hiking Time: 2.5 hours

The trail is pure sand, and cactus lines parts of the path—the Illinois version of a desert. At noon on a sunny, summer day, the turkey vultures circling overhead may bring to mind Death Valley—only forested.

Caution: The trail is sand and can sometimes be very hard to negotiate. Horses also use parts of it, so watch where you step. Take along water for this hike!

Trail Directions: Stop at the first parking area, on the south side of 2500 N, just after you pass the road to Jake Wolf Fish Hatchery. Begin the trail at the south edge of the parking area [**1**] on a forest road. The trail will curve left twice, but before the second curve, catch your first glimpse of prickly-pear cactus. At .3 mi. come to a trail intersection; go right [**2**]. At this point the trail is marked with yellow and blue squares.

Ignore the fire lanes on your left at .6 mi. and again at .7 mi. At .9 mi., at the trail intersection, go right [**3**].

At 1.15 mi. [**4**] begin to go downhill on a vegetated, old dune. Look for a faint trail off to your left between 1.25 and 1.3 mi. (and two trail markers, one on a curve). If you hit the curve in the trail, you have gone too far. Take this faint trail for a side spur to a quiver prairie [**5**]. The path will be lined with oaks and suddenly you find yourself in a large open area (a bowl), lined with scrubby oaks and filled with prairie grasses. On the ground black moss grows with cactus. If you see this, you have discovered the quiver prairie. Afterward, retrace your steps to the trail.

The trail will curve to the right between two large red oaks. The trail curves left at 1.6 mi. [**6**] and goes through a more mature forest, still dominated by oaks. At 2 mi. [**7**] you'll come to a trail intersection; go left, following green trail markers (squares) on a trail for hikers only. Within a few feet is another intersection; go right (straight leads you to a camp-site).

The trail has narrowed, and the mixed woods gives way to pines. The trail suddenly widens with an open area on the right and lots of prickly-pear cactus. At 2.35 mi. pass by a path on your left. Also ignore the trail off to your right at 2.55 mi. At 2.8 mi. you will come to the intersection of several trails [**8**]. Go left on the trail nearest to you. This trail is now marked with blue, and cedars will soon line the path. Another trail intersection occurs at 3 mi. [**9**]; continue straight ahead through the cedars on the blue trail.

Yet another trail intersection appears at 3.15 mi.; go left [**10**], staying on the blue trail, hike into an oak woods, and then go uphill, walking in a gully. The brown trail will be to your left; ignore it.

At 3.5 mi. come to another trail intersection. Take a short spur to stand atop a sand dune and view the expanse of forest below. Retrace your steps to the trail and go right [**11**] on a narrow path through some large oaks, winding your way downhill. At 3.7 mi. go left and up a dune. The trail forms a T at 3.85 mi.; go right on a wide path through scrub oak forest and up another dune [**12**]. Pines again line the trail.

At 4.15 mi. the blue trail intersects with the yellow one; continue uphill on the trail now marked blue/yellow [**13**]. Both sides of this undulating trail are lined with cactus. Before the trail curves left and skirts a paved road, look to your left at a large open patch of ground. In May, this is a carpet of pale-blue sand phlox (4.45 mi.) [**14**]. The trail next skirts the road, winding through oak woods with trees that range from very small to very large.

At 4.9 mi. the trail finally curves away from the road, and at 5.15 mi. it curves right and heads upward [**15**]. At a Y-intersection at 5.3 mi. you'll find yourself back at [**2**]. Go right and retrace your steps to the parking area.

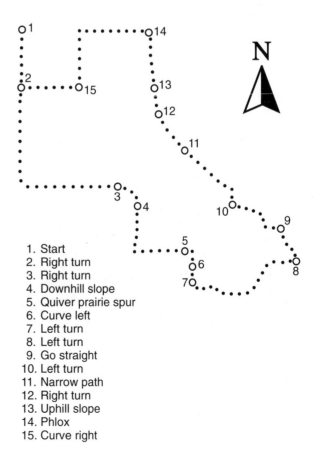

1. Start
2. Right turn
3. Right turn
4. Downhill slope
5. Quiver prairie spur
6. Curve left
7. Left turn
8. Left turn
9. Go straight
10. Left turn
11. Narrow path
12. Right turn
13. Uphill slope
14. Phlox
15. Curve right

Henry Allen Gleason Nature Preserve 👢👢

Distance Round-Trip: 1.15 miles

Estimated Hiking Time: .75 hour

Botanist Henry A. Gleason, known worldwide for his publication The New Britton and Brown Illustrated Flora of the Northeastern United States and Adjacent Canada, *explored the sand areas around Havana in the early 1900s while a student at the University of Illinois. Let's retrace his steps to discover and explore Devil's Neck.*

Caution: There is no formal trail, but the well-worn path is easy to follow. Stay on the path, however, as too many offshoot trails will damage the habitat.

Trail Directions: Park at the sign off Topeka Road for the Henry Allen Gleason Nature Preserve and begin the trail here [**1**]. At .1 mi. you should encounter a brown Illinois Nature Preserve sign. This will also mark the first indication that you are about to explore an unusual area. A large dune, about 60 feet high and covered with prickly-pear cactus and little bluestem, looms in front. Enter through the gate [**2**] and head up the well-worn path over the sand dune.

At .2 mi. enter a grove of blackjack oaks. Take a look at their leaves, said to resemble a duck's feet. At .25 mi. you are high enough on the dune to enjoy a vista of the farmland below. The vegetation around you consists of switch grass, little bluestem, an occasional blackjack oak, and the ever-present cactus. Take an abrupt right [**3**] and continue to follow the faint trail.

You are skirting the large dune on your left. Look for false Solomon's seal under the oaks. At .4 mi. you will come to a trail intersection; go left and up the dune [**4**]. Once on top, the trail disappears. Go to your right (gently) and explore Devil's Neck, the 60-foot-high dune overlooking the Illinois River valley.

Gleason writes about his first visit here on August 17, 1904, "By far the most interesting visit was to the Devil's Neck, a large wild expanse of blow sand, where we found many interesting things, especially unlimited quanti-ties of *Cristatella jamesii* [a species of clammyweed] and a few plants of *Lesquerella spathulata* [silvery bladder pod] hitherto known only from Northwestern Nebraska and Montana."

Go right, walking along the top, and at .5 mi. go down into the blowout on the left, being careful not to disturb the sand [**5**]. If your visit is in May, look for the silvery bladder pod—a yellow mustard. Although the plant is not the typical showy wildflower, it is important. This is its only location for hundreds of miles, the only other eastern site for this plant being in Minnesota. Head across the blowout to further explore the area. Go right again and begin to walk along the rim. Look for showy, orange butterfly weed, listen for the call of the dickcissel, watch for the colorful wings of grasshoppers, and observe the sulphur, buckeye, and monarch butterflies. Hike the perimeter of the blowout until you are near the point where you descended into it. From here take one final look at the impressive view and go left and back down the dune. Soon you will be back at [**4**].

Go left, and continue on the original path. The trail ends at a fence (.75 mi.) [**6**]. Climb over the chain and go right, walking on an old road that skirts the preserve. As you walk, look for a less rare and less welcome mustard—garlic mustard—a nonnative plant that is taking over many Illinois woodlands.

Shortly after receiving the news that the sand dune where he first saw *Lesquerella* in Illinois would be a nature preserve named after him, Gleason wrote to the chairman of the Nature Preserves Commission, "Sixty-seven years have rolled by since my first discovery of *Lesquerella* in Illinois. We had no cars in those days, and my trips entailed a four-mile walk out, another one back, and probably five or six hours' work on those bare dunes of sun-burnt sand. But when I was last there, in 1966, *Lesquerella* was still growing on top of the highest dune as before, and doubtless has been growing since the Xerothermic Period, at least five thousand years ago."

At 1.05 mi. you are back at [**2**]; go left and retrace your steps to the parking area. Although this trail wasn't long in distance, you hiked in time to a piece of the state's botanical history, back through the time of Gleason and back some 5,000 years.

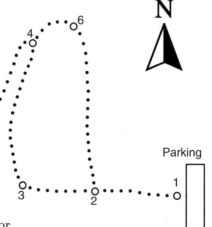

N

1. Start
2. Gate
3. Right turn
4. Left up dune
5. Blowout
6. Fence

Parking

34. Argyle Lake State Park

- Discover the parklike setting of a unique plant community—oak openings.
- Look for trees with the kind of large, gnarled, outreaching limbs that attacked Dorothy and her friends in *The Wizard of Oz*.
- Enjoy a hike redolent of northern woods and bursting with spring wildflowers, especially bird's-foot violet.

Area Information

The hills and valleys of Argyle Lake State Park encompass what once was known as Argyle Hollow, part of the old stagecoach route between Galena and Beardstown. The lake now occupies most of Argyle Hollow.

Although the hollow is gone, land preservationists are helping maintain another area of the park as travelers on a stagecoach journey might have seen it—an oak opening. This kind of habitat, a transition zone between prairie and forest, used to occur in several parts of the state. Early travelers described such oak openings:

> Green groves, arranged with the regularity of art, making shady alleys, for the heated traveler. . . . Among the "oak-openings" you find some of the most lovely landscapes of the West. . . . Here, trees grouped or standing single—and there, arranged in long avenues as though by human hands, with slips of meadow between.

What is your impression of this landscape and the opening at mile 3.35? Were the early visitors wrong? Take time to admire this once common habitat, so rare today.

Directions: Argyle Lake State Park is located west of Macomb. Travel Route 136 west from Macomb to Colchester and follow the signs north into the park.

Hours Open: The site is open year-round, except on Christmas and New Year's Day.

Facilities: Modern camping facilities with showers are found here, along with picnicking, a concession stand and restaurant, boating, fishing, and horseback riding.

Permits and Rules: Part of the trail is located in a dedicated Illinois Nature Preserve: No pets are allowed on the trails. Do not pick or disturb the wildflowers.

Further Information: Site Superintendent, Argyle Lake State Park, 640 Argyle Park Road, Colchester, IL 62326; 309-776-3422.

Other Areas of Interest

Located in Schuyler County, 30 minutes from Macomb, **Weinberg-King State Park** offers camping, fishing, hunting, equestrian trails, and picnicking. Williams Creek runs through the park, and along with the rolling terrain it provides habitat for an abundance of wildlife. For more information call 217-392-2345.

© Michael Jeffords

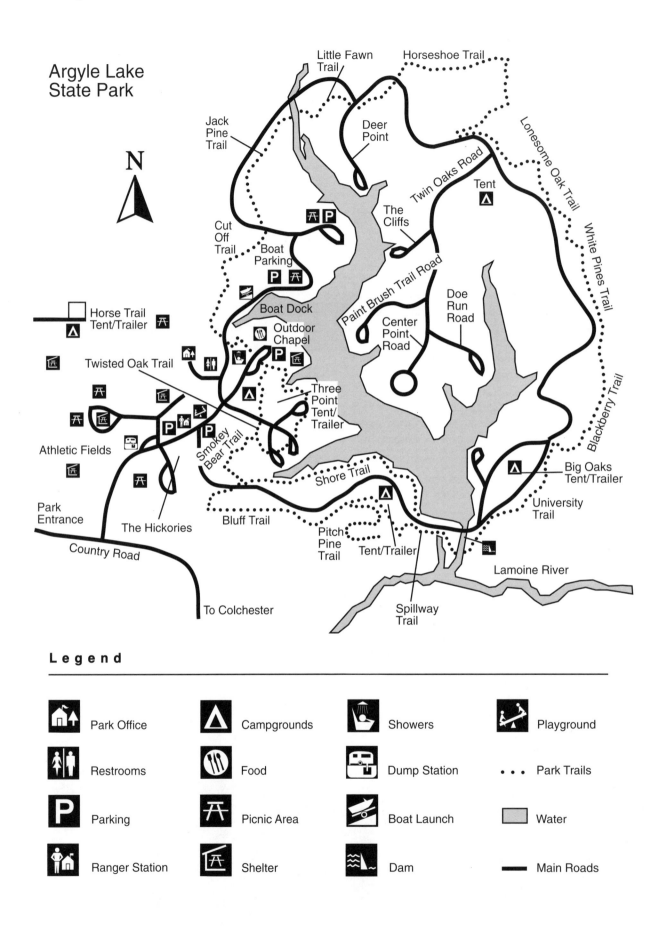

Argyle Lake State Park

Little Fawn Trail

Horseshoe Trail

Jack Pine Trail

Deer Point

N

Twin Oaks Road

Tent

Lonesome Oak Trail

White Pines Trail

Cut Off Trail

The Cliffs

Boat Parking

Paint Brush Trail Road

Doe Run Road

Boat Dock

Horse Trail
Tent/Trailer

Outdoor Chapel

Center Point Road

Twisted Oak Trail

Three Point Tent/Trailer

Blackberry Trail

Athletic Fields

Smokey Bear Trail

Park Entrance

Shore Trail

Big Oaks Tent/Trailer

University Trail

The Hickories

Bluff Trail

Country Road

Pitch Pine Trail

Tent/Trailer

Lamoine River

To Colchester

Spillway Trail

Legend

	Park Office		Campgrounds		Showers		Playground
	Restrooms		Food		Dump Station	...	Park Trails
P	Parking		Picnic Area		Boat Launch		Water
	Ranger Station		Shelter		Dam	—	Main Roads

Trail of Many Names 👢👢👢👢

Distance Round-Trip: 5.75 miles

Estimated Hiking Time: 3.25 hours

The hike through (and aroma of) pitch and white pines evokes summers spent in the far northern woods, but the trail's oak opening is a sight nearly unique to Illinois.

Caution: The trail can be very muddy. Logs sometimes lie in the pathway, and some roots are exposed.

Trail Directions: The route circles the lake and links together several smaller trails, each with its own name. Although you can start at any trailhead, this guide begins at the Bluff Trail trail board. From there go left [1]. The trail parallels the road as you hike through a red pine plantation. Soon the path becomes the Pitch Pine Trail, with an appropriate change in tree species. At .25 mi. cross the wooden plank bridge over the small creek and bear to the right [2]. Go right again at a rock and a log in the path and head toward the picnic area.

At the picnic area go right, skirting the edge of the forest and the picnic grounds. The trail soon heads back into the woods and curves left at .5 mi. [3]. From here, go down wooden steps to a trail intersection, and go left where you will encounter a switchback and an uphill trek. As the trail heads back down, the parking area for the Spillway Trail will be on your left; the spillway will soon appear at .65 mi. [4]. After crossing a rocky overflow area, the trail heads into floodplain woods. Soon you must cross the spillway using the shallows and immediately go left up a cement draw to the road. Follow the park road uphill for a short distance.

At the top of the hill the trail reappears on the right. Head into the woods and through more pines (.85 mi.) [5]. From here the trail descends, crosses a wooden bridge, and heads left. As you hike through this second growth of oak-hickory woods, look for large oaks. In spring, seek out mayapple, spring beauty, and Virginia bluebells. Notice the old coal-mining pit on your left (1.2 mi.) [6]. Coal was mined here beginning in 1850, using drift mines with tunnels only 36 inches high! If you look on the trail you can still see bits of coal. The trail now heads up a steep, reinforced grade. Notice all the Jack-in-the-pulpits around you; by late summer their fruit (bright red berries) will be all that remains.

At the trail intersection at 1.35 mi. go right and through the pines [7]. A picnic area is on your left. The trail forks at 1.65 mi.; go left and come to an intersection where you should continue straight [8]. This segment of the trail is named White Pine and will lead in and out of old pine plantings. Enjoy the carpet of needles and the fragrance of the pines. Two miles brings you out of the pines and downward; go right [9]. After crossing two wooden footbridges, go right again. You are now hiking on a ridge overlooking the road.

Descend the wooden steps at 2.15 mi., go to the right [10] and cross another bridge. The trail now heads up. Within .1 mi. you will come to an intersection; go right and uphill again [11]. Do the oaks in this section of the trail remind you of anything? (Hint: ever see *The Wizard of Oz*?) At 2.45 mi. another trailhead comes in; go right [12] (on your left there is a toilet and the road). You are now on Horseshoe Trail. The trail skirts the metal guide rail on the road, goes back into the woods, crosses a bridge, and heads upward on wooden steps.

At 2.7 mi. you'll encounter another bridge and more steps [13]. At the trail's intersection at 2.9 mi., go left [14]. You will be hiking through a very disturbed woods—honeysuckle and multiflora rose line the path, and the clean, open understory is gone. When you reach the intersection at 3.1 mi., go left. The trail will emerge on the park road [15]; cross it and begin on the other side. Soon you will recross the road as the trail heads toward an Illinois Nature Preserve—Argyle Hollow Barrens (3.35 mi.) [16].

Take time to savor this rare plant community—an intermediate stage between prairie and forest. Early visitors described these openings as well-kept parks. The large white and black oaks have open crowns, and the vegetation underneath them comprises prairie plants such as little bluestem. Instead of the normal spring wildflowers, look for bi-colored, bird's-foot violets growing among the mounds of lichens and moss. Around Labor Day, look for the large, yellow blossoms of false foxglove. Stop and admire how the large oaks grow up and down the ravine. At 3.5 mi. head down the steps, away from this special place, and cross a bridge [17].

The trail comes out on the road. Take a short spur to your right to see another example of a drift coal mine with an information sign. If you are tired from hiking, imagine what spending 16 hours in that mine must have been like! Retrace your steps and rejoin the trail on the left as it goes uphill at 3.6 mi. [18]. During spring, this hillside is covered with flowers; identifying them may take your mind off the steep climb. At the top, go left on a trail through rich woods with lots of bloodroot. On your left is a view of the lake. The Cutoff trailhead is at 3.75 mi.; go left [19]. You will again cross the road and head down to walk through a successional forest; for a short distance, the path is made of shale.

Look to your left (4.05 mi.) [20] where water from a drainpipe has eroded the shale, allowing you to see several layers. At 4.15 mi. take the trail off to the right [21]. You will soon go down wooden steps and cross an old, one-lane road. The trail comes out near the park road and boat rental area (4.4 mi.) [22]. Cross the road and go up the other side on wooden steps. You can pause at the top to see a large oak tree on the left. Continue upward, and the trail soon comes out at the campground. Cross the road and go back into the woods at campsite 8A.

At 4.65 mi. go down the wooden steps, bear right, and cross a bridge [23]. On your left is the lake and on your right is a hill—covered in spring with wild ginger and large patches of yellow bellwort. The trail soon heads up and you reach a lake overlook (4.8 mi.) [24]. From here, the trail heads uphill on railroad-tie, reinforced steps. By early May the ground is covered with wild geranium. About a quarter of the way up ignore a faint trail to the left, the remains of an old nature trail. Once at the top, go left and pass through an old picnic area with a parking circle on the right [25].

You will come to a trail board at 5 mi.; go right, skirting the campground as you walk through woods. At several points the trail will go in and out of the campground. You will come off a bridge and go left at 5.25 mi. [26]. Within .25 mi. go down steps and cross the park road [27]. Notice the coal pieces in the trail

as you hike this final section. On your left is a sandstone-over-shale bluff. From here you begin a long switchback, go through a final pine plantation, and soon return to your vehicle.

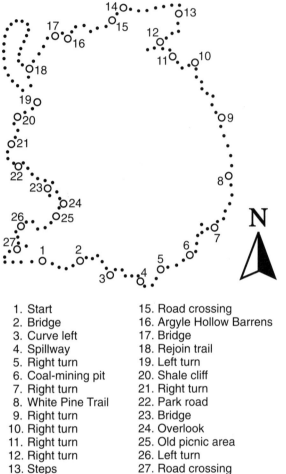

1. Start	15. Road crossing
2. Bridge	16. Argyle Hollow Barrens
3. Curve left	17. Bridge
4. Spillway	18. Rejoin trail
5. Right turn	19. Left turn
6. Coal-mining pit	20. Shale cliff
7. Right turn	21. Right turn
8. White Pine Trail	22. Park road
9. Right turn	23. Bridge
10. Right turn	24. Overlook
11. Right turn	25. Old picnic area
12. Right turn	26. Left turn
13. Steps	27. Road crossing
14. Left turn	

35. Siloam Springs State Park

- Hike to the deafening din of spring peepers (frogs).
- Enjoy idyllic ravines with fern-covered hillsides and rushing streams.
- Pass by an oak opening.
- While the curative springs may be gone, a hike on one of the park's trails may just cure whatever ails you.

Area Information

Siloam Springs State Park, an area of rolling hills, prairies, and forests, is one of the larger parks in the state. It was named by Rev. Reuben McCoy, a minister from the neighboring town of Clayton, for the Pool of Siloam where the miracle of the blind man occurred. The reverend saw a similarity to the healing efficacy of these Illinois waters.

The springs that issued from the ravine slopes had a high mineral content and were believed to be the cure-all for everything from cancer and kidney problems to drunkenness. A little community grew up around the springs, and the Siloam Forest Hotel resort (built in 1884) offered a bath house, swimming, and a pool to make the waters readily available to the public.

The village suffered when the railroad—and medical science—passed it by. The springs became contaminated and were sealed off. The present picnic area is where the small village once stood, and all that remains of the park's past are two stone foundations—one of which can be viewed from the Red Oak Trail.

Directions: Siloam Springs is 25 miles east of Quincy and north of where Adams, Brown, and Pike counties intersect. From Route 104, go north on 2873 E to the park entrance on the east side.

Hours Open: The site is open year-round except on Christmas and New Year's Day.

Facilities: A concession stand offers boat and canoe rentals; there are campgrounds with showers and electricity, a picnic area with shelters and grills, horse trails and equestrian camping, and hunting.

Permits and Rules: Pets must be leashed at all times.

Further Information: Site Superintendent, Siloam Springs State Park, RR 1, Box 204, Clayton, IL 62324; 217-894-6205.

Other Areas of Interest

Siloam Springs is a little more than an hour's drive from **Nauvoo** (see park #38) to the northwest, **New Salem** (see park #32) to the northeast, and **Argyle Lake State Park** (see park #34) to the north.

Park Trails

Crabapple Trail —.6 miles—This is a linear trail that follows McKee Creek and heads north toward the lake. Rock outcrops along the creek and a pleasant meandering stream are highlights.

Prairie Bluff Trail —1 mile—This trail may be accessed from the Crab Apple Creek Trail. It crosses McKee Creek, goes up a hill (with a great view at the top), and heads toward the lake's earthen dam.

Siloam Springs
State Park

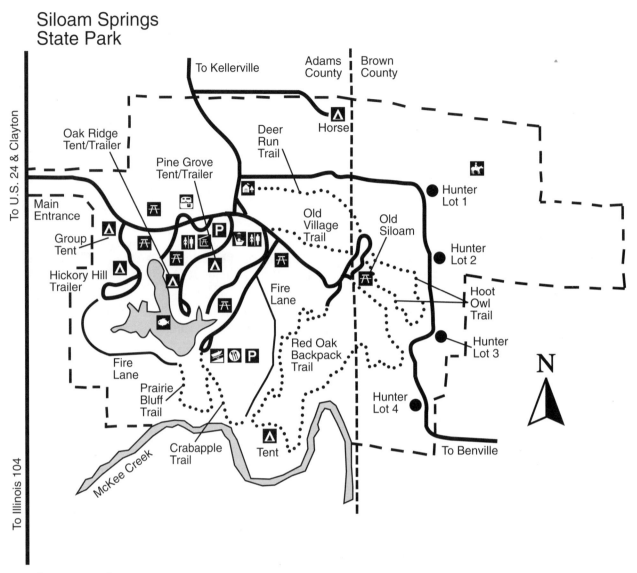

Legend

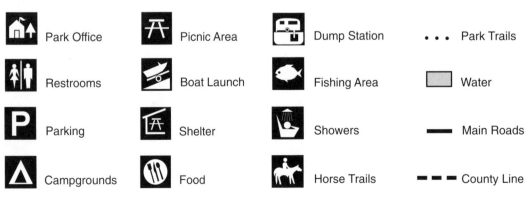

Park Office	Picnic Area	Dump Station	• • • Park Trails
Restrooms	Boat Launch	Fishing Area	Water
Parking	Shelter	Showers	—— Main Roads
Campgrounds	Food	Horse Trails	– – – County Line
			– – – Park Boundary

Red Oak Backpack Trail

👢👢👢👢

Distance Round-Trip: 4 miles

Estimated Hiking Time: 2 hours

Hike this trail only in dry weather! In the rain I encountered a world of raging, impassable streams; mud slides; and a maze of bewildering, water-filled, false trails.

Caution: The trail can be very muddy and slick when wet, and some stream crossings may be difficult in wet weather.

Trail Directions: Begin at the trail board in the Old Siloam Picnic Area at the end of the park's loop road. The trail ascends on an old roadbed through fern-lined bluffs [1]. The trail is marked with six-by-six poles and a yellow hiker at every quarter mile. By .2 mi. the ascent is over and you are hiking on top of a ridge [2] through a mixed woods with a nice spring understory (especially the anemone). The trail soon passes through an early successional woods with lots of dogwood, elderberry, and sumac.

At .55 mi. go to the right [3] and pass an old mining pit with water in it on the left. Soon the path goes downhill and skirts a park road. The road disappears by .75 mi., and pines line the trail. Look for bracken fern at 1.05 mi. [4]. This fern, which continues to produce new, wavy, dark-green leaves all season, usually indicates poor, barren soils.

From 1.65 to 1.75 mi. the trail goes through a unique area in Illinois—an oak opening [5]. Oak openings are an intermediate texture between prairie and woodlands. They are usually grassy and free of brush, with trees growing widely spaced or in clumps, similar to a city park, but unique because it is not planted by man. On your right the trees are all elms; on the left, mature oaks. Look closely at the ground in early spring for bicolor, bird's-foot violet. As the trail begins to head down, leaving the oak opening, buckeyes appear as an upper understory shrub. This is a fairly steep descent, so use caution. (While keeping your mind on the trail, during May also look for phlox and columbine.)

After the descent you'll see that the woods give way to a shrubby, grassy area. At 2 mi. cross the creek [6]. When the water is low, this presents no problem. If you happen to hike during or after a heavy rainfall, you might have to retrace your steps and find a suitable log on which to cross. The trail now heads up and out of the floodplain. Did you notice the buttercups near the stream? Their generic name (*Ranunculus*) means "little frog," the plants so-named

because of their affinity for moist areas.

Another creek crossing occurs at 2.15 mi. [7], and to the right are the remains of Old Stone House, worth a look. Follow the creek, lined with shrubs and saplings. The trail soon heads upward at 2.25 mi. and you are walking through autumn olive (a weedy, introduced tree), big bluestem, and Indian grass. At 2.5 mi. the trail passes a pine plantation on the left [8] and a backpacker campsite (with privy toilets).

The trail intersects a forest road at 2.4 mi. [9]; go right. You'll wander between pines on the left and autumn olive and prairie grasses on the right. In spring, look down and discover pussytoes. The flower head resembles an off-white kitten's paw. Notice that no other plants grow near the pussytoes. It puts out a growth inhibitor to assure that each pussytoes has enough nutrients and water. The trail curves left at 2.75 mi.

At 3 mi. [10] the trail heads to the right, and a forest road emerges to join the trail. At 3.1 mi. go right; at 3.35 mi. the trail heads right again and down [11], through a mixed woods. Wind your way downhill with help from steps placed near the end of the descent. Once down, you are on level ground in a floodplain woods. In rainy weather, there really may be a flood! Cross the creek several times until the final crossing at 3.7 mi. [12]. Look to your right at the shale outcrop and to the left at a sandstone outcrop. From here you will walk on a crushed-rock path back to the picnic area.

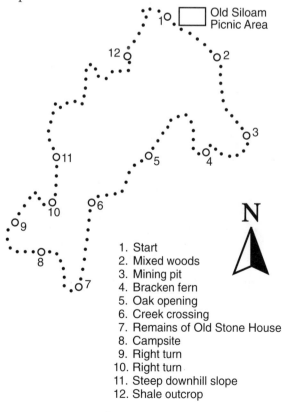

1. Start
2. Mixed woods
3. Mining pit
4. Bracken fern
5. Oak opening
6. Creek crossing
7. Remains of Old Stone House
8. Campsite
9. Right turn
10. Right turn
11. Steep downhill slope
12. Shale outcrop

Hoot Owl Trail 👢👢👢👢

Distance Round-Trip: 1.5 miles

Estimated Hiking Time: .75 hour

A fern-covered hillside along a rushing stream is an idyllic hike after a rainstorm. The greens glisten, the stream drowns out all other noises, and, of course, the trail is slick as glass!

Caution: This trail can be very muddy.

Trail Directions: Begin at the trail board near the end of the loop at Old Siloam Picnic Area and immediately start an ascent [1]. This section of the trail is braced with railroad ties. As you head up, look at the large white oaks on either side. During spring, the trail will be lined with mayapples, rattlesnake fern, and anemones. Some parts of the hillside are covered with Christmas fern. Take advantage of the small overlooks to peer into the ravine below and perhaps catch a glimpse of the trail's namesake.

At .15 mi. [2] the trail has leveled off, and you are hiking on top of a ridge with a great view to the left.

In spring, when trees just begin to leaf out, this ravine is absolutely beautiful! On your right, look into the woods for large-canopied oak trees, better known as "wolf" trees. A bench is provided at the quarter-mile point; soon after, the ravine on the left disappears, only to be replaced by an equally impressive ravine on the right. A pine plantation is on the left and the trail skirts a park road at .5 mi. [3]. The trail curves to the right at .65 mi. where you again see the road and a sign [4]. By .75 mi. you are finally away from the road and into a woods dominated by oak and elm saplings. Pines will again appear and soon more saplings. If you look closely, however, you can find several large, old oak trees.

At 1.05 mi. you are again on a ridge with a ravine forest on either side [5]. Continue to look down into the beautiful ravines as you hike on this dry, narrow ridge. Keep an eye out for violet wood sorrel. The trail splits at 1.35 mi. [6]. To the right is an overlook (take advantage of this); then go left, between the two large white oaks. The descent begins near 1.4 mi. [7] on a trail reinforced with railroad ties. By 1.5 mi. the trail is back on level ground at a play area near the trail board.

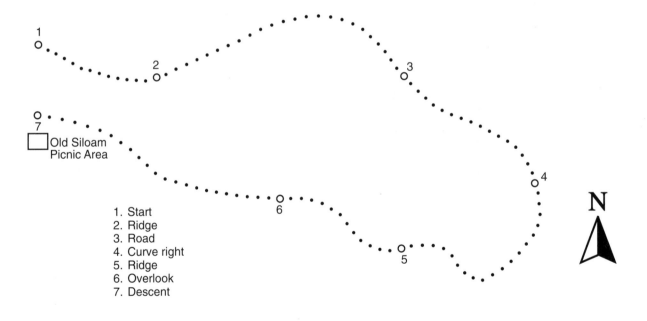

Old Siloam
Picnic Area

1. Start
2. Ridge
3. Road
4. Curve right
5. Ridge
6. Overlook
7. Descent

N

36. American Bottoms

- Experience the peaceful solemnity of an ancient site.

- Discover a culture that one thousand years ago was more powerful and sophisticated than any other—north of Mexico—in the Western Hemisphere.

- Climb the largest, prehistoric earthen structure in the Western Hemisphere for a great view.

- Bring your binoculars and bird books as you hike a trail "strictly for the birds."

Area Information

The 70 miles of the American Bottoms along the Illinois side of the Mississippi River floodplain (south of where the Missouri River enters) is a montage of swales, ridges, backwater lakes, and river terraces. When Charles Dickens visited the area in 1842 all he could hear was the loud chirping of frogs and all he could see on "the unwholesome, steaming earth" was mud, mire, brake (overgrown marshland), and brush.

From 1300 B.P. to 800 B.P. this area was the site of a great Mississippian civilization built on agriculture. Corn and other cultivated crops, combined with the region's bountiful wildlife, formed a stable, year-round food supply. Results of the long habitation were permanent structures: monumental earthen mounds in three shapes: conical, ridge-top, and platform. The prehistoric city is referred to as **Cahokia**, named for the Native Americans in the late 1600s who lived nearby, and it was the center of Mississippian culture. With a population of 20,000, Cahokia was one of the great urban centers of the world. It wasn't until 1800 that a city in the United States was again that sizable.

Horseshoe Lake formed when the Mississippi River overflowed its banks, changed direction, and cut a new channel. The old river section was now cut off from the flowing river and a U-shaped, ox-bow lake formed. Horseshoe Lake served as a food source for the early residents of Cahokia, supplying fish, fowl, and wild vegetables.

Directions: Cahokia Mounds is east of St. Louis and west of Collinsville on the Collinsville Road; it can be reached from exit 24 off I-255 or exit 6 off I-55/I-70. Follow the signs to the site.

Horseshoe Lake State Park can be reached from exit 6 off I-55/I-70 by heading north on Route 111 for 3.5 miles. The park entrance will be on the left.

Hours Open: Cahokia Mounds is open year-round from 8 A.M. to dusk. The interpretive center is open 9 A.M. to 5 P.M. and closed during major holidays. **Horseshoe Lake** is open year-round.

Facilities: Cahokia Mounds has an interpretive center with outstanding exhibits about the area. An admission charge of $2 for adults and $1 for children has recently been implemented. Access to the grounds is free. A picnic area is provided. **Horseshoe Lake** offers picnicking with shelters, fishing, boating with a 25-hp limit, a concession stand, camping (48 tent and trailer sites), pit toilets, and hunting.

Permits and Rules: In Cahokia Mounds all pets must be leashed. Do not leave children unsupervised. It is unlawful to remove or disturb plants or artifacts from the site. Do not climb the slopes of any mounds. Use the stairway to climb Monk's Mound. At **Horseshoe Lake** no plants, flowers, shrubs, or trees may be removed or damaged. Pets must be on a leash no longer than 10 feet.

Further Information: Cahokia Mounds State Historic and World Heritage Site, P.O. Box 681, Collinsville, IL 62234; 618-546-5160. **Horseshoe Lake State Park**, 3321 Hwy. 111, Granite City, IL 62040; 618-931-0270.

Other Areas of Interest

Located in East St. Louis, **Frank Holten State Park** is within site of the Gateway Arch. This park offers picnic facilities, a concession stand, two lakes for fishing and boating, a golf course, and a variety of recreation areas for baseball, track, soccer, and basketball. For more information call 618-874-7920.

As you drive through the area, take note of the leafy plant growing in the fields that is neither corn nor soybeans. This area is the world's leader in horseradish production. For a taste of the pungent radish and to learn about its culture and cultivation, attend the **International Horseradish Festival** held the first weekend in June at Woodland Park in Collinsville. For more information call 618-344-2884.

American Bottoms

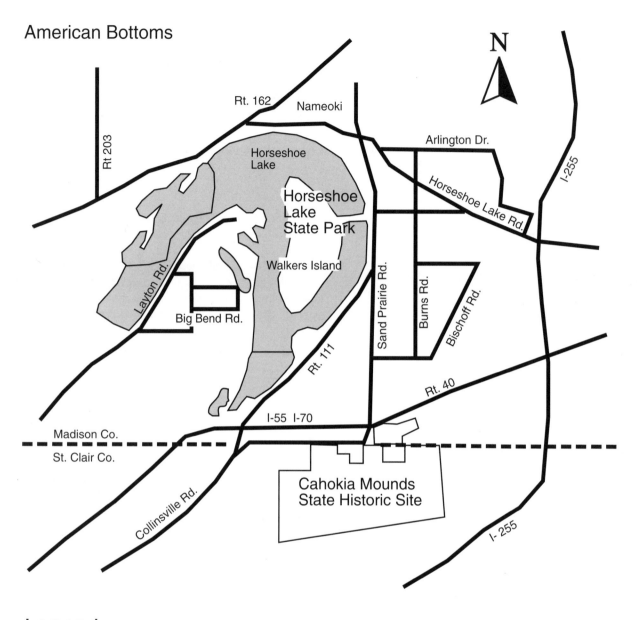

L e g e n d

  Water

──── Main Roads

▬ ▬ County Line

Cahokia Mounds 👢👢👢

Distance Round-Trip: 5 miles

Estimated Hiking Time: 2.5 hours

At one time it was a bustling habitation surrounded by a vast silence. Today, it is a vast silence surrounded by bustling habitation.

Caution: Thefts are very high in this area, so make sure all valuables are locked and out of sight in your vehicle (or kept with you). You will cross a four-lane highway twice—watch for traffic!

Trail Directions: The interpretive center is well worth the time before hiking as it will give you an insight into Mississippian civilization. Begin the hike at the back door of the center and take the path that is farthest to the left [**1**]. The trail will be marked with barn-red posts. The numbers of this hike do not correspond with those in the trail book that can be purchased at the center. At .15 mi. the trail joins a crushed-rock path; go right and then left at the fork [**2**]. In front of you is Mound 60, a rectangular platform mound. The small mound off to your right is Mound 56.

Go to the left after passing cement marker #4. On your right is a swampy area called a borrow pit, the largest one at the site. Soil was gathered from here to build many of the mounds. The trail next passes Mound 72 at .4 mi. [**3**], a seven-foot-high ridge-top mound. Note that Mound 72's orientation is diagonal instead of east-west or north-south like the others.

From here the trail will wander through a flood-plain woods on the left and the same borrow pit on the right. At 1.05 mi. go left, following the grassy, mown path. Within a short distance you will pass a pair of mounds called Little Twin Mounds [**4**]: One is a platform and the other, a conical mound. From here the trail winds through a grassy field with large pin oaks and hackberry trees. At 1.25 mi. go left into a grassy expanse without trees [**5**]. In the distance ahead you can see Woodhenge, a solar-horizon calendar.

After crossing the four-lane highway (Collinsville Road) at 1.7 mi. [**6**] you enter the parking area for Woodhenge. Continue north (straight ahead) and skirt the reconstructed Woodhenge. Continue north until you reach the bed of old Cahokia Creek. The trail will skirt the creek and then angle uphill to the right at 2.1 mi. [**7**]. While hiking here you will pass two conical and two platform mounds before crossing Sand Prairie Lane at 2.6 mi. [**8**].

On the opposite side of Sand Prairie Lane look to the south (right); the large, square platform mound is probably the true Monk's Mound, where Trappist Monks lived from 1809 to 1813. Angle to the north

(left) as you continue to follow the path. You will hike by two conical mounds before beginning to skirt the base of Monk's Mound. This mound contains 22 million cubic feet of earth that were dug with stone tools and carried from the borrow pits in baskets on people's backs.

At marker 21 go left (3 mi.) [**9**] and encircle a replica of the stockade wall. The stockade enclosed the heart of the city, an elite neighborhood. After encircling the stockade; go left again through a grassy meadow (east). You are walking through an area that has been greatly altered, first by the floods of the 1940s and 1950s when the landowners used the mounds as fill, and later by the encroachment of development. Nine conical mounds are still somewhat visible, whereas four more have been mostly destroyed.

Follow the mown path as it curves and heads back toward Monk's Mound. Hike toward the Monk's Mound parking lot to a side spur that leads up to the mound. Use the gray, weathered steps (about 155) to climb the mound at 3.5 mi. [**10**]. It rises in four terraces; a massive ceremonial building stood on the highest terrace. Smaller structures were built on the lower terraces. Once you're at the top of this flat-topped mound, use the diagrams to interpret the area.

Descend the mound and retrace your steps back to the parking area at 4 mi. [**11**] and follow the road to Collinsville Road (the four-lane highway). Use extreme caution as you cross it; then angle left and continue to follow the grassy path. Although there is not much to see now, this area contained several mounds. Note that the trailer park on the left sits on a mound. The depressions to your right are borrow pits. At marker #27 (4.75 mi.) [**12**] go right and back to the interpretive center.

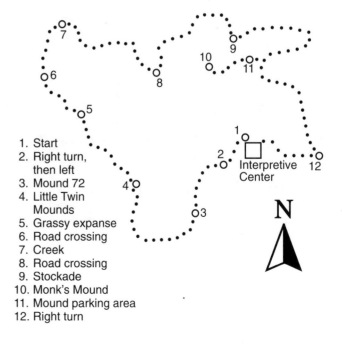

1. Start
2. Right turn, then left
3. Mound 72
4. Little Twin Mounds
5. Grassy expanse
6. Road crossing
7. Creek
8. Road crossing
9. Stockade
10. Monk's Mound
11. Mound parking area
12. Right turn

Horseshoe Lake 👢

Distance Round-Trip: 4 miles

Estimated Hiking Time: 2 hours

Here's your chance in the land-locked prairie state to circumnavigate an island on a trail that is strictly for the birds!

Caution: After spring rains, the only way to navigate parts of the trail is by wading with shoes off or in knee-high boots. The trail wanders near the campground; please be courteous to the campers.

Trail Directions: Use the guide provided with the park map to help you enjoy your birding adventure. The trail begins .1 mi. north of the first parking area, after you cross a causeway onto the island. Head north at the large cottonwood and the trail sign [**1**]. On your left is a field used for wildlife food plantings; on your right is the lake. The dominant trees on this trail will be silver maple, hackberry, and cottonwood. As you hike, note the bluebird boxes; these birds were once a common site, even in towns. Since the introduction of the house sparrow, however, bluebirds have become strictly rural.

Search the branches hanging over the water—you might be rewarded with a sighting of a black-crowned night heron. Although related to the great blue heron, this bird is short and chunky. As the name suggests, it feeds at twilight and during the night. Watch the purple martins and barn swallows as they swoop over the water, eating mosquitoes and pesky flies. These birds spend so much time in the air that their feet are small and weak; they can barely walk on them. During the fall and winter, scan the water for diving ducks that overwinter here.

At 1.2 mi. [**2**] you will pass a gravel road on your left. The trail at this point begins to head away from the lake and skirt wet areas surrounded by trees, called hardwood ponds. Look in open areas in the woods for good-sized tree specimens. Listen for the rustling of leaves and the playful chatter of fox squirrels. At 1.65 mi. you are at the south end of a hardwood pond [**3**], and the trail curves to the right. If you are hiking during the spring, take a look at the small trees in the area; many of them will have silken nests, homes of the eastern tent caterpillar. During the day the tent caterpillars feed, traveling through the branches in search of food (leaves). As they travel they lay down a line of silk. In the evening they follow this silken line back to their tent.

Be on the lookout for the Eurasian tree sparrow. This sparrow was introduced from Europe in the 1870s in St. Louis, Missouri. The birds live in hedgerows and willow areas, and are only found in eastern Missouri and west-central Illinois. At 2.2 mi. [**4**] go right and cross the hardwood pond. The lake will soon be in view again on your right as the path heads into the woods. At 2.65 mi. cross a bridge; the trail then forks. Go to the right for a short side spur into a marsh [**5**]. If you are quiet you'll have a chance to view skittish and noisy American coots as they appear to be running on water while fleeing from you. Also look for nesting blue-winged teals here.

After exploring the marsh with your binoculars, retrace your steps and take the trail to the right into an open area (campground) that is soon hidden by a barrier of vegetation. At 3 mi. search the large marsh on the right for great blue herons [**6**]. It's possible to see more than 30 of them here, silhouetted by the lingering daylight. Also look closely along the trail for beaver (I saw my first Illinois beaver here!) Their lodge is visible from the trail. After crossing two wooden bridges, the campground is again visible on the left. Continue to follow the trail near the marsh on the right.

At 3.45 mi. [**7**] cross a final bridge. Soon the trail ends at the parking area near the causeway. With luck, you added the Eurasian tree sparrow and the black-crowned night heron to your birding life list.

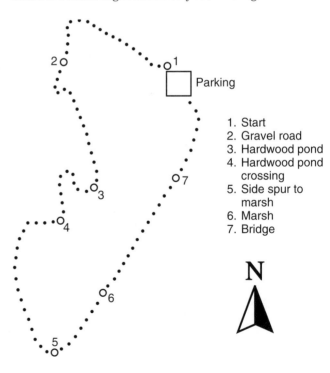

1. Start
2. Gravel road
3. Hardwood pond
4. Hardwood pond crossing
5. Side spur to marsh
6. Marsh
7. Bridge

37. Pere Marquette State Park

- Brush up on your botany as you look for ferns, green dragons, and doll's eyes.
- See spectacular views of the Illinois and Mississippi rivers.
- Experience the highest highs and the lowest lows, all within a few feet.
- Discover loess.

Area Information

Pere Marquette State Park lies at the confluence of the Mississippi and Illinois rivers, just southwest of the glacial boundary in western Illinois. It is the state's largest park, consisting of 8,000 acres that include limestone and loess bluffs, second-growth timber, and hill prairies.

The park was originally named Piasa Bluff State Park to commemorate the two drawings of the Piasa Bird discovered near the park. The name was later changed to Pere Marquette, in honor of Father Jacques Marquette, a French missionary who in 1673 was among the first group of Europeans to reach the confluence of the Mississippi and Illinois rivers. Father Marquette noted that these bluffs' "height and length inspired awe."

One of the extraordinary features of the park is *loess* (rhymes with bus), which are deposits of windblown silt. As the glaciers advanced, they acted like giant grist mills, grinding and pulverizing much of the rock and earth into very fine, dust-sized particles. Forests along major river valleys trapped this wind-blown dust, and the material accumulated to form high bluffs. One of the characteristics of loess is its tendency to stand in vertical walls that don't erode. This has resulted in two of the park's higher peaks—McAdams Peak and Lovers Leap.

Directions: The park is 5 miles west of Grafton on Route 100 and about 25 miles northwest of Alton.

Hours Open: The site is open year-round.

Facilities: The Lodge and Conference Center includes a restaurant, indoor pool, guest rooms, and a 700-ton stone fireplace. For information call 618-786-2331. The park has camping, along with rent-a-camp facilities, horseback riding, boating, fishing, picnicking, and hunting.

Permits and Rules: Pets must be kept on a leash at all times.

Further Information: Site Superintendent, Pere Marquette State Park, Route 100, P.O. Box 158, Grafton, IL 62037; 618-786-3323.

Other Areas of Interest

Sam Vadalabene Bike Trail is a paved, linear bicycle trail that follows the Great River Road from Alton to Pere Marquette State Park. Hikers are also welcome to use the trail, which includes interesting points along the way (especially the small town of Elsah, listed in the National Register of Historic Places). For more information call 800-258-6645.

From December 1 to March 1 watch for wintering **bald eagles** in this area: downriver from Alton at the mouth of the Missouri River, up the Mississippi to Winfield Lock and Dam, and up the Illinois River to Pere Marquette State Park. On a good cold day, dozens of wintering bald eagles may be seen. For eagle-watching information call 618-463-0766.

Park Trails

Goat Cliff Trail —2 miles (one way)—This linear trail is a continual uphill climb. Along the way you will discover the Cap au Grès fault, where the land once rose out of the sea, limestone cliffs containing ancient sea creatures, and scenic vistas.

Ravine Trail —1 mile (one way)—The trail is along an intermittent stream and contains a bench near the top.

Hickory Trail —.75 mile (one way)—This is considered the main trail of the park as it links with the other park trails. The trail goes from McAdams Peak to Twin Shelters.

Hickory North Trail —1 mile—The trail connects with Hickory Trail and Hickory South. Hikers will wind over hills and down valleys.

Hickory South Trail —1.5 miles—This trail connects with the Fern Hollow Trail and Hickory North Trail. It also provides access to Twin Shelters Overlook and the lodge.

Rattlesnake Trail —.75 mile— Although named for this unpopular reptile, the chances of a sighting are practically nil. Rattlesnake Trail skirts rocky bluffs and outcrops and connects with Fern Hollow Trail and the park road.

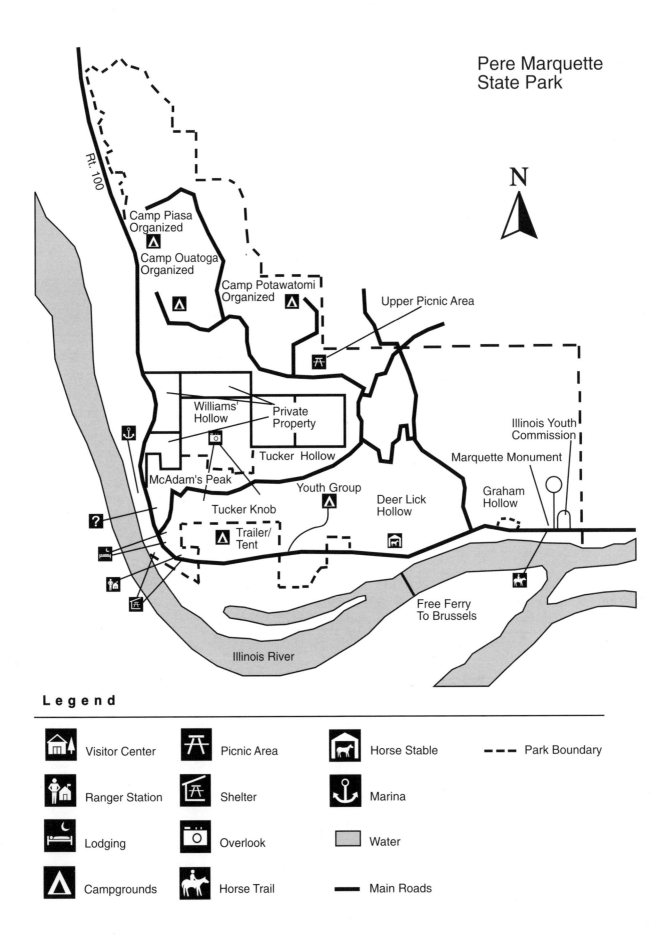

Pere Marquette State Park

N

Rt. 100

Camp Piasa Organized

Camp Ouatoga Organized

Camp Potawatomi Organized

Upper Picnic Area

Williams' Hollow

Private Property

Tucker Hollow

Illinois Youth Commission

Marquette Monument

McAdam's Peak

Tucker Knob

Youth Group

Deer Lick Hollow

Graham Hollow

Trailer/ Tent

Free Ferry To Brussels

Illinois River

Legend

Visitor Center	Picnic Area	Horse Stable	---	Park Boundary
Ranger Station	Shelter	Marina		
Lodging	Overlook	Water		
Campgrounds	Horse Trail	Main Roads		

Dogwood–Oak Trails

Distance Round-Trip: 2.25 miles

Estimated Hiking Time: 1.25 hours

Walk in feet-deep layers of loess while looking across the valley at an area that never saw a glacier.

Caution: Roots and limbs are scattered about the trail: Try not to trip! The trail crosses the park road with traffic.

Trail Directions: Begin the trail at the Visitor's Center trail board and follow the blue rectangles painted on the trees (blazes) [1]. The trail, supplied with reinforced steps, immediately ascends. Before .1 mi. you'll reach a trail intersection; continue straight ahead. On your left are great views of the fish and wildlife area as you pass through a maple-basswood forest growing on rolling ravines.

Take advantage of the Mississippi River Overlook at .25 mi. [2]. At .35 mi. [3] the trail intersects with the Ridge Trail; go left, still following the blue blazes. Within .05 miles come to another trail intersection, but continue straight ahead, following the sign to McAdams Peak [4]. Along this segment look for small patches of crested iris during the spring. At .45 mi. [5] you should see a large oak tree; take a side spur to your left and view a small prairie opening called a *hill prairie*. In the spring look for clumps of puccoon—these orange-yellow flowers are related to Virginia bluebells. The spur comes back out and rejoins the trail.

At .55 mi. [6] several trails intersect; go left to the McAdams Peak Overlook, only a few feet from the intersection [7]. McAdams Peak is 372 feet above the Illinois River and is named for the McAdams family. William, the father, removed 100 Native American skeletons from this vicinity for the Smithsonian, and John, his son, was instrumental in acquiring this property for a state park. From the overlook you can see the Illinois River and its bottomland and the unglaciated hills of Calhoun County.

Retrace your steps back to [6] and go to your left, following Goat Cliff Trail (blazed in yellow paint) [8]. Immediately as you begin to descend, look to your right where you'll see loess. Take time to touch and feel the silt. It is firm, yet crumbly; easy to dig, yet it holds together. If you take a closer look, you'll notice the loess has a uniform texture and is free from rocks.

Along this trail in spring look for larkspur, both the common purple and an unusual white form. On your left is a loess hill prairie. At .95 mi. [9], by a large dead tree, the trail goes off to the left. Follow it as it twists and turns uphill. At 1.05 mi. steps to the left lead to an overview of the area and benches; stop for a view [10]. On your way up notice the girdling and

burning of trees. The area around you is a hill prairie in the process of being restored. Without fire, these open areas would soon be taken over by unwanted trees, and a unique part of our landscape lost.

Go back down the steps and go left; the trail will soon rejoin the original trail at 1.2 mi. [11]. From here go right, retracing your steps back to [6] at 1.3 mi. and then continuing straight. Join the Hickory Trail, marked with red blazes. At 1.35 mi. [12] take the spur to your right, marked by a worn path, a cement bench, and marking post. The path will take you up stone steps to view a hill prairie from a place called Twin Mounds Overlook. Here the hill prairie is dominated by Indian grass and little bluestem. This spur soon rejoins the main trail.

At 1.45 mi. [13] you will encounter another trail intersection; go right. You are now following the Oak Trail, which is marked with pink blazes. As the trail descends look to your right at the loess deposits. This part of the trail is deeply eroded as it cuts through the loess and skirts the bottom of the hill prairie you just explored. At 1.75 mi. [14] cross the park road. The trail on the opposite side passes through a disturbed area.

The trail will soon come to another junction; go right at 1.8 mi. [15]. The trail (Hickory Trail) is now marked by a red blaze with a white circle and passes through a mixed hardwood forest. Look for ferns along the trail as you continue to the right and downhill. Soon you are on level ground and following a ravine with bluffs along either side. Watch out for stinging nettle!

After encountering a stone retaining wall on your left built by the Civilian Conservation Corps, you will again cross the park road at 2.25 mi. [16] and finish at the Visitor's Center parking area.

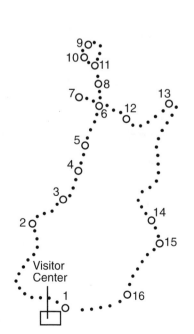

1. Start
2. Mississippi River Overlook
3. Left turn
4. Go straight
5. Hill prairie side spur
6. Trail intersection
7. McAdams Peak Overlook
8. Left turn
9. Left turn
10. Overlook
11. Left turn
12. Right turn
13. Right turn
14. Road crossing
15. Right turn
16. Road crossing

Fern Hollow Trail

Distance Round-Trip: 3 miles

Estimated Hiking Time: 1.5 hours

Hiking on this rolling, woodland trail is not without peril. You will encounter wolves, rattlesnakes, and dragons—in this instance, a tree, a fern, and a flower. But like their real counterparts, they can be very difficult to find.

Caution: Branches sometimes block the trail and roots are exposed. The trail is very slippery when wet.

Trail Directions: Park at the Flagpole Overlook, the second overlook parking area at the top of the bluff. It is on the right. Head south through the parking area, cross the park road, and the trail will appear a few feet down the road (.05 mi.) [**1**]. The trail is marked by a red circle with a white dot. Begin hiking through a maple woods along a deep ravine. On your left look for rattlesnake fern, with its lacy, bright-green, triangular leaves.

At .3 mi. [**2**] come to a trail intersection and go right. The trail is now marked by orange circles. For the next .1 mi. look for small limestone outcrops and fragile fern as it lines the trail. Keep an eye out for patches of doll's eye at .55 mi. [**3**] and throughout the hike. In the fall, the fruits of these plants are shiny white berries, each with a black dot, that resemble the china eyes once used in dolls. These berries are very poisonous. Doll's eye is viewed by ecologists as an indicator of a good woods. Not far from the first patch of doll's eye are a pair of large oaks on your left. From here the trail soon heads upward.

A bench is set at .8 mi. [**4**]. In the spring look here for large clumps of bellwort, wild ginger, and large patches of doll's eye mixed with mayapples. As you cross the stream at .9 mi. [**5**] admire the ravine forest on the right. Here look for maidenhair ferns with feathery, flat fronds borne on glistening black stalks. The trail crosses the park road at 1.3 mi. [**6**] and reenters the woods on the other side. You are still following the orange circles as you hike in a mixed, second-growth woods.

At 1.4 miles ignore a trail to the left and continue straight ahead [**7**]. You will enter an immature forest at 1.6 mi. [**8**]: Note the smaller trees and the remains of an old homestead. The trail begins to head downward at 1.7 mi. and the forest also begins to improve [**9**]. Before you round the curve in the trail, look to your right for a large "wolf" tree (1.75 mi.) [**10**]. (Wolf trees are usually oaks with wide-spreading canopies, indicating that at one time the area was more open.)

After sighting the wolf tree, again look for rattlesnake fern. If your visit is during the late spring, also look for green dragons with their incomplete whorl of leaves and unique flower structure underneath (supposedly the dragon's tongue). Two miles brings a gully crossing [**11**], and for the next .25 mi. the trail is lined with Christmas ferns. At 2.25 mi. [**12**] you leave the fern-lined hollow—the trail's namesake—and hike upward. On your left note a farm pasture as you hike through disturbed woods.

At 2.7 mi. [**13**] you will head upward on an eroded path. The view of the pasture is gone. Look on your right for another wolf tree as you climb steadily upward. Near the top is another trail going off to the right at 2.9 mi.; take it [**14**]. The trail is again marked by a red circle with a white dot. Within .05 mi. you will come to the park road [**15**] and have completed the trail. Go left back to the parking area and enjoy the view from Flagpole Observation Area.

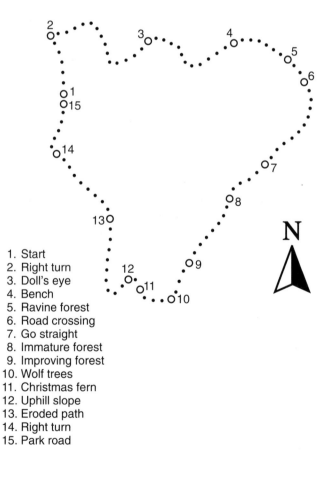

1. Start
2. Right turn
3. Doll's eye
4. Bench
5. Ravine forest
6. Road crossing
7. Go straight
8. Immature forest
9. Improving forest
10. Wolf trees
11. Christmas fern
12. Uphill slope
13. Eroded path
14. Right turn
15. Park road

38. Nauvoo

- Celebrate the traditional stages and roles in a woman's life.
- Search for stones that were once part of the Temple.
- Hike among the rubble—the sun, moon, and stars—of a failed Utopian society.
- Visit a city that was once the largest in the state.
- Learn about the day-to-day lives of early Mormons.

Area Information

Nauvoo, located on a rise above a horseshoe bend in the Mississippi River, was the religious, governmental, and cultural center of the Church of Jesus Christ of Latter-Day Saints (Mormon) from 1839 to 1846. Joseph Smith, its prophet-leader, first described the area as "literally a wilderness. The land was mostly covered with trees and bushes and much of it so wet . . . that it was impossible for teams [of horses] to get through." But he also saw the value of the area as a trading port. Initially the site was named Commerce, but once the Mormons purchased it, they changed its name to Nauvoo, meaning "beautiful place or pleasant land." It would be the religion's third attempt to build "God's City" on the frontier.

Construction of the Temple began during 1841; it was to "rise out of the bluffs as a beacon to all of God's People in their last days of life on earth." The Temple, which took five years to complete, was the tallest structure in Illinois, and it was declared to be an architectural wonder. Yet not everyone who viewed it was impressed. Josiah Quincy, son of the president of Harvard, viewed the area in 1844:

> Perhaps it would of [sic] required a genius to have designed anything worthy of that noble site. The city of Nauvoo, with its wide streets, sloping gracefully to the farms enclosed on the prairie seemed a better temple to Him who prospers the work of industrious hands than the grotesque structure on the hill, with its queer carvings of moons and suns.

By 1844 the town's population had reached 12,000, and Nauvoo was the largest city in the state. Yet all was not well, for neighbors resented the community's religion and prosperity. Tension between the Mormons and their neighbors broke loose when Joseph Smith and his brother were murdered in the Carthage Jail in 1844. By September of 1846 most of the Mormons had left, looking for yet another site on which to build "God's City."

Directions: Nauvoo is located near the banks of the Mississippi River along Route 96. The Latter-Day Saints Visitor Center is at the north end of the restored village.

Hours Open: The site is open year-round. The Visitor Center hours are Monday to Saturday, 9 A.M. to 7 P.M., and Sunday, 11 A.M. to 6 P.M.

Facilities: The Visitor Center contains artifacts, an audiovisual presentation, and a scale model of the 1846 city. It also offers restrooms, water, and maps.

Permits and Rules: Some of the homes are privately owned and cannot be toured. Please respect the owners' privacy.

Further Information: Nauvoo Visitor Center, P.O. Box 215, Nauvoo, IL 62354; 217-453-2233.

Other Areas of Interest

Three years after the Mormons' exodus, another Utopian community attempted to settle at Nauvoo—the Icarians. Although their communal lifestyle proved to be unworkable, they had a lasting effect on the community. They introduced grape growing and wine making to the area. The first vineyard planted at Nauvoo exists in **Nauvoo State Park**. You can also fish, boat, picnic, tour the museum, and camp. A 1.5-mile trail winds around the lake and the wooded areas. For more information call 217-453-2512.

Area Trail

1844 Martyrdom Trail: Nauvoo to Carthage 👢—23 miles—The trail begins at the Latter-Day Saints Visitor Center and follows the route that Joseph Smith and his brother took to the Carthage Jail. Before hiking here you must register two weeks in advance. For further information contact Martyrdom Trail Committee, P.O. Box 223, Nauvoo, IL 62354; 217-453-6543.

Historic Nauvoo 👢

Distance Round-Trip: 4 miles

Estimated Hiking Time: 2 hours (with a few house tours)

"Half encircled by a bend of the river, a beautiful city lay glittering in the fresh morning sun; its bright new dwellings, set in cool green gardens, ranging up around a stately domeshaped hill, which was crowned by a noble marble edifice."
—Colonel Thomas Kane, 1846

Caution: There are no sidewalks for part of the trail so walk along the side of the road. Many of the sites have interpretive guides; interact with them as much or as little as you like. Each is a wealth of information, but usually will talk for 20 minutes or more at each site.

Trail Directions: Park at the Latter-Day Saints Visitor Center. Begin the hike in the garden at the Emma and Joseph Smith Statue [1]. At *Fulfillment* go left and begin hiking on Young Street. Cross Partridge and Wells streets before going right on Bluff Street (.4 mi.) [2].

On your right at .45 mi. is the Temple Information Center. After visiting the center, go across the street to the site of the original temple [3]. Enter at the gate in the middle of the block and tour the site.

After touring the temple site, exit from the south gate and go right on Mulholland Street [4]. Cross Wells and head downhill. The sidewalk will soon end, so use the side of the road and exercise caution. At .9 mi. go left on Partridge Street [5]. On your right is a large grove of cottonwoods. Cross White and Hotchkiss streets. Notice a prairie restoration in progress on the right, and at 1.2 mi. view the Hiber C. Kimball home on the right [6].

Continue walking down Partridge. At 1.3 mi. go right on Kimball [7], passing one of the seven brickyards that were in operation during the town's heyday. Go left on Hyde. On your left at 1.4 mi. is the Joseph Coolidge home. From the Coolidge home, go right onto Parley [8], and at 1.5 mi. go left onto Main [9]. On your left is the Mansion House.

Cross Water Street and look on your left for a piece of Temple stone that has been incorporated into the flagstone path. Nauvoo House is on your left as the street dead-ends into the Mississippi River (1.7 mi.) [10]. Climb up on the bluff and look around, then proceed north on the other side of the circle. Go up the steps in front of the Smith Family Homestead. At Water Street go left, and as you turn the corner, note the Nauvoo Survey Stone at your feet.

At 1.8 mi. go left into the Smith Family Cemetery [11], following the brick path. Retrace your steps back to Water Street and continue on past the Red Brick Store, the William Marks home, and the Aaron Johnson home. On your left is the Mississippi River. At 2.35 mi. Water Street curves to the right, leaving the river behind, and soon dead-ends into Parley [12].

On your right at this junction is the *Monument to Exodus*. Continue north on Parley, which was the street used for the exodus. The Seventies Hall is on your left at 2.7 mi. [13]. This building is a reproduction.

Adjacent to the Seventies Hall is the Webb Blacksmith. Cross Granger Street and at 2.85 mi. go left on Main [14]. For the next .3 mi. you will walk through what was once the business district of the settlement.

The Cultural and Masonic Hall is the last building before the sidewalk gives way on Main Street [15]. Continue past the hall, walking along the side of the street (3.15 mi.). Soon you will pass the Visitor Center. At 3.6 mi. go left on Broadway and then right at the fenced-in area [16].

Here is one of the four quarries used as a source of the temple's limestone. At the southwest corner you are able to peer into the old quarry, now water-filled. From here retrace your steps back to the Visitor Center and parking area.

Nauvoo

Historic Nauvoo

Cultural Hall

Seventies Hall — Webb Blacksmith

Kimball Home

Mississippi River

1. Start
2. Right turn
3. Temple site
4. Right turn
5. Left turn
6. Kimball home
7. Right turn
8. Right turn
9. Left turn
10. Mississippi River
11. Smith Family Cemetery
12. Exodus site
13. Seventies Hall
14. Left turn
15. Cultural and Masonic Hall
16. Stone quarry

South

The southern part of Illinois is defined as the area south of Interstate 70.

Topography

The terrain in the south shows the influence of glaciation, either by its earlier presence or by its total absence. Parts of the region were affected by glaciation—not from the most recent Wisconsinan glacier but from the earlier Illinoian glacier some 200 thousand years ago. South of a line from Fountain Bluff on the Mississippi River to the Shawneetown Hills near the mouth of the Wabash rise the Shawnee Hills, a landscape untouched by glacial ice.

North of the Shawnee Hills the topography is gently rolling with steep bluffs rising along the Mississippi. As the river nears the southern border of Illinois, however, it grades into a broad floodplain with oxbow lakes. The Shawnee Hills feature east-to-west sandstone escarpments with bluffs, ravines, overhangs, cliffs, and canyons. South of the Shawnee Hills the land is a broad plain, once the northernmost extension of the Gulf of Mexico. Today, it is occupied by the Cache River.

Major Rivers and Lakes

The Mississippi River borders the state's western boundary; the eastern and southern boundary is completed by the Wabash and Ohio rivers respectively. The Wabash, in fact, forms the boundary of Illinois and Indiana for nearly 200 miles. It is the second-largest tributary of the Ohio (and one of the first routes the early French used in settling here). The Ohio, which serves as the boundary between western Kentucky and southernmost Illinois, used to be a shallow, free-flowing river. These days it is a series of deep, navigational pools maintained by 20 locks and dams.

Interior rivers are numerous. The Big Muddy has a series of impoundments along its course: Rend Lake (the second-largest man-made lake in the state), Crab Orchard Lake, Kinkaid Lake, and Lake Murphysboro. The Saline River flows into the Ohio, whereas the Little Wabash contributes water to its larger cousin, the Wabash. Among southern Illinois creeks are Bay,

Lusk, Hayes, Big, and Big Grand Pierre Creeks, which are small in length and drainage area but flow through scenic areas and are clear and mostly spring-fed. They may be the most aesthetically pleasing streams in Illinois.

The Cache River Basin, which early settlers referred to as "inaccessible and a drowned land," marks the geographical point where the last invasion of the sea into the Midwest reached its northernmost limit. It lies a few miles from the southernmost extent of the old continental glaciers. This basin has been designated a wetland of international importance. Horseshoe Lake, a former bend of the Mississippi River, is located in the lower Cache Basin and is the largest natural lake in the southern part of the state.

Common Plant Life

Just as forests were few and far between in the central part of Illinois, prairies were mostly absent from the south. If prairie did occur, it was given special names—Fults Hill Prairie, Looking-Glass Prairie, and Twelve-Mile Prairie. In the north, it was the woodlands that stood out on the landscape (Funk's Grove, Big Grove, Ten-Mile Grove) and received special attention. The prairies found in southern Illinois are similar to those found in the central part of the state. Loess hill prairies occur along the bluffs of the Mississippi River, and are dominated by sideoats grama, little bluestem, vervain, and leadplant.

Along the Wabash grows the last stronghold of the eastern deciduous forest. Oak, beech, sweet gum, and tulip trees occur in the lowlands. The floodplains are characterized by oaks—Shumard, pin, overcup, swamp white, and bur. Along the stream banks are silver maple and sycamore trees. The understory consists of large colonies of larkspur, mayapple, bloodroot, and blue-eyed Mary.

In the upland forests of the Shawnee Hills white and black oak and shagbark hickory flourish. Dryer areas have post, blackjack, and scarlet oaks. Beech, tulip tree, and sugar maple prefer the ravines; the floodplains support sycamore and Kentucky coffee tree. Interesting wildflowers include French's shooting star, white trillium, celandine poppy, phacelia, squirrel corn, and yellow trout lily. On the dry escarpments a variety of lichens and mosses grow, along with yellow star grass and bluets.

The cypress swamps have vegetation more typical of Louisiana. They hold extensive tracts of bald cypress (the oldest trees east of the Mississippi), tupelo gum, and pumpkin ash. Buttonbush and lizard's tail ring most of the swamps and wet areas. Red iris, the state flower of Louisiana, is found in the southern swamps of Illinois, as is spider lily (a mid-August bloomer). Duckweed covers the swamp surfaces, whereas yellow pond lily and American lotus blanket large portions of shallow lakes.

Common Birds and Mammals

Any remaining large tract of old forest is home to the pileated woodpecker. This bird is heard more often than it is seen, its cries echoing through the woods. Redheaded woodpeckers are numerous. Near wet areas, look for prothonotary warblers; coots; great, little blue, and green-backed herons; yellow warblers; and the common yellowthroat. The impoundments of Rend Lake and Crab Orchard Lake are home to thousands of Canada geese and snow geese each winter.

The area's most notorious reptile may be the cottonmouth. Other notable herpetofauna include the loud-voiced green tree frog, innumerable tiny toads, skinks sunning on the sandstone, frogs covered with duckweed, rustling box turtles, and hundreds of red-eared slider turtles basking on logs in the swamps and lakes.

Among the mammals look for white-tailed deer, raccoons, gray squirrels, white squirrels (in Olney), coyotes, beaver, woodchucks, and the illusive bobcat. Many interesting and unusual insects (besides the pesky mosquito) include tiger and zebra swallowtails, lichen grasshoppers, and large walking sticks.

Climate

The mean average temperature is 35 °F in January and 79 °F in July. Rainfall averages 45 inches per year, with the highest totals in May (4.6 inches). The mean average snowfall is 9 to 15 inches, with fewer than 10 days a year having 3 or more inches of snow on the ground. Some years no snow is recorded. The land along the Ohio and lower Mississippi rivers has the warmest and wettest climate in Illinois.

Best Features

- Size and diversity of the tree species
- Shawnee National Forest
- Sandstone escarpments and related formations
- Swamps of the Cache
- Spring wildflowers with a southern flavor
- Biennial migration of the herpetofauna
- Ravines, shelter caves, cliffs, and canyons
- Clear, rock-bottomed, spring-fed streams

© Michael Jeffords

39. Robeson Hills Nature Preserve

- Discover ridges topped with a beautiful beech-maple woods.
- Enjoy masses of common and uncommon spring wildflowers.
- Develop an appreciation for the American beech.
- Savor topflight fall colors.
- Delve into the depths of Dark Hollow.

Area Information

Robeson Hills comprises approximately two square miles and rises 85 feet above the Wabash River. A prominent feature of the Wabash River bottomland, the site is the last rise of the Cumberland Mountain Range before it fades into the prairies. The area is characterized by narrow, flat-topped ridges; steep slopes; and deep ravines. The hills are named after William Robeson, who purchased the land in 1875.

As with any terrain that has hills and hollows, it is not without its legends. Most concern an area called Dark Hollow, a deep, timbered ravine. It is rumored that a fortune in silver bars lies buried in its dark recesses. Another story describes a man on horseback who met his demise and was left headless. This headless rider purportedly resides in the cavernous depths of Dark Hollow. Whether you come to seek the solitude of nature or to discover the legends of Dark Hollow, Robeson Hills is certainly both far off the beaten path and a unique part of the Illinois landscape.

Directions: From the junction of highways 1 and 50 in Lawrenceville, take Highway 50 east 7.4 miles to Highway 33; go south (right). Travel south for 2.1 miles and take a left, still on Highway 33. Take another left at 1.7 miles (difficult to see) and head up a narrow, one-lane gravel road that winds to the parking area. You will see white, triangular signs for the nature preserve before you see this entrance. The entrance is not marked with any type of sign.

Hours Open: The site is open year-round.

Facilities: The area has a few picnic tables, parking, and a trash receptacle, but no restrooms.

Permits and Rules: The trails are located in the area of the park that is a dedicated Illinois Nature Preserve: No pets are allowed on the trails. Do not pick or disturb the wild flowers, and do not deface the beech trees.

Further Information: Vincennes University, 1002 North 1st Street, Vincennes, IN 47591-9986, 812-882-3350.

Other Areas of Interest

Located in southeastern Illinois between Olney and Lawrenceville, **Red Hills State Park** is an area of wooded hills, deep ravines, and Red Hill itself—the highest point of land between St. Louis and Cincinnati. The area has plenty of picnic sites with tables and grills, six playgrounds, and camping (complete with electricity, showers, and flush toilets). Hunting, fishing, and boating are allowed at the park. Six miles of hiking trails wind through the park. For more information call 618-936-2469.

Located west of Route 1 and two miles south of Marshall, in Clark County, **Lincoln Trail State Recreation Area** is named after the trail that Abraham Lincoln's family followed en route from Indiana to Illinois. Of historical significance, the area also includes American Beech Woods, an Illinois Nature Preserve. Facilities include picnic sites, water, camping, boating, fishing, and a concession stand. Sand Ford Nature Trail is a 2-mile trail that explores an oak-hickory forest. For more information call 217-826-2222.

Beech-Maple Trail 👢👢👢

Distance Round-Trip: 1 mile

Estimated Hiking Time: 45 minutes

The beeches are always photogenic, but during spring they are exceptionally so. Their gray bark in contrast to a pair of Jack-in-the-pulpits at their base or when surrounded by lush, green ferns made me forget all about mystical, headless riders.

Caution: During the fall, leaves can obscure the trail, so watch your step. Trails are also steep and narrow.

Trail Directions: Begin to the left (south) of the parking area [1]. The first few steps parallel the road and overlook the Wabash River. Before the trail heads downhill, you will come to a large white oak; this specimen happens to be 350 to 400 years old. At .1 mi. the trail heads downhill [2]—a steep descent. You will cross a small creek at .25 mi. [3], an excellent area for wildflowers in spring. Around April 15 look for woodland phlox, larkspur, prairie trillium, and the uncommon sessile trillium. Although the two trillium species resemble each other, a discerning eye can note that the sessile trillium's flower lacks a stalk. The flower appears to arise directly from its three leaves.

After crossing the creek, head uphill. It is a relatively steep climb, but once on top you experience an inspiring beech-maple forest—a sight more common in the east. The smooth, pearl-gray bark, only half an inch thick, is the most identifiable characteristic of the beech. The trail next veers to the right. Unfortunately, the beech's bark has made it an irresistible temptation to visitors with pocket knives. As you hike among these trees, you will see several trees that have been defaced—*do not add your name!* The beech has rapid formation of wound cork (the tree's equivalent of a scab) and cuts or wounds are quickly sealed over, thus preserving the record in the bark and, unfortunately, in the tree.

At .4 mi. the trail crosses a small bridge. At .5 mi. head downhill and cross Scout Bridge, an interesting suspension bridge over a ravine [4]. The trail then curves to the left and goes up. At .6 mi. note the huge beech tree on the right [5]. Beech trees are found in groups, as they can grow from the surface roots of another tree. Make a game of counting how many beech trees you find in this area. If you are here in the fall, look for beechnuts. The small, triangular morsel is 50 percent fat, and early settlers would use these nuts to fatten their holiday turkeys and pigs. The beechnut was the number-one food preference of the extinct passenger pigeon. A bird would land on the outer limbs of the beech, seize the nut in its bill, fan backwards with its wings, pull the nut from the tree, and swallow it whole. A pigeon could eat a cup of nuts at a feeding.

You will soon pass a large thicket of scouring rush on your left. Note the joints along the stem. At .75 mi. you complete your sojourn in the beech woods, and the trail comes out on an old road [6]. Go right and walk back to the parking area. On your right you'll see woods and on your left, an old field. A German visitor in 1833 commented on the beech forest, ". . . the most splendid I had yet to see in America." Do you agree?

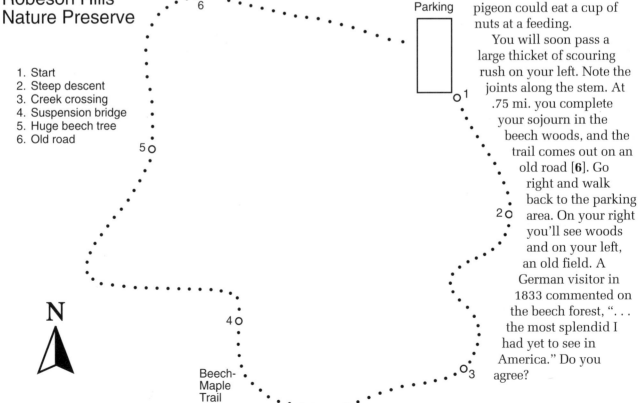

**Robeson Hills
Nature Preserve**

1. Start
2. Steep descent
3. Creek crossing
4. Suspension bridge
5. Huge beech tree
6. Old road

Parking

Beech-
Maple
Trail

N

40. Beall Woods

- Discover one of the best examples on the entire North American continent of a nearly virgin deciduous forest—the Forest of the Wabash.

- Bring a tree identification guide to help identify more than 64 species of trees that can be found along the trails.

- Listen for the call of the pileated woodpecker and look for these large woodpeckers throughout the park. Dusk is a good time to encounter a woodpecker.

- Experience a sense of the past as you view photos at the Red Barn Nature Center of the last great denizens (the giant trees) of these woods.

- Enjoy some of the premier fall colors in Illinois.

Area Information

In presettlement days, the eastern border of Illinois contained the great trees that made up the last stronghold of the eastern deciduous forest. These primeval woods, considered by some to be one of the wonders of the world, had trees over 130 feet tall, with trunks 6 feet or more in diameter; poison ivy and wild grape hung like monstrous suspension cables from their branches.

Although not readily apparent to the casual observer, traces of this magnificent forest still remain in Beall Woods, a national landmark in southern Wabash County. Sixty-four tree species have been identified here, and some three hundred trees have trunks with diameters greater than 30 inches at chest height. Six state champion trees can also be found here.

To appreciate this region of Illinois requires a sense of the past. Here was the last citadel of the eastern deciduous forest before the onset of the endless prairie, a home to giant trees and lush vegetation. Beall Woods, a remnant of the Forest of the Wabash, helps recapture the forest that our pioneering ancestors saw.

Directions: Beall Woods is in southeastern Illinois on Route 1 near Keensburg, about 10 miles north of I-64. From Keensburg, take a blacktop road 1.5 miles east to the park.

Hours Open: The site is open year-round except on Christmas and New Year's Day.

Facilities: Red Barn Visitor Center has excellent photos of the ancient woods. Restrooms are also located here. There are no camping facilities, but picnicking, and fishing in the small lake, are allowed.

Permits and Rules: The trails are located in the area of the park that is a dedicated Illinois Nature Preserve: No pets are allowed on the trails.

Further Information: Site Superintendent, Beall Woods Conservation Area, RR 2, Mount Carmel, IL 62863; 618-298-2442.

Other Areas of Interest

Olney has two areas of interest. One is the now-famous white form of the gray squirrel found in Olney City Park; white squirrel symbols are found everywhere in this small town. Bird Haven is a second attraction, a memorial to Robert Ridgway, an early Smithsonian ornithologist who documented the great trees that grew along the Wabash. An arboretum with more than 74 varieties of trees, Bird Haven is an excellent place for bird watching. For more information about both sites call 618-392-2241.

Park Trails

Tulip Tree Trail 👢—1.5 miles—This is a wide loop trail that traces Coffee Creek along a small bluff. The trail has a cassette tape for visually impaired hikers and is wide enough for disabled visitors.

Ridgeway Trail 👢—1.75 miles—This trail is a living memorial to Robert Ridgway, a Smithsonian naturalist who studied these woods during the 1870s. Due to a bridge outage, the trail is presently closed: Check with the park naturalist for the trail's status.

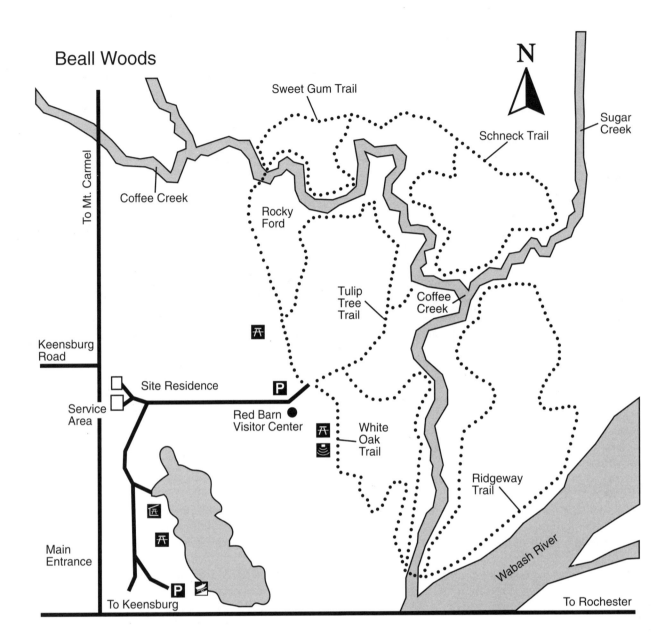

Beall Woods

N

Sweet Gum Trail

Schneck Trail

Sugar Creek

Coffee Creek

Rocky Ford

To Mt. Carmel

Tulip Tree Trail

Coffee Creek

Keensburg Road

Site Residence

P

Service Area

Red Barn Visitor Center

White Oak Trail

Ridgeway Trail

Main Entrance

Wabash River

P

To Keensburg

To Rochester

Legend

Amphitheater	Shelter	Water
P Parking	Boat Launch	Main Roads
Picnic Area	••• Park Trails	

Sweet Gum and Schneck Trails 👢👢👢

Distance Round-Trip: 3 miles

Estimated Hiking Time: 1.75 hours

It's as if you are hiking in the perfect photograph. The sky is blue and the air crisp; to your right is a young buck browsing on the last greenery of the season. Surrounding him is a golden, leaf-strewn carpet and the undulating hills of the forest.

Caution: Crossing Rocky Ford during wet weather could result in wet feet. Poison ivy grows in large patches in some parts of the woods. Neck strain is a distinct possibility on the trail if you keep looking up to see the large trees.

Trail Directions: Begin at the north end of the parking area for the Red Barn Visitor Center on the Sweet Gum Trail. The trail signs are a green sweet-gum leaf and a white triangle [**1**]. To reach the Schneck Trail you must cross Rocky Ford and continue on the Sweet Gum Trail that connects with the Schneck Trail. At .07 mi. [**2**] the Sweet Gum and Tulip Tree trails intersect; continue straight. After a few steps you will pass a sign explaining that the stagecoach from Vincennes, Indiana, to Shawneetown used to pass this area.

Soon Coffee Creek comes into view, and the understory of the woods is full of poison ivy. Cross Coffee Creek using Rocky Ford at .3 mi. [**3**]. Use the cement steps to enter the creek, walk across a bedrock slab, and proceed up the wooden steps on the opposite side. Immediately after the trail climbs out of the creek, it forks—go right.

On your right is Coffee Creek (.4 mi.) [**4**], which gets its name from leaf tannins that turn it brown. Note how the creek has undercut the bedrock. On the opposite bank beech trees are perched precariously. By .5 mi. [**5**] the trail no longer follows Coffee Creek. At .75 mi. [**6**] a path to the Schneck Trail intersects the Sweet Gum Trail. Notice the huge oak on the right that has been struck by lightning. Go right at this intersection to explore the Schneck Trail, marked with a pink flower.

The trail is the namesake of Dr. Jacob Schneck, a Mount Carmel physician and botanist who documented the huge trees during the mid-1800s. At .9 mi. [**7**] you will reach the loop, Schneck Trail. Go to your right. You will be hiking the loop backward, so all the trail signs are facing the other way. Coffee

Creek is again on your right, and the understory is a pure stand of poison ivy. Stay on the smooth dirt trail!

Coffee Creek makes a large bend at 1.1 mi. [**8**] and the trail follows along, meandering through the woods with sinuous curves and sweeps. At 1.3 mi. note the junction of Coffee Creek and Sugar Creek [**9**]. Sugar Creek is now on your right, and is much smaller and shallower.

The trail heads upland out of the creek's floodplain (1.85 mi.) [**10**], and the poison ivy soon disappears to be replaced by pawpaw. Soon you have finished the loop (1.95 mi.) and are back at [**7**]. On the way back to Sweet Gum Trail, look for two giant twin oaks looming ahead (at 2 mi.) [**11**]. Pause here to reflect on the statement made by Dr. Schneck in 1876: "The time is not distant when there will scarcely be left a sample of those monuments of centuries of growth."

You are now back at the intersection of Sweet Gum and Schneck trails (2.2 mi.) [**6**]. Return by the Sweet Gum Trail. As you walk along, note the line where poison ivy begins and ends—an indication of where floodplain and upland forest meet. At 2.5 mi. recross Rocky Ford [**12**] and head back to the parking area.

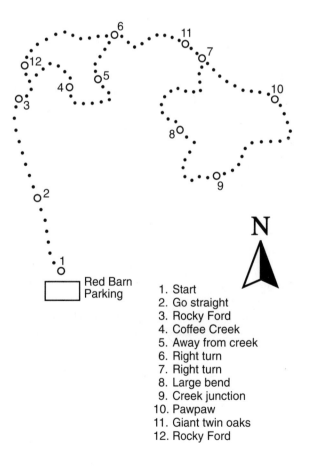

Red Barn Parking

N

1. Start
2. Go straight
3. Rocky Ford
4. Coffee Creek
5. Away from creek
6. Right turn
7. Right turn
8. Large bend
9. Creek junction
10. Pawpaw
11. Giant twin oaks
12. Rocky Ford

White Oak Trail 👢👢👢

Distance Round-Trip: 1.75 miles

Estimated Hiking Time: 1.5 hours

Painted on the floor of the Red Barn Visitor Center is a large, yellow circle 16 feet in diameter. It is a "small" remembrance of one of the last great trees (see [8] on the hike). Many large trees will be encountered on the trail, but they pale in comparison with this ghost of the past.

Caution: You risk getting your feet soaked if you hike the side spur during a wet spring. Be careful not to walk into a ravine while looking up to see the canopies of the large trees.

Trail Directions: The trailhead is found north of the Red Barn Visitor Center. Begin the trail at the sign board [1]. The trail is marked with a painted, green oak leaf and a white arrow. It begins as a wide dirt path but soon narrows. At .02 mi. [2] the trail splits from Tulip Tree Trail. Go to your right.

At .15 mi. [3] a large white arrow appears and the path again splits; go left. You are now walking on top of a ridge. After a few steps you will come to a series of wooden-platform overlooks with steps leading downward. During fall, winter, and early spring when the leaves are off the trees, you are able to see the huge grape and poison ivy vines—the "suspension cables" that Ridgway saw and marveled at.

The steps have brought you to down to Coffee Creek. For the next .4 mi. the path skirts the creek [4]. Take time to look at the huge oaks arching overhead, the immense sycamores in the distant woods, or the tall, straight sweet gums. The torn logs on the ground and the large squarish holes in some of the trees were made by pileated woodpeckers. Listen for their call and hammering on the trees. If you are quiet, you may be rewarded with a glimpse of these denizens of ancient woods.

At .75 mi. [5] come to an intersection and go left (straight) across a wooden bridge over a small ravine. This is a side spur to the trail that will take you to the intersection of Coffee Creek and the Wabash River. After crossing the bridge continue straight toward the river, disregarding a service path leading uphill.

Ahead you will pass a huge sycamore tree whose beauty is spoiled by an adjacent oil well. Go left, past the oil well, and walk along the Wabash River.

Note the width of the Wabash while traversing its banks (.9 mi.) [6]. Since you left the official White Oak Trail, you have been walking in a floodplain woods. Here the trees are cottonwood, silver maple, and sycamore. After .05 mi. you are at the point where Coffee Creek empties into the Wabash River (.95 mi.) [7]. Your side trip has been completed, so recross the bridge to [5], but this time walk up a series of wooden steps. At the top are a pair of wooden benches and a plaque telling the story of the large sycamore depicted by the circle in the visitor's center [8].

You now are surrounded by an upland forest, and the trail will snake through the woods for the next .25 mile [9]. Take note of the huge oaks with an understory of pawpaw and of the equally impressive tulip trees.

At 1.4 mi. [10] you will cross a service road. Continue hiking straight and leave the big trees behind. You are now passing through a reforestation plot (small saplings). Note the stark contrast between the two woods! The path is mostly straight and soon rejoins a path returning to the Red Barn Visitor Center.

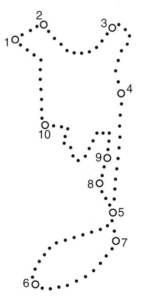

1. Start
2. Right turn
3. Left turn
4. Coffee Creek
5. Wooden bridge
6. Wabash River
7. Mouth of Coffee Creek
8. Storyboard
9. Upland forest
10. Service road

41. Rim Rock/Pounds Hollow Recreation Complex

- Explore crevasses, streets, and shelter bluffs with names like Fat Man's Misery and Ox-Lot Cave, all "constructed" of Pounds sandstone.
- Look for the elusive beaver as you discover its dens and favorite feeding areas.
- Find out why the Illinois Native Plant Society calls this a super site for spring wildflowers.

Area Information

In earlier times before the recreation area was built, this area was known simply as the Pounds, a mesa-like rock structure with a rounded surface on top and sufficient soil for growing crops. Two valleys met at its north end to form Pounds Hollow. At the southern end and toward the top, mysterious rocks were strewn about and were said to be the remnants of a prehistoric fortification. Twenty families lived here during the late-19th century and kept their livestock in Ox-Lot Cave. The fertility of the soil soon gave out, however, and they abandoned the area.

The Rim Rock/Pounds Hollow Area you see today was developed by the Civilian Conservation Corps during the Great Depression. The CCC planted a cedar grove on top of the Pounds to help stabilize the abandoned farmland and built steps and stone walls. The crown jewel of their work was the construction of Pounds Hollow Lake, accomplished by covering the bed of a steam railroad.

The Rim Rock Recreation Trail was created in 1962–63 with money from the Illinois Federation of Women's Clubs.

Directions: Rim Rock/Pounds Hollow is southeast of Harrisburg in Saline County. From Harrisburg follow Illinois 145/34 to Illinois 34; turn east (left) onto Karbers Ridge Road (1065 N), drive through the town of Karbers Ridge (4 miles from the area), and follow the National Forest signs to the site.

Hours Open: The area is open year-round. The picnic area is open from 6 A.M. to 10 P.M. A swimming beach is open only in the summer and the campground is open from April 1 to December 15.

Facilities: Picnicking, camping with drinking water, swimming, boating, and fishing. A concession stand has row- and paddleboats for rent and also manages the swimming area and showers.

Permits and Rules: Pets must be leashed. No pets, bottles, cans, or coolers are permitted on the beach. Rappelling and rock climbing are prohibited. No horseback riding is allowed on the Rim Rock National Recreational Trail or on the Beaver Trail between Rim Rock and Pounds Hollow.

Further Information: Elizabethtown Ranger District, Shawnee National Forest, RR 2, Box 4, Elizabethtown, IL 62931; 618-287-2201.

Other Areas of Interest

The **Illinois Iron Furnace Recreation Site** is located 7 miles south of Karbers Ridge. The Illinois Iron Furnace was the first charcoal-fired iron furnace in the state. During the Civil War this furnace was the principal supplier of iron for the Union's ironclad ships. A .5-mile loop trail that follows scenic Big Creek is north of the site. For more information call 618-287-3222.

Located south of the intersection of Route 1 and Route 146, **Cave-In-Rock State Park** offers a lodge, restaurant, and a cave with a colorful history. It has been used by river bandits, outlaws and murderers, and Hollywood producers (appearing in *How the West Was Won*). Two trails, Hickory Ridge and Pirate's Bluff, total 1.75 miles. For more information call 618-289-4325.

Park Trails

Beaver Trail 👢👢—7.5 miles (one way)—This trail, which can be accessed from Indian Wall Picnic Area, descends into the hollow and goes right at an intersection, following Beaver Creek to Pounds Hollow Lake and the beach. It continues to circle the lake until reaching the dam, where it heads east and crosses Karbers Ridge blacktop. From the blacktop the trail uses old forest and gravel roads. Beaver Trail ends at Camp Cadiz, which has camping facilities, restrooms, and water.

River-to-River Trail 👢👢👢👢👢—146 miles—The River-to-River Trail honors the routes of the pioneers, running east-west, beginning at Battery Rock on the Ohio River, and ending at Devil's Backbone Park on the Mississippi. This trail passes just south of the Rim Rock/Pounds Hollow Area and has a trailhead at Camp Cadiz. For more information call the River-to-River Trail Society at 618-252-6789.

Rim Rock/
Pounds Hollow
Recreation Complex

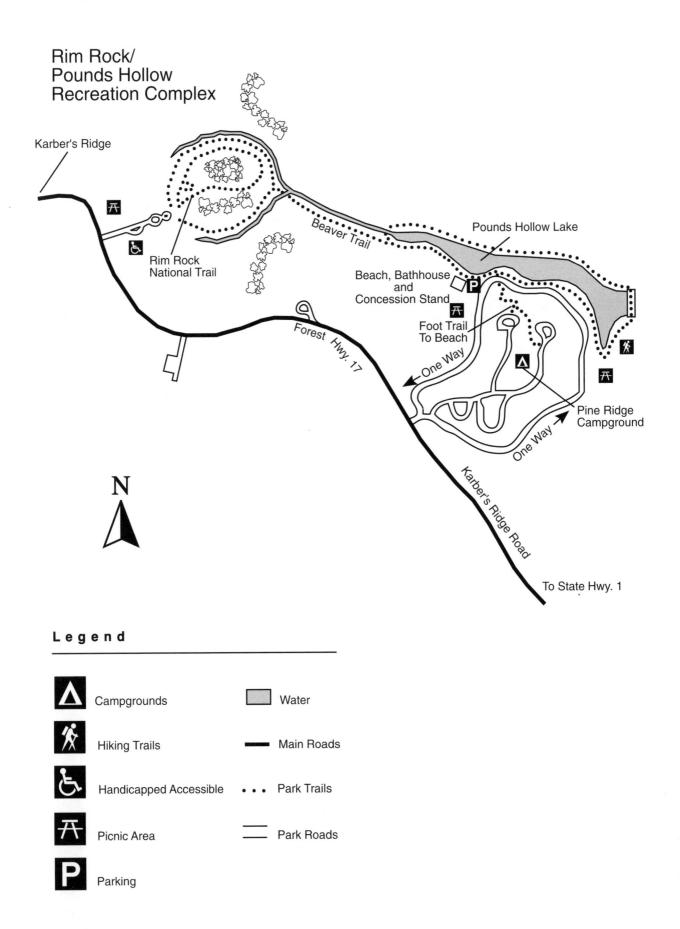

Karber's Ridge

Rim Rock
National Trail

Beaver Trail

Pounds Hollow Lake

Beach, Bathhouse
and
Concession Stand

Foot Trail
To Beach

One Way

One Way

Pine Ridge
Campground

Forest Hwy. 17

Karber's Ridge Road

To State Hwy. 1

N

Legend

△ Campgrounds

🚶 Hiking Trails

♿ Handicapped Accessible

🎪 Picnic Area

P Parking

▨ Water

▬ Main Roads

• • • Park Trails

═ Park Roads

Rim Rock National Trail

🥾🥾🥾🥾

Distance Round-Trip: 2 miles

Estimated Hiking Time: 1.5 hours

Walk among walls built 1,500 years ago by Native Americans, 200 years ago by European settlers, 60 years ago by the Civilian Conservation Corps—not to mention the most powerful builder, those geologic forces that shaped the Pounds sandstone millions of years ago.

Caution: Once you have descended into the valley, be aware of many large tree roots and rocks in the trail. Be careful near bluff edges.

Trail Directions: Park at the Rim Rock National Trail parking area and take the middle trail from the informational kiosk. The trail is paved with flagstone and heads straight uphill [**1**]. Within a few yards you'll encounter steps and an informational sign explaining and speculating about the remains of an ancient stone wall built by Native Americans. The wall extends almost 150 feet across the bluff top.

Continue on the trail and pass through a cedar grove planted by the CCC in 1939 to stabilize the sod [**2**]. At .3 mi. pause at a bench and look north. From here you can see Pounds Hollow Lake. Steps lead down to an observation deck (.4 mi.) [**3**] from which you can peer into the ravine forest below.

For an interesting side spur take a few minutes to walk down and hike among the giant boulders. Squeeze through moss-covered, rock walls and become lost in a maze of sandstone. Once you've found yourself, retrace your steps back up and rejoin the original trail. (You can explore Ox-Lot Cave later.) During the spring, along the neat flagstone trail, look for shooting stars and wood betony lining the way. Another name for wood betony is lousewort (farmers believed any animals that encountered it would become covered with lice).

As you hike along, look to your right through the gnarly branches of ancient cedars for the smooth, gray, upper branches of beech. On your left is a dry, oak-hickory woods, and on your right at .7 mi. [**4**] is a plant community called a *barrens*. The term barrens often was applied to habitats perceived to be unproductive. In truth, barrens are usually very dry with thin soil. The surface is usually a mosaic of bare rock, those plants that can tolerate the dry soil, and stunted, gnarled trees such as post and blackjack oaks.

You encounter the Indian Wall again, this time on your left (.85 mi.) [**5**], and the first half of the trail is completed. As you come off Rim Rock Trail, immediately go to the right and down Lower Pounds Trail: The first half of this trail is unmarked but fairly easy to follow. On your right are the bluffs, topped by barrens. Go right, up some fairly cryptic stone steps, and skirt the base of the bluff (1.15 mi.) [**6**]. As you emerge from a tunnel of rocks, the forest composition has changed; springtime brings the first installment of a multitude of spring wildflowers.

After skirting the base of the bluff and scrambling over a boulder field, another set of stone steps [**7**] are hidden among the huge rocks at 1.3 mi. Like the last set, these also were made by the CCC. Soon you will head upward and come upon Ox-Lot Cave (1.4 mi.) [**8**]. A sign provides details on the colorful past of this large rock overhang. Continue on the trail to an intersection at 1.55 mi. [**9**]; go right and around the bluff. At this point the trail leads through a veritable garden of spring wildflowers. From the earliest harbinger-of-spring to white trilliums, all your favorites can be found.

As you skirt the bluff note the smooth, gray bark of the large beeches. They present a biography of the valley through the names carved in them, but please do not add yours! At 1.85 mi. [**10**] you will cross the first of a series of large and small bridges. The trail ends at 2 mi. and you are back at the kiosk.

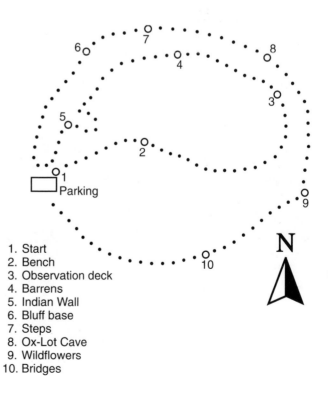

1. Start
2. Bench
3. Observation deck
4. Barrens
5. Indian Wall
6. Bluff base
7. Steps
8. Ox-Lot Cave
9. Wildflowers
10. Bridges

Beaver Trail 👢👢👢👢

Distance Round-Trip: 4 miles (including a .5-mile side spur)

Estimated Hiking Time: 3 hours

The trail is appropriately named, for gnawed stumps, dams, lodges, and wood chips are everywhere. The only thing missing is a glimpse of the elusive rodent. Instead of the beaver, I had to settle for a path of wood chips leading from a fresh-cut stump to the beaver's dining table, the shallow water at the edge of the lake.

Caution: Part way around the lake the trail will become fairly faint with many logs and rocks to negotiate. If the water is high, two places require log crossings. Remember when you cross the sandstone ledges that the surfaces may be wet and slippery.

Trail Directions: From the kiosk at Rim Rock National Trail take the trail farthest to the right at a sign indicating Beaver Trail [1]. The trail begins as a crushed-limestone path through a dry, oak-pine woods. Within the first .15 mi. [2] the trail crosses a series of wooden bridges and leads downward. A set of stone steps leads to huge sandstone bluffs on the left; others will soon appear on the right.

The forest between the bluffs supports a profusion of spring wildflowers, and as the trail nears the bluffs, both rocks and wildflowers seem to tumble down the slopes. You encounter a trail intersection at .4 mi. [3]; go right.

You will now cross a series of footbridges before reaching Pounds Hollow Lake. At the fourth bridge (.55 mi.) [4] a small waterfall sometimes (during spring) cascades down the rocks on the right; on the left you can see spicebush and beavers' damage to the tree. Go up the wooden steps and then to the left, still following the limestone path. Take time to admire the bald cypress growing in the ravine as you walk along a ridge that separates the wetland on the left from a dry, oak-hickory forest on the right.

On the left at .7 mi. note the gray, weathered remains of an old beaver dam and cross the final bridge before beginning to skirt Pounds Hollow Lake [5]. At .9 mi. [6], as you pass the wastewater-treatment plant, admire the stone wall built by the CCC during the late 1930s.

When you reach the Pounds Hollow Recreation Area at 1 mi. [7], the trail passes a beach and bathhouse. Follow the trail down the steps along a flagstone path, cross a bridge, and continue following the flagstone path as you skirt the lake on the left and picnic areas on the right. At 1.2 mi. [8] the last picnic area is passed and the flagstone path ends.

Continue along the lake: Although the path is not marked, a faint trail is present. Just keep the lake on your left! Find a convenient place to cross the narrow cove at 1.6 mi. [9], without getting wet feet. On the other side go left and continue to hike around the lake.

At 1.75 mi. [10] you will come to the spillway. If your visit is in spring, take a short side spur and go straight. Head downhill and bear to the right, following a wide trail. A short walk (about .5 mi. round-trip) on this path will yield a profusion of Virginia bluebells, yellow trout lily, and spicebush. Having had your fill of flowers, retrace your steps to the spillway and earthen dam, cross it, and go left (2.2 mi., including the spur) [11]. Continue to skirt the lake on the left.

The trail here, although faint, is easily followed. By now you have passed the picnic area and bathhouse on the opposite side (2.9 mi.) [12]. Close to the trail find a beaver lodge.

At 3.25 [13] ignore the orange tape and arrow, markers for a horse trail. Instead, continue straight ahead through moss, lichens, and sandstone. On your left is a picturesque view of a large cypress, beaver dam, and a pond. A few feet from this view the trail heads down, using sandstone rocks as steps. Where the stream narrows to a single channel (3.4 mi.) [14] head farther downward on a series of sandstone rock terraces. The trail passes between the bluff and stream.

At 3.5 mi. practice your balance-beam routine and cross the stream on a large log [15]. From here you will rejoin the limestone path, and at the intersection [3] go left, retracing your steps back up the bluff and to the parking area.

1. Start
2. Wooden bridges
3. Right turn
4. Waterfall
5. Old beaver dam
6. CCC wall
7. Bathhouse
8. Flagstone path ends
9. Cross cove
10. Spillway
11. Left turn
12. Beaver lodge
13. Cypress in pond
14. Rock terraces
15. Stream crossing

N

42. Garden of the Gods Recreation Area

- Discover a fairyland of rock formations, including Camel Rock, Noah's Ark, Table Rock, and Mushroom Rock.
- Step onto the rock ledges, gaze over the vistas, and create your own nicknames for the fantastic rock formations.
- Wind through the woods and encounter sandstone bluffs, huge boulders, and rugged sandstone knuckles.
- See spectacular fall color provided by huge, old-growth oaks, maples, and tulip trees.
- Hike part of the River-to-River Trail, crossing southern Illinois from Battery Rock on the Ohio River to Devil's Backbone on the Mississippi River.

Area Information

The massive Pennsylvanian sandstone escarpments of Garden of the Gods stand ancient, weathered, and exposed. A visit can leave one thirsting for water, with only a hand-pump drinking fountain to be seen. Still, evidence is everywhere that water has influenced these formations. The sandstone was deposited by a warm sea some 270 to 310 million years ago. Glacial meltwater and rain moved along the joints and planes of the sandstone, expanding crevices into fissures, fissures into clefts, and eventually creating the pinnacles, curiously carved boulders, rock shelters, tunnels, and deep valleys.

In addition to the rocky outcrops with exotic names, some cliff faces are decorated with dark-reddish swirls (made of iron) and raised designs called Liesegang Rings. Chemical changes caused the iron to solidify as rust between the rock particles; the sandstone is held together by these raised, dark bands of iron, and it has resisted weathering.

Directions: Garden of the Gods is southeast of Harrisburg in Saline County. From Harrisburg follow Illinois 145/34 to Illinois 34, turn east (left) onto Karbers Ridge Road (1065 N). At 2.8 miles turn east (left) at 250 E Garden of the Gods Road. At 1.4 mi. take another left into Garden of the Gods Recreation Area. There should be a National Forest sign and several brown highway signs to indicate the way.

Hours Open: The site is open year-round. The picnic area and observational trail are open from 6 A.M. to 10 P.M.

Facilities: A picnic area with grills, tables, and toilets and a 12-site campground with drinking water, fire grills, toilets, and tables are maintained year-round.

Permits and Rules: Pets are allowed only on a leash. No food or drink is allowed on the observation trail.

Further Information: Elizabethtown Ranger District, RR 2, Box 4, Elizabethtown, IL 62931; 618-287-2201.

Other Areas of Interest

Located between Garden of the Gods and Pounds Hollow (see park #41), north of Karbers Ridge, **High Knob Recreation Area** provides picnicking and hiking. High Knob is a 929-foot hill of Pennsylvanian sandstone. A 1-mile loop trail follows the northwest side of the knob rim. The River-to-River Trail may be accessed at the base of the knob near the entrance. There are also several unmarked, short, interconnecting loops. For more information call the Elizabethtown Ranger District at 618-287-2201.

Park Trails

Indian Point Trail —2 miles—This is a linear trail that leads to an overlook.

Lower Trail —2.5 miles—The valley beneath the rock formations can be explored by using this trail, accessed from the picnic-camping area.

After a quarter-mile the trail will bend right where it circles a bluff, crosses the park road, and enters a valley beneath rock formations. At 1.5 miles go right at an intersection that leads you past Shelter Rock. After a half-mile go right to Anvil Rock and soon enter the parking lot near the picnic-camping area.

Garden of the Gods Recreation Area

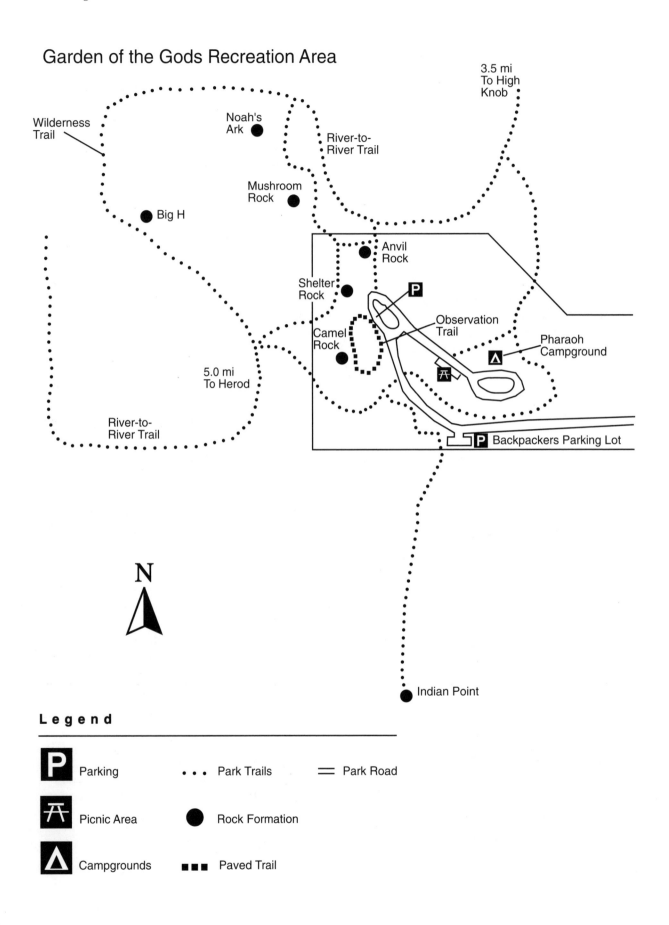

Legend

P Parking

・・・ Park Trails

═ Park Road

Picnic Area

● Rock Formation

Campgrounds

■■■ Paved Trail

Observation Trail 👢👢

Distance Round-Trip: .25 to .50 mile (depending on the number of spurs hiked)

Estimated Hiking Time: .75 hour

Camel Rock is the poster child for the region. A trip to southern Illinois without viewing Camel Rock is like going to Yellowstone and not seeing Old Faithful.

Caution: The trail and parking lot can be crowded during weekends in summer and fall.

Trail Directions: Begin the trail at the information signs off the parking lot [1]. The beginning of the trail is paved with flagstones. Take a right at the information sign. Although the walk won't be a wilderness experience, the scenery is worth the effort.

Within less than .1 mi. [2] you will come to a narrow squeeze through the rocks. Give it a try! Down the path from the squeeze is a great example of Liesegang Rings and an explanation of the phenomenon [3].

At .12 mi. the trail forks; go right [4]. This is a short, side spur enabling you to take in the view—which, at one time, was only forest as far as the eye could see. The large, bare slash on the horizon represents a strip mine. Retrace your steps back to the main trail.

At .2 mi. go right at a fork to another side spur [5]. Pause at Devil's Smokestack, a huge pillar formed when the softer sandstone around it washed away. The smokestack measures 30 feet. Retrace your steps and go to the left to begin a gentle climb to a rock-top vista.

A short observational trail appears at .3 mi. [6] and leads to a view of Camel Rock. After viewing this most famous of southern Illinois' landmarks, head downhill. Table rock appears on your left. Another observational spur leads to the right at .4 mi. [7] and provides a nice view of the forest to the south. Retrace your steps back to the original trail and head back.

Congratulations! Within .5 mi. you have seen and experienced the most prominent features of Garden of the Gods and warmed up your leg muscles for the more challenging Wilderness Trail.

1. Start
2. Narrow squeeze
3. Liesegang Rings
4. Right turn
5. Devil's Smokestack
6. Camel Rock
7. Observational spur

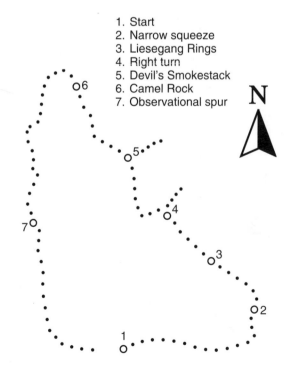

© Sue Post

Wilderness Trail 👢👢👢👢

Distance Round-Trip: 3.5 miles

Estimated Hiking Time: 2.25 hours

Wind your way through the dense woods and encounter unique sandstone formations, rugged rock knuckles, and eroding outcrops framed against the fall backdrop of a blue sky and the red and gold accents of ancient oaks, beeches, and maples.

Caution: Parts of this trail are also used by horses (don't neglect to dodge the horse apples!) so the path can be uneven. The trail is also very steep in places; don't be surprised if you must scamper over an occasional downed tree across the path.

Trail Directions: The trail begins to the north of the parking area for the Observational Trail. Enter an area enclosed by a split-rail fence, and begin the trail at the Garden of Gods Wilderness Trail sign [**1**]. The trail starts out as a crushed-gravel road, which soon gives way to a well-trampled dirt path. At the Anvil Rock sign (.1 mi.) take a left [**2**]. You can see this formation from the path or take a short spur to the left to examine the rock and its Liesegang Rings more closely. Walk through the tunnel in the rock and rejoin the main trail.

The trail is hard packed and wanders through an oak-hickory forest with many sandstone outcrops. At .4 mi. take a short side spur to Mushroom Rock. If the sign is missing, go left at the gnarled cedar [**3**]. Backtrack and continue onward. Take time in this area to step onto the ledges and use your imagination to name the many rock formations. Another side spur appears at .6 mi., leading to the Noah's Ark formation. Take this left to examine the arklike formation on top of a narrow rock pedestal [**4**]. Backtrack again and continue on the trail.

The trail next goes up and down a series of small rock outcrops and comes to a junction at .75 mi. Go left onto the River-to-River Trail, which at this point is a deeply eroded path [**5**]. The trail will be marked with either a blue i or a large white diamond with a blue i in the center. This segment passes through a little canyon with large rock outcrops.

At 1 mi. the trail begins a climb [**6**]. Note the nice honeycomb pattern on the sandstone. A sandstone bluff is on your right; to the left are rolling hills with many sandstone knuckles and outcrops. At 1.2 mi. (the big H sign) look around for a rock formation resembling an H. Immediately after the H, the trail forks (1.25 mi.); go right, up and through the rocks [**7**], and follow the markers on the trees to stay on the path.

You have now left the bluffs and will wind through the woods. Note the understory, carpeted with Christmas fern in spots. At 1.75 mi. a series of rock boulders leads you into a valley [**8**]. On your left is a sandstone bluff, and beech trees with huge, gray trunks grow along the stream. In the valley you begin a series of stream crossings, crisscrossing back and forth in a hollow or valley full of large beech trees (2 mi.) [**9**]. You can expect to get your feet wet in springtime. Take time to admire the valley's large oak, tulip, and beech trees—giants from a bygone era.

At 2.4 mi. the trail begins to climb out of the hollow [**10**]. The trees are smaller, and red cedar trees appear. This area is definitely drier. A trail intersection appears at 2.8 mi. [**11**]. Go left (a sign indicates you are heading toward High Knob). As you head east on this dirt path, you will pass a moss-covered sandstone bluff to your right. Ahead is a series of boulder steps that go up to a large shelter cave. The trail soon widens, becoming strewn with boulders, steep and tricky to walk.

A large rock looms ahead at 3.3 mi., and the trail comes to a T; go to the right [**12**], returning to the original trail leading to Anvil Rock. From Anvil Rock it is a short hike back to the wooden fence and the parking lot.

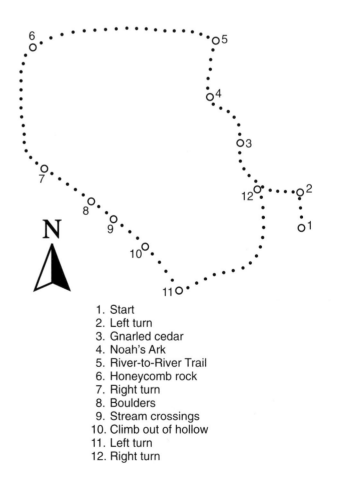

1. Start
2. Left turn
3. Gnarled cedar
4. Noah's Ark
5. River-to-River Trail
6. Honeycomb rock
7. Right turn
8. Boulders
9. Stream crossings
10. Climb out of hollow
11. Left turn
12. Right turn

43. Northern Shawnee Hills

- Discover and explore the unique plant communities of barrens and glades.
- Meet the patriarch of the Shawnee Hills—Stone Face.
- Commune with Stone Face as you enjoy one of the best scenic vistas in the Shawnee.
- Hike on a pioneer roadway and stop at a popular watering hole of the old times.

Area Information

The original Shawnee Hills area wasn't the solid, forested land that we are familiar with today. Before European immigrants settled here, much of the landscape was quite open and grassy. They called these grassy openings in the forest *barrens,* rightly assuming the soil must be poor to produce such a scanty growth of timber. Barrens are found on rocky, dry, south-facing slopes that have only a thin layer of soil covering the rocks. Vegetation includes small, gnarled, and twisted blackjack and post oaks. Prairie grasses and the occasional blazing star grow under the oaks.

Glades, another plant community found in woods openings, are open expanses of bedrock on a bluff top. Here the dominant tree is red cedar. Although prairie grasses such as little bluestem occur, the ground is just as likely to be covered with moss and lichens that crunch like eggshells as the hot, dry summer wears on.

Both communities, barrens and glades, were maintained by fire. In 1922 botanist H.A. Gleason observed, "Large areas of barrens were converted into forest by magic when the fires that had maintained them were stopped and the oak sprouts became trees." So don't be surprised, when you visit either Gibbons Creek Barrens or Stone Face, to find the ground is blackened: Diligent and patient volunteers are trying to restore and maintain a bit of history.

Directions: Gibbons Creek Barrens is located north of Herod on Illinois 34. From the post office in Herod continue north on Route 34 for 1.3 miles to a gravel entrance road on the right side of the highway. Enter and proceed .2 miles to a small parking area with a large wooden sign. **Stone Face Recreation Area** is also north of the small town of Herod. Go north on Illinois 34 to the town of Rudiment. From here follow the directional signs to Stone Face for about 4 miles along a gravel road. The entrance to Stone Face is Forest Road 150, and it is about .25 mi. long.

Hours Open: Gibbons Creek Barrens is open daily from 8 A.M. to 6 P.M. **Stone Face** is open from dawn to dusk.

Facilities: There are no facilities at either site.

Permits and Rules: Both areas are nature preserves; do not remove any plants or animals from the sites.

Further Information: Gibbons Creek Barrens, The Illinois Nature Conservancy, 8 S. Michigan Ave., Suite 900, Chicago, IL 60603; 312-346-8166. **Stone Face Recreation Area,** Shawnee National Forest Headquarters, 901 S. Commercial Street, Harrisburg, IL 62946; 618-253-7114.

Other Areas of Interest

Located southeast of Harrisburg, **Saline County Conservation Area** is a combination of Saline River bottomland and the northern Shawnee Hills. Springs, rocky creeks, and Glen O. Jones Lake are some of the area's highlights. The site accommodates camping, hunting, picnicking, boating, fishing, and hiking. Three trails are located here: Lake Trail, 3 miles that encircle Glen O. Jones Lake; Wildlife Nature Trail, .75 mile; and Cave Hill Trail, 3 miles (linear) that end at Cave Hill. For more information call 618-276-4405.

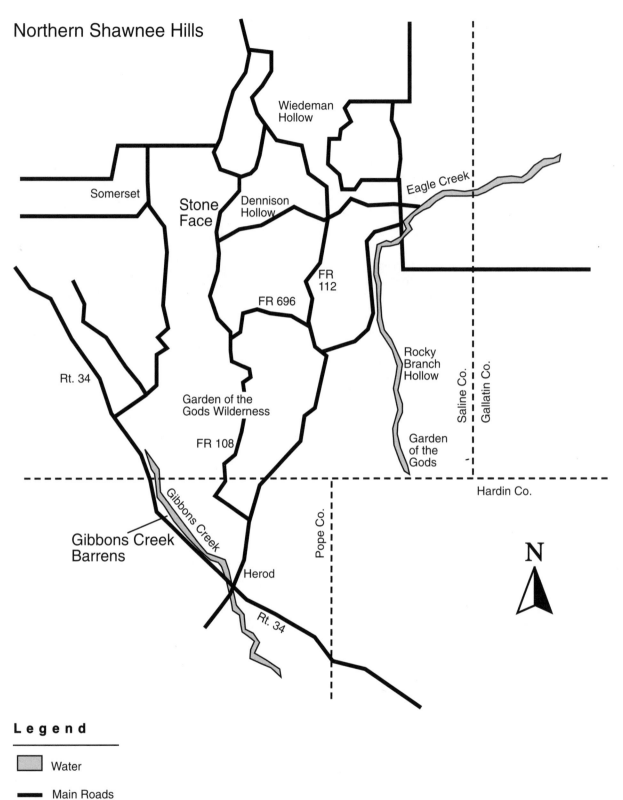

Northern Shawnee Hills

Wiedeman Hollow

Somerset

Stone Face

Dennison Hollow

Eagle Creek

FR 112

FR 696

Rt. 34

Rocky Branch Hollow

Saline Co.

Gallatin Co.

Garden of the Gods Wilderness

FR 108

Garden of the Gods

Hardin Co.

Gibbons Creek

Gibbons Creek Barrens

Pope Co.

Herod

Rt. 34

N

Legend

Water

Main Roads

County Line

Gibbons Creek Barrens

👢👢👢👢👢

Distance Round-Trip: 2.25 miles

Estimated Hiking Time: 2 hours

At the beginning you may experience a smug sense of calm—this trail is only a pleasant, wildflower-strewn path next to a creek. Once you hit the main route, however, it's up, up, and up, with nothing on the forest floor except plentiful oak leaves of various shapes and sizes. Oh, my aching calves!

Caution: At times this trail may seem more of a cross-country scramble as you traverse a boulder-strewn hillside and navigate over or under fallen logs. Watch for loose rocks, roots, and logs.

Trail Directions: Begin the trail at the large sign in the parking area [1]. The trail is marked with blue blazes and begins as a wide, grassy strip; to the left is a patch of giant cane. The trail soon crosses a bridge, and in the spring the ground is littered with spring wildflowers—Virginia bluebells, toothwort, Dutchman's-breeches, and shooting star. At .15 mi. [2] a side spur leads right and to a spring. Retrace your steps back to the main trail.

The main trail follows an old roadway used by settlers to go from Golconda to the northern prairie country. Go left at the sign that indicates Barrens and Main Trail (.25 mi.) [3]. From here the trail heads up a steep slope through an oak woods. At .35 mi. [4] you'll come to a junction with a sign (the sign may be lying on the ground) indicating the Barrens Trail, Short Cut Trail, and parking area. Go right, taking the short spur to the barrens. Notice how the trees along this spur are smaller and the soil is much rockier, with boulders scattered about; prairie grasses, such as big and little bluestem, have also appeared. This is a barrens. The trees, although just as old as those in the valley below, are short and twisted due to their excessive exposure to the sun and lack of moisture.

After discovering the barrens, retrace your steps to the intersection (.8 mi.) [4]. Continue on the main trail and hike upward. Once at the top note how disturbed the woods are. Here the trees are smaller and the understory is full of shrubs and vines—this part of the trail was an old clearing, and you are now hiking on an old wagon trail that leads to a homesite, which you'll reach at 1.2 mi. [5].

A few feet past the homesite is the spur to a sandstone glade; go right to explore this unique plant community. The spur ends at the glade. Retrace your steps to rejoin the main trail and go right (1.3 mi.).

On the trail note the odd, swirly shapes on the dead trees (which look like something out of the *Wizard of Oz!*). Soon you are away from the homesite and the strange trees, and the woods improve. The trail, marked with blue blazes and yellow ribbons, begins to go downward. At 1.5 mi. [6] a stony gap appears and the trail leads down through it; follow the blazes and ribbons. Use caution as you descend. Small sandstone outcrops occur in the area around the trail. About three-fourths of the way down, you'll skirt a large sandstone outcrop.

The descent ends at Gibbons Creek (1.65 mi.) [7]; go right. The trail now follows the left bank of the creek. Cross a small tributary to Gibbons Creek (which usually is dry). At 1.75 mi. [8] go right and upward at the giant boulder in the trail: Local legend claims that this large boulder was a hiding place for whiskey during Prohibition. You may need to climb under one log and over another here. The trail next traverses a ridge overlooking Gibbons Creek. Look to your right as you hike this section. You are walking over the rocks of another barrens (1.85 mi.) [9]. Look for the small and gnarly oaks, prairie grasses, and forbs such as little bluestem, Indian grass, asters, and goldenrod.

At the base of the ridge, the main trail comes onto a fairly level path that will led back to the parking area (2 mi.) [10]. The area you just hiked is regularly burned to help restore the original vegetation to its open condition and eliminate shade-tolerant maples and the shrubby understory. You soon are back to the intersection (2.15 mi.) [3]; cross the bridge and complete the hike.

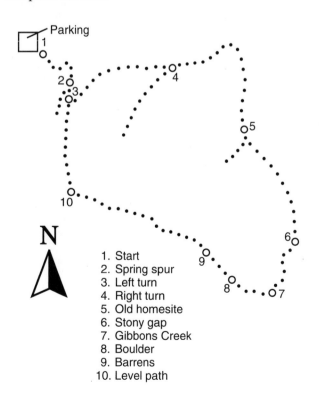

1. Start
2. Spring spur
3. Left turn
4. Right turn
5. Old homesite
6. Stony gap
7. Gibbons Creek
8. Boulder
9. Barrens
10. Level path

Stone Face ⚘⚘⚘⚘

Distance Round-Trip: 1.75 miles

Estimated Hiking Time: 1.25 hours

It's just you and Stone Face here, taking in the spectacular views of the Shawnee Hills and the Saline River Valley.

Caution: Large chunks of rock and roots in the trail can trip you. The descent after viewing Stone Face is quite rocky—use caution.

Trail Directions: The crushed-limestone trail begins at the parking area and forks within a few feet; go right and uphill [1]. As you trek upward through the oak-hickory woods, note the large sandstone boulders littering the hillside. At .15 mi. [2] the trail angles to the left, still climbing. The trail comes to the bluffs at .3 mi. [3]; go left. From an airplane this ridge looks like a thin, gray line through a sea of green. From the ground, however, the bluffs are much more imposing and formidable.

The trail soon intersects with the path that will lead downward (.35 mi.) [4]. Continue straight ahead. The trail (no longer crushed limestone) goes under a large chunk of sandstone. As you skirt the bluff, note the maze of moss that covers it. Walk under a small shelter cave before coming to a faint trail intersection at .5 mi. [5]. Although the trail appears to go left, go right and uphill. You will be walking atop the same bluff that you skirted a few minutes ago.

Soon you reach the first of several sandstone outcrops with great views. A wooden fence is provided to protect you from falling over the edge. Straight ahead is Stone Face (.7 mi.) [6], surveying his domain and guarded by scrubby sentinels of post oak, blackjack oak, and red cedar. After experiencing the view and Stone Face (more impressive than New Hampshire's famous Old Man of the Mountains), continue walking on top of the bluff. The area to your left has been burned and cut in an effort to restore the original vegetation—a barrens community. Look for gnarled and stunted post oak (its leaves have five to

seven rounded lobes, the two middle lobes being the largest) and blackjack oak (its leaves are broadest at the tip and have three bristle-tipped lobes). In summer look for blazing star and white prairie clover in this area.

Just before the power lines, look to the right at a large blackjack oak (.85 mi.) [7]. Continue straight. The trail begins a descent until it comes out on bare sandstone; still continue straight. At 1.1 mi. [8] head downward and pick your way through the rocks. About one-third of the way down, go to the right, cautiously skirting the bluff and following a rocky path. If you are hiking during a wet period, you are likely to see small waterfalls coming off the rocks. Look at the bluff with its upward-thrust folds and faults.

At 1.3 mi. [9] the trail skirts a huge chunk of rock that has broken off from the main bluff. Soon you rejoin the limestone path (1.4 mi.) [10]. Follow it to 1.55 mi. [4] where the trail forks; go left and head downward and back to the parking area.

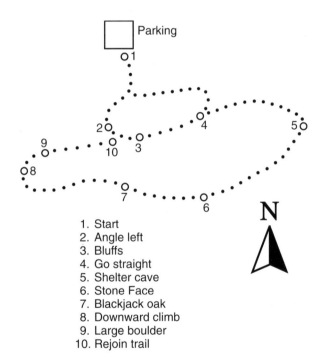

1. Start
2. Angle left
3. Bluffs
4. Go straight
5. Shelter cave
6. Stone Face
7. Blackjack oak
8. Downward climb
9. Large boulder
10. Rejoin trail

44. Lusk Creek and Hayes Creek Canyons

- Visit one of the most beautiful stream valleys in southern Illinois.
- Play hide-and-seek with cerulean-throated, eastern fence lizards.
- Bring your moss, lichen, and fern field guides—these canyons are excellent places for viewing lower-plant life.
- Enjoy the spring flowering trees—redbud, dogwood, and shadbush—against bare canyon walls.
- View waterfalls, gorges, slip slopes, cliffs, and dripways.

Area Information

Whereas glaciation was the major force creating the topography of much of Illinois (including many canyons in the Shawnee Hills cut by meltwater from glaciers farther north), streams were responsible for deepening and shaping the sandstone valleys of the Shawnee Hills. Lusk Creek and Hayes Creek are excellent examples of beautiful scenery along the courses of southern Illinois streams.

Lusk Creek cuts through massive sandstone blocks along a valley lined with cliffs ranging from a few feet to almost 100 feet high. Steep slopes are clothed with mosses, lichens, and deciduous trees. On high ledges, miniature wildflower gardens have gained a foothold in soil-filled cracks. Lusk Creek itself is an outstanding stream with deep, blue-green rocky pools, gravelly riffles, and cold springs.

Hayes Creek flows over beds of sandstone. A tributary stream to Hayes Creek (entering from the east) has cut deeply into its sandstone bed to form a steep gorge at the escarpment (steep, rocky slope). Where the two streams merge visitors will find a double waterfall named Double Branch Hole. Here at Hayes Creek you have the opportunity to walk on and discover the life of a sandstone escarpment. The small, gnarled, and twisted trees, cushions of moss and lichens, and camouflaged insect and reptilian life here make the area look like the netherworld surface of a distant planet.

Directions: Lusk Creek Canyon is 4 miles northeast of Eddyville. From Eddyville on Illinois Route 145 turn right (east) onto County Road 5, the Eddyville blacktop. Follow the blacktop .25 mile and turn on the first road to the left—County Road 126. There should be a sign indicating Lusk Creek. Follow this road until you come to the Lusk Creek parking area on the left.

Hayes Creek Canyon is located 1.1 miles from Eddyville. From Illinois 145 go through the village of Eddyville. Just past a horse campground you should find a small parking area on the left.

Hours Open: The sites are open year-round.

Facilities: Lusk Creek has a privy toilet. There are no facilities at **Hayes Creek**.

Permits and Rules: Part of the trail at **Lusk Creek** is located in a dedicated Illinois Nature Preserve: No pets are allowed on the trail. At both sites the removal of plants and animals is prohibited.

Further Information: (For both sites) Vienna Ranger District, Shawnee National Forest, P.O. Box 567, Vienna, IL 62995; 618-658-2111.

Other Areas of Interest

Located near the tiny town of Robbs in Pope County, **Millstone Bluff Archeological Site** has the most accessible rock carvings (petroglyphs) in southern Illinois. A .5-mi. interpretive trail helps you discover and learn about the culture of the Woodland and Mississippian Indians. View a stonewall, a former village, burial grounds, petroglyphs, and an ancient plaza. For more information call 618-253-7144.

Lusk Creek

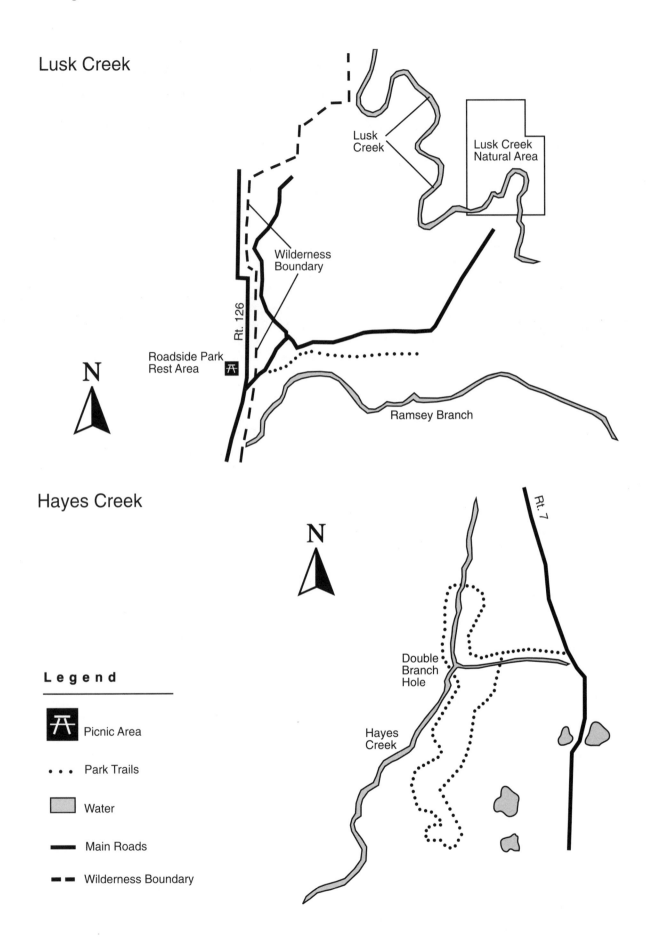

Lusk Creek

Lusk Creek Natural Area

Wilderness Boundary

Rt. 126

N

Roadside Park Rest Area

Ramsey Branch

Hayes Creek

N

Rt. 7

Double Branch Hole

Hayes Creek

Legend

Picnic Area

• • •   Park Trails

Water

Main Roads

Wilderness Boundary

Lusk Creek Canyon 👢👢👢

Distance Round-Trip: 3.5 miles

Estimated Hiking Time: 2.25 hours

Discover Lusk Creek Gorge, a place where Lusk Creek slithers through the steep-sided cliffs like a turquoise snake.

Caution: The trail can be very muddy and uneven due to horse traffic. Logs sometimes block the trail, and exposed roots can trip the unwary. In the preserve, the trail is very close to the edge—use common sense.

Trail Directions: The trail begins across the road from the parking area at a metal gate [**1**] and is marked with white arrows, though these are few and far between. At first the trail is lined with old, gnarled cedars and thickets of honeysuckle and multiflora rose. At .3 mi. [**2**] you will come to a crossroads—continue straight ahead on the small path into a pine plantation. The trail will soon come to an old forest road—go left. Remember this site for the return trip!

The remains of an old homestead are on the left, complete with daffodils (.4 mi.) [**3**]. You next hike through another pine plantation along the now-cushiony trail. Look for Christmas ferns in the understory. The common name refers to the fern's being green at Christmas time (settlers gathered the evergreen fronds for holiday decorations). Some botanists think the plant's sterile leaflets resemble Christmas stockings.

Here and there the symmetry of the pines is broken by a large maple or oak. Take a short side spur to examine a woodland pond on your right (1.15 mi.) [**4**]. Water lilies float on the top, while just under the water's surface (in spring) are salamander egg masses made of tiny, gelatinous balls, each with a dot indicating the developing larval salamander. Watch water striders "walk on water," using the surface tension of the pond to keep them afloat. Before returning to the trail look around the water's edge for dragonflies, damselflies, and large, lazy tadpoles.

The trail soon (1.55 mi.) comes upon an open area surrounded by a fence used for tying up horses [**5**]. A few yards down the trail is the entrance to Lusk Creek Canyon Nature Preserve; enter it, using the series of stone and log reinforced steps. At the bottom of the

steps the pine plantation has been replaced with ancient cedars and the cushions of pine needles, replaced by mats of lichens and mosses.

Follow the narrow path down. On your left look for a large, lichen-encrusted, sandstone boulder. At 1.8 mi. [**6**] the trail ends at Indian Kitchen Canyon. Here the water is a fantastic turquoise color. Continue descending, using the stones and logs, and explore the edge of Lusk Creek. Next go right. The trail will come precipitously close to the edge. On your left is Lusk Creek, backed by bare canyon walls; on the right are moss- and wildflower-covered rocks.

Any sign of the trail soon ends (1.85 mi.) [**7**]. The cliff is farther from the creek here, but the rocks on the right are to the edge. The curious and adventuresome may continue to explore Lusk Creek in the summer by wading in (be careful of the plant life). Eventually you must retrace your steps to the trail that led into the canyon. Before heading back up, explore the area straight ahead on a short trail.

On the left you can get a close-up view of moss and ferns. Note the spores underneath the fern fronds and the fruiting bodies of the mosses (1.9 mi.) [**8**]. Interrupting the carpeting of green moss are the bright red fruits of partridgeberry. Although the name suggests they are relished by partridges, the berries are not an important foodstuff for wildlife. Continue to explore at your leisure. The trail will soon disappear, so retrace your steps back to where you entered the valley [**6**].

Once you exit the Nature Preserve [**5**], retrace your steps back through the pines. The trail where you enter the pines back to the parking area is faint: It is a few yards past the homestead (the clear area with bricks and daffodils) at about 3.15 mi.

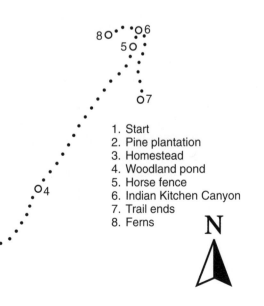

1. Start
2. Pine plantation
3. Homestead
4. Woodland pond
5. Horse fence
6. Indian Kitchen Canyon
7. Trail ends
8. Ferns

N

Hayes Creek Canyon 👢👢👢

Distance Round-Trip: 2 miles

Estimated Hiking Time: 1.5 hours

On a gray, spring day the landscape is foreign. The rocks are covered with cushions of moss and lichen. The areas of the pink sandstone known as dripways are a deep-maroon color, caused by excess water trickling toward the gorge below. Balls of male crane flies writhe across the sandstone in an ancient mating ritual, and the gnarled, twisted, lichen-covered cedars and blackjack oaks hide the fact that they are hundreds of years old.

Caution: The trail can be very muddy and rutted; horses share it, so watch where you step. The moss on the wet rocks is very slippery! A small piece of the trail is on private land, with signs posted—please show respect and courtesy.

Trail Directions: The trail begins to the left of the pull-off and soon crosses under a power line [**1**]. Go perpendicular to the small creek (left). After .1 mi. the view of the horse campground disappears and an oak-cedar forest is on both sides of the trail.

The trail forks at .3 mi. [**2**]; take a short side spur to the left and explore the sandstone outcrop. While walking along the sandstone, angle to your left to explore the miniature waterfalls and creek, which erodes through the sandstone. Once you have finished exploring, retrace your steps and rejoin the trail. Although the trail is unmarked, horse traffic has made the path easy to follow.

The trail winds briefly through cedar and is away from the canyon. It soon goes to the left and downward, emerging on a sandstone ledge that makes a smooth, hard hiking path (.6 mi.) [**3**]. On your left note the canyon and a small waterfall. The smooth ledge soon becomes a series of rock terraces that lead down to Hayes Creek. Angle to your left, climb down the terraces to the water (.7 mi.) [**4**], and follow the creek downstream (left). Note how the creek flows across solid bedrock instead of gravel or cobble.

Continue down the creek until you come to a crossing at .85 mi. [**5**]. There is a small rock ford at two small, muscular-looking trees (blue beeches). As soon as you cross the creek, join the horse trail. At this point you will be hiking in Hayes Creek Canyon. The trail will soon recross the creek (.9 mi.). Find a suitable spot to cross and continue hiking through a mesic (moist) ravine and hardwood forest.

Before you cross the creek again, take a short side spur to Double Branch Hole (1 mi.) [**6**], where you can see two waterfalls emptying into a spectacular circular canyon. Retrace your steps to the creek and

cross it. The trail ascends, skirting the bluff on the left.

The trail leads under a shelter cave. On your right the trail passes by huge chunks of sandstone that have broken off from the main bluff.

At 1.15 mi. [**7**] you emerge from this city of boulders with the creek to your right and the bluff to your left. The trail soon angles to the right, heading toward a large chunk of sandstone and then again to the left, skirting the bluff. Another shelter cave appears at 1.2 mi. [**8**] and the trail forks. Go uphill, skirting the bluff (1.35 mi.) [**9**]. Once the trail forks, walk to where the rock outcrop is no longer visible on the hillside. (Note a short stretch of fence and also signage that this is private land.) Work your way to the top of the ridge (only a short distance) to avoid hiking on private land.

Once on top rejoin the horse trail and go left. The trail soon goes to the right through the woods and away from the bluff (1.5 mi.) [**10**]. To your left you can see the top of a large boulder. You will pass a fence and a very small waterfall, both on your left. At 1.7 mi. [**11**] cross the rock bed of a small creek and go up the other side.

When you come to the second bedrock streambed (which leads into Double Branch Hole), leave the horse trail, go left, and follow it downstream. You are now walking on a lichen and moss covered sandstone ledge (1.8 mi.) [**12**]. You may have to leap across several rivulets in spring. Soon you reach the area you explored earlier on a side spur, only this time on the opposite side of the canyon. Beware of the wet dripways, which are algae-coated and very slick! Cross the creek (1.85 mi.) [**13**] and head up into the forest where you will rejoin the main trail—go to the right and retrace your steps to the parking area.

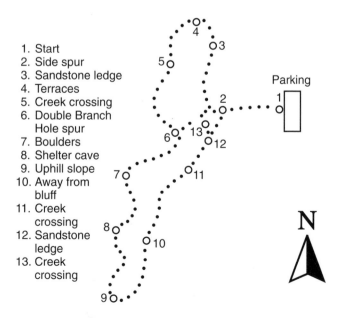

1. Start
2. Side spur
3. Sandstone ledge
4. Terraces
5. Creek crossing
6. Double Branch Hole spur
7. Boulders
8. Shelter cave
9. Uphill slope
10. Away from bluff
11. Creek crossing
12. Sandstone ledge
13. Creek crossing

45. Bell Smith Springs Recreation Area

- Follow an ever-narrowing valley to a spectacular, stream-carved gorge.
- View canyons, a natural stone bridge, and diverse rock formations.
- Look for grasshoppers that resemble lichens and eastern fence lizards camouflaged against rocks, soil, and lichen-covered trees.
- Search in the nooks and crannies between giant boulders to discover some of the area's 700 species of wildflowers and ferns.
- Enjoy a profusion of redbud, dogwood, and early spring butterflies.

Area Information

Bell Smith Springs is a world of vertical sandstone cliffs, clear rocky streams, outstanding rock formations, and a lush spring flora. Located in the Shawnee National Forest, Bell Smith Springs was named after its former owner.

The region is an area of contrasts. Sandstone ledges are windswept and scorched by the summer sun. Blankets of lichens and moss help insulate the rock against the extremes of heating and cooling. Moisture brings slick, dark, algae-covered streaks (called dripways) to the sandstone shelves. In contrast to the harsh ledges, the canyons are dark, cool, and green. Beech trees, their gray tree trunks resembling huge elephant legs, occupy preferred spots next to the stream. Large clumps of yellow trout lily on inaccessible canyon shelves make one wish for the dexterity of a mountain goat to allow a closer inspection.

Directions: Drive south from Harrisburg on Route 145 and turn right (west) on Forest Route (FR) 402 at Delwood. After about 4 miles on this gravel road you will come to a T junction with FR 447. Turn left and proceed south past Teal Pond to FR 848. Turn right onto FR 848. At the park-entrance sign, go 1.6 miles farther to a right turn that leads to Hunting Branch Picnic Area. To reach the main parking area for Bell Smith Springs, continue to the end of FR 848.

Hours Open: The site is open-year round. Teal Pond campground is open year-round, and Redbud campground is open from March 15 through December 15. Hunting Branch Picnic Area is open from March 15 through October 31 from 6 A.M. to 10 P.M.

Facilities: Camping (tent and RV), fishing, and picnicking are available, with restrooms at the campgrounds and parking areas.

Permits and Rules: The cutting of live trees, shrubs, and other vegetation is prohibited. Weapons, firearms, and fireworks are not to be discharged in the campground or picnic areas. Pets should be confined to a leash and not allowed in the water.

Further Information: Vienna Ranger District, Shawnee National Forest, Vienna, IL 62995; 618-658-2111.

Other Areas of Interest

Accessed from FR 402, **Burden Falls**, a seasonal, 100-foot waterfall, plunges into a deep canyon each spring but dries to a trickle by midsummer. A linear trail along the south-bluff's bank allows the curious a closer look. For more information call the Vienna Ranger District at 618-658-2111.

Park Trails

General Area Trail or the White Trail 👢👢👢—1.4 miles—This trail can be accessed either at Hunting Branch Picnic Area or the parking area at the end of FR 848. The trail, marked with white diamonds painted on trees or rocks, goes through the center of the park and passes by Devil's Backbone, a cliff area. Farther on, deep, spring-fed pools offer a welcome respite on hot summer days. The trail eventually leads to the site of the spring for which the area was named.

Natural Bridge Trail or the Yellow Trail 👢👢👢— 1.5 miles—This trail begins and ends at the parking area at the end of FR 848. The trail is marked with yellow diamonds on trees or rocks and begins with a descent into Bay Creek Canyon using a series of steps cut into the rock face. The trail explores the area above and below the natural bridge, a sandstone formation 30 feet high, 20 feet wide, and more than 125 feet long that formed through centuries of water erosion.

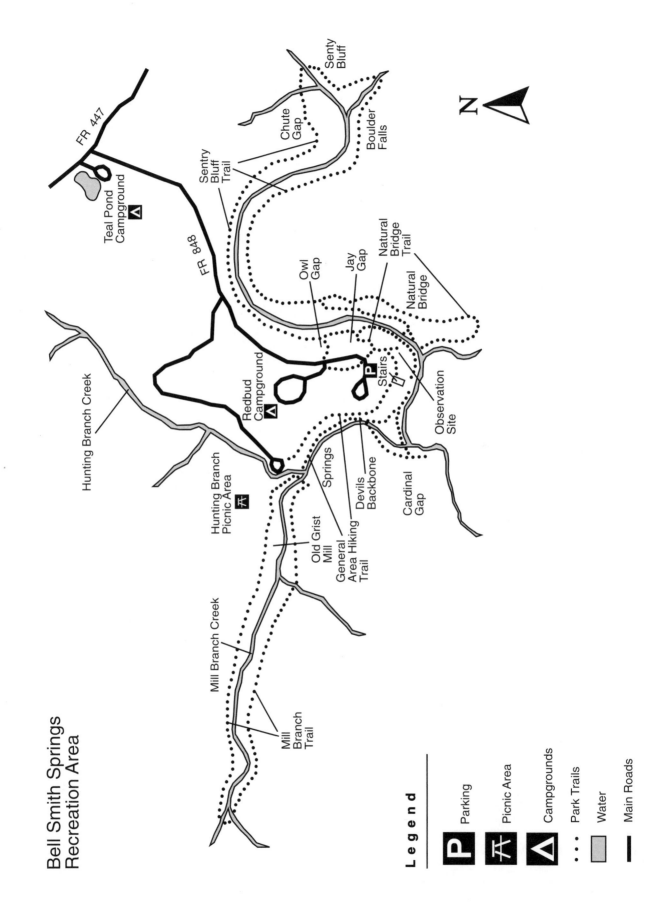

Bell Smith Springs
Recreation Area

Legend

P	Parking
🛆	Picnic Area
△	Campgrounds
· · ·	Park Trails
▨	Water
—	Main Roads

Mill Branch Trail 👢👢

Distance Round-Trip: 2 miles

Estimated Hiking Time: 1 hour

Mill Branch Trail offers the opportunity to play hide-and-seek with the lichen grasshopper and the eastern fence lizard—they will do the hiding—and to experience the unique habitat of a sandstone ledge.

Caution: The sandstone ledges are slippery when wet. Stay off the cushions of lichens and mosses to help protect them.

Trail Directions: The trail begins near Hunting Branch Picnic Area at a parking lot before you reach the picnic grounds. The picnic area is on the other side of a concrete ford through the creek. Start your hike at a tree marked with both white and orange diamonds [**1**]. Immediately cross a creek—which can be a challenge in wet weather or the spring. Mill Branch Trail is marked with orange diamonds.

After a few steps the trail will fork at a yellow, metal pole sporting a No Camping sign [**2**]; proceed to the right. The trail climbs a series of rocky steps and crosses outcrops of lichen-covered sandstone, with cushions of moss on either side. Look for trail markers on trees or painted on the rocks.

On your right is a dry, oak-hickory woods with many red cedar trees. In the spring note the diminutive flowers of yellow star grass. In the fall single stems of blazing stars can be seen here. To your left is the flat-bottomed stream valley of Mill Creek that varies from a raging torrent in the spring to a series of quiet, leaf-strewn pools in the fall. As you proceed, note that the valley becomes deeper, narrower, and rocky—more canyon-like. Along the trail be alert for eastern fence lizards, especially in spring when males have a bright-blue brooding patch.

At .5 mi. you will cross a series of small, intermit-

tent streams that can be full in the spring [**3**]. The trail is just a narrow, rocky path at this point, and the trail markings are very faint. Two large chunks of sandstone boulders appear on your left at .8 mi. [**4**], providing a perfect place to observe Mill Branch Creek and look for the lichen grasshopper (whose pattern mimics the colors of the lichens on which it sits).

After this brief side trip, the trail soon crosses the sandstone (.9 mi.) [**5**], marked here with white diamonds (these may be just faded orange ones). Walk cautiously on the ledge, especially if there is a thin layer of moss. The trail, still on the sandstone ledges, begins to descend toward Mill Branch Creek.

At 1 mi. the trail leaves the ledges to pass through the woods and, within a few steps, crosses Mill Branch Creek and heads up the other side [**6**]. You can expect to get your feet wet here during spring hikes. The trail on the south side of Mill Branch winds farther from the stream and into the woods. Temporarily off the hot sandstone, it passes through a cool woods composed mostly of oaks and hickories, but also of maples and an understory of Christmas fern.

After about .5 mi. the trail descends onto a sandstone shelf [**7**], marked by faded white diamonds. You should see a series of pools in the sandstone one below the other—like stair-steps—as you cross the feeder stream and come out of the woods to the right.

At 1.75 mi. you will cross a small rocky stream. From here the trail subtly forks [**8**]. The oak tree on the left has both an orange and a white diamond; remember that you are on the orange trail, so go downward. (The white trail continues straight ahead and becomes very narrow, with a large drop-off to the left.) The orange trail winds its way down into the valley. Note the partridgeberry with its bright-red fruit growing among the mosses. You now enter the streambed of Mill Branch Creek. Cross the stream [**9**] and at 1.95 mi. you return to the No Camping sign [**2**]. Cross the stream and you'll arrive back at your vehicle.

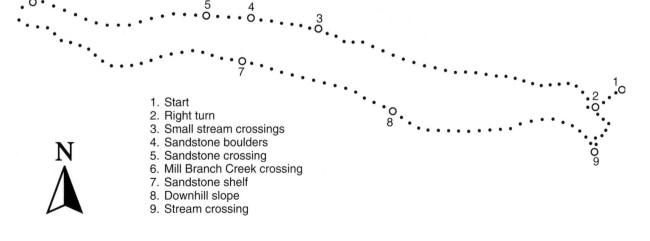

1. Start
2. Right turn
3. Small stream crossings
4. Sandstone boulders
5. Sandstone crossing
6. Mill Branch Creek crossing
7. Sandstone shelf
8. Downhill slope
9. Stream crossing

N

Sentry Bluff Trail 👢👢👢

Distance Round-Trip: 3.5 miles

Estimated Hiking Time: 2.5 to 3 hours

Make sure you take time to enjoy the sluggish, leaf-strewn stream called Bay Creek. The beech-lined banks, set against a backdrop of rocky bluffs and a brilliant blue, fall sky, can be found only on the blue trail at Bell Smith Springs!

Caution: Take extra care when crossing the creek, as the algae-covered rocks are very slippery when wet. Watch your step on the trail; tree roots have eroded from the soil of the path and can catch an unsuspecting toe. In a few places the trail comes perilously close to the bluff edge.

Trail Directions: The trailhead is located off the parking area past Redbud Campground at the end of FR 848. A paved walkway leads down to a brown information board. Continue downhill from the sign on the asphalt trail. After a few steps the trail forks; go to the right. A yellow diamond will designate the beginning of a short hike on the yellow trail [1], which will soon lead to our destination, the blue trail.

At .05 mi. the trail descends into Bay Creek Canyon using a steep rock staircase. At the foot of the steps is a shelter cave [2]. At the bottom of the staircase, go left and follow the yellow diamonds.

At .3 mi. cross a creek [3]. On the far side are stone steps leading up and to your left. The trail here carries both blue- and yellow-diamond markers. On your right you should see a massive stone cliff fronted with large beech trees.

As you walk along Bay Creek, skirting the bluff, note the huge boulders that have sheared off from the sandstone wall during an earlier time (.4 mi.) [4].

At .6 mi. the yellow and blue trails divide. The yellow goes right, to the natural arch, whereas the blue goes left [5]. A short side trip (.3 mi.) to the natural arch is

well worth the effort. The trail to the arch is uphill and leads one though the treetops of the ravine forest. Natural Arch [6] is a partially eroded shelter cave. The trail leads across the top of the arch; take care not to get too close to either edge. Then retrace your steps back to the junction of the blue and yellow trails [5].

At 1.25 mi. notice on the left that Bay Creek has undercut the rock face, creating shelter caves. In places, the stone walls abruptly end in the water [7].

At 1.5 mi. the trail narrows and runs near the edge of the bluff [8] before a slope downward into the ravine. At 1.75 mi. the trail skirts a sandstone wall that is being undercut, the early stages in the formation of a shelter cave. At the base of the wall are geological formations called Liesegang Rings (colorful, concentric, raised rings in the rock) [9]. From here the trail again heads uphill.

The valley floor soon comes up to meet the trail (2 mi.). The once impressive ravine is now nothing but a boulder-strewn streambed [10]. Cross the stream on small boulders and note that this side appears to be hotter and drier.

At 2.25 mi. you will come to a series of sandstone rock terraces leading down into a valley. The trail is quite steep, requiring a little mountaineering, and it can be treacherous. Walk across the ledge and climb carefully down on the terraces [11]. Blue diamonds are painted on the rocks to lead you downward. Cross a small creek, enter the woods on the other side, and go up a small incline. Turn left here. A blue, spray-painted NO to the right affirms that the trail proceeds to the left. Follow the blue diamonds emblazoned on trees along a dirt trail through an oak-hickory forest.

At 2.4 mi. Chute Gap [12] is marked by a brown Forest Service sign. A little farther along and to your left is an impressive view of the ravine [13]. Here the trail begins to narrow.

At 3 mi. the trail heads uphill with a series of short switchbacks [14]. A trail to Owl Gap veers off to the right at 3.4 mi.; stay on the blue diamond trail [15]. At 3.5 miles you will come to the asphalt path by a metal sign for Jay Gap [16]. A few steps ahead are the brown park information board and the parking area denoting the end of your hike.

1. Start
2. Shelter cave
3. Creek crossing
4. Boulders
5. Right turn
6. Natural Arch
7. Sheer bluffs
8. Bluff edge
9. Liesegang rings
10. Streambed
11. Terraces
12. Chute Gap
13. Ravine
14. Switchbacks
15. Go straight
16. Asphalt path

Parking

N

46. Dixon Springs State Park

- Discover Lover's Leap, Album Rock, Alligator Rock, Pluto's Cave, and Honey Comb Rock among the overhangs, outcrops, and cliffs.
- Take your rain gear. In rainy weather, rivulets are everywhere—cascading down the hills and creating hundreds of waterfalls.
- Look for large patches of prickly-pear cactus.
- Enjoy an idyllic setting—a babbling stream, large boulders cloaked with ferns, wildflowers strewn about, and large trees arching overhead.
- Visit the Chocolate Factory across from the park entrance for a sweet treat to end your hike.

Area Information

Dixon Springs State Park is located on a giant block of sandstone that extends northwesterly across Pope County. Rapid erosion has exposed the rock in various forms (including giant streets and a canyon) and given rise to imaginative names.

Native Americans who camped here called this area "the great medicine water," referring to the many springs. By the late 1880s a small community had grown up here and a large hotel had been built—the Dixon Springs Hotel Company. The area was a 19th-century health spa, and with the hotel open from June to September, visitors came from all around to take advantage of the springs that, according to one advertisement, "had been curing the ills of mankind for several years." If you couldn't afford the trip, you could have five gallons of this miracle water shipped to you for 50 cents.

The hotel no longer exists, and, with the exception of the churches, the community has also disappeared. Swimming in the springs has been replaced with swimming in a modern pool. To modern-day visitors of Dixon Springs, however, another advertisement for the hotel still rings true: "The cool quiet nights, invigorating mountain air, and sparkling spring water make this the ideal spot of recreation for the tired business man and his family."

Directions: Dixon Springs State Park is located 10 miles west of Golconda on Illinois 146 near its junction with Illinois 145.

Hours Open: The site is open year-round except on Christmas and New Year's Day.

Facilities: A campground has electricity and will accommodate both tents and trailers. A baseball field, swimming pool with lifeguard and water slide, concession stand, and picnicking are all part of the day-use area.

Permits and Rules: Pets must be kept leashed at all times.

Further Information: Site Superintendent, Dixon Springs State Park, RR #2, Golconda, IL 62938; 618-949-3394.

Other Areas of Interest

Located 12 miles east of Vienna, **Lake Glendale Recreation Area** features swimming, boating, fishing, camping, and hiking. Two 3-mile hiking trails lead around Lake Glendale and to and around Signal Point Bluff. For more information call the Vienna Ranger District at 618-658-2111.

Park Trail

Ghost Dance Canyon Trail 🥾🥾🥾—1 mile—The trail begins south of the swimming pool parking area and leads hikers down Hill Branch and along the east canyon wall. Use extreme caution when crossing the stream as the rocks are very slippery.

Pine–Oak–Bluff Trails 🥾🥾

Distance Round-Trip: 1.7 miles

Estimated Hiking Time: 1 hour

The brown sandstone is quite striking, having weathered to fantastic shapes and a gray-green patina caused by mosses and lichens. Small saplings try to set roots on precarious footholds— the soil being less than one-inch thick.

Caution: Tree roots are at the surface on parts of the trail. During the rainy season streambeds may be hard to cross.

Trail Directions: The trailhead is .2 mi. down a gravel road past the white churches. Begin at a brown trail sign for Pine Tree Trail [**1**]. Brown trail markers and signs are infrequent, but the path is not hard to follow. The trail begins as a wide path through a pine plantation carpeted with pine needles. You soon exit the pines to a grassy area. Follow the trail sign and arrow. The path narrows and the composition of the woods becomes oak, hickory, maple, and cedar.

At .35 mi. the trail bears to the left [**2**]; follow the marker for the Bluff Trail. At .55 mi. the trail crosses a stream, and on the opposite side it begins to skirt a sandstone bluff [**3**]. The bluff is topped with cedars, and the forest on your right is mostly young oak and hickory trees recovering from some past disturbance. After the stream crossing you'll find a mature, second-growth forest of mature, good-sized trees in place of the recovering forest. A large patch of prickly-pear cactus on the left at .7 mi. [**4**] attests to the dryness of the bluff.

Along this segment of the trail you are likely looking left at the bluff to admire its honeycomb erosion and cigar-shaped, mud dauber tubes; don't neglect the right side also, which gives view into a stream valley. It is quite pretty in the fall, especially when the last rays of sunshine filter through the golden brown and yellow leaves. At .75 mi. the trail skirts a small shelter bluff; as you walk by, touch the rock and feel it crumble in your hand [**5**]. You next pass under a shelter bluff, recross the stream, and enter a woods dominated by white oaks (.8 mi.) [**6**].

Ignore the arrow pointing downhill and straight ahead and go instead to your left, continuing to hike through an oak woods (.85 mi.) [**7**]. A large thicket of pawpaws is on the left and a grove of cedars, on the right. At 1 mi. you will pass a large white oak, festooned with cable-like poison ivy. The oaks soon give way to vine-covered cedars (at an old farm site), which in turn make way for oaks again. At 1.4 mi. cross another stream, and the trail soon passes the Vienna Boys' Detention Camp—quite hidden by the woods [**8**]. Don't pick up any hitchhikers. You will soon cross a wooden bridge.

Just before the ranger station, take a right (1.7 mi.) [**9**], cross the creek, and head uphill. You will emerge at a grove of pines near where you parked your vehicle.

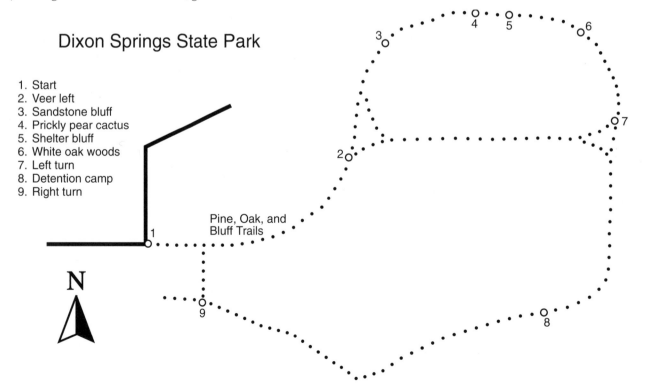

Dixon Springs State Park

1. Start
2. Veer left
3. Sandstone bluff
4. Prickly pear cactus
5. Shelter bluff
6. White oak woods
7. Left turn
8. Detention camp
9. Right turn

Pine, Oak, and Bluff Trails

N

47. Fort Massac State Park

- Walk in the footsteps of George Rogers Clark and his band of Long Knives.
- Visit the first state park in Illinois.
- Tour a reconstructed fort and museum.
- Watch a sunset or the barge traffic on the Ohio River, a river that is busier than the Panama Canal.
- Discover the giant pin oaks of floodplain flatwoods.

Area Information

The Fort Massac State Park area, strategically overlooking the Ohio River, probably was the site of a fort as early as 1540. The first documentation of a fort, however, occurred in 1757 when the French built here during the French and Indian War. The French occupied the fort until after they surrendered to the British in 1765. The fort, then abandoned, subsequently burned to the ground. The British elected not to rebuild or regarrison the fort, an oversight they may have regretted: It allowed George Rogers Clark and his band of Long Knives into Illinois at Massac Creek during the Revolutionary War. What followed was a march of 100 miles until the small band of patriots was able to capture Kaskaskia and claim the entire Illinois Territory for the state of Virginia.

Another kind of history is also located here: a nature preserve that presents the landscape much as George Rogers Clark saw it. In the preserve you will find a unique forest community—a pin oak flatwoods—growing on hardpan, clay soil that is very moist in the spring but dry and rock-hard in the summer. The appearance of these flatwoods is probably much the same today as it was in the late-18th century because trees do not live excessively long in a flatwood forest. They undergo a regular cycle of 150 to 200 years, and when they reach a certain size, the trees inevitably blow down because of their shallow root penetration in the clay soil.

Directions: Take exit 37 off I-24 west to U.S. Route 45. The park is 2.5 miles west of the interstate, near Metropolis. The trailhead, however, must be accessed by heading east after exit 37 on U.S. Route 45 to the first road that heads right. Follow it to a dead-end; the trailhead will be on your right by a small parking area.

Hours Open: The site is open-year round except on Christmas and New Year's Day. The fort's hours are 10 A.M. to 5:30 P.M. daylight savings time and 10 A.M. to 4:30 P.M. central standard time.

Facilities: The park includes a fort and museum complex, campground, boat ramp, and picnic areas.

Permits and Rules: Part of the trail is located in a dedicated Illinois Nature Preserve: No pets are allowed on this trail.

Further Information: Site Superintendent, Fort Massac State Park, 1308 E. 5th Street, Metropolis, IL 62960; 618-524-4712.

Other Areas of Interest

For two days during October, a re-creation of the lifestyles and atmosphere of the late 1700s occurs at the **Fort Massac Encampment**. You can witness mock battles and Voyageur canoe races, meet traders and crafts people, and be a part of the state's colorful past. For more information call 618-524-4712.

Visit **Metropolis** (the only city in the United States with this name), the official home of Superman. Tour the Superman Museum, the largest collection of the superhero's memorabilia. For more information call 800-949-5740.

Hickory Nut Ridge Trail 🥾🥾

Distance Round-Trip: 2.5 miles

Estimated Hiking Time: 1.75 hours

If you doubt plastic should be recycled, hike this trail after a spring of high water when you can experience the flotsam and jetsam coughed up by a giant river!

Caution: The trail can be very muddy. Logs, driftwood, and other river debris can block a large area of the trail and require wading through or crawling over.

Trail Directions: Begin the hike at the locked gate and follow the gravel road west. On either side is a disturbed woods cloaked in Japanese honeysuckle [1]. At .1 mi. [2] a trail leads to the left—take it and follow a pleasant, grassy path. Soon (.25 mi.) [3] the trail is blocked by upright railroad ties; walk around them and continue on.

On your left (during floods) is the backwater of the Ohio River and Seven Mile Creek. Look to your left among the sycamores for a great blue heron *rookery*. The largest trees are usually chosen for nesting, and a rookery is used by dozens of heron generations. The nests (a jumble of sticks and twigs) may be four-feet wide and a couple of feet deep. You may experience an odd mix of sounds here—the primeval squawks of the herons and the roar of distant semis from the I-24 bridge.

Where Seven Mile Creek enters the Ohio, you begin to encounter Ohio River debris (.45 mi.) [4], a curious mix of mussels, driftwood, and cast-off plastic. (The trail is about 50 yards from the river.) During winter and spring, look up into the tall trees. The only thing green in the canopy is mistletoe, a partially parasitic plant attached to the tree. Its seeds

are covered with a poisonous substance that is toxic to humans, but not to birds. In fact, birds spread mistletoe seeds in their droppings and by wiping their beaks on branches.

For the next .5 mi. watch your step and pick your way through a tree graveyard—driftwood is everywhere. The bleached remains of trees and the more-than-occasional bleach bottle and other plastic debris litter the area, but will disappear at the next flood event to continue their journey elsewhere. To your right is a low spot within a low spot (.65 mi.) [5], that is, a cypress pond in a floodplain woods. As you walk under the overpass for I-24 (ignoring another trail off to the right), look for a stand of giant cane (.8 mi.) [6].

At 1.05 mi. [7] the trail proceeds away from the river and debris and ascends along a river terrace. Marvel here at the straight, tall pin oaks in this flatwoods. Pin oaks thrive in this Ohio River valley. With a shallow root system and absence of a prominent taproot, pin oak does quite well in this claypan soil.

Look for Massac Creek off to the left as the trail comes out on the park road (1.3 mi.) [8]. Go right and hike on the abandoned park road. Along here think of how George Rogers Clark and his Long Knives left the Ohio River near Fort Massac, beginning their overland trek to Kaskaskia to defeat the British. This is what the forest looked like during that epic event in American history.

From 1.55 to 2.1 mi. you will pass a series of trails off to the right and left. Ignore these and stay on the abandoned park road; most of these are access trails for hunters. At 1.6 mi. [9] the road stops curving (at the 10-mph sign). Note the change in the woods: The large trees have disappeared to be replaced by shrubs, small trees, and Kentucky bluegrass. The trail goes under the overpass at 1.85 mi. [10], and soon you are back at the parking area.

Fort Massac State Park

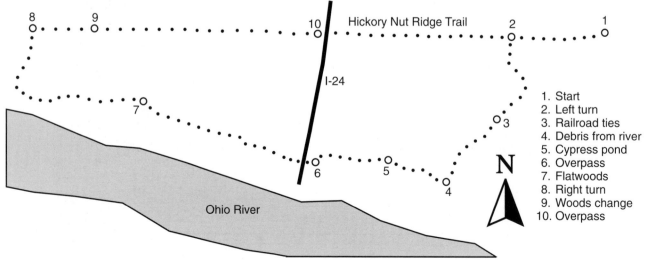

1. Start
2. Left turn
3. Railroad ties
4. Debris from river
5. Cypress pond
6. Overpass
7. Flatwoods
8. Right turn
9. Woods change
10. Overpass

48. Jackson Hollow

- Discover shelter caves, massive tumbled rocks, tall cliffs, crevasses, and clear pools of sparkling water.
- Bring your plant field guide to help identify Indian pipe and beech-drops, two of the many unusual plants found here.
- Enjoy a magnificent display of fall colors.
- Experience how an insect must feel just before it is stepped on!

Area Information

Jackson Hollow consists of a main hollow with four tributary valleys, forming one gigantic hole in the forested Shawnee Hills. The valley forest is walled in by huge cliffs made of sandstone. Called "the most beautiful valley in Illinois" by some people, this area features clear pools, huge blocks of rock that lie strewn from the cliffs to the creek, large and small undercuts or shelter caves, crevasses to explore, rocks that continuously drip water, and cool shade on a hot summer's day.

Orange Jackson, who would treat all of the neighborhood children to candy and oranges at Christmas time, owned this area at one time. The family house is gone, but the Jackson name lives on in the canyon. As an old ad for the area states, "It is easy to use superlatives when describing Jackson Hollow—it is that kind of place."

Directions: Jackson Hollow is near the Pope and Johnson county lines. From I-24 take exit 16 east to Illinois 146 at Vienna and drive one-third mile to Illinois 147. Travel 8 miles to the small town of Simpson. Go north on Forest Road (FR) 424 just east of the post office in Simpson. Along this road you will pass the Trigg fire tower. Immediately after the River-to-River Trail crossing, FR 1770 will be on your right and a horse camp on the left. Park along the road and begin the trail on FR 1770.

Hours Open: The site is open year-round.

Facilities: There are no facilities.

Permits and Rules: All rules applicable to the Shawnee National Forest apply here.

Further Information: Vienna Ranger District, Shawnee National Forest, Vienna, IL 62995; 618-658-2111.

Other Areas of Interest

Located en route to Jackson Hollow, **Trigg Tower** is one of the few, old, fire lookout towers that you may climb. For a bird's-eye view of the area take a few minutes to climb the 100-plus steps. For more information call 618-658-2111.

© Michael Jeffords

Jackson Hollow Trail

Distance Round-Trip: 3 miles

Estimated Hiking Time: 2 hours

The first mile may lull you into complacency, but after you work your way down into the valley through a cleft in the rocks, you are prepared to scramble over rocks and logs and hike in one of the more beautiful hollows of southern Illinois.

Caution: The trail into the hollow is steep and treacherous. Work your way down carefully.

Trail Directions: Begin the trail at FR 1770 [1]. You may park at the side of the road near a horse camp. The road and trail lead through a young forest overrun with honeysuckle and multiflora rose. The road soon curves left and enters a pine plantation. At .5 mi. [2] note a large, double-stemmed white oak.

The trail is lined with pines again at .6 mi. [3], and soon leads to an opening (perhaps an abandoned farmstead) on the left occupied by an impressive tulip poplar. The road ends in a grassy clearing at .9 mi. [4]. Pass through the clearing and go right, following a faint trail that follows the bluff's top. (If you go straight, you will see Jackson Hollow below but there is no way down to it.) The trail begins a descent at 1.2 mi. [5] and ends in a cleft in the rocks that allows you to *carefully* work your way down into Jackson Hollow. Be very cautious, as the way is steep and treacherous!

Once safely in the hollow, proceed to the left on a faint trail that skirts the base of the bluffs. You may have to traverse boulders and fallen trees for a few hundred feet before finding the faint trail. At 1.35 mi. [6], immediately to your right and down the slope, is an absolutely massive sandstone boulder that appears to lean precariously downhill. You may wish to take a side trip down to experience this large rock from under the leaning overhang—and to get the feeling of how an insect must feel just before being stepped on! From here you can continue to follow the creek (to the left; although there is no trail, it is relatively easy going) or return to the original trail at the base of the bluff.

Take time to explore the bluff and its many interesting rock formations. During spring the valley floor is carpeted with wildflowers (Dutchman's-breeches, blue cohosh, etc.). The woods in the valley is a typical beech-maple forest, but many oaks are interspersed within it. At one point along the bluff you will pass through a very narrow cleft that could have no name other than Fat Man's Squeeze. At about 1.5 mi. [7] head downhill from the bluff and join an unmarked but very wide trail that leads through the valley. Proceed left on this trail. You may begin to see rock climbers or horses along this section.

The trail splits at 1.65 mi. [8]. The spur to the right leads to a large railroad culvert under the tracks that traverse the hollow. Go left and cross Bay Creek (the same creek that runs through Bell Smith Springs). You will cross the creek again at 1.95 mi. [9] and pass a huge beech tree with a small sign on it (denoting it as a wildlife tree). Soon afterward the trail heads upward. Proceed to the right and note how the previously wide valley is rapidly narrowing. You are now walking on the right side of the creek.

Look for a magnificent tulip poplar at 2.4 mi. [10] as you walk through a moist, mixed hardwood forest. The bluffs and boulders are no longer visible. Three stream crossings follow in relatively rapid succession, and you will end up on the left side of the stream. The trail heads upward and curves to the left between large boulders at 2.55 mi. [11]. Note the pale yellow corydalis blooming along this area in the spring. This portion of the trail shows heavy horse use, so stay alert.

The trail now curves to the right and within a few feet an intersection appears—go left. Note the pines off to the left. The trail soon heads into the pines and is deeply rutted by horse traffic. At 2.75 mi. [12] it heads up a series of sandstone terraces and soon intersects with a gravel road. Go left along the road to FR 1770 and your vehicle.

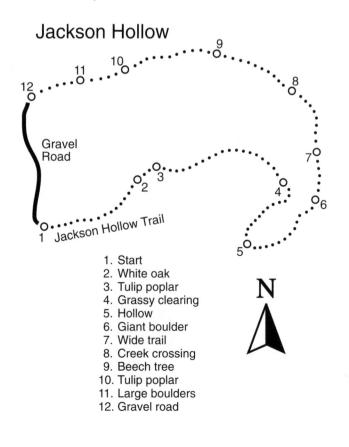

Jackson Hollow

1. Start
2. White oak
3. Tulip poplar
4. Grassy clearing
5. Hollow
6. Giant boulder
7. Wide trail
8. Creek crossing
9. Beech tree
10. Tulip poplar
11. Large boulders
12. Gravel road

49. Mermet Lake Conservation Area

- Look for hundreds of red-eared slider turtles basking on every available log.
- Observe grass pickerels in the water as they silently fan their tails among the moss and debris, hoping to elude predators.
- Brush up on your herpetofauna: Banded water snakes sun in the shrubs; snapping, slider, softshell, or box turtles cross the paths; and frogs and toads keep up an endless serenade.
- Enjoy unfamiliar wildflowers such as copper iris, American lotus, lizard's tail, and the elusive purple-fringed orchid.

Area Information

Mermet Lake Conservation Area used to be a cypress swamp, and you can see remnants of that in a few old cypress trees standing in the middle of the lake. In 1962 a newly constructed system of levees created this lake for duck hunting. Each fall the lake's level is dropped two inches to accommodate the hunters. After the hunting season, the level is restored. The area also has 200 acres of grains planted in the open fields to attract waterfowl. Even though Mermet is a hunters' lake, more than 90 percent of the visitors are fishermen, casting for largemouth bass, channel catfish, or sunfish.

Although Mermet Lake is managed for waterfowl, other types of wildlife are abundant. On any warm, sunny day—spring, summer, or fall—every available log is crammed with turtles, their necks outstretched as they bask. Snakes entwine themselves in the branches of shrubs to catch the sun's warming rays. Mink may be seen running along the downed logs in the wet woods, and great blue herons lurk in the shadows for unsuspecting fish.

Directions: Mermet Lake is off U.S. 45 in Massac County, 14 miles northwest of Paducah, Kentucky. From the north, take exit 16 off I-24 onto Illinois 146. Illinois 146 quickly intersects with U.S. 45. Go south (left) on U.S. 45 for 9 miles to Mermet Lake. From the south, take I-24 to the Metropolis exit at U.S. 45. Take U.S. 45 north for 11 miles to the lake.

Hours Open: Although the site is open year-round, during duck season it is open only for hunting, and at that time all trails and the road are closed.

Facilities: Picnicking, pit toilets, fishing, boating, and hunting are available, but there is no drinking water on the premises.

Permits and Rules: One of the trails is in an area that is a dedicated Illinois Nature Preserve: No pets are allowed in this area.

Further Information: Site Superintendent, Mermet Lake Conservation Area, RR 1, Belknap, IL 62908; 618-524-5577.

Park Trail

Mermet Nature Preserve Trail—.75 mile 🥾—This is a loop trail through a southern Illinois swamp and is the easiest access to a cypress swamp in the state. A boardwalk is provided to give you a close look, and trees are labeled for you to learn Illinois' water-loving trees.

Mermet Lake Conservation Area

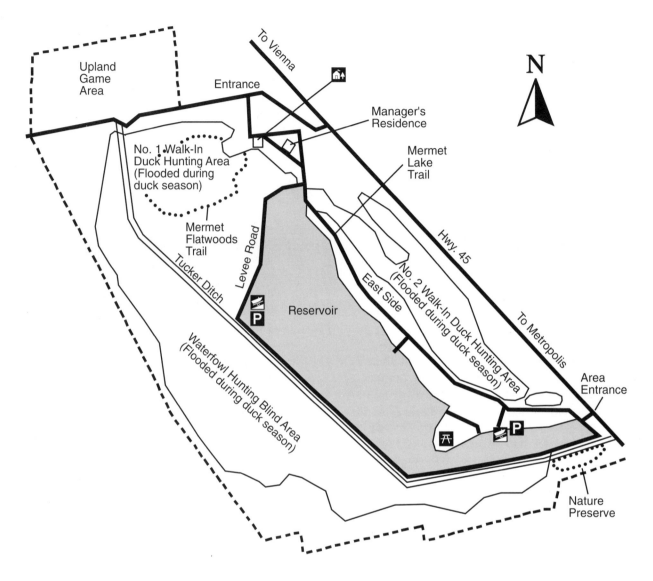

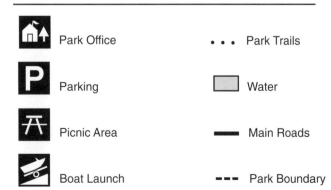

Legend

Park Office		• • •	Park Trails
Parking		▨	Water
Picnic Area		▬▬▬	Main Roads
Boat Launch		- - -	Park Boundary

Mermet Flatwoods Trail 🥾

Distance Round-Trip: 1.3 miles

Estimated Hiking Time: 1 hour

Anybody with even a remote interest in botany will find this trail absolutely fascinating. It contains a most curious mixture of species—tallgrass prairie forbs, sand prairie wildflowers, southern swamp lilies, sea oats, and even a relative of black pepper!

Caution: At various times this trail will be either extremely wet or impassable. Check at the area headquarters for trail conditions.

Trail Directions: The trail begins near a group of maintenance buildings at a small parking area. The loop trail is a flat, easy walk with selected trees identified. Almost immediately you enter an Illinois flatwoods, a type of woods most people have not experienced [1]. Flatwoods are forests that grow on hardpan clay soil, which is very moist in the spring and very dry and hard during the summer. When the trees reach a certain size, they inevitably get blown down because of their shallow root penetration in the clay soil. At .1 mi. note the large and diverse oaks and an American elm. Once very common, this species is now rare due to Dutch elm disease. Along the trail you will encounter a great diversity of trees, including post and black oak. At .15 mi. a small clump of yellow primrose brightens the forest floor. Notice, also, how tall and straight the trees grow in this habitat. Soon you will see a large tree that has toppled over (.25 mi.) [2], an example of the large trees' inevitable fate in a flatwoods. Observe its flat, shallow root structure and the small pond that has been created by its fall.

At .3 mi. the trees show evidence of fire. This is undoubtedly a management tool that accounts for the parklike appearance of the woods and the presence of prairie plants. Along this part of the trail keep an eye out for eastern box turtles, a common resident. Here also note the spiderwort growing in the understory (this plant is more familiarly associated with dry, sand prairies). Near the midpoint of your hike (.5 mi.) [3] a clue to the area's past history appears—an old, wire fence deeply embedded in a large tree. Around .65 mi. [4] look for another typical prairie species, false wild indigo (*Baptisia*), an unusual occurrence in

this type of habitat! Yellow primrose also grow along this stretch. Soon (.75 mi.) [5] you will encounter one of the most spectacular flowers found in Illinois: wild spider lily. If you are hiking in mid-August this impressive clump will likely be in full bloom. Note also the extremely open nature of the forest. Add a few picnic tables and the area would have the appearance of a well-manicured park.

The trail passes through a wet area at (.85 mi.) [6] and by a colony of iris (which may include the unusual red or copper iris, a species more common farther south). At .9 mi. a colony of sea oats (more commonly associated with Florida beaches) droops gracefully along the trail, followed almost immediately by a clump of rattlesnake master (another prairie species). The trail crosses a short boardwalk over a small wetland at 1 mi. [7]. If you're observant, from here until the trail's end you can find several types of sedges and a large mockernut hickory. Near the hickory (1.2 mi.) [8] appears a magnificent stand of an unusual plant called lizard's tail, which is related to an old-world species that produces black pepper. Lizard's tail is the only member of its family found in Illinois, and it blooms in mid-June. The trail soon exits the woods (1.3 mi.), and you will have completed your botanical potpourri.

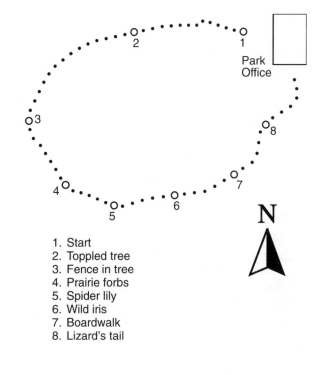

1. Start
2. Toppled tree
3. Fence in tree
4. Prairie forbs
5. Spider lily
6. Wild iris
7. Boardwalk
8. Lizard's tail

Mermet Lake Trail 🥾

Distance Round-Trip: 4.8 miles

Estimated Hiking Time: 2.5 hours

Near dusk a great blue heron fishes in an open pool, camouflaged by the lengthening shadows of the dying cattails. Goldeneyes and redheads (the duck variety!) swim nearby, while geese looking for a safe haven fly overhead. A hawk surveys the activity from a leafless, bald cypress.

Caution: This is a one-way, multipurpose trail that you will share with bicyclists, cars, snakes, and turtles—keep alert.

Trail Directions: While driving into Mermet, check the open, grassy area near the park office for upland sandpipers. Park at the entrance to the Nature Preserve and begin the hike there [1]. You will follow the levee road around the lake. Directly on the right is a good spot for viewing turtles as they bask on nice, sunny days. As reptiles, turtles maintain body temperature by relying on external sources of heat. Notice that some of them bask by stretching out their extremities; this encourages any parasites, such as leeches, to drop off. To your left look for mink running along downed logs in the wet woods.

The first of many fishing pull-off spots is at .2 mi. [2], this one directly in front of a buttressed cypress. On your left is a shrubby, floodplain woods. At .4 mi. note the first of several duck hunting pull-offs; you can see the blind in the distance [3]. Keep your eyes open for turtles—slider, snapping, and softshell—crossing the road. Also begin to look for water snakes basking in the shrubby overgrowth on the left (.55 mi.) [4].

At .9 mi. go right and stay on the levee road [5]; a grassy levee goes off to the left and into the woods. Another fishing pull-off is on the right. The road narrows at 1 mi. so use caution. On your left, if it's wet, look for waterfowl—when it's dry, this is a favorite haunt of deer. In summer, water primrose will be blooming in the ditch. Look on your left at 1.4 mi. for a large beaver mound: These industrious engineers go into high gear beginning at dusk [6].

Take advantage of the many pull-offs to scan the lake and surrounding area for activity. Look for grass pickerels and turtle snouts as these animals come up for air. You can also chat with the local people for a taste of southern Illinois

color. At 2 mi. continue to go right along the curve in the road [7]. Straight ahead is a small cypress pond. On the left are two grass levees leading into a hunting area. Look for kingfishers here. Kingfishers are excitable and aggressive birds who express their displeasure by giving a call that has been compared to a New Year's Eve noisemaker.

Take advantage of the pull-offs at either 2.3 or 2.5 miles [8]. By the end of June this area is usually covered with American lotus. Look for red-eared sliders shingled on submerged logs like an ancient slate roof. Scan the lotus with binoculars. Who knows what lurks among those large leaves. The road forms a T at 2.8 mi.; go right, following the levee [9]. The area on the right is a transition zone of cattail and lotus. Look for red iris on the left, blooming by mid-May, and for little green herons. On the right check the shrubs for basking snakes. You can see a great lotus bed on the right at 2.9 mi. and an attempt at reforestation on the left. The white tubes on the seedlings are to protect them from deer.

At 3.8 the road enters the woods [10]; look for little bluestem along here. By 4.25 mi. you are in the open again, with a boat launch and toilet to the right [11]. Check the ponds on the left for geese with their goslings in May. At 4.7 mi. [12] watch the ditch on the left near the remnants of a bridge for snakes. On the right is another good area for turtle viewing. From here it is a short walk to your vehicle. No matter what the season or time of day there is always something interesting going on at Mermet, even if it is only chatting with the locals about the size of the fish that got away.

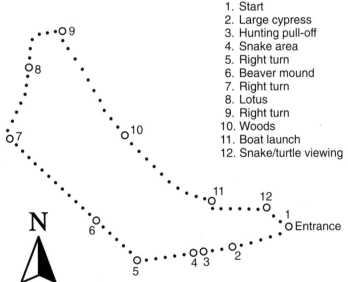

1. Start
2. Large cypress
3. Hunting pull-off
4. Snake area
5. Right turn
6. Beaver mound
7. Right turn
8. Lotus
9. Right turn
10. Woods
11. Boat launch
12. Snake/turtle viewing

50. Ferne Clyffe State Park

- View sandstone canyons, deep gorges, shady dells, shelter caves, unique rock formations, and intermittent (seasonal) waterfalls.
- Discover Hawk's Cave, the largest of the park's shelter caves. This structure is an immense undercut in the sandstone with a large overhanging ledge that forms a natural amphitheater.
- Look under the vast overhang of Hawk's Cave for the circular depressions of antlion pits and the sinuous patterns of snakes in the dust.
- Explore Round Bluff Nature Preserve and discover many of the park's 700 species of plants.
- Experience alleyways between large boulders carpeted with spring wildflowers.

Area Information

Ferne Clyffe State Park lies just south of where the Illinoian glacier stopped its southward advance. The park's massive sandstone outcroppings, although untouched by the ice, were not unaffected. Glacial meltwaters from the receding ice widened and deepened canyons and carved terraces, steps, and shelter bluffs in the canyon walls. Round Bluff, a massive sandstone outlier, stands alone, an island separated from the other bluffs in the park. Hawk's Cave, a shelter cave hewn by wind and water, is a vast overhang 150 feet long and nearly as high.

In the spring, assemblages of wildflowers and ferns line the trails descending into and traversing the ravines—mayapple, yellow trout lily, Dutchman's-breeches, and squirrel-corn. The latter species covers the valley floor with lush, feathery foliage. Large sandstone blocks have separated from the canyon walls and created blind alleys and narrow passages within the forest. On top of these blocks are isolated islands of wildflowers, many of them never experiencing human footprints.

In the 1920s Ferne Clyffe State Park was considered the most beautiful spot in Illinois. Today, it still is an area not to be missed during a visit to southern Illinois!

Directions: Located on Illinois 37, one mile south of Goreville and 12 miles south of Marion, the park is easily accessible from I-57 or I-24. Take exit 7 from I-24 and head west to Route 37. The park entrance is a short distance south on Route 37. From I-57, take exit 40 and then drive east to Route 37 and south to the entrance.

Hours Open: The park is open year-round except for Christmas and New Year's Day.

Facilities: Picnicking, RV and tent camping, fishing, and horseback riding are available.

Permits and Rules: Round Bluff is a dedicated Illinois Nature Preserve. No pets are allowed on the trail or in the nature preserve, and within the nature preserve no hunting, camping, fires, picnicking, or rock climbing are allowed.

Further Information: Site Superintendent, Ferne Clyffe State Park, P.O. Box 10, Goreville, IL 62939; 618-995-2411.

Other Areas of Interest

Dutchman Lake, near Vienna, was constructed during the early 1970s. The main recreational activities are fishing and boating, with some primitive camping. A faint, unmaintained 2-mile trail follows the northeast shoreline and the sandstone bluff tops. Highlights of the trail include seasonal waterfalls and vistas of Dutchman Lake. For more information call the Vienna Ranger District at 618-658-2111.

Park Trails

Rebman Trail 👢—.25 mile—A level, loop trail (named for the area's former owner) leads by a small waterfall. A marker dedicated to Miss Rebman marks the beginning of the trail.

Blackjack Oak Trail 👢👢👢—1 mile—This linear trail with two steep climbs traverses Deer Ridge. Impressive vistas and blackjack oaks among the dry bluff tops are worth the climb.

Ferne Clyffe Lake Trail 👢—1 mile—An easy loop circles the lake's shoreline, giving anglers ample opportunity to cast their lines.

Happy Hollow Trail 👢👢👢—5 miles—This trail (for both horses and hikers) winds through woods and wildlife food plantings, and it has several creek crossings.

Happy Hollow Backpack Trail 👢—.5 mile—A linear trail leads campers to a primitive camping area.

Happy Hollow Horse Trail 👢👢👢—8 miles—This horse trail leads from the horseback camping area to the Happy Hollow Trail.

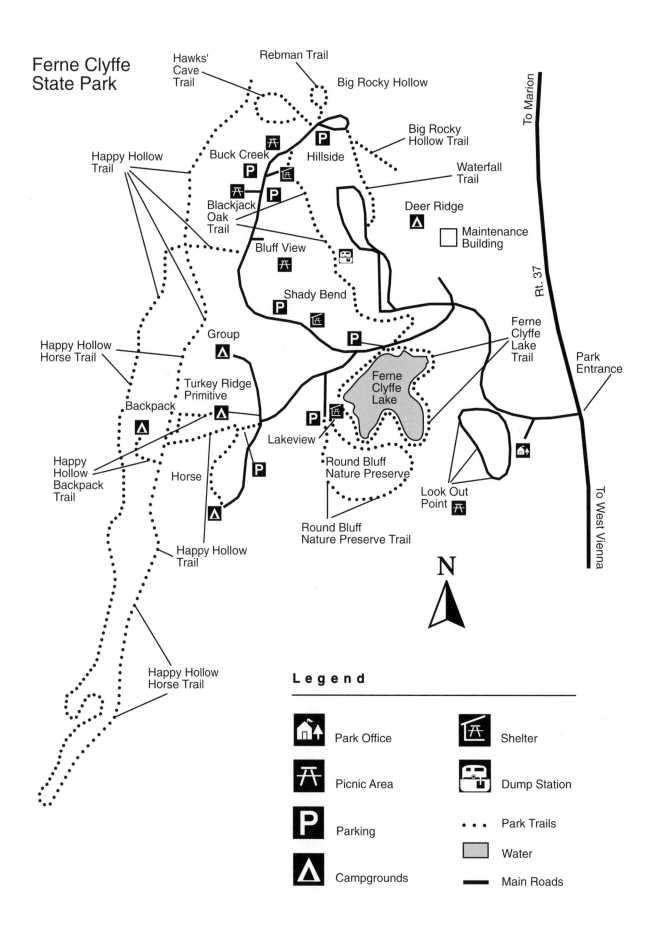

Ferne Clyffe
State Park

Hawks'
Cave
Trail

Rebman Trail

Big Rocky Hollow

Big Rocky
Hollow Trail

To Marion

Buck Creek

Hillside

Waterfall
Trail

Happy Hollow
Trail

Deer Ridge

Rt. 37

Blackjack
Oak
Trail

Maintenance
Building

Bluff View

Shady Bend

Ferne
Clyffe
Lake Trail

Happy Hollow
Horse Trail

Group

Ferne
Clyffe
Lake

Park
Entrance

Backpack

Turkey Ridge
Primitive

Lakeview

Happy
Hollow
Backpack
Trail

Horse

Round Bluff
Nature Preserve

Look Out
Point

To West Vienna

Happy Hollow
Trail

Round Bluff
Nature Preserve Trail

N

Happy Hollow
Horse Trail

Legend

Park Office

Shelter

Picnic Area

Dump Station

P Parking

Park Trails

Campgrounds

Water

Main Roads

Hawks' Cave–Blackjack Oak–Waterfall Trails 👢👢👢👢

Distance Round-Trip: 3 miles

Estimated Hiking Time: 2 hours

An overweight dog joined us for part of the trail and soon was wheezing and puffing; he turned back. What a shame, as he missed both the bird's-eye view of Round Bluff from the overlook and the antlion pits of Hawk's Cave.

Caution: Watch your step on the trail: Tree roots and rocks have eroded from the soil of the path. You might get your feet wet crossing a couple of streams.

Trail Directions: The trailhead is found at the end of the park's loop road in a parking area. Cross Buck Creek using the ford [**1**] and look on your left for a trail board pointing to Hawk's Cave. The gravel trail begins with a bridge crossing and heads uphill.

At .1 mi. [**2**] the trail forks; go to the right. After hiking through a mixed hardwood forest for .3 mi., you'll see Hawk's Cave [**3**], a huge shelter cave. In the spring, look under the dripline for French's shooting star, a wildflower once thought to grow only in Illinois. If visitors have been few, check the dust for the dendritic patterns of snakes or for ant lion pits. Antlions are immature insects that dig pits to trap prey. Each pit has a voracious larva waiting at the bottom with open jaws for its next meal!

After exploring the cave continue on the rocky trail. At .4 mi. a giant boulder resides near the path [**4**]. During wet weather look for slimy salamanders slithering across the trail. By .55 mi. you have finished the loop of Hawk's Cave Trail [**2**]. Retrace your steps to the trailhead.

Recross Buck's Creek and walk on the road along the parking and picnic area [**5**] for a short distance. Go past a large chunk of sandstone and observe the top. In spring it will be carpeted with wildflowers. You will soon see a sign on the left for Blackjack Oak Trail [**6**].

The trail immediately begins an uphill climb on a grassy path. After a few steps another trail intersects this one. Go to your left, as the trail to the right leads back to the picnic area. For the next .25 mi. you will be hiking uphill. In spring look for bluets in the rock pockets. At the top the trail crosses rock outcroppings interspersed with gravel. At 1 mi. [**7**] follow the trail to your right to a sign for Blackjack Oak Trail. Immediately past the trail sign is an overlook on your right, complete with a park bench to enjoy the forest panorama below.

Continue on the path along a ridge. At 1.4 mi. [**8**] the trail emerges from the forest with an impressive view of the lake and Round Bluff Nature Preserve. Within less than .1 mi. follow a sign leading left to Deer Ridge Campground (1.5 mi.) [**9**].

Soon the paved road of the campground will appear (1.6 mi.) [**10**]. Take a left and follow the road to an intersection by the sanitary dump; take the middle road and follow the right arm of the campground loop road. By 1.9 mi. you should see a marker leading to the Waterfall Trail [**11**] on your right—hike in.

The rocky, dirt trail descends through a dry, oak-hickory forest. After .25 mi. look to your right at a large beech tree (2.15 mi.) rising out of the ravine below. Its trunk resembles an elephant's leg. On your left is a sandstone bluff [**12**]. Giant boulders have eroded away from the cliff and are slowly working their way down the hill. At one such boulder (2.2 mi.) the trail veers left (a well-worn path appears on the right—this is not the trail!) [**13**]. Go left and head uphill; the path will be boulder-strewn, with an impressive vertical rock face on the left.

At 2.3 mi. [**14**] the trail turns 90 degrees, goes through a pair of large beech trees, crosses a creek, and joins the Waterfall Trail. It then passes through a deep, cool ravine that abruptly narrows. The trail ends (2.6 mi.) in a box canyon with a waterfall; in the fall, however, all that will be found is the wet face of a cliff footed by a small, still pool [**15**]. Hike out on the same trail you entered, but do not turn at [**14**]—continue straight this time. The trail will lead to the parking area on the loop road, and at 3 mi. you should be at your vehicle.

1. Start
2. Right turn
3. Hawk's Cave
4. Large boulder
5. Picnic area
6. Blackjack Oak Trail
7. Overlook
8. Overlook
9. Left turn
10. Campground road
11. Waterfall Trail
12. Bluff
13. Veer left
14. Right turn
15. Waterfall

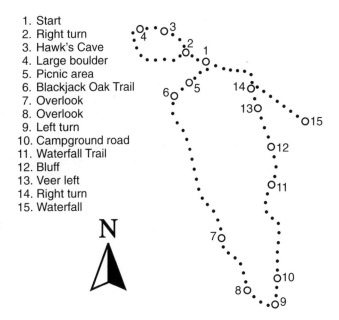

Round Bluff Nature Preserve Trail 👢👢👢

Distance Round-Trip: 1 mile

Estimated Hiking Time: 1 hour

Hiking this trail on a dry autumn day may yield a box turtle or two, but it gives little hint of the moistness of spring or its attendant wildflower diversity. The feathery foliage of Dutchman's-breeches and squirrel-corn carpet areas of the canyons, their patterns broken only by Jack-in-the-pulpits poking through.

Caution: Watch your step on the trail and slippery stairs; tree roots and rocks have eroded from the soil of the path.

Trail Directions: The trail begins near the Lakeview Picnic Shelter and parking area. Start your hike at the large Nature Preserve sign [1]. Here you can pick up a trail guide. The numbers on the trail guide map do not correspond to those found in this book.

The trail begins as a mowed path but soon becomes hard-packed dirt. A hiker's silhouette on a brown post marks the trail. Round Bluff, a 300-million-year-old sandstone knob, is immediately visible on your left. The roots of several red cedars have eroded out of the soil and crisscross the path. At .1 mi. [2] the bluff is at the trail edge. At this point find a series of steps. Look up and observe that the cedars have branches only on the side away from the cliff's face. This is the portion of the tree that receives sunlight.

A side spur appears on the left at .3 mi. [3]. Take the short trail and examine the champion winged elm of Illinois. Back on the trail you'll encounter another side spur at .4 mi. [4] that leads to a glade community (a dry bedrock opening in the forest). If you decide to explore this area, take care: Trampling can be harmful to the vegetation. Beyond the spur the trail descends with a series of wooden, erosion-control steps. You are now on the northern side of the bluff where, during the spring, the best displays of wildflowers occur.

At .5 mi. [5] cross a spring, the only one in the nature preserve. Here the trail traverses up and down.

Take time to look left at the interesting cracks and crevices in the sandstone. Hike under an overhang at .7 mi. [6], which might be wet during spring. Facing you is a steep set of steps. Before going down them, note a crack in the sandstone that is cloaked with ferns, lush and green even in the dry summers.

Beginning at .8 mi. [7] note the impressive sandstone bluff and the erosional patterns etched into the rock. Close observation may yield a skull or a monkey face. From this point on appear spectacular assemblages of spring wildflowers. Stay on the trail, for nowhere else can you avoid stepping on a trout lily, spring beauty, Jack-in-the-pulpit, or hay-scented fern. At .85 mi. [8] cross a bridge over a small stream. In early April this area in front of you is a carpet of Dutchman's-breeches and squirrel-corn.

At 1 mi. [9] you encounter the Lakeview Picnic Shelter and parking lot. The area has picnic facilities, a water fountain, and pit toilets.

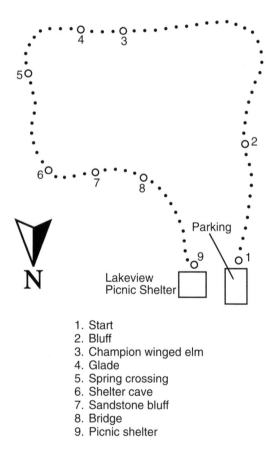

1. Start
2. Bluff
3. Champion winged elm
4. Glade
5. Spring crossing
6. Shelter cave
7. Sandstone bluff
8. Bridge
9. Picnic shelter

51. Cache River State Natural Area

- Visit the watery home of cypress and tupelo trees.
- Walk into a swamp on a floating boardwalk.
- View a landscape more typically associated with the bayous of Louisiana.

Area Information

The Cache must be actively sought to be experienced. The Cache River watershed, a result of thousands of years of geologic action, is divided into three parts: the Upper Cache River, the Lower Cache River, and the Cache River Basin itself. The Cache River Basin marks the geographical point where the last invasion of the sea (some 30 million years ago) reached its northernmost limit. In the original United States Land Survey, this area was referred to as "inaccessible, a drowned land." Due to the efforts of conservation groups and concerned citizens, the area is today protected and no longer inaccessible.

The Cache River has three dedicated nature preserves and two National Natural Landmarks along it. Some of the oldest and largest trees in Illinois and the United States grow in its floodplain. This distinguished group includes the largest tree in Illinois (a bald cypress) and the oldest living stand of trees east of the Mississippi River.

From Little Black Slough and Heron Pond, examples of southern swamps at the northernmost limits of their range, to the southern exposure of Wildcat Bluff, where a hill prairie looks onto the floodplain forests and upland woods, the area is truly unique. Eighteen miles of hiking trails offer a sampler of the diverse wetlands, grasslands, and forests that make up the Cache River State Recreation Area.

Directions: The Cache River State Natural Area has several different areas and covers over 10,000 acres. To reach the Site Headquarters from Vienna, Illinois, at the junction of Highways 45 and 146, take Highway 45 south 5 miles to Belknap Road; turn right (west) and go to the town of Belknap. Turn right onto 300 N. (the Dongola-Belknap Road). In the town turn right (north) at a large white church on the right side of the road. Follow the gravel road .9 miles to the park office. To reach the trailhead parking area (Tupelo Trail and others) follow a gravel road through a gate on the north side of the office for .6 mile. To reach Heron Pond from Vienna at the junction of Highways 45 and 146, take Highway 45 south 5 miles to Belknap Road, turn right (west) and go 1.5 miles to a gravel road (Heron Pond Lane); turn right onto Heron Pond Lane and go north .5 mile to a large parking area.

Hours Open: The site office is open daily from 8:00 A.M. to 4:00 P.M. All sites are open year-round.

Facilities: Site office, canoe access, and privy toilets are available.

Permits and rules: Several areas within the Cache River State Natural Area are state nature preserves: Heron Pond-Wildcat Bluff, Little Black Slough, and Section 8 Woods. Pets, hunting, trapping, fires, camping, picnicking, and rock climbing are not allowed in nature preserves.

Further Information: Site Superintendent, Cache River State Natural Area, 930 Sunflower Lane, Belknap, IL 62908; 618-634-9678.

Park Trails

Little Black Slough Trail 👢👢👢—5.5 miles—This trail can be accessed from the Wildcat Bluff, Heron Pond, or Marshall Ridge trails. A rock ford 1.5 miles west of the Wildcat Bluff access permits crossing the Cache River to Boss Island. This crossing, however, can only be made during periods of low water.

Lookout Point Trail 👢—1 mile—Access this trail off Route 146 west of Vienna. The trail winds along the edge of a hillside barren and provides an overview of the Cache River.

Linkage Trail 👢—2.4 miles—Trail access is through Heron Pond, Wildcat Bluff, or Marshall Ridge. Linking the Heron Pond Trail with the Little Black Slough Trail, this trail features the state champion (largest example of its species in the state) cherry-bark oak tree.

Marshall Ridge Trail 👢—2.8 miles—This trail winds through reforested fields north of Marshall Ridge and connects with the Linkage Trail to provide access to Heron Pond and Little Black Slough. Trail access is through the Marshall Ridge Access Area.

Lower Cache River Swamp Trail 👢—2.5 miles—Trail access is between Route 37 and Perks; you should see signs off the Perks' blacktop. The trail parallels the Cache River and Cypress Creek, allowing foot access to a cypress and tupelo swamp. Dusk offers a springtime serenade of tree frogs. Wet conditions may make parts of this trail impassable.

Cache River State Natural Area

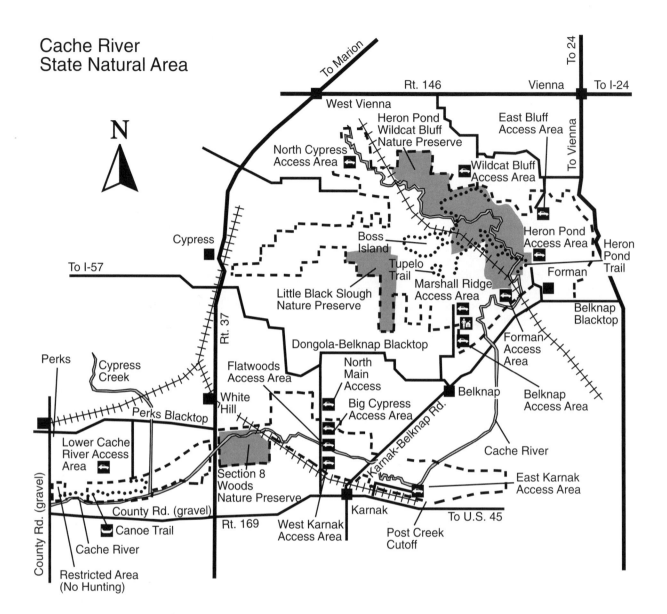

Legend

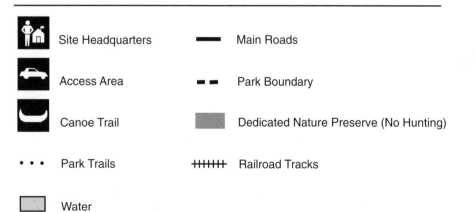

Site Headquarters	——— Main Roads		
Access Area	‑ ‑ Park Boundary		
Canoe Trail	Dedicated Nature Preserve (No Hunting)		
• • • Park Trails	++++++ Railroad Tracks		
Water			

Heron Pond Trail (Todd Fink Trail) 👢

Distance Round-Trip: 1.9 miles

Estimated Hiking Time: 1.25 hours

With the aid of a boardwalk you can experience the strange, silent, primeval world of a southern Illinois swamp. Early visitors who lacked the luxury of a boardwalk described this swamp as a "cheerless miserable place" or, more simply, "the pit of hell." Your experience is sure to be much more enjoyable.

Caution: This area is one of the few places in Illinois where the snake you see in the water is probably a poisonous water moccasin or cottonmouth! Cottonmouths are especially fond of basking on the trail during summer. In the spring, the several water crossings along the trail will likely soak your feet.

Trail Directions: From the parking area the trail begins at the brown, park-information board [1]. Here a large map shows the extent of the Cache River Natural Area; a box nearby has trail guides. Use the trail guides to add to your enjoyment of this unique hike, though the numbers on the trail-guide map do not correspond to those found in this book.

Blue blazes and occasional metal posts with a hiker symbol mark the trail. The hike begins on a limestone path that winds its way downhill. At .06 mi. [2] note a large boulder with a plaque dedicating this area as a National Landmark. A suspension bridge crosses the junction of the Cache River and Dutchman Creek. After crossing the bridge, follow the trail through a floodplain forest of large maples and sycamores.

From .25 mi. to .5 mi. you will encounter a series of large, stepping-stone bridges [3]. In dry weather these help prevent the swamp (on your left) from draining into the channeled Cache River on your right. During wet springs, this area is sometimes under water and the rocks turn slippery, so use caution. After the fourth stone

bridge, fingers of the swamp are visible from the trail on your left.

At .5 mi. leave the trail, step onto the boardwalk [4], and enter the realm of a cypress-tupelo swamp. All around are cypress trees with their knobby knees supporting small islands of plants. Cypress trees are one of the few evergreens that lose their needles in fall. Water tupelos are rounder at the base and have more common, deciduous-looking leaves. The green carpet on the swamp is duckweed. Take a close look at it for any small or large frogs camouflaged by the mantle of duckweed. Most visitors are likely to see a sinuous path in the duckweed-covered water, a telltale mark that a water moccasin has been here (water moccasins swim on the surface). For a lucky few, the originator of this trail may be seen basking on a partially submerged log! In spring, bright yellow prothonotary warblers nest overhead. At the end of the boardwalk turn around and retrace your steps to the trail and proceed to the left.

At .65 mi. the trail forms a V, and a park sign lists trail options [5]. Take the left fork, following the edge of Heron Pond (the swamp). Along this muddy trail, look at cypress knees for closer observation. Heron Pond soon ends and the trail curves to the right [6]. (Even though you may see a blue blaze ahead of you, the trail has recently been rerouted, so go to the right!) The trail goes uphill and winds its way through a beautiful woods.

At 1.1 mi. a metal trail marker gives you several hiking options [7]. A short side trip left (200 feet) leads to the state champion cherry-bark oak tree [8]. Walk around the tree on crosscut log sections to marvel at its size. From here you have the option of continuing on with the trail leading you to the site office and to Little Black Slough or backtracking 200 feet and rejoining the Heron Pond trail and eventually the parking area.

Backtrack and rejoin the Heron Pond Trail and continue to follow the blue blazes. After a few steps a service road appears on the left; bear to the right following a white-limestone rock trail. At 1.25 mi. you will rejoin the main trail [5]. You have just completed the loop and will hike back past the boardwalk, keeping an eye out for pileated woodpeckers. Continue back, recross the series of stepping-stone bridges, cross the suspension bridge, and finally climb uphill to the parking area.

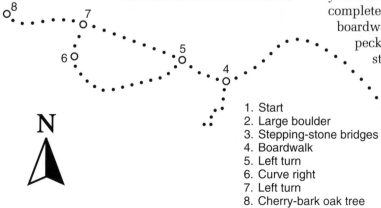

1. Start
2. Large boulder
3. Stepping-stone bridges
4. Boardwalk
5. Left turn
6. Curve right
7. Left turn
8. Cherry-bark oak tree

N

Tupelo Trail 👢👢

Distance Round-Trip: 2.5 miles

Estimated Hiking Time: 1.5 hours

Hike to Little Black Slough for great wildlife view-ing. The leaves of tall trees glisten against the backdrop of an incredibly blue sky. A bluebird fusses in a dead tupelo tree, woodpeckers fly between tree holes, a hawk screams overhead, a young raccoon yawns and stretches in a feathery cypress tree, and an elusive wild turkey skitters across the trail. All this happens along the Tupelo Trail each autumn.

Caution: During a wet year portions of the trail may be under water, so come prepared in the spring. The trail is fairly new, so there could be downed trees to scramble over and the trail may be faint in places. Be warned that this part of southern Illinois has poison-ous snakes: the copperhead, timber rattlesnake, and water moccasin.

Trail Directions: Park your vehicle at the Marshall Ridge Access Area and begin the trail in the north-west corner of the parking area [**1**]. The trail will have brown metal markers with the white silhouette of a hiker. Your hike begins on a crushed-rock road with a rolling, pastoral scene to the left and woods to the right.

After .25 mi. the trail forks and the crushed rock ends [**2**]. A sign points left for the Tupelo Trail. Begin hiking down an old dirt, forest road that passes through a dry, oak-hickory forest. During an excellent nut-crop year, this stretch of trail is like walking on ball bearings! Check the woods for large tulip and sweet gum trees with multiple trunks. At .75 mi. the trail forks and heads straight or to the left [**3**]. Con-tinue straight ahead into an old open field.

The trail soon reenters the woods, turning left and no longer following the forest road. At 1 mi. it heads downhill [**4**]. Watch your step, as the trail's leaves may cover treacherous rocky outcroppings. The trail here is faint. Bear to the left after a large rock outcrop-ping and cross a small creek. The woods are now dominated by maples and sweet gums. Beware of the large, cable-like vines going up the trees; these are poison ivy!

Straight ahead at 1.1 mi. you see the swamp's edge [**5**]. Only dead tupelo trees are visible, and the swamp is skirted by lizard's tail, which blooms during the summer. Look for woodpeckers among the dead snags and for tiny frogs along the water's edge. For the next half mile the trail will skirt the edge of this tupelo-dominated swamp. A few cypress trees soon begin to appear, along with live tupelo trees. Although the swamp on the right receives much of your attention, the woods to the left are impressive too, having many large, straight-trunked oaks and tulip trees.

Take time to view the swamp. This is one of the truly primeval landscapes found in Illinois. At 1.4 mi. the trail begins an ascent, although still skirting the swamp on your right [**6**]. The path becomes narrow and rocky. On the left are large patches of Christmas fern on a hill covered with rock outcroppings.

The trail goes up (1.5 mi.) [**7**] leaving the swamp behind. At the crest of the small hill is an intersection with two hiking signs. Go to the right. At 1.65 mi. [**3**] you will come to another intersection. You have just completed a short loop, discovering the watery world of a tupelo swamp. Hike to the right on the same trail through the dry oak-hickory forest. A .5-mi. walk brings you back to [**2**] and the Tupelo Trail sign. Take a right on the crushed-rock path, returning to the parking area.

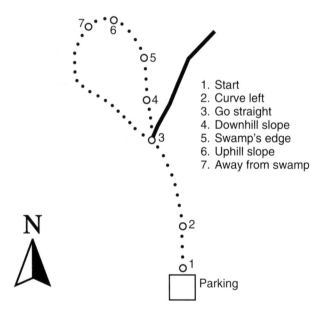

1. Start
2. Curve left
3. Go straight
4. Downhill slope
5. Swamp's edge
6. Uphill slope
7. Away from swamp

52. Created Lakes of the Southwest Shawnee National Forest

- Visit a super site for spring wildflowers, recommended by the Illinois Native Plant Society.
- View the effects groundwater has created in the form of collapsed coves and Liesegang Rings.
- Look for sunning skinks (lizards) and cavorting chipmunks.
- Hike through a sandstone glade.
- Discover that human-made lakes aren't just for fishing.

Area Information

Although many lakes exist (and most of them have intriguing, provocative names) in the Shawnee Hills of southern Illinois, none are natural. Crab Orchard Lake was built by the Civilian Conservation Corps; Lake of Egypt, a power-plant lake, was built to cool a steam-generating plant. Kinkaid, Cedar, Devil's Kitchen, and Little Grassy were constructed for water supplies and recreation. These lakes offer more, however, than muskie, trout, walleye, bluegill, or a constant supply of drinking water. Many have excellent hiking trails—paths to hike as well as fascinating, rugged opportunities to interact with some of nature's finest.

Directions: Cedar Lake is located 11 miles south of Murphysboro. Take Route 127, which is 9 miles south of Murphysboro. Turn east (left) onto Dutch Ridge Road and follow the signs for 2 miles to the trailhead. **Devil's Kitchen Lake** is located southwest of Carbondale. Take Route 13 east from Carbondale to the Refuge/Spillway Road and wind around Crab Orchard Lake for several miles; a park sign will direct you to **Devil's Kitchen Lake**. Once there, go straight on the road that skirts the lake. The parking area for the trail will be on your left.

Hours Open: Both sites are open year-round.

Facilities: Cedar Lake has boating and fishing. **Devil's Kitchen Lake** has boating, fishing, picnicking, and camping.

Permits and Rules: The trails at **Cedar Lake** skirt private property; please respect the owners' land.

Further Information: Cedar Lake, District Ranger, Murphysboro Ranger District, Shawnee National Forest, 2221 Walnut Street, Murphysboro, IL 62966; 618-687-1731. **Devil's Kitchen Lake**, Refuge Manager, Crab Orchard National Wildlife Refuge, P.O. Box J, Carterville, IL 62918; 618-997-3344.

Other Areas of Interest

Located between Marion and Carbondale, **Crab Orchard National Wildlife Refuge** is a combination of forests, wetlands, and grasslands. An average of 120,000 geese overwinter here annually. Bald eagles not only winter here, but a few also stay to nest. The area offers many recreational opportunities, including photography, wildlife observation, bicycling, picnicking, hunting, fishing, swimming, and camping. For further information contact Refuge Manager, Crab Orchard National Wildlife Refuge, P.O. Box J, Carterville, IL 62918; 618-997-3344.

Located northwest of Murphysboro, **Kinkaid Lake** offers the only muskie fishing in southern Illinois. In addition to various water activities, Kinkaid Lake also features a 15-mile (one-way), linear hiking trail. The trail skirts the south side of the lake, investigating finger coves and passing between the lake and exposed sandstone outcrops. A 3-mile loop trail has been developed within Johnson Creek Recreation Area. For further information contact District Ranger, Murphysboro Ranger District, Shawnee National Forest, 2221 Walnut Street, Murphysboro, IL 62966; 618-687-1731.

Park Trail

Cedar Lake Trail 👢👢👢👢—10 miles (one-way)—Cove Hollow Trail is just a segment of a much longer trail that skirts the western boundary of Cedar Lake and hikes around Little Cedar Lake. In addition to rolling terrain, the hike provides nice views and the opportunity to cross Little Cedar Lake on a natural-stone outcrop spillway. For further information contact District Ranger, Murphysboro Ranger District, Shawnee National Forest, 2221 Walnut Street, Murphysboro, IL, 62966, 618-687-1731.

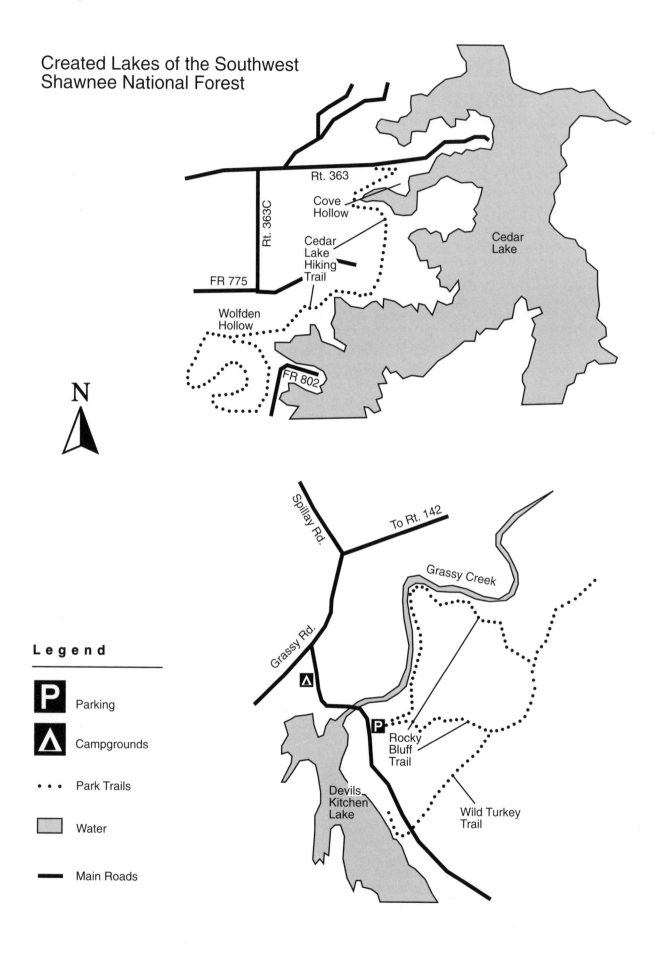

Created Lakes of the Southwest Shawnee National Forest

Rt. 363

Rt. 363C

Cove Hollow

Cedar Lake Hiking Trail

Cedar Lake

FR 775

Wolfden Hollow

FR 802

N

Spillay Rd.

To Rt. 142

Grassy Creek

Grassy Rd.

Rocky Bluff Trail

Devils Kitchen Lake

Wild Turkey Trail

Legend

P Parking

A Campgrounds

• • • Park Trails

Water

Main Roads

Cove Hollow Trail—Cedar Lake 👢👢👢👢👢

Distance Round-Trip: 5.5 miles

Estimated Hiking Time: 3 hours

Hike between large, sliding slabs of sandstone while seeking sunning skinks!

Caution: The trail skirts private land; stay on the well-marked trail. Several areas are steep, rocky, and slippery when wet.

Trail Directions: Begin the trail to the right of the signboard indicating Pomona Road and Little Cedar Lake Dam [1]. The trail is marked by white diamonds on trees and immediately descends on sandstone steps. Cedar Lake soon comes into view. Go between the bluffs and chunks of broken sandstone to another set of sandstone steps and descend into the valley. The trail angles right.

Cove Hollow, a shelter cave, is on your right at .15 mi. [2]. During the rainy season, it is topped with a small waterfall. While hiking in this ravine look for Jack-in-the-pulpit, which blooms during the spring. By late summer all that is left of it is a cluster of fiery-red berries. Cross the small stream using rocks as stepping stones (.35 mi.) [3]. Look for a large beech tree to the right of the stream and, during early spring, note the yellow trout lilies growing in pockets on the side of the bluff.

At the double white diamond (.7 mi.) [4] go left (not right!), and soon the bluffs and the lake are hidden by cedar, pine, and honeysuckle. The bluffs, however, quickly come back into view; nearby, look for a large tulip tree with a white diamond. Also look for orange-tip butterflies, a species that might be mistaken for cabbage butterflies if not for the males' being adorned with brilliant orange! Females, alas, are somewhat duller in color. As larvae, the orange-tip butterflies feed on toothwort and other mustards.

The looming bluff on the right at 1.25 mi. [5] has several nearby signs indicating private land. For the next .75 mi. the trail will pass by the bluffs and large chunks of broken sandstone. In the jumble of rocks, look for skinks basking in the sun and chipmunks scurrying, squeaking, and otherwise cavorting about. Look at the understory for pawpaw trees with large, tropical-looking leaves and for goldenseal, a type of buttercup.

At 2 mi. you will come to a trail intersection [6] with plenty of signage (trail names and mileage points); go right and head upward. You are now hiking along the ridge above Wolf Den Hollow and through a very dry, oak-hickory forest. As you walk up, the hollow becomes narrower. Cross a stream (2.3 mi.) [7] and try the other side of the hollow, again heading upward. At 2.4 mi. [8] go to the right, following the white diamonds. Once up, go left; you are now walking along the opposite ridge top. Cedar Lake will soon come into view on your right.

At 2.7 mi. [9], you will begin to descend from the ridge and will be hiking along the edge of a bluff. Within .1 mi. you will pass through the first of two *sandstone glades*. Sandstone glades are open expanses of exposed sandstone covered with lichens and moss. These hot, dry exposures support gnarly, short, blackjack oak; prickly-pear cactus; bluets; and false garlic. After the second glade, the trail continues downward on a slippery switchback.

Three miles brings level ground and another trail intersection [10]. Go left, skirting the bluff you just hiked along. Through the trees you are able to catch glimpses of Cedar Lake on your right. Before a small shelter bluff at 3.1 mi. [11], look for a large oak root that has become one with the bluff, and is now covered with lichens and moss. At 3.25 mi. find a bluff overhang [12]. During spring look for clumps of French's shooting star, a rarely occurring relative of the prairie shooting star with a fondness for growing under the driplines of bluff overhangs.

From the overhang, hike through a field of sandstone boulders, up and then down (being careful not to turn an ankle!). Cross a stream at 3.5 mi., and you are back at an earlier intersection [6]. Retrace your steps to the parking area. While hiking back, enjoy the calm serenity of Cedar Lake on the right and look for any missed skinks, chipmunks, interesting erosional patterns on the sandstone (*Liesegang Rings*), and wildflowers.

1. Start
2. Cove Hollow
3. Stream crossing
4. Left turn
5. Bluff
6. Right turn
7. Stream crossing
8. Right turn
9. Bluff edge
10. Left turn
11. Shelter bluff
12. Bluff overhang

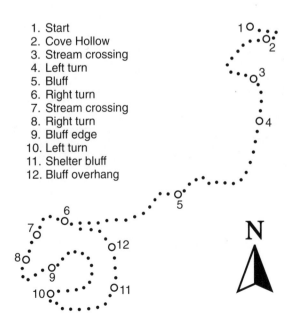

Rocky Bluff Trail—Devil's Kitchen Lake 👢👢👢👢

Distance Round-Trip: 1.4 miles

Estimated Hiking Time: 1 hour

Like someone who likes to eat dessert before dinner, I did the sweetest part of the trail first. I couldn't wait to see the colorful wildflowers or the mouthwatering waterfall!

Caution: The trail can be very muddy. Fallen saplings often block the way, and roots are exposed. Some of the rocks can be very slippery.

Trail Directions: Park on the left side of the road and begin at the trail board [1]. Go left and head downward, using the steps and a metal handrail to aid with the steep descent. Within 100 feet look to your right for a great waterfall, especially if a heavy downpour has occurred before your visit! Continue down small stone steps with another handrail to aid a stream crossing.

Again look to your right at the small canyon and waterfall. Note a large alcove and a collapsed, smaller alcove above at its head (.10 mi.) [2]. The waterfall helps to remove debris. The alcove was formed by a process called *groundwater sapping*—when groundwater seeps out from a cliff's face and undermines the cliff. Erosion at the seepage face creates an alcove, and, as the back of the alcove retreats, the overhanging rock is undermined and eventually collapses in an interesting geological formation. In the spring the ground here is carpeted with wildflowers of every imaginable hue: This may just be the best wildflower display in the state!

Continue straight over a wooden bridge (.2 mi.) [3]; on your left in the spring are acres of blue-eyed Mary's along Grassy Creek. These relatives of snapdragons are one of the few spring wildflowers that must come up each year from seed (annuals). The trail skirts Grassy Creek at .3 mi. [4]. On the left look for signs of nature's engineer: downed trees and muddy slides made by beavers. At .4 mi. [5] the trail skirts a sandstone bluff on the right. Try to spot the small circular depressions in the sand caused by antlion larvae. These very effective snares trap all manner of small insects for prey. An antlion awaits each of its hapless victims at the bottom of the pit with open jaws! Also notice the dark, concentric rings on the bluffs; called Liesegang Rings, they are caused by groundwater flowing through the sandstone, eroding it, and leaving behind mineral deposits.

As you skirt the bluff, you will walk under a shelter cave and soon step onto a point overlooking Grassy Creek. Enjoy the view before heading uphill.

At .5 mi. [6] you will come to a blind corner of sandstone; here you should head up. Head up on the reinforced rock steps to a ridge top overlooking Grassy Creek. Here the understory is fragile fern, mayapple, and larkspur.

All too soon the views of sandstone, Grassy Creek, and wildflowers are gone, replaced by a floodplain woods. At .75 mi. [7] cross a bridge before heading up into an oak-hickory forest. Look to your right for a great view of the ravine. One mile [8] brings you to a trail intersection; go right. Within a few yards you will encounter another intersection; go right again onto a wide grassy path. Note, but ignore, the large, wooden arrow pointing in the opposite direction.

The grassy path soon becomes a narrow trail through the woods. Look to your right into the ravine woods below. The trail forks at 1.1 mi. [9]; take the left fork and head downhill where you will encounter another wooden footbridge. Another stream crossing occurs at 1.25 mi. [10], where the stream runs across sandstone slabs; use caution to cross it. The trail continues straight ahead through a planting of pines (you will find informational signage along this section).

Another sandstone slab stream crossing is at 1.35 mi. [11]. It's slick, so be careful not to join the waterfall to the right! From here the trail soon ends, completing the loop. If you're visiting in the spring, have a second helping of dessert—take the few extra steps to enjoy the waterfall, collapsed alcove, and profusion of wildflowers once again.

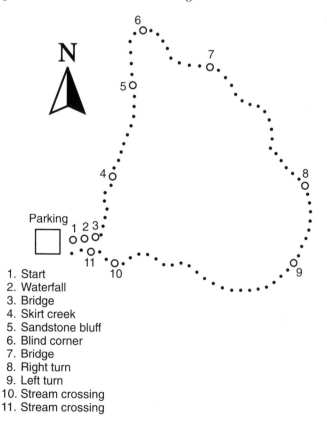

1. Start
2. Waterfall
3. Bridge
4. Skirt creek
5. Sandstone bluff
6. Blind corner
7. Bridge
8. Right turn
9. Left turn
10. Stream crossing
11. Stream crossing

53. Giant City State Park

- Walk through the narrow, echoing aisles of the Giant City.
- Look for the names of Union and Confederate soldiers carved in the sandstone walls of Giant City.
- View Devil's Standtable, a Native American stone fort, and a unique water tower with a 50-foot-high observation deck.
- Bring a plant guide to help identify some of the park's 800 species of flowering plants and 30 kinds of ferns. The best place for plant identification is Fern Rocks Nature Preserve.
- Enjoy some of the best fall colors in Illinois.

Area Information

At one time this region was under a warm inland sea that reached as far as the Gulf of Mexico. Slowly the sea receded, landforms emerged, streams began to cut deep valleys, and, over the millennia, striking sandstone formations were created. Faulting and folding of the sandstone formed structures unique to the park, with names like Whale's Mouth and Devil's Standtable. Perhaps the most unique feature, however, is Giant City—the park's namesake.

In Giant City the massive rock formations create walls so perfect they appear to be constructed by machine. The sections of rock form cool, shaded streets and alleys, thus resembling a "giant city." During the Civil War, the cliffs and canyons became a haven for soldiers of both Union and Confederate armies; their names are still visible in the soft sandstone walls.

Perhaps the crown jewel of the park is Fern Rocks

Nature Preserve, named for the abundant ferns that adorn its sandstone walls. These sandstone escarpments continuously drip water and leave driplines on the valley floor, the habitat for French's shooting star. Fern Rocks also has a profusion of blue-eyed Mary's, and its gentle slopes are carpeted with white trillium and celandine poppy.

Whether you seek to climb trails to high places, stand and marvel at a precariously balanced rock, or try your luck at locating some of the 800 species of flowering plants, Giant City State Park offers many wonders and can provide many weekends of eventful exploration.

Directions: Giant City State Park is located 12 miles south of Carbondale. From Carbondale take U.S. 51 south to Makanda Road; go left (east) and follow the signs to the park.

Hours Open: The site is open year-round except on Christmas and New Year's Day. The trails close at dusk.

Facilities: The park offers fishing, boating, horseback riding, swimming, rappelling, camping, picnicking (both tables and shelters), children's playgrounds, limited hunting, and a lodge with a dining room.

Permits and Rules: Trillium Trail in Fern Rocks is in a dedicated Illinois Nature Preserve: No pets are allowed on the trail. In the rest of the park, pets must be leashed at all times.

Further Information: Site Superintendent, Giant City State Park, 336 S. Church Road, Makanda, IL 62958; 618-457-4836. For information about the lodge or reservations call 618-457-4921.

Park Trails

All the park trails have trail guide pamphlets available from the Park Office.

Stone Fort Nature Trail—.4 miles—This is a loop trail that explores a remnant Native American stone fort; the view from the bluff provides a great overview of the north end of the park. The trail goes uphill adjacent to a small, flowing stream—a good place for bird watching (look for summer tanagers).

Indian Creek Shelter Nature Trail—.75 miles—Hike along Indian Creek and explore a virgin forest and shelter bluff (cave) used by Native Americans from 400 to 1100 A.D.

Post Oak Trail—.33 miles—Along this wheelchair-accessible trail you will discover Makanda Sandstone and its corresponding bluffs, moist- to dry-upland forests, and a good population of prickly-pear cactus.

Red Cedar Hiking Trail—16 miles—The trail may be covered in a day. If you are taking two days to hike the trail, however, you must be on the trail by noon of the first day and obtain a camping permit. The trail traverses the park's perimeter. Some of its highlights include Indian Creek, Stonefort Cemetery, drift coal mines, Old Makanda, sandstone bluffs lining the stream valleys, a small waterfall, and numerous rock outcrops.

Giant City State Park

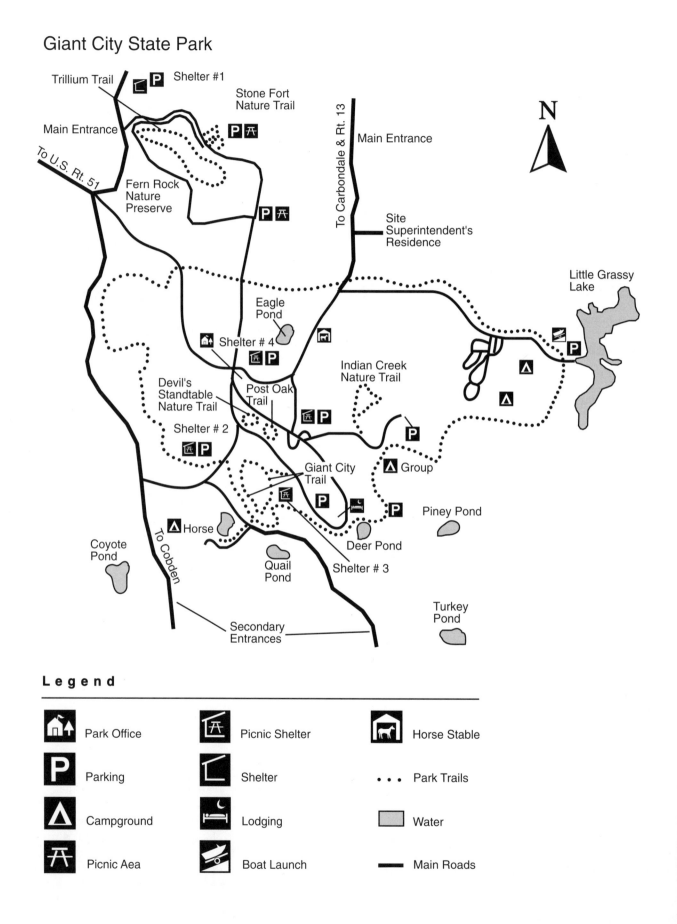

Trillium Trail

Shelter #1

Stone Fort Nature Trail

Main Entrance

To U.S. Rt. 51

Fern Rock Nature Preserve

To Carbondale & Rt. 13

Main Entrance

N

Site Superintendent's Residence

Little Grassy Lake

Eagle Pond

Shelter # 4

Indian Creek Nature Trail

Devil's Standtable Nature Trail

Post Oak Trail

Shelter # 2

Giant City Trail

Group

Horse

Piney Pond

Coyote Pond

To Cobden

Quail Pond

Deer Pond

Shelter # 3

Turkey Pond

Secondary Entrances

Legend

Park Office	Picnic Shelter	Horse Stable
P Parking	Shelter	• • • Park Trails
Campground	Lodging	Water
Picnic Aea	Boat Launch	— Main Roads

Giant City Trail

Distance Round-Trip: 2 miles

Estimated Hiking Time: 1.33 hours

It is little wonder that early visitors, accustomed to small log cabins, found these rock formations singularly frightening and mysterious, and dubbed the site a "giant city." Even to eyes accustomed to imposing skyscrapers, this landscape is still impressive.

Caution: Many tree roots and large rocks have eroded from the trail—watch your step. The trail crosses a park road, so also watch for cars.

Trail Directions: Trail guides are available at the park office, but the numbers in this book do not correspond to those in the guides. Park at the Giant City Trail Parking Area and begin at the trail board. You will immediately cross a bridge over Giant City Creek [**1**]. The trail is marked with white and orange, spray-painted arrows. At .1 mi. the trail forks [**2**]; go right and head upward. Just ahead, sandstone bluffs form a stone wall.

Near the top of the bluff continue right and pass blocks of rock that have broken off from the bluff. To whet your appetite for what is to come, leave the trail that skirts the bluff. You will be walking through the outskirts of Giant City, a veritable sandstone suburbia (.3 mi.) [**3**]. Pass through an alleyway of rocks and go left to rejoin the trail that encircles the bluff.

At .35 miles the trail forks again; go left for a close and personal view of the bluffs [**4**]. Squeeze through to the other side and skirt the bluff. Soon you will hit the wall, so-to-speak, and encounter what looks like a dead-end. Go left and you are in downtown Giant City (.5 mi.) [**5**].

Take care walking the streets of Giant City; follow all directional arrows. In lieu of billboards, this city has names and dates carved into the sandstone walls. Seek out the oldest name and date you can find, but please refrain from adding yours to the walls. You exit the city, fittingly, by walking under an arch.

From the balanced rock go down the wooden steps and follow the orange arrows. Soon you enter the drier side of the bluff. At .65 mi. the trail heads upward again, with steps fit for giants [**6**]. Benches are provided to enjoy the view from the top or to rest. The trail next heads down.

When you encounter a bench on the left and a large boulder in the middle of the trail with arrows pointing both ways, go left (.85 mi.) [**7**]. Cross a footbridge to view a dark hole in the rock, leading who knows where. Go right, cross another bridge,

and encircle the large boulder. Continue following the trail downward until you are back at the beginning trail board.

Go left past restrooms and walk along Giant City Creek (1 mi.) [**8**]. At times you will be walking between two streams, soon crossing the small one on the right and then recrossing the main stream when both merge. At 1.2 mi. [**9**] you will come to Shelter #2 and a grassy play area. Walk by the shelter and the swings and cross the stream on the second bridge on your right. From here you will come into a parking area; walk left until you see the sign for Devil's Standtable Trail across the road. Begin the trail at 1.35 mi. [**10**].

After a short uphill climb, you will again come to the familiar sandstone bluffs. A shelter cave soon comes into view, formed because the softer sandstone in the lower part of the bluffs eroded faster than the upper layer (permeated with iron ore) (1.45 mi.) [**11**]. Jump over a stream and continue to a large, free-standing pillar called Devil's Standtable, or Mushroom Rock (on your left). This was once a large block of the bluff that cracked loose during some earlier movement of the earth. The softer areas of the sandstone have eroded, leaving the large base and the iron-embedded cap (1.5 mi.) [**12**].

At Devil's Standtable the trail forks; go right and soon you are back at the road. Cross the road and head back into the parking area, recrossing the bridge and skirting the stream. Notice the stream's bottom: The water flows over huge slabs of sandstone, creating miniature waterfalls. By the time you return to the trail board for Giant City, the stream will have narrowed and the bottom will be only rocks and gravel.

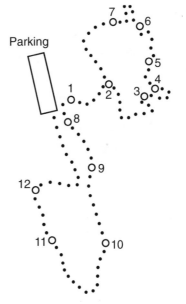

1. Start
2. Right turn
3. Suburbs
4. Bluffs
5. Downtown
6. Steps
7. Left turn
8. Left turn
9. Shelter #2
10. Devil's Standtable Trail
11. Shelter cave
12. Devil's Standtable

Trillium Trail 👢👢👢

Round-Trip Distance: 1.75 miles

Estimated Hiking Time: 1 hour

In the spring, Trillium Trail lives up to its name. Within the first few steps you can see not only the familiar prairie trillium but also graceful, arching white trilliums that line the path and mingle with the abundant spring flora.

Caution: During the wet season the rocks can be very slippery.

Trail Directions: Begin the trail to the left of the signboard for Fern Rocks Nature Preserve and start the trek upward [1]. The trail is a well-worn path, occasionally marked by a black post with white arrows. Note the huge chunks of sandstone ahead of you and to the right. The vertical separations in the rock were caused by glacial meltwaters. In the spring, within the first .1 mi. your senses are inundated with flowers of every hue. The familiar and unfamiliar grow together—squirrel-corn, celandine poppy, white trillium, mayapple, and spring beauties [2]. Search the rock ledges for precariously perched yellow trout lilies.

At .2 mile the trail crosses a bridge [3] and passes by blocks of sandstone that have broken off from the main bluff. The bluffs are layered; the lower part is Makanda Sandstone whereas the top is Drury Shale. A fine layer of loess rests on top of the shale. The blocks break off, due to erosion of the underlying softer layer. Note the different shapes the boulders take—from large and square to ultrathin. After crossing the bridge, look to the right to see how an intermittent waterfall has smoothed the surface of the rock and created stair steps.

The trail passes very close to the road and appears to fork at .3 mi.; stay to the right [4]. Pass between the bluff and a large broken chunk of sandstone and come to a series of rock steps leading upward. Along here each spring look for both Dutchman's-breeches and squirrel-corn growing in the protected corners of the bluff. Be alert both for bumblebees and bumble-bee sphinx moths, a harmless look-alike (mimic). They can be seen pollinating the same plant.

You come to another bridge at .7 mi. [5], but before crossing it, admire the profuse spring flowers. From here the trail begins an upward climb, first over stone chunks and finally on wooden steps; go right at the top of the steps.

You will be on top of the bluffs, and the lush spring understory has disappeared. Around you will be a dry forest dominated by red and white oaks and hickory. At 1.1 mi. [6] you will come to a fork; go left, and when you come off the hill, go left again. Along the bluff top look for the metallic green of tiger beetles. They will always manage to stay one step ahead. Look also for small, white butterflies with orange-tipped wings. Appropriately called orange-tips, they are more typical of the Southwest than Illinois.

As you cross the bridge at 1.3 mi. [7], peer into the crevice below, created when a section of bluff split apart. From the bridge the trail descends back into the lush, green ravine forest. As you hike here, look for some of the 30 species of ferns that occur in the park. Most of these fern species are located in the preserve, hence the name Fern Rocks. By 1.75 mi. the trail has wound back down, returning you to the trail board.

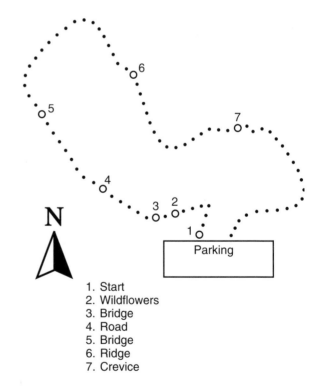

N

1. Start
2. Wildflowers
3. Bridge
4. Road
5. Bridge
6. Ridge
7. Crevice

54. Trail of Tears State Forest

- Bring a plant identification guide to help identify some of the more than 620 species of flowering plants and ferns, including one of the best displays of squirrel-corn and celandine poppy in the state.
- Listen for the call of the pileated woodpecker and look for these large woodpeckers throughout the park.
- See one of the last-remaining fire towers in southern Illinois.
- Appreciate the hard work of the Civilian Conservation Corps as you use one of its log and stone shelters or walk past a stonework stabilization wall.
- Contemplate Robert Frost's poem "The Road Not Taken" as you pass many fire trails heading off into the distant forest.

Area Information

Southern Illinois has more kinds of trees than does all of Europe. You can get a glimpse of this arboreal variety at Trail of Tears State Forest—huge beeches in ravine forests, dry hill-top forests of black and white oak, and isolated clumps of the uncommon red buckeye in the adjoining nature preserve. Nearly all species of trees found in southern Illinois occur at Trail of Tears.

Originally known as the Turkey Farm, Trail of Tears was established as set-aside lands for the growing of timber for forest products, for watershed protection, and for outdoor recreation. More than 40 fire trails are open for hiking and exploration all year.

The forest's present name memorializes the tragic time when Native Americans from the Cherokee, Creek, and Chickasaw nations were displaced from their reservations in the southeast and forced to move to Oklahoma. They overwintered in makeshift camps 4 miles south of the forest's southern boundary.

Directions: Trail of Tears State Forest lies in western Union County, 5 miles northwest of Jonesboro. Access to the forest is from Illinois 127 in the east and Illinois 3 in the west. Take Trail of Tears Blacktop from either of these highways to reach the forest.

Hours Open: The site is open year-round.

Facilities: The forest has picnic areas (including two large and two small shelters), camping (both tent and backpack), and hunting.

Permits and Rules: No pets are allowed on the trail in Ozark Hills Nature Preserve. Elsewhere, pets must be kept on a leash at all times. Motorized vehicles and bicycles are not allowed off the paved or gravel roads. All-terrain vehicles are prohibited and large recreational vehicles are discouraged. Indiscriminate killing of snakes is prohibited.

Further Information: Site Superintendent, Trail of Tears State Forest, Route 1, P.O. Box 1331, Jonesboro, IL 62952; 618-833-4910.

Other Areas of Interest

Lincoln Memorial Picnic Grounds is located in Jonesboro. The only town in the north to be occupied by the Union troops during the Civil War, Jonesboro hosted the third senate debate between Lincoln and Douglas (held in 1858), and a monument here commemorates the site. A half-mile loop trail is available. For more information call 618-833-8576.

Trail of Tears State Forest

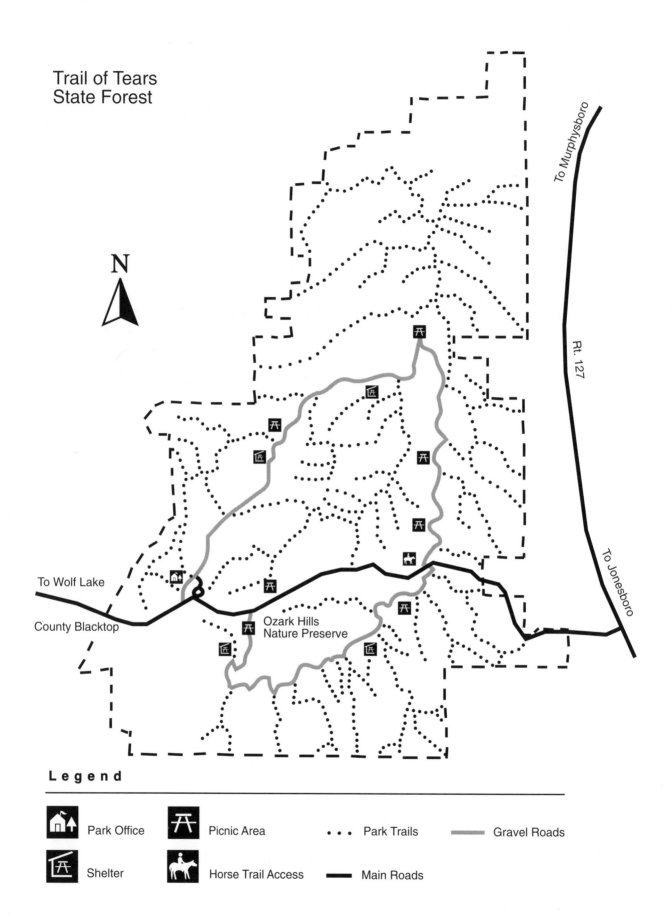

N

To Murphysboro

Rt. 127

To Jonesboro

To Wolf Lake

County Blacktop

Ozark Hills
Nature Preserve

Legend

Park Office

Shelter

Picnic Area

Horse Trail Access

• • • Park Trails

Main Roads

Gravel Roads

Fire Trails #21 to 29 👢👢👢👢👢

Distance Round-Trip: 7 miles

Estimated Hiking Time: 3 hours

This trail is a treat (and challenge) for legs and feet as you will climb many hills. Look for missed morels, their tops dried and no longer tasty. Listen to the screaming screech (no, those aren't your calves) of a pileated woodpecker. All the while take time to ponder that mysterious fire trail not taken.

Caution: The trail starts on a road that is open to traffic from May 1 to December 24. Look out also for fallen branches and tree roots on the trail.

Trail Directions: Travel east on the county road through the forest, passing a horse camp area where horses are tied up for the evening. The road then curves; look to the left for a one-way gravel road that is sometimes closed, depending on the time of year. Park by the side of this road. Start the hike at the gate and immediately begin climbing uphill [1]. On either side are ridges of dry, oak-hickory woods with an occasional smooth, gray-barked beech. Although the woods have been cut, an occasional large tree is still visible. Fire trails are trails maintained to access the inner forest.

First [2] you pass fire trails #16-20 and campsites N-1 to N-5. Along the gravel road look for a black bird, the size of a crow, with a bright, poppy-red crest. This is the pileated woodpecker, a common resident of Trail of Tears State Forest. At 1.5 mi. you will come to a large picnic area [3]. Go to the right, through the area, and join fire trials #21-29. This part of the hike is also a horse trail, so watch your step!

Shortly after fire trail #29, fire trail #21 appears at 2 mi. [4]. Here you will ascend a short rise, come to a T, and go left. Fire trail #22 will be on your right as the trail heads downward. On springtime hikes, look for a large patch of yellow-flowered bellwort. A major fire trail intersection appears at 2.25 mi. [5]. Continue straight ahead, ignoring the trails to the right and left. Be sure to look left, however, into the deep, forested ravine below.

After a stimulating, uphill climb you'll encounter fire trail #24 on your right at 2.5 mi. [6]; at the intersection go left (fire trail #25 will be on the right). From this vantage, LaRue-Pine Hills (see park #56) is straight ahead. At 2.65 mi. you will come upon an unmarked fork in the trail [7]. Follow the horse trail signs to the right.

Fire trail #26B is to the right as you walk along a narrow path on top of a ridge. By 2.95 mi. [8] the trail forks; curve to the left. If there are no leaves on the trees, take advantage of the great view to the right.

Prepare for a climb up and down a hill. As you descend, look to the right to see the ridge you just climbed.

Begin a steep descent down a deeply rutted path at 3.6 mi. [9], passing from the realm of the oaks to that of the beeches. Once into the beech grove, the trail goes to the right. But before you turn, note the exposed and eroded bluff of chert (flint) in front of you and the huge beech. A horse-trail sign is visible across the stream (it leads back to the horse camp, so ignore it). Crossing the stream provides another opportunity to study the chert. Here the bedrock is limestone, not sandstone as in other parts of the Shawnee National Forest.

Cross the stream again and look to your right for some great examples of beeches with gray, exposed roots gripping the hillside. Cross the stream again, go left, and skirt a large beech tree. During the summer the stream may be nothing more than a few wet pools. This area has not been well-traveled and the beeches have a clean slate—no names are carved into them. Before climbing to reenter the domain of the oaks, take a last, lingering look at the beeches (3.8 mi.) [10]. At the intersection at 3.95 mi. [11] pause to catch your breath; then go left. Fire trail #27A appears on the right at 4.35 mi. [12]. Continue on and you will have come full circle when you come out on fire trail #27 at 4.65 mi. [13]. Go right and hike past fire trails #23, 28, 22, 21, and 29. A final uphill climb returns you to the picnic area (5.35 mi.) [3]. Retrace your steps back down the gravel road you entered, looking back along the way for tiger swallowtails, spring azure butterflies, and small flies that look like fuzzy bees (called bombyliids).

At 7 mi. you are back where you started. Remember Robert Frost, and perhaps one day you will return to explore those many other paths not taken.

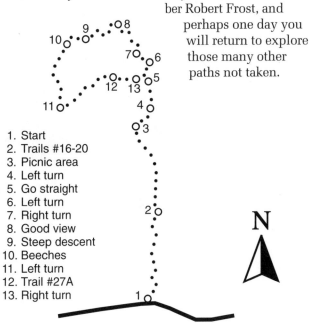

1. Start
2. Trails #16-20
3. Picnic area
4. Left turn
5. Go straight
6. Left turn
7. Right turn
8. Good view
9. Steep descent
10. Beeches
11. Left turn
12. Trail #27A
13. Right turn

Ozark Hills Nature Preserve

Distance Round-Trip: 3 miles

Estimated Hiking Time: 1.25 hours

Although the early spring was dry, I marveled at the green "waterfalls" provided by masses of mayapple flowing down the ravines.

Caution: From May 1 to December 25 the road for the hike is open to traffic. Sticks, branches, and limbs may litter the trail.

Trail Directions: Park at the main day-use area across from the white barn (a turkey and deer check-station in season). Begin the hike at the yellow gate (closed to vehicular traffic from December 26 to April 30) [**1**]. Note the chert slopes with large beech trees and the rich spring understory. Celandine poppy and squirrel-corn are especially abundant.

Most of the hike is on a one-lane gravel road. At .25 mi. [**2**] you will cross a series of bridges built by the Civilian Conservation Corps. After the third bridge, the trail begins an uphill climb. As you labor upward note the ridge on the left. You are passing through a mature second-growth forest. As the climb continues, the rich flora at the bottom gives way to scattered patches of understory plants. At the intersection at .4 mi. [**3**] go left and continue uphill. On the right is a campsite. Within .1 mi. fire trail #2 will appear on your right.

The forest's fire tower (no long used) appears at .8 mi. [**4**]. Look left to see down into the valley. Con-

tinue upward from the fire tower, passing fire trails #3-5. Look for a sign on the left indicating the boundary of the nature preserve (1.2 mi.) [**5**]. As you pass by fire trails #6–8, enjoy the quiet: The only sounds are the wind through the trees and the birds' singing. Fire trails #9–10 appear near 1.8 mi. [**6**], along with a shelter, toilet, and camping area. In springtime at this point you can discover scattered patches of bellwort (a lily with a yellow, dangling flower).

Another shelter is passed before you reach the entrance to Ozark Hills Nature Preserve at 2 mi. [**7**]. It is named after this area's geologic similarity to the Ozark region of Missouri. Go left, and the gravel path soon gives way to a leaf-strewn, rolling woodland trail. Note the ridges on either side of the path and watch as squirrels leap across the path into trees on the opposite side.

The ridges on the right have disappeared, and the trail leads downward (2.6 mi.) [**8**]. A small grove of red buckeyes is just ahead. Red buckeyes are fairly rare in Illinois and inhabit the rich woodlands of a few southern areas. The trail ends at these red-flowered trees. Proceed left and downhill, passing through a line of wild cane, a bamboo-like plant. Soon you will come to an open grove of maples and a ball field (2.75 mi.) [**9**]. Angle to the right on a gravel road; on your left is a small creek.

You are again immersed in a lush spring flora. Look on the hillside for waterleaf blooming in May. At the yellow gate you reach at 2.85 mi., go around or under and then left . Soon you will pass a double-trunked sweet gum on the right as you head back to the parking and picnic area.

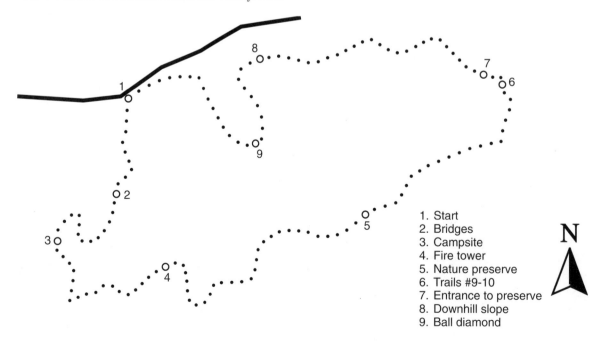

1. Start
2. Bridges
3. Campsite
4. Fire tower
5. Nature preserve
6. Trails #9-10
7. Entrance to preserve
8. Downhill slope
9. Ball diamond

N

55. Hamburg Hill

- Discover one of the best examples of an American beech forest in the state.

- Bring your binoculars to watch the antics of the American coot, scan the sky for great blue herons heading to their rookery, and seek the rarely sighted tricolored heron.

- Become an entomologist for the day and observe tiger beetles, tiger swallowtails, whirligig beetles, dragonflies, and many more of the area's myriad species of insects.

- Look for plants and animals more reminiscent of Louisiana than Illinois—bald cypress, American featherfoil, and the green tree frog.

Area Information

The first quarter-mile of this trail gives no hint of what lies ahead—a scintillating example of a beech forest, multitudes of spring wildflowers, and an interesting swamp where hiking is literally "on the edge." The swamps and bluffs at Hamburg Hill meet abruptly, as they do at LaRue-Pine Hills (see park #56), but here the bluffs are not so imposing. Here also, on any warm spring or fall day, is the opportunity for sightings of numerous migrating reptiles and amphibians.

In springtime hundreds of tiny frogs hop in front of you and soon you are immersed in the life of the swamp and surrounding forest—watching birds, insects, and mammals and enjoying a hike that is literally between two separate worlds.

Directions: Hamburg Hill is located south of Jonesboro in Union County. From Jonesboro go south on Route 127 for 2.1 miles to County Road 9 (Old Cape Road/Plank Hill Road); turn right and drive 5.3 miles south and west. The road follows Harrison Creek. The parking area for the trailhead is the first right (a muddy, rutted pull-in) past the fourth one-lane bridge.

Hours Open: The site is open year-round.

Facilities: None

Permits and Rules: Killing of snakes is prohibited.

Further Information: Jonesboro Ranger District, Shawnee National Forest, Jonesboro, IL 62952; 618-833-8576.

Other Areas of Interest

Located at the western edge of the state, **Union County Conservation Area** was established to replenish and maintain the declining goose populations. During five months of the year you can see 85,000 geese here. Thousands of these overwintering birds can be viewed along the Refuge Drive. For more information call the Refuge Manager at 618-833-5175.

Thebes Courthouse is a Greek Revival structure (in Thebes, off Route 3), an example of one of the state's early courthouses. According to local legend, the escaped slave Dred Scott may have been imprisoned in the town's jail. For more information call 618-764-2600.

© Michael Jeffords

Hamburg Hill Trail 👢👢👢

Distance Round-Trip: 7.2 miles

Estimated Hiking Time: 4.5 hours

It is a perfect spring day. The birds are singing, frogs are hopping into the water in front of you, an abundance of phlox lends its heady fragrance to the air, and tiger swallowtails are everywhere, flitting from flower to flower. What a way to spend the day —hiking Hamburg Hill!

Caution: The trail is used by off-road vehicles; sometimes it has large ruts and is very muddy. Hiking during the week is recommended to avoid the recreational vehicles. Downed trees across the path are also a problem. Crossing the creek in springtime almost guarantees getting wet feet, and by late spring the woods are teeming with poison ivy.

Trail Directions: Begin the trail by crossing the creek and follow an old forest road [1]. The line of hills that appears on your right is known as Atwood Ridge; the swamp on your left is the Union County Conservation Area (.15 mi.) [2]. Here the swamps of the lower Mississippi River valley meet the bluffs of the Shawnee Hills.

At .35 mi. venture close to the water [3] and look for the cast skins of dragonflies, left behind when they molt from nymph to adult, floating mats of duckweed, and masses of whirligig beetles. A small hollow in the woods on the right (.6 mi.) [4] has several giant beech trees.

At 1 mi. the shrub zone of the swamp has appeared, and the trail detours into the woods and then back down [5]. The trail again climbs into the woods at 1.25 mi. [6], taking you to a ridge above the swamp. The limestone bluffs on your right are dominated by huge old tulip trees.

Come off the ridge at 1.45 mi. [7] and walk through a floodplain forest. Soon the swamp will appear again (on the left). Cypress trees are found close to the path at 1.5 mi. [8] and floating in the swamp just beyond them is one of the state's more unusual plants, American featherfoil.

For the next mile the trail undulates through upland and floodplain woods (1.6 mi.) [9]. Ignore the side trails to the left and right— these have been made by all-terrain vehicles. At 2.6 mi. [10] you leave the swamp, and the trail merges with a small stream, crisscrossing it several times. Here the floodplain woods have been replaced by a thick stand of young tulip trees.

The small tulip trees gradually disappear; by the 3-mi. point they have been replaced by large beech trees on both sides of the trail [11], some of the finest examples of beech trees in the state. As the trail climbs, the beeches get smaller until they finally disappear (3.25 mi.). Near the top of the hill a short, squatty, water tank becomes visible on the right [12]. The trail ends at a metal barricade on Forest Road 266A (3.6 mi.) [13]. You have just climbed Hamburg Hill.

Turn and retrace your steps. But this time spend less time viewing the dramatics of the swamp, ridge, and forest and more time enjoying the subtler things. Play catch with the green tiger beetles. They allow you to get only so close before they fly off. Repeat this activity until you or the beetles tire of the sport.

Look for puddle clubs of butterflies. Puddle clubbing is a gathering of bachelor male butterflies at a moist spot on the ground or at a particularly delectable scat. It is thought that these males, by being together, are creating a "super male" to attract the fancy of passing females.

Once the swamp is on your right look for the green tree frog. This bright-green frog with a cream-colored stripe along its sides evokes images of Florida. Look at the vegetation in and around the water; during the day the frogs crouch motionless, relying on their coloration to protect them.

At 7.2 miles you are back at the stream crossing [1]. Why not take off your shoes and wade across the cool stream, giving your feet a well-deserved reward?

Hamburg Hill

1. Start
2. Swamp
3. Water's edge
4. Large beech trees
5. Woods
6. Ridge
7. Floodplain forest
8. Featherfoil
9. Undulating trail
10. Crisscross stream
11. Beech forest
12. Water tank
13. Hamburg Hill

Hamburg Hill Trail

Upper Bluff Lake

Harrison Creek

Parking

Plank Hill Rd.

N

56. LaRue-Pine Hills

- Why does the snake cross the road? Find out by hiking the trail along the base of the bluff.

- Enjoy spectacular views from Inspiration Point.

- Bring your reptile and amphibian guides to help you identify the 59 species of snakes, salamanders, turtles, frogs, lizards, and skinks that live here.

- Discover a beautiful, winding forest road and coves carpeted with wildflowers.

- Enjoy some of the best fall colors in Illinois against the backdrop of white limestone bluffs.

Area Information

LaRue-Pine Hills is a 5-mile by 2-mile strip of land running north-south in the Shawnee National Forest. Designated in 1970 as the National Forest Service's first Ecological Area and in 1991 as a National Research Natural Area by the Department of the Interior, LaRue-Pine Hills is a fascinating melting pot of widely different habitats. Limestone cliffs like those in the Missouri Ozarks, swampland reminiscent of Louisiana, and densely wooded coves like those of the Appalachians coexist here.

In a 4-square-mile area twelve hundred plant species are found—35 percent of all the known Illinois plant species. Ninety percent of the state's known mammal species occur here, including the illusive bobcat, which routinely ranges over the rugged forest ridges. The rare eastern wood rat, a type of pack rat, lives at the base of the bluffs.

For a month each spring and fall the road at the base of the bluffs is closed to vehicular traffic to allow the many species of reptiles and amphibians that hibernate among the rocks along the bluff a safe route for migration into and out of the swamp. LaRue-Pine Hills is the most diverse natural area of its size in the Midwest—an Illinois biological Garden of Eden.

Directions: LaRue-Pine Hills is 3 miles north of the small town of Wolf Lake and is best reached from Route 3. Of the three entrances to the area, the easiest is the Big Muddy River Levee Road. As you drive on this road look to your left along the Big Muddy River at the aftermath of the flood of 1993: Many of the large trees are dead. When you round a large curve in the road, the bluffs of LaRue-Pine Hills literally spring into view. At the intersection, go right to the base of the bluff trail (Forest Road 345) or left to Inspiration Point Trail.

Hours Open: The site is open year-round. One of the best times to visit is when Forest Road 345 is closed for the herptile migration—in April and October.

Facilities: Pit toilets and several picnic areas are available. Pine Hills campground is located on Forest Road 236, one mile east of Wolf Lake.

Permits and Rules: Permits must be obtained for any collecting within LaRue-Pine Hills.

Further Information: Jonesboro Ranger District, Shawnee National Forest; Jonesboro, IL 62952; 618-833-8576.

Other Areas of Interest

Located west of Route 127, the famous **Bald Knob Cross** was built as a monument for peace. This is the highest landmark in Union County. For more information call 618-893-2344.

Devil's Backbone Park, on the Mississippi River in Grand Tower, is quite scenic and boasts a sandbar beach and several rock formations: Devil's Backbone, Devil's Bake Oven, and Tower Rock. A .5-mi. linear trail traverses the Backbone. For more information call 618-565-2454.

Park Trail

Observation Overlook Trails—Forest Road 236, along the bluff top of Pine Hills, gives access to a series of Overlook Trails. Ranging in length from .2 mi. to .75 mi. and offering stunning vistas of the area, these trails afford views of the shortleaf pines that the park is named after (a species found in only one other location in the state).

LaRue-
Pine Hills

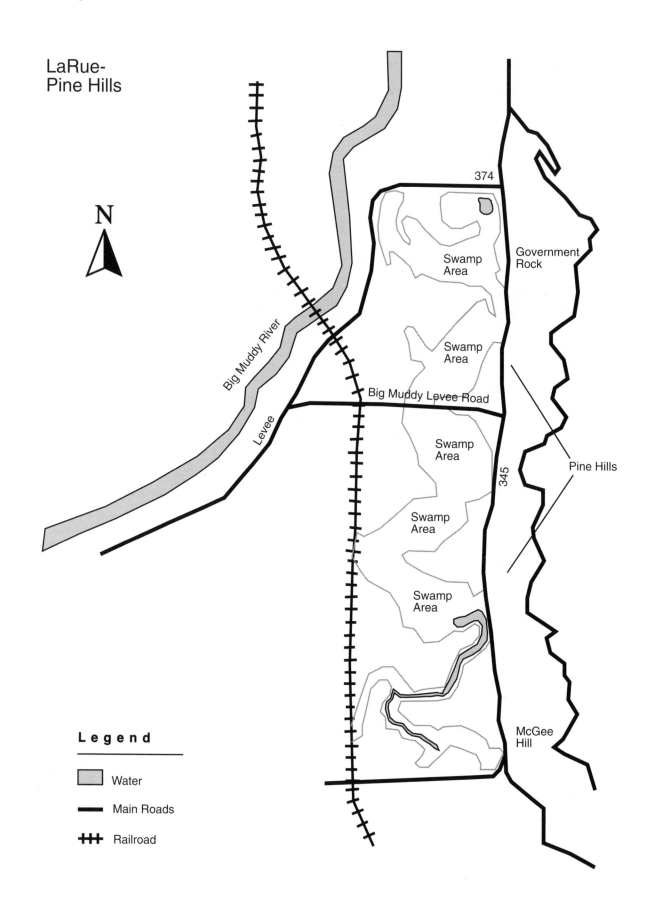

N

Big Muddy River

Levee

374

Government
Rock

Swamp
Area

Swamp
Area

Big Muddy Levee Road

Swamp
Area

345

Pine Hills

Swamp
Area

Swamp
Area

McGee
Hill

Legend

Water

Main Roads

Railroad

Base of the Bluff Road (or Tigers, Zebras, and Snakes) 🥾

Distance Round-Trip: 5 miles

Estimated Hiking Time: 3 hours

Whether the trail is so flooded that you hike it in hip boots, or so dusty that your tennis shoes kick up miniature dust devils, hundreds of tiny frogs will celebrate your presence. They hop along in front of you, so watch where you step!

Caution: You're likely to encounter poisonous snakes; take care and leave them alone. Collecting or disturbing them is prohibited! Three species of poisonous snakes inhabit LaRue-Pine Hills: copperhead, timber rattlesnake, and cottonmouth. The best times to hike the road are April and October when the profusion of wildflowers or the fall colors are at their best and the road is closed to vehicular traffic for the snake migration. At other times you may be sharing the road with the occasional car.

Trail Directions: The Big Muddy Levee Road comes to a T at the bluffs of LaRue-Pine Hills; go right and park in the Winters Pond Picnic Area. Before beginning the hike, observe the bird life of Winters Pond (which is actually a borrow pit for the levee road). From Winters Pond head through the picnic area and turn right onto the road at the base of the bluffs [**1**]. It will be gated when the road is closed. This is a linear hike, so concentrate on the swamp going out and the cliffs coming back.

The forest to the right is a floodplain woods with water-tolerant trees. At .3 mi. [**2**] the swamp first comes into view. It soon will be at the edge of the road, if not over the edge! Take time to study the green carpet of duckweed covering the water.

By .5 mi. [**3**] the swamp has receded from the road, leaving small, vine-entangled trees in its place. These single trees soon become an impenetrable, vine-covered thicket. A spur leading into the swamp appears to your right at .6 mi. [**4**]. Take the .5-mi. round-trip into this watery world. As you walk, beware of mud, downed trees, and snakes. The trail ends in a cypress pond. After observing the small swamp and many redheaded woodpeckers, retrace your steps back to the main trail road (1.1 mi.).

At 1.25 mi. [**5**] look for large patches of trout lily. The spots on the leaves are said to resemble those on a trout—the only type of trout you will find here, unfortunately.

Although the imposing bluffs are on the left, precariously close to the path, continue viewing the swamp and walking on the right (1.5 mi.) [**6**]. You encounter open water and a beaver dam at 1.9 mi. [**7**]. Farther down the road note the large trees. A gate that closes the road for migration is the turnaround point at 2.5 mi. [**8**]. During the hike back, study the right side again; this time it will feature rocky bluffs and a sea of flowers.

As soon as you turn around to head back, you can see the imposing white bluffs. Just like the swamp, the bluffs come and go from view. Springs are evidenced by small streams coming from the bluffs. Look for chipmunks taking advantage of these springs for a cool drink. The upland forest on top of the bluffs is as dry and green/brown as the swamp was green and lush (2.75) [**9**].

You come close-up with the limestone bluffs at 3 mi. [**10**] and can actually touch the rocks. At 3.35 mi. [**11**] you'll see the first of several small ponds along the base of the bluffs. Look closely at the sticks lying in the road near these ponds (especially those that weren't there on the trip out): They might not be sticks at all, but migrating cottonmouth snakes or yellow-bellied water snakes!

For the next mile look for snakes on the road, for bright-yellow tiger swallowtails, or for black-and-white-striped zebra swallowtails. On the right at 4.75 mi. you encounter the last of the ponds [**12**]. As you continue to hike listen to the noisy symphony of sounds around you. Five miles finds you back at Winters Pond Picnic Area.

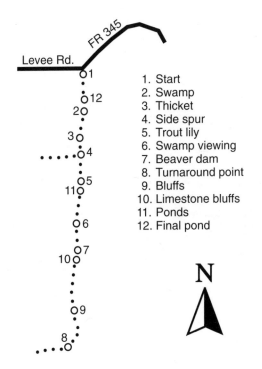

1. Start
2. Swamp
3. Thicket
4. Side spur
5. Trout lily
6. Swamp viewing
7. Beaver dam
8. Turnaround point
9. Bluffs
10. Limestone bluffs
11. Ponds
12. Final pond

Inspiration Point Trail 👢👢👢👢

Distance Round-Trip: 1.5 miles

Estimated Hiking Time: 1 hour

Like the snakes that bask on the LaRue-Pine Hills Road, this trail slithers up the side of the cliff like one long S-shaped serpent.

Caution: You may have to navigate downed trees. At the top of the bluff the fence is there for a reason; do not go too near the edge.

Trail Directions: Big Muddy Levee Road dead-ends into the bluffs; turn left and soon turn right. Park on the right at the McCann Springs Picnic Ground. The trail begins by crossing a narrow footbridge; go left off the bridge [**1**]. During the spring the area immediately after the bridge supports a lush spring flora. Look here for your favorite spring wildflowers.

Within the first .1 mi. note the large, gray beeches and straight-trunked tulip trees. These straight trees indicate an old-growth forest—centuries of undisturbed growth. At .3 mi. [**2**] the trail begins to climb upward with a series of switchbacks. The upward trek yields close-up views of the abundant mayapples. As you climb, note which mayapple stems have two leaves. Only those stems with two leaves will flower this year.

Soon the lush, green understory is left behind as you head upward into a dry, oak-hickory forest (.4 mi.) [**3**]. Look down into the ancient valley as you hike upward. Stay on the main trail, ignoring the many "unofficial" side trails. The .5-mi. mark yields the first of two fenced overlooks [**4**]. What a view! From here you can see the old channel of the Big

Muddy River and an aerial view of the swamp. Continue the climb.

The second fenced overlook (.55 mi.) [**5**] provides a better-than-treetop view. At the end of the railing the trail forks—go right for yet another spectacular view. Then circle back down and rejoin the main trail. Note the carpets of cleft phlox in spring. At .7 mi. [**6**] a bench is provided for you to contemplate (and rest). The trail ends at a parking area .75 mi. from the start [**7**]. Retrace your steps back to McCann Springs Picnic Ground. During the hike back, while still among the tree tops, look for chickadees as they scold from the cedars, or watch as they build nests and forage for food. At 1.2 mi. use caution while snaking your way back down into the palette of green where the chickadee's chirps will be replaced by chorusing frogs.

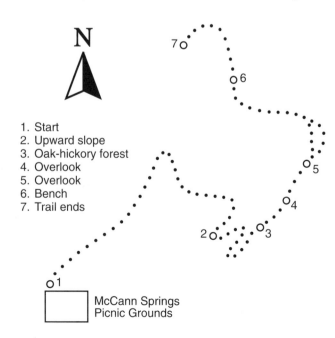

1. Start
2. Upward slope
3. Oak-hickory forest
4. Overlook
5. Overlook
6. Bench
7. Trail ends

© Michael Jeffords

57. Little Grand Canyon

- Discover sheer cliffs, deep canyons, and moist ravines.
- Experience a unique canyon that opens onto the Mississippi River floodplain.
- See what happens when a canyon meets a 500-year flood event!
- Watch where you step amid spring wildflowers that literally carpet the canyon floor.
- Revel in scenic vistas provided by trail overlooks.

Area Information

Three sides of Little Grand Canyon are made up of the cliffs and bluffs known as Hickory Ridge, bordering the Mississippi River valley. On its western side the canyon ends at the Big Muddy River, a tributary of the Mississippi. From the river's floodplain the canyon bluffs rise more than 300 feet.

During the 1930s the area was known as the Hanging Gardens of Egypt or Rattlesnake Den. The gardens nickname referred to the abundance of wildflowers found on the canyon floor, the rattlesnake moniker to the snake den that was once among the best in the eastern United States. Snake collectors from around the country came here for choice reptiles. Too much collecting and people's intolerance of the remaining few have greatly reduced the reptile population.

The best way to view Little Grand Canyon is from the loop trail. The trail encompasses every inch of the rise from the valley floor to the top of Hickory Ridge. Traverse the canyon through steep sandstone creek beds, using the subtle stone steps carved by the Civilian Conservation Corps (CCC), and encounter wildflowers and wildlife all along the trail.

Directions: Little Grand Canyon is 8 miles southwest of Murphysboro, between Illinois 127 and Illinois 3.

From Murphysboro go south on Route 127 for 5 miles. Turn right at Etherton Road and travel 3 miles to Poplar Ridge Road (the last mile is gravel), then turn right onto Little Grand Canyon Road, and follow it to the entrance. The routes are well marked with brown directional signs.

Hours Open: The site is open year-round from 6 A.M. to 10 P.M.

Facilities: Picnic area and privy toilets

Permits and Rules: Be careful with fire; pack all trash and remove it. It is illegal to take or kill any snake in the Little Grand Canyon Area.

Further Information: Shawnee National Forest, Murphysboro Ranger District, 618-687-1731 or Shawnee National Forest, Supervisor's Office, 901 S. Commercial Street, Harrisburg, IL 62946; 618-253-7114 or 800-699-6637.

Other Areas of Interest

Located 1 mile west of Murphysboro, **Lake Murphysboro State Park** is situated among wooded, rolling hills. The well-stocked, star-shaped lake is but one draw to the park. A 3-mile trail explores part of the lake, a ravine, and a ridge. You may wander some of the many unofficial paths looking for patches of native orchids—yellow lady's-slipper, showy orchis, purple fringeless, twayblade, coral root, and ladies' tresses. For more information call the State Park at 618-684-2867.

Pomona Natural Bridge near the small town of Pomona spans 90 feet across a ravine and is one of the few natural bridges east of the Mississippi River. Take time to traverse the .3-mi. loop trail to view the rock formation and ravine. For a treat, stop at the vintage Pomona General Store. For more information call the Murphysboro Ranger District at 618-687-1731.

Loop Trail 👢👢👢👢👢

Distance Round-Trip: 3.6 miles

Estimated Hiking Time: 2 hours

This trail follows a valley and becomes so steep that you must descend (and climb out) by the series of stone steps carved not by the ancients but by the CCC.

Caution: You will be climbing on wet sandstone, so use extreme caution as it is very slippery. The trail also passes along the top of some very imposing cliffs. Stay on the trail!

Trail Directions: In the center of the parking area note the concrete blocks, all that remains of the Hickory Ridge Lookout Tower. Begin the hike to the right of the tower remains [1] and descend a series of steps. The trail is marked by white blazes on trees. Continue downhill. On either side are mixed hardwoods dominated by oaks and augmented by many beech saplings. At .35 mi. [2] find an overlook from which you can see the tops of trees (sycamore and beech) growing in the ravine forest below. On the opposite bluff is a habitat called a barrens, where the habitat is basically exposed rock with scrubby, gnarled cedar trees and a few prairie grasses.

When you have passed the overlook and headed left on the trail, note a cleft in the rock below and to the right. This cleft is actually the trail into the canyon! You are soon walking down the rocky *defile* (a narrow passage), aided by the occasional steps cut into the canyon floor (.5 mi.) [3]. You go right and then left, looking for the easiest path down—the steps carved by the CCC in the 1930s.

From the defile you enter a deep, green valley. Go left and cross a creek using stepping stones (.55 mi.) [4]. You have entered a ravine forest dominated by giant beech trees. Each spring the understory is a carpet of spring wild-flower favorites—wild onion, trillium, squirrel-corn, and many others. On the left is a meandering stream backed by interesting, colorful bluffs. You'll be crossing the stream at least four more times, using rocks as bridges. After the final crossing, the path leads away from the stream and you should begin to notice that most of the large trees are dead (1 mi.) [5].

The trail begins to head uphill and to the left at 1.25 mi. [6], away from the devastated trees. On your right note the Big Muddy River and the mouth of the canyon. The tree deaths were caused by the flood of 1993. The trees that stood away from the flood's reach did fine, but an esti-mated 18 to 37 percent of the mature trees near

the Mississippi River were killed during the flood.

At 1.45 mi. [7] the trail enters a valley with bluffs on both sides. From here you soon cross two small streams and head up another rocky defile. Use a similar set of cryptic stairs carved into the sandstone (1.6 mi.) [8]. A few steps may require giant strides. Cross the canyon and head up the opposite side. You will be walking upward along a ridge, with the valley below on your right.

Take advantage of the view (and catch your breath) at River Bottom Overlook at 2.15 mi. [9]. From this bird's-eye vantage you can see where the Mississippi River valley meets the Shawnee Hills. Look for the old channel of the Big Muddy River (a channelized stream) that is now an oxbow lake.

From the overlook, continue upward as you hike along Viney Ridge on top of the Chalk Bluffs. Once again note the rugged, magnificent valley to your left, full of wildflowers each spring and great colors each fall. In the valley below, all the species coexist in a colorful mosaic; here on the ridge, look for small, isolated patches of single species—cushions of Dutchman's-breeches, mayapples tumbling into the valley, or small groupings of toothwort.

The top of the ridge is finally reached at 2.6 miles [10] where a bench is provided before you begin the undulating trek along a series of ridges. As you hike the remaining mile, look into the forest below, which is reminiscent of the cove forests of the Appalachians. The hike ends at the remnants of the old fire tower.

Little Grand Canyon

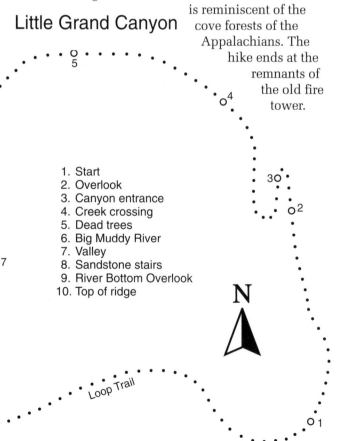

1. Start
2. Overlook
3. Canyon entrance
4. Creek crossing
5. Dead trees
6. Big Muddy River
7. Valley
8. Sandstone stairs
9. River Bottom Overlook
10. Top of ridge

Loop Trail

N

58. Piney Creek Ravine Nature Preserve

- Discover sandstone bluffs, clear streams, and waterfalls.

- Bring a plant identification guide to help you identify more than 440 plants that grow in the preserve—including species that would be more at home in Missouri than Illinois.

- Hike through a native, shortleaf pine forest. This is one of only two places in Illinois where shortleaf pine is found.

- Visit an Illinois extension of the Missouri Ozarks.

- Explore what may be the most beautiful ravine in Illinois.

Area Information

Although at first glance Piney Creek Ravine may appear indistinguishable from the sandstone ravines of the Shawnee National Forest, it is distinctive. This area underwent the scraping and grinding of the glaciers many years ago; the ravines of the Shawnee National Forest were spared such icy depredations. Piney Creek Ravine was created in a relatively short time, carved by glacial meltwaters eating their way through the soft sandstone.

Sandstone cliffs enclose both sides of Piney Creek, and its bottom is a solid layer of sandstone—not the more familiar cobbles, sand, or mixture of both found in other area streams. In addition, the sandstone bottom is marked by long, deep grooves. Occasionally Piney Creek drops off into small, clear pools. In other places the creek is so close to the sandstone walls that it splashes against the vertical surfaces, providing a constantly moist habitat for ferns in cracks and crevices. As abruptly as the sandstone cliffs begin, they taper off; after a short distance they disappear entirely, replaced by a flat, floodplain woods.

A major portion of the trail skirts Piney Creek. Take time to discover its bottom, waterfalls, and undercuts, and although the stream appears tame, use extreme caution. Its rocks are quite beautiful, yet very slippery and totally unforgiving to the careless hiker.

Directions: From Highway 4 at the northwest end of Campbell Hill, take the blacktop road 3.8 miles west. Turn and go north .7 miles to Shiloh Hill; then continue south 1.8 miles to West Point Church Cemetery. The nature preserve is .4 miles west of the road.

Hours Open: The ravine is open year-round but closes at dusk.

Facilities: The site has a picnic table with a trash receptacle.

Permits and Rules: This trail is in a dedicated Illinois Nature Preserve: No pets are allowed. Remove nothing from the preserve.

Further Information: Site Superintendent, Randolph County Conservation Area, Route 1, Box 345, Chester, IL 62002; 618-462-1181.

Other Areas of Interest

Numerous outdoor recreational activities can be found at **Randolph State Fish and Wildlife Area,** located 5 miles northeast of Chester. These include picnicking, boating, hunting, fishing, and camping. The area features several short hikes, including an interpretive nature trail designed by a local Boy Scout troop. For further information contact Site Superintendent, Randolph County Conservation Area, Route 1, Box 345, Chester, IL 62002; 618-462-1181.

Piney Creek Trail 👢👢👢👢

Distance Round-Trip: 2.5 miles

Estimated Hiking Time: 2.25 hours

While there is plenty to see at any time of the year, during the early spring this trail is subtly beautiful—the gray rocks are covered with green, circular lichens and buried in the burnished leaves of past autumns.

Caution: The rocks are beautiful but extremely slippery when wet! Use common sense and respect the trail.

Trail Directions: Begin the trail to the left of the parking area [1], along a wide grass swath between two fencerows. At .15 mi. [2] the right fencerow ends, and you will come to a large grassy area; walk diagonally across this to the preserve entrance. A large white sign indicates the trailhead; the trail in the preserve is marked by faint orange circles on trees.

Wooden steps from the trail sign lead downward (.3 mi.) [3], and you soon encounter a glade community on your right. A glade is an opening in the woods with an expanse of sandstone. The exposed rocks are covered with mosses and lichens, and cedars are the dominant tree. On your left is a dry, oak-hickory forest. During spring, look for pussytoes along this segment of the trail, flowers that have a woolly stem and a cluster of white, fuzzy flowers that resemble a cat's paw.

At .4 mi. [4] the trail heads downward and crosses a stream (and a bedrock streambed). Rejoin the trail on the opposite side and head uphill. Soon the trail will fork; go right and continue uphill. Look left across the ravine where you can see shortleaf pine, found in only two locations in Illinois. As you hike along the ridge top, look left (especially in winter and spring) for a great view of a waterfall (.65 mi.) [5]. You will hear the waterfall before it comes into view. In the valley below are some gray rocks covered with green lichens. Just past the view of the waterfall, cross a stream on stepping stones.

A trail intersection appears at .85 mi. [6]; go left and downward, pausing to look into the ravine below. After a small descent, the trail heads left (to the right is another trail to the stream). Before continuing left, however, wander down on the right trail to the stream, cross over on its wide, bedrock bottom (the streambed is very slick, so use caution), and follow it upstream. This short spur ends at small waterfall. Retrace your steps, rejoin the trail, and head downward. Cross the stream on the giant slabs of bedrock, looking to your left at the giant undercut. Join the trail on the other side (note the faint, orange markings on the trees).

As the trail heads upward, glance at the stream and its narrow channel cut through the rock (1 mi.) [7]. The trail will proceed through a grove of shortleaf pines: The trees have slender, drooping branches and trunks covered by a light, cinnamon-red bark that is broken into large, scaly plates. Away from the creek, you are hiking through a dry, oak-hickory forest. Sightings of Piney Creek are infrequent, with only glimpses of the bluff through the trees but a constant sound of rushing water.

At 1.35 mi. you will head downhill into another stream valley [8]. The spring flora that was absent on the dry, upper ridge top are now present—spring beauty, trout lily, and prairie trillium. The trail heads upward at 1.65 mi. [9] and skirts a sandstone bluff. Note the colors and erosional patterns on the bluff to the right. Do you detect an ancient bison petroglyph? The trail leads away from the bluff and again crosses a stream and small tributary. Look to your right at the undercut as you use rocks to aid in the stream crossing. A small waterfall has formed where the tributary joins the creek.

Head uphill (steep) after the crossing, and soon you are back to [4] at 1.85 mi. Go to your right and retrace your steps out of the preserve, through the grassy area, and back to your vehicle.

Piney Creek Ravine Nature Preserve

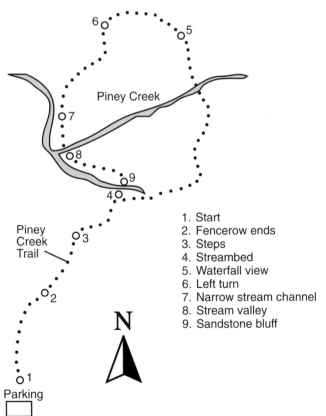

1. Start
2. Fencerow ends
3. Steps
4. Streambed
5. Waterfall view
6. Left turn
7. Narrow stream channel
8. Stream valley
9. Sandstone bluff

59. Fults Hill Prairie

- Enjoy spectacular views of the surrounding countryside.
- Discover a hill prairie and its unique vegetation.
- Practice your mountain-goat maneuvers as you climb up and down the steep trail.
- From a bird's-eye perch, look for bald eagles during the winter and turkey vultures and hawks year-round.

Area Information

To most people, prairies are flat grasslands. It is not the topography, however, that distinguishes a prairie, but the vegetation. Prairies growing on pronounced slopes are called hill prairies. Located high on a west-facing bluff overlooking the Mississippi River, Fults Hill Prairie is one of those special prairies. John Marks, a Wisconsin botanist, dubbed hill prairies "goat prairies" because of their being located on slopes so "steep that only a nimble goat could graze them." It was this attitude and inaccessibility that helped hill prairies survive. They were too difficult to farm and very few animals had the dexterity to graze them. Thus, by the 1950s hill prairies were the largest remnants of virgin prairie left in Illinois.

With the cessation of fire, however, the hill prairie landscapes have been taken over by trees and shrubs from adjacent woodlands. Only the occasional prairie plant gives any indication of the area's former glory. If your visit to Fults Hill Prairie occurs just after a burn has taken place, do not despair for the land; volunteer stewards are managing this grassland to keep a piece of vegetation history in Illinois alive and well. Fults Hill Prairie was dedicated as the state's 30th Nature Preserve in 1970. In 1986 the preserve was designated as a National Natural Landmark by the U.S. Department of the Interior.

Directions: Fults Hill Prairie is located along the Mississippi River bluffs near the town of Fults, about 25 miles south of Belleville. You can reach it from Bluff Road (a blacktop road), which joins Maeystown Road northwest of the area, and finally Illinois 3. From the south end of Fults, take Bluff Road southeast 1.6 miles to a small parking area and a preserve sign.

Hours Open: The site is open year-round.

Facilities: A picnic table and garbage can are found in the small parking area.

Permits and Rules: The trail is located in a dedicated Illinois Nature Preserve: No pets are allowed on the trail. Do not disturb or remove anything from the preserve.

Further Information: Illinois Department of Natural Resources, Natural Heritage Biologist, 4521 Alton Commerce Parkway, Alton, IL 62002; 618-462-1181.

Other Areas of Interest

Located in Monroe County, **Illinois Caverns** was originally called "Mammoth Cave of Illinois." The caverns have 6 miles of passages that are open to the public for exploration, but a permit is required to enter. For further information, contact Illinois Caverns, Site Interpreter, RR 4, Waterloo, IL 62298; 618-458-6699.

Listed on the National Register of Historic Places, **Maeystown** is mostly populated by direct descendants of its first inhabitants, immigrants from Germany. Following an old German custom, many of the homes have been built of locally quarried limestone and set directly into the hillsides. For more information call 618-458-6600.

Fults Hill Prairie Trail

Distance Round-Trip: 1.6 miles

Estimated Hiking Time: 1 hour

No wonder these are called goat prairies! The hike upward constantly proves the appropriateness of the name, as only a nimble goat or equally adept hiker could readily navigate the steep upward climb. Thankfully, there are plenty of resting spots along the way to take in the view and catch your breath.

Caution: The trail is very steep and lacks guard rails near the bluff edge. Use common sense and do not get too close to the edge.

Trail Directions: Begin the trail at the parking area—go right and begin to hike uphill [1]. In the spring, find an abundance of larkspur and phlox carpeting the hill. At .1 mi. [2] take advantage of the overlook for a great view of the Missouri hills across the way (Mississippi River valley). Another overlook within a few yards provides a bird's-eye view of Kidd Lake Marsh, a small remnant—dominated by cattails and cordgrass—of the huge wetlands that used to occupy the bottomland. The area supports a small population of venomous cottonmouth snakes; it is the northernmost occurrence of the species in Illinois.

At the top (.25 mi.) [3] the woods have changed from mixed to a dry, oak-hickory forest with some cedars. To your right is a glimpse of the hill prairie before the trail heads back into the woods. At .35 mi. the trail forks—go right for an overview and visit a small piece of prairie. Then retrace your steps and take the other fork [4]. Soon you are walking along the top of the bluff surrounded by dogwoods and, unfortunately, poison ivy. As you hike the ridge, zebra swallowtails may keep you company.

At .6 mi. [5] go left, following a wide path through small saplings. In the spring, look for the solitary stems of bellwort; gaze upward to see great blue herons flying to the adjacent marsh or turkey vultures gliding on the thermals. The trail begins to head uphill at 1.1 mi. [6] and will soon curve to the left. Enjoy a fabulous view once you exit the woods (1.2 mi.) [7]! You are in the midst of a hill prairie.

Little bluestem, sideoats grama, and big bluestem are the dominant grasses. The purples of lead plant, purple prairie clover, purple coneflower, and vervain and the yellows of puccoon and coreopsis break up the green carpet.

The trail splits within a few yards—go right to explore the prairie. Continue to the right to explore a long finger of prairie on a narrow goat trail. In the spring, look for white blue-eyed grass, a diminutive relative of the iris. In the fall, the pink blossoms of autumn wild onion grace the path. At 1.35 mi. you will come to an overlook [8]; the path skirts the edge of the bluff and begins to descend. Watch your step as you head downhill and use the open areas as overlooks.

Soon the hill prairie is left behind as you head back into the woods. The trail joins another path at 1.5 mi. [9]. Go right and continue downward until you cross a footbridge. Around the bridge each spring is a profusion of phacelia, a plant often encountered in the Great Smoky Mountains.

After crossing the bridge, you have completed the loop and are back at the parking area.

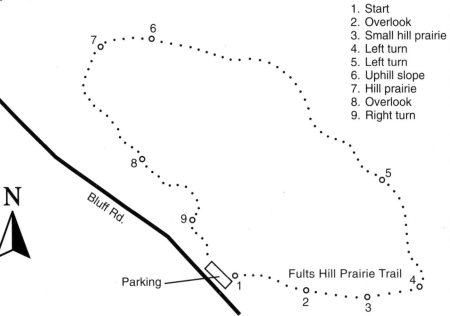

Fults Hill Prairie

1. Start
2. Overlook
3. Small hill prairie
4. Left turn
5. Left turn
6. Uphill slope
7. Hill prairie
8. Overlook
9. Right turn